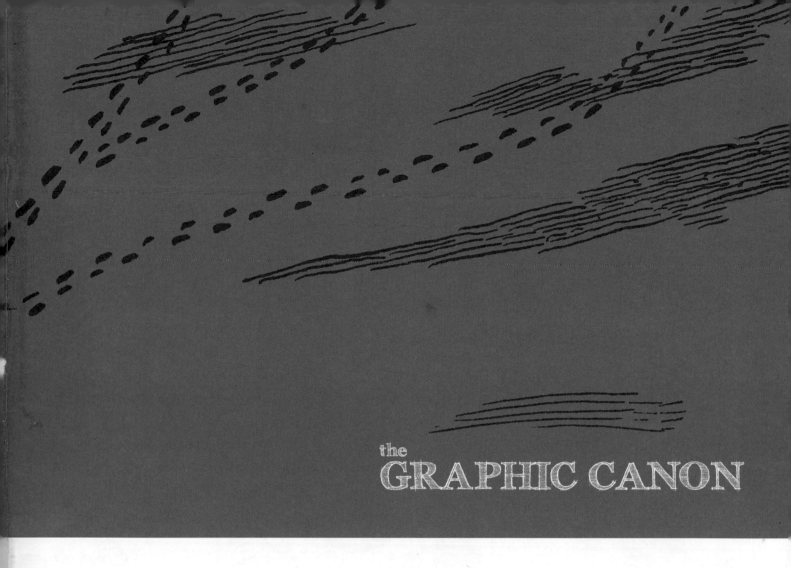

the
GRAPHIC CANON

Volume 2

One shade more, one ray the less.

Had half impair'd the nameless grace

Volume 2

FROM "KUBLA KHAN"
TO THE BRONTË SISTERS
TO *THE PICTURE OF DORIAN GRAY*

the GRAPHIC CANON

Edited by
RUSS KICK

SEVEN STORIES PRESS
New York

For permissions information see page 498.

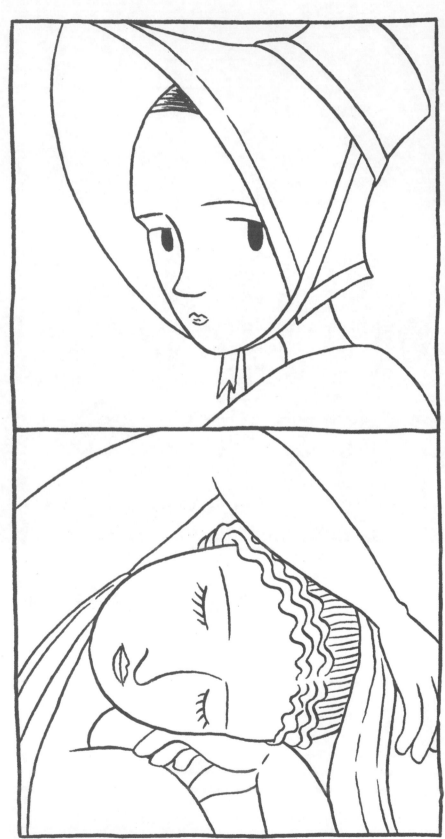

A SEVEN STORIES PRESS FIRST EDITION

SEVEN STORIES PRESS
140 Watts Street
New York, NY 10013
www.sevenstories.com

College professors may order examination copies of Seven Stories Press titles for a free six-month trial period. To order, visit www.sevenstories.com/textbook or send a fax on school letterhead to (212) 226-1411.

Book design by Pollen/Stewart Cauley, New York
Cover art by Huxley King with Terrence Boyce
Back cover art by John Porcellino

Library of Congress Cataloging-in-Publication Data
The graphic canon, volume 2: from Kubla Khan to the Brontë sisters to The picture of Dorian Gray / edited by Russ Kick. — A Seven Stories Press 1st ed.
p. cm.
Includes index.
ISBN 978-1-60980-378-0 (pbk.)
1. Comic books, strips, etc. — History and criticism.
2. Literature — Adaptations.
3. Graphic novels in education.
I. Kick, Russell.
PN6714.G736 2012
741.5'69 — dc23
2012013176

Printed in Hong Kong

9 8 7 6 5 4 3 2

CONTENTS

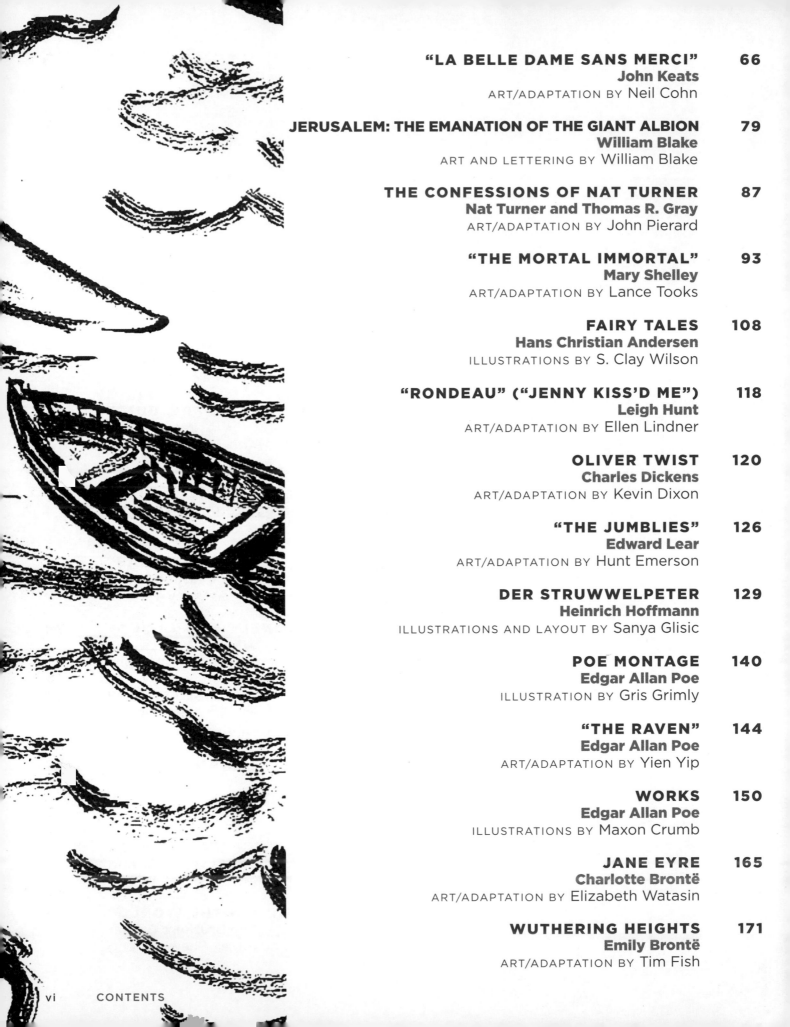

Three Panel Review
Lisa Brown

A TALE OF TWO CITIES
by Charles Dickens
It was the BEST of TimeS, it was the WORST of Times...
Actually, it was really just...
um, Liberté?
NON!
NON!
OUI.
PLOP!
the WORST of times.

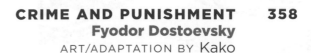

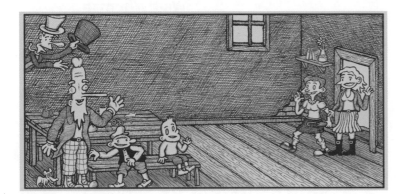

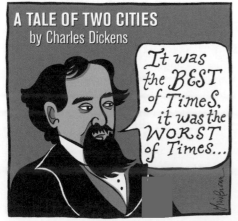

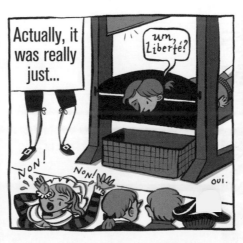

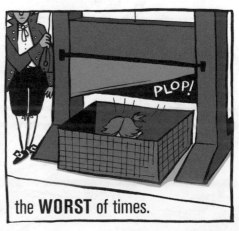

Three Panel Review
Lisa Brown

MADAME BOVARY by Gustav Flaubert
Sigh.
My husband bores me.
Mon amour!
Sigh.
I bore my lovers.
Mon amour!
© 2011 LISA M. BROWN | DIST. BY TRIBUNE MEDIA SERVICES, INC.
Hey, is that ARSENIC?

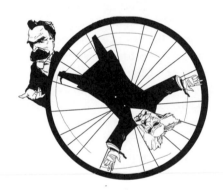

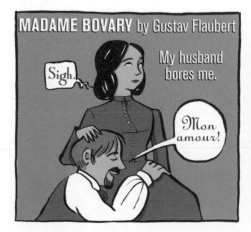

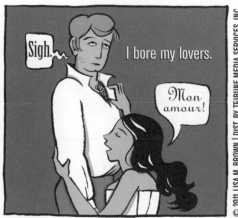

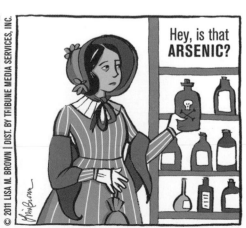

ACKNOWLEDGMENTS

IT TAKES A LOT OF PEOPLE TO MAKE A BOOK, ESPECIALLY a gigantic anthology. Endless gratitude goes to Dan Simon, founder and president of Seven Stories Press, who immediately shared my vision for *The Graphic Canon* and, by his second email to me, was already discussing the nitty-gritty details. I originally pitched an over-sized 400-page book, but much later in the process, when I later told Dan that it could easily be expanded to 500 or even 600 pages, he expanded it, all right—to two volumes. Then, weeks later, to three. From 400 pages each to 500. From some color to color throughout. From mostly reprints to mostly new material. We both like to think big.

Huge thanks to editor and fellow night owl Veronica Liu, who was so much fun to work with that it didn't feel like work at all, even when she found loads of errors I had embarrassingly overlooked or when she lovingly cracked the whip as I let this or that task fall by the wayside. Merci beaucoup to everyone on Seven Stories' all-star team: Astrid Cook, Liz DeLong, Gabe Espinal, Jon Gilbert, Phoebe Hwang, Silvia Stramenga, Anne Rumberger, Linda Trepanier, Ruth Weiner, Crystal Yakacki, and all the interns. Gracias to Karin Bolender for copyediting, Jordyn Ostroff for putting together a fantastic "Further Reading" section, and everyone at Random House Publisher Services for the distribution.

Hugs go to my parents, Ruthanne & Derek, Kiki, Sky, Terrence & Rebekah, Darrell, Billy Dale, Cat & David, Kelly & Kevin, Mary, Z, Hawk, Songtruth, Fred & Dorothy, Jeff & Christy, Jenny, Christine, the Sharps, and the Boyces. I raise a glass to Gary Baddeley and Ralph Bernardo at Disinformation. I bow to the people who led me to artists—Paul Buhle, Molly Kiely, Onsmith, Molly Crabapple, Ed Choy, and Zak Smith.

A tip of the hat to Lorraine Chamberlain, Tony Bennett at Knockabout Comics, Clive Bryant at Classical Comics, Malcolm Whyte at Word Play publications, Maria Singer at the Yale Center for British Art, Ty King and Alena Gribskov at Writers House, James Sturm at the Center for Cartoon Studies, Bob Niegowski at Rodale Books, Sari Levy-Shore at Levy Creative Management, Valerie Merians and Dennis Loy Johnson at Melville House, Andrew Furlow at Icon Books, Emma Hayley at SelfMadeHero, and Charlotte Sheedy, Meredith Kaffel, and Mackenzie C. Brady at the Charlotte Sheedy Literary Agency.

Major thanks are due to everyone who gets this book made and into your hands: the paper-makers, the truck drivers, the printers, the distributors and wholesalers, the booksellers. . . . And of course the many trees who gave their all.

I'm grateful to all the authors, poets, and playwrights who gave us these works of literature. Many of them sacrificed their personal freedom, economic well-being, sanity, relationships, livers, and lives to illuminate the human condition. And I reserve a special place in my heart for all the artists here, who enthusiastically produced amazing work. Without you guys, *The Graphic Canon* couldn't exist.

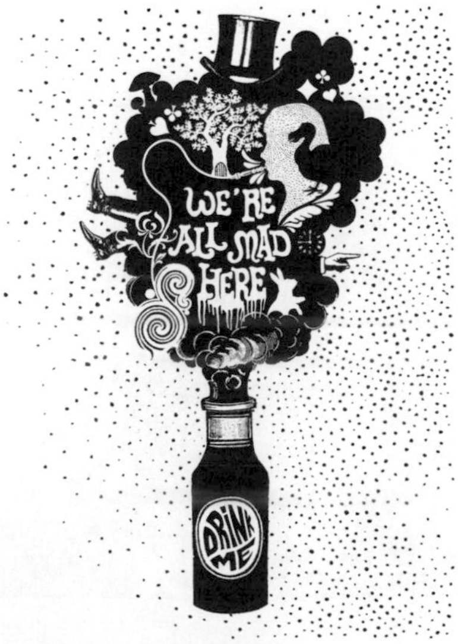
WE'RE ALL MAD HERE
DRINK ME

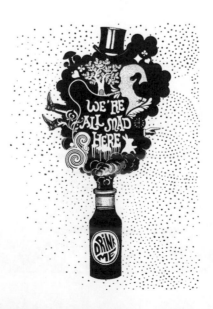

EDITOR'S INTRODUCTION TO VOLUME 2

WELCOME TO THE SECOND VOLUME OF *THE GRAPHIC Canon*, wherein comics artists and illustrators graphically adapt over fifty works of literature from the 1800s. If you read the introduction to the first volume, you know that the idea for the *Canon* came to me in a flash. I was standing in a bookstore when I fully realized how many great works of lit were being graphically adapted—but also how many had yet to be adapted. Being an anthologist, my immediate thought was to put together a huge literary anthology of fiction, poetry, plays, essays, letters . . . with the twist being that they would be visually adapted.

There's a long history of using written works as the basis for other art forms. Literature has provided fuel for paintings, plays, operas, symphonies, songs, movies. . . . In the nineteenth century, master engraver Gustave Doré created iconic images for *The Divine Comedy*, "The Rime of the Ancient Mariner," the Bible, and many other works. Six theater productions of *Oliver Twist* were staged in the same year the novel was published. Salvador Dalí created several sets of paintings based on classic works, including *Romeo and Juliet*, *Don Quixote*, and *The Divine Comedy.* Billie Holiday's jazz staple "Strange Fruit" started out as a poem. Kate Bush's first single—a huge international hit that launched her career—was "Wuthering Heights," which is based on the novel and includes some direct quotes. *Apocalypse Now* is a retelling of Joseph Conrad's *Heart of Darkness*, and MGM's 1939 *The Wizard of Oz* is one of the very few movie adaptations that has exceeded the fame of the classic book on which it was based. And you might've heard of a couple of Broadway musicals called *Les Misérables* and *The Phantom of the Opera*. The long-running PBS series *Masterpiece Theatre* (now just *Masterpiece*) has been raking in awards since 1971 when it began airing British TV productions of classic works, including *Bleak House*, *Moll Flanders*, *Jude the Obscure*, *The Last of the Mohicans*, *Vanity Fair*, and *Anna Karenina*.

And now it's time for comics—a.k.a. sequential art—to show what it can do, and *The Graphic Canon* is part of that. From 1941 to 1971, the comic book series Classic Comics (later becoming Classics Illustrated) produced 169 issues that adapted classic works of literature. Lots of baby boomers have fond memories of this series, but frankly they weren't that great. As a rule, the artwork was uninspired—not bad, but nothing to take note of—and the works were stripped down and sanitized. It was a very workman-like transcription of the most superficial highlights of the work. The Classics Illustrated line has been relaunched twice in recent years, with brand-new adaptations often containing wonderful artwork and sophisticated approaches by the likes of Bill Sienkiewicz, Gahan Wilson, and Rick Geary.

In the 1970s, Marvel filled the void with Marvel Classics Comics, a monthly title that adapted a new work in each of its 30+ issues. More recently, the industry giant launched Marvel Illustrated—each classic work is adapted as a limited series, then collected as an oversized hardcover, then as a smaller softcover.

Currently, Tom Pomplun's Graphic Classics concern has published over twenty volumes of consistently high-quality comic adaptations of literature, with each 144-page book devoted to a single writer or genre. In the UK, Classical Comics puts out full-length adapta-

Three Panel Review
Lisa Brown

LITTLE WOMEN
by Louisa May Alcott
JO: SMART
INK
MEG: SWEET
AMY: SPOILED
BETH : DEAD

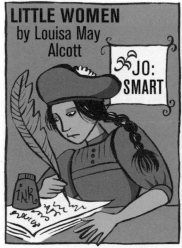

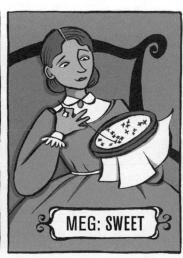

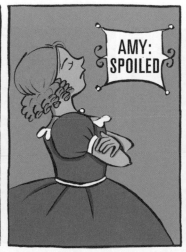

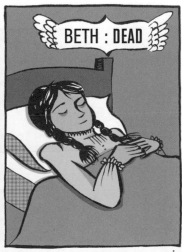

tions of classroom favorites such as *Hamlet* and *Frankenstein*, while SelfMadeHero has a line of often gritty and challenging adaptations (*Tristram Shandy*, *Heart of Darkness*), plus a line of manga Shakespeare. Robert Berry's Throwaway Horse produces meaty digital comic adaptations of *Ulysses* and other works. Short adaptations have been showing up within larger comics for decades; publishers Wiley and Sterling regularly put out books along these lines; and there's the occasional self-published minicomic or a graphic novel from one of the big corporate publishers.

There's a lot going on in this realm, but up till now no one had brought together a huge variety in one place. When it comes to the original, all-text works of literature, we've had humongous, eon-spanning anthologies for ages. Anyone who's taken English 101 knows the exertion of carrying around the brick-like tomes from Norton, Oxford, Longman, and others. I wanted to create something like that—a kaleidoscopic take on literary art, artistic literature. It would start with *The Epic of Gilgamesh* and end in the late twentieth century, and it would cover fiction, poetry, plays, and nonfiction in a rainbow of languages from around the globe. It would collect some of what had already been done, but mainly it would contain new pieces, filling in a lot of gaps. No graphic novel of *Paradise Lost*? Hardly anything from the ancient Greek playwrights—no *Lysistrata* or *Medea*? No "Kubla Khan" or anything from Lord Byron? Only one Dickinson poem? No *Crime and Punishment* set during the original, Tsarist time period? Nothing from James Joyce's *Dubliners* or T. S. Eliot's "The Waste Land"? These omissions, and many more, needed to be corrected.

Classic literature is more exciting, relevant, and subversive than it generally gets credit for being. Its boring image is largely due to the way it's taught by an educational system that sucks the life out of these investigations of the human condition and makes them into dry things to be dissected and quizzed on. But these works are powerful probings of universal questions, wrapped in beautiful writing and populated by amazing characters. It's no wonder they're used as the basis for so much visual and performing art. I was excited to see what would happen when some of the best current artists were given the entire literary canon to play with, interpret, build upon. I knew we'd end up with new things, with meetings of visual and literary minds that would create works of art that stand on their own. I was gratified by one of the first reviews of Volume 1, a glowing recommendation from *Kirkus Reviews* that ended on this note: "If artists, as British sculptor Anish Kapoor famously said, make mythologies, then this volume is genuinely a marriage of equals."

Another early review of Volume 1 picked up on another, perhaps more subtle, agenda of mine. *Booklist* said that the anthology "showcase[s] the extraordinary potential of the artform itself," that "there is a new visual idea on nearly every turn of the page." It concludes that Volume 1 is "a breathtaking glimpse of this young medium's incredible future." Mission accomplished. Not only did I set out to find the best artists I could, I wanted a blistering diversity of styles and approaches. As I've said before, we're truly living in a golden age of comic art, graphic novels, and illustration in general. The sheer number of talented artists at work—and their inventiveness—is off the charts. There's no way to even keep track of them all.

One purpose of *The Graphic Canon* is to showcase this burgeoning of brilliance. In other words, no matter what the theme of the pieces is—even if this were a three-volume anthology about love or current events or dogs—I wanted to excite and overload your visual cortex to the point of transcendent bliss. These artists are bringing something new to the table, each creating a delectable dish that can be savored on its own . . . but put them all together and, let me tell you, you have a smorgasbord on your hands, a cornucopia of artistic goodness overflowing your retinas. So, leaving aside the literature aspect, I hope that the *Canon* shows a good deal of what comic art and illustration are capable of, and goes a little way in helping propel them in new directions.

To be honest, there are other agendas at play in *The Graphic Canon*. Easter eggs and Trojan horses abound. Unannounced, and sometimes unintended, themes weave in and out. The array of artists is crucial, though largely serendipitous. The pairing of certain artists with certain works seems to have added layers of meaning. The interesting, synchronistic way that some works bump against each other in the chronological presentation can be enlightening or hilarious.

It's a rich tapestry. But it's also simply an enjoyable feast for the eyes and brain. So, please, dig in.

RUSS KICK

Three Panel Review
Lisa Brown

THE SCARLET LETTER
by Nathaniel Hawthorne
ADULTERESS
APOSTATE
© 2011 LISA M. BROWN | DIST. BY TRIBUNE MEDIA SERVICES, INC.
AFTERMATH

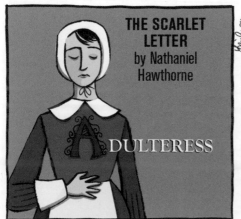

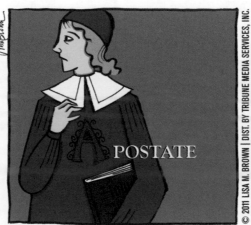

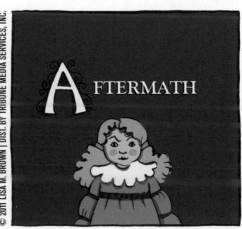

"Kubla Khan"

Samuel Taylor Coleridge

ART/ADAPTATION BY **Alice Duke**

"KUBLA KHAN" MIGHT HAVE THE MOST FAMOUS backstory of any work of literature. Coleridge claims that he was tripping on opium when all the images from the poem appeared before him as practically tangible things, while at the same time around 300 lines of poetry describing these people and places spontaneously popped into his head. Coming out of this narcotic dream, he proceeded to write down—essentially, transcribe—"Kubla Khan." He was famously interrupted by an unexpected visitor at the farmhouse in Somerset, England, and when he returned to pen and paper an hour later, the images and lines had dissipated.

The poem apparently was composed in 1797, definitely not later than 1800, yet for reasons unknown it wasn't published until 1816, and then only at the insistence of Lord Byron. It was almost universally savaged upon release but has gone on to become one of the most famous, admired, and debated poems in the world. In *A Coleridge Companion*, University of Georgia professor John Spencer Hill writes:

> It must surely be true that no poem of comparable length in English or any other language has been the subject of so much critical commentary. Its fifty-four lines have spawned thousands of pages of discussion and analysis. "Kubla Khan" is the sole or a major subject in five book-length studies; close

to 150 articles and book-chapters (doubtless I have missed some others) have been devoted exclusively to it; and brief notes and incidental comments on it are without number. Despite this deluge, however, there is no critical unanimity and very little agreement on a number of important issues connected with the poem: its date of composition, its "meaning," its sources in Coleridge's reading and observation of nature, its structural integrity (i.e., fragment *versus* complete poem), and its relationship to the Preface by which Coleridge introduced it on its first publication in 1816.

Say what you will, there's no denying that it's a magical, powerful poem packed with rich, mysterious imagery. After hearing Coleridge recite it, the poet Charles Lamb wrote that he did so "so enchantingly that it irradiates & brings heaven & Elysian bowers into my parlour while he sings or says it." Artist Alice Duke—who specializes in illustrations of the fantastic, including work by Lovecraft and Poe—says that she was "feverish and ill" while completing this adaptation, which was probably the perfect, semi-delirious state of mind to be in.

SOURCE

Hill, John Spencer. *A Coleridge Companion*. London: Macmillan Press, 1983.

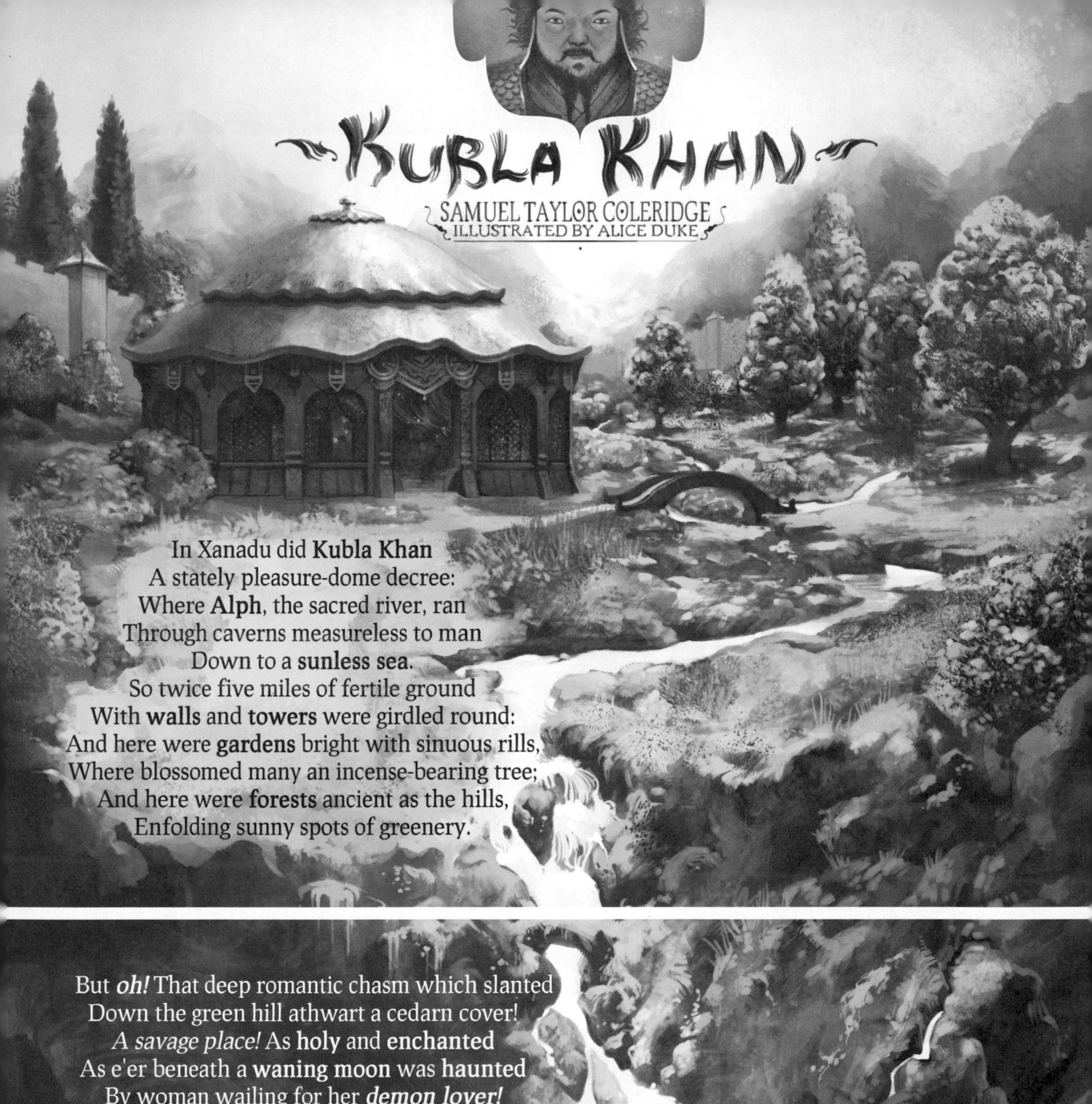

KUBLA KHAN

SAMUEL TAYLOR COLERIDGE
ILLUSTRATED BY ALICE DUKE

In Xanadu did **Kubla Khan**
A stately pleasure-dome decree:
Where **Alph**, the sacred river, ran
Through caverns measureless to man
Down to a **sunless sea.**
So twice five miles of fertile ground
With **walls** and **towers** were girdled round:
And here were **gardens** bright with sinuous rills,
Where blossomed many an incense-bearing tree;
And here were **forests** ancient as the hills,
Enfolding sunny spots of greenery.

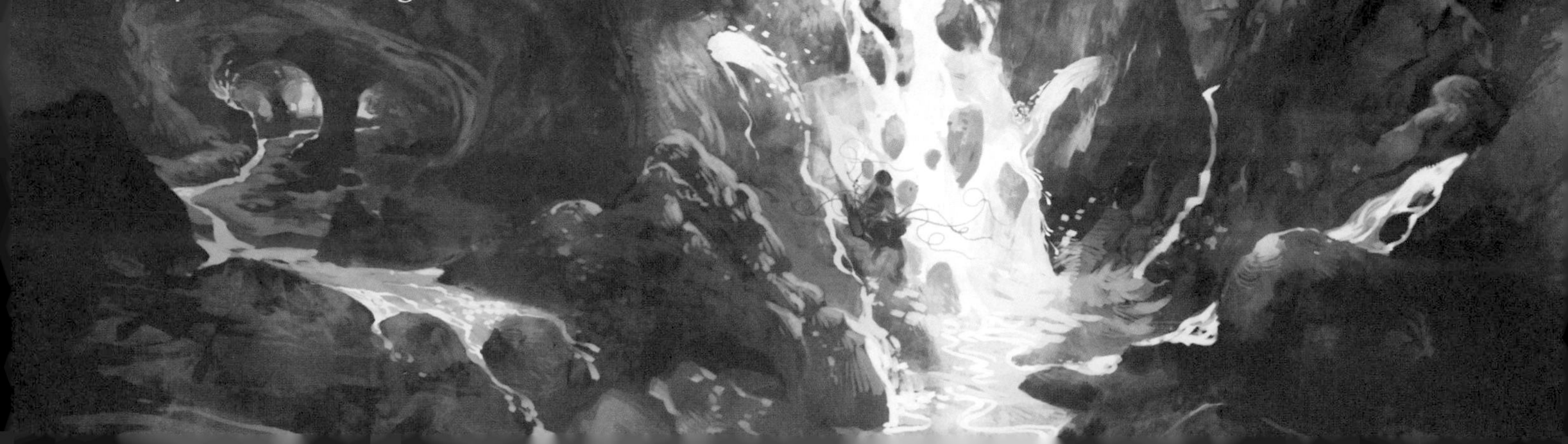

But ***oh!*** That deep romantic chasm which slanted
Down the green hill athwart a cedarn cover!
A savage place! As **holy** and **enchanted**
As e'er beneath a **waning moon** was **haunted**
By woman wailing for her ***demon lover!***

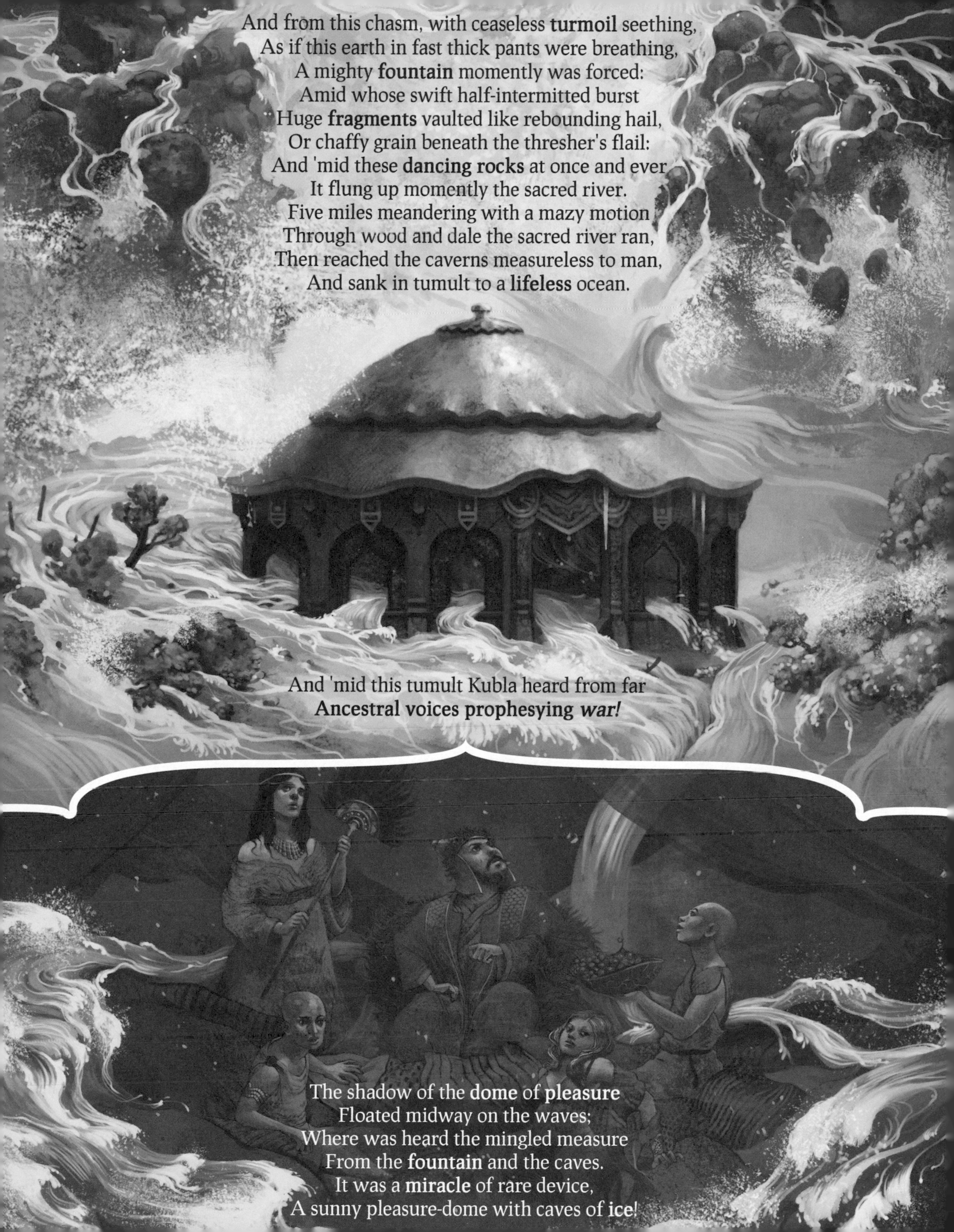

And from this chasm, with ceaseless **turmoil** seething,
As if this earth in fast thick pants were breathing,
A mighty **fountain** momently was forced:
Amid whose swift half-intermitted burst
Huge **fragments** vaulted like rebounding hail,
Or chaffy grain beneath the thresher's flail:
And 'mid these **dancing rocks** at once and ever
It flung up momently the sacred river.
Five miles meandering with a mazy motion
Through wood and dale the sacred river ran,
Then reached the caverns measureless to man,
And sank in tumult to a **lifeless** ocean.

And 'mid this tumult Kubla heard from far
Ancestral voices prophesying *war!*

The shadow of the **dome** of **pleasure**
Floated midway on the waves;
Where was heard the mingled measure
From the **fountain** and the caves.
It was a **miracle** of rare device,
A sunny pleasure-dome with caves of **ice**!

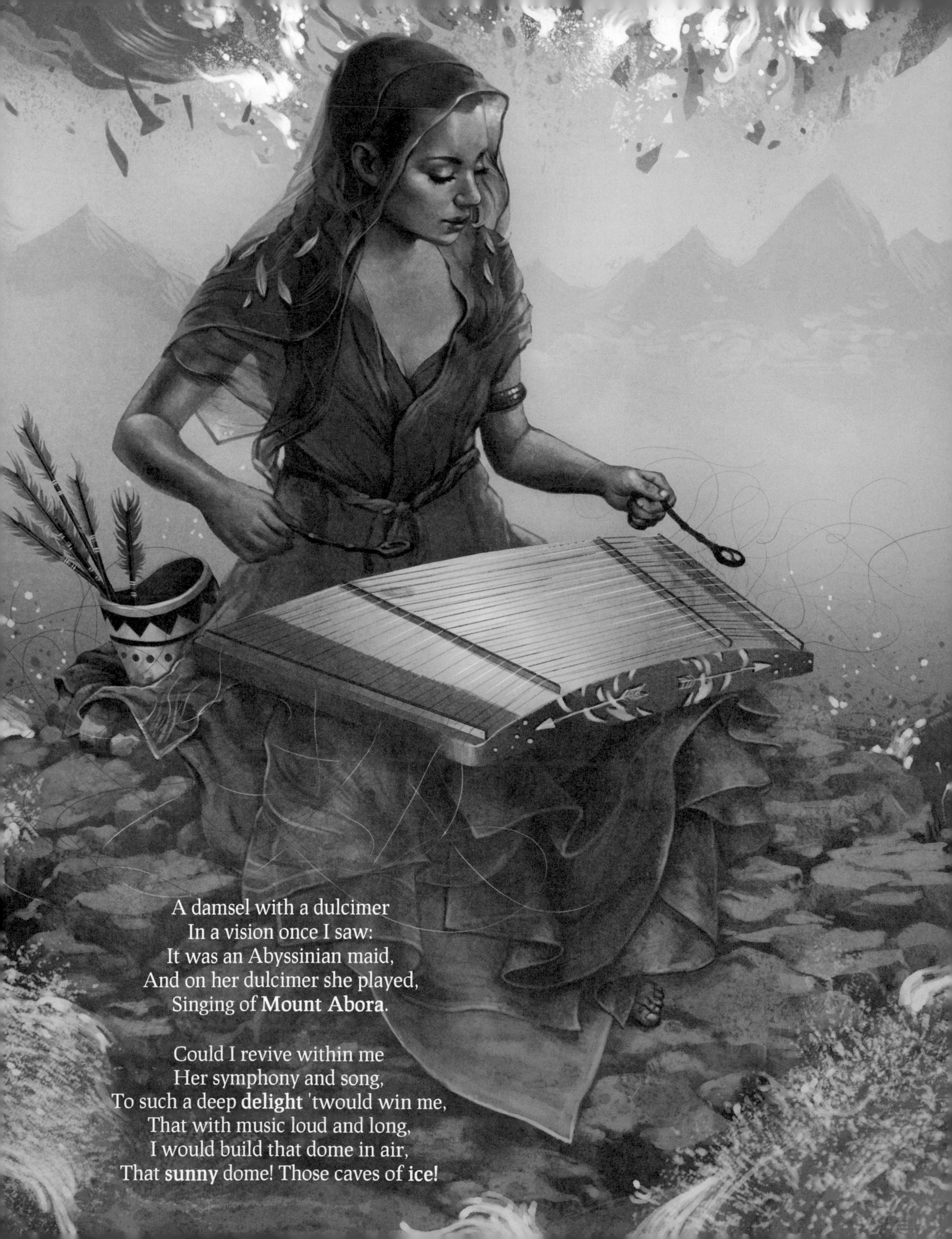

A damsel with a dulcimer
In a vision once I saw:
It was an Abyssinian maid,
And on her dulcimer she played,
Singing of **Mount Abora**.

Could I revive within me
Her symphony and song,
To such a deep **delight** 'twould win me,
That with music loud and long,
I would build that dome in air,
That **sunny** dome! Those caves of **ice!**

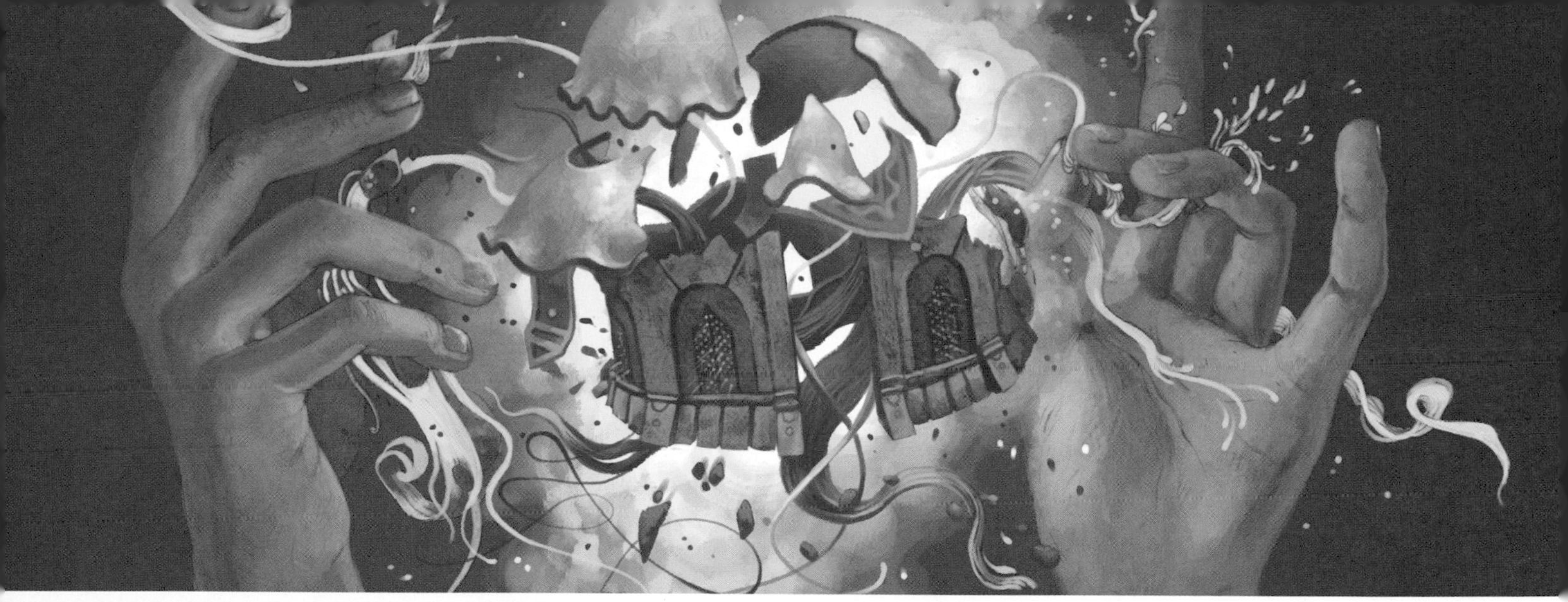

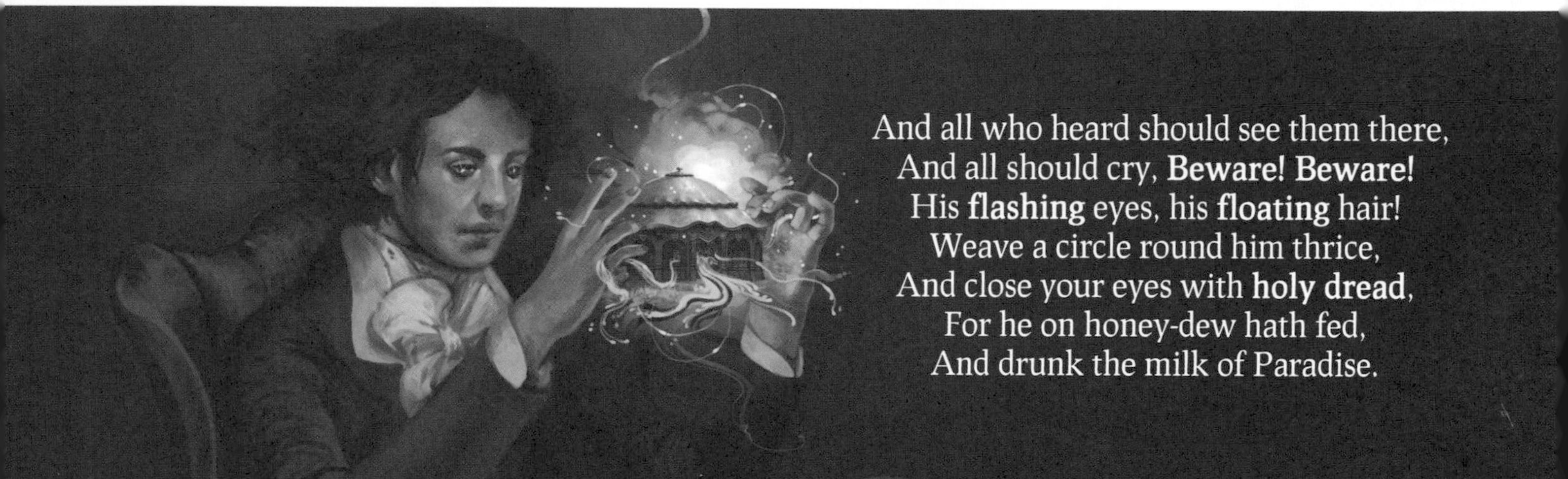

And all who heard should see them there,
And all should cry, **Beware! Beware!**
His **flashing** eyes, his **floating** hair!
Weave a circle round him thrice,
And close your eyes with **holy dread**,
For he on honey-dew hath fed,
And drunk the milk of Paradise.

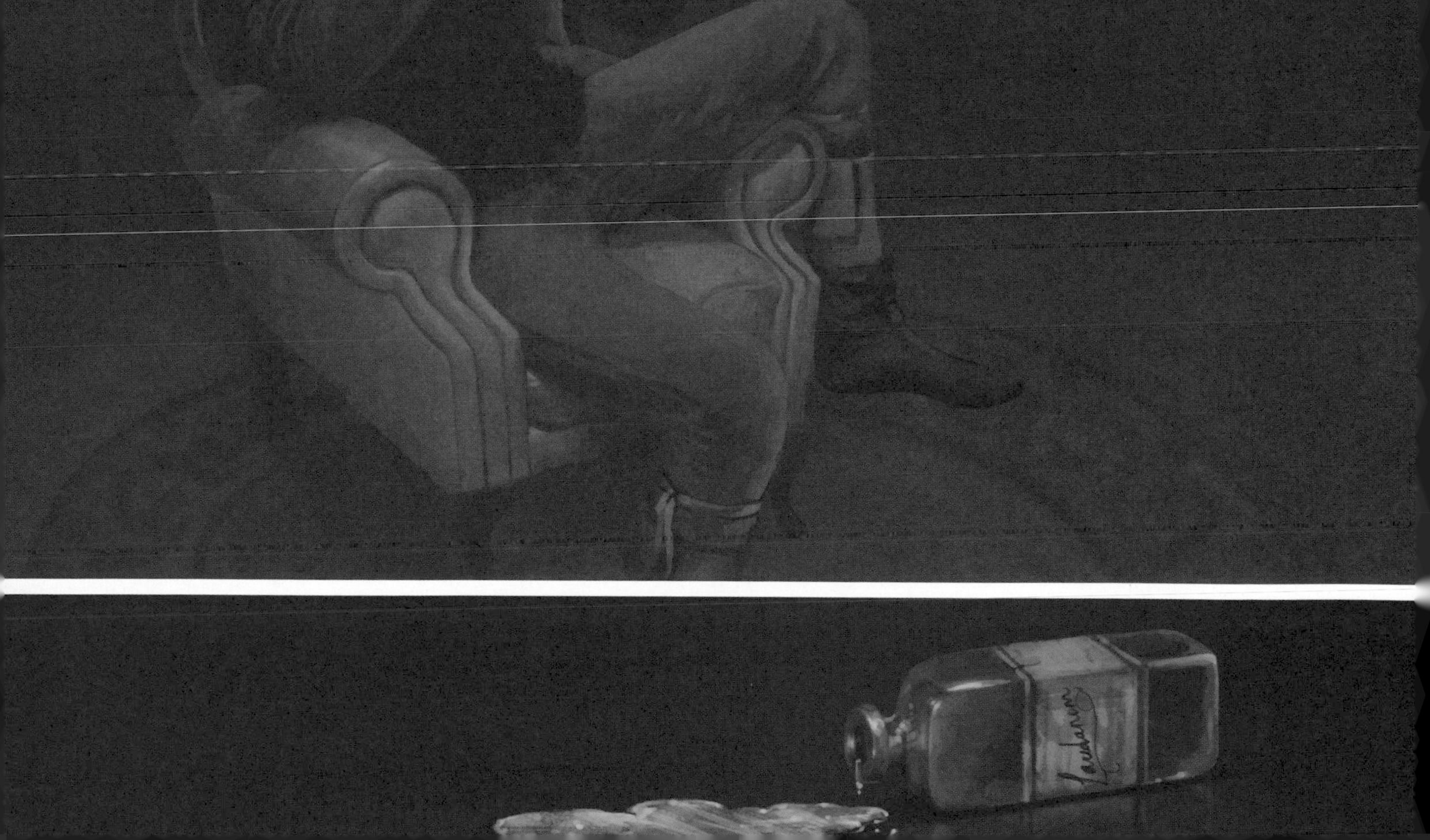

"The Rime of the Ancient Mariner"

Samuel Taylor Coleridge

ART/ADAPTATION BY **Hunt Emerson**

SOME POETS AND WRITERS ATTEMPT TO WRITE an amazing work of literature. Others simply want to make some money by cashing in on a publishing trend and end up writing a classic of the Western canon. Coleridge and his friend/collaborator William Wordsworth came up with an idea during one of their long walks along Britain's Devon coast: together they would write a ballad—a form that had recently become very popular—rife with supernatural and Gothic elements (also a big sensation at the time), then sell it for five pounds to *Monthly Magazine.* Wordsworth contributed some important ideas and a couple of lines, but soon withdrew and let Coleridge run with it. In his hands, it turned into something else—twice as long as a typical ballad, filled with archaic words and odd diction, and conveying an unclear message. It never did make it into a magazine, instead appearing as the first poem in *Lyrical Ballads*, the collection of poems separately written by Coleridge and Wordsworth that launched the Romantic movement in England in 1798.

Strangely enough, it's a quite non-Romantic poem in form and style, and no one knew what in God's name to make of it, so, predictably, it was torn to shreds by critics, contemporaries, and, at one point, even Wordsworth himself. Its strange, bulky presence at the very start of *Lyrical Ballads* almost torpedoed the book's reception, and later editions moved it much further inside.

The poem is relayed by a wedding guest who gets buttonholed by a half-crazed sailor who tells him of his bizarre experiences at sea, which famously involve an albatross around his neck and water, water everywhere, but not a drop to drink. "The Rime of the Ancient Mariner" is overwhelmingly dark and weird (though with a strong theme of spiritual redemption), but British comics legend Hunt Emerson has found the humor in it. Or, rather, he's made some humor for it in his full-length adaptation. Here we present the crucial second part of the tale. In Part One, the mariner's ship is trapped in the South Pole, but an albatross appears—a good omen to sailors: "We hailed it in God's name"—and immediately the ice cracks and a favorable wind blows, allowing the ship and her crew to get back to safe, though foggy, waters, as the albatross follows them. Suddenly, the mariner shoots and kills the albatross with a crossbow. (Just why he did such a stupid and cruel thing to a creature that everyone believed had saved them is one of the biggest mysteries in literature, and has provided fuel for endless grad student papers.) Part Two shows us the immediate aftermath of the mariner's callous act.

SOURCE

Hill, John Spencer. *A Coleridge Companion*. London: Macmillan Press, 1983.

part the second

"THE RIME OF THE ANCIENT MARINER" SAMUEL TAYLOR COLERIDGE HUNT EMERSON

7

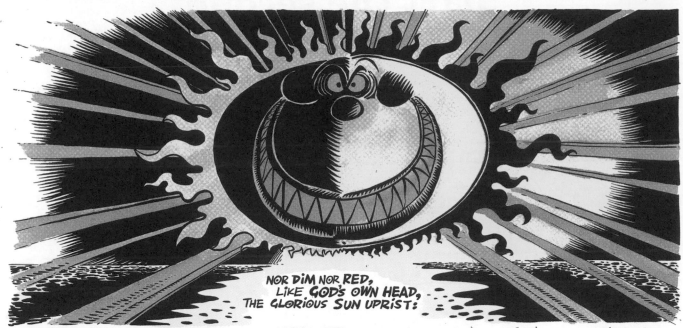

NOR DIM NOR RED,
LIKE GOD'S OWN HEAD,
THE GLORIOUS SUN UPRIST:

THEN ALL AVERRED, I HAD KILLED THE BIRD
THAT BROUGHT THE FOG AND MIST...

'TWAS RIGHT, SAID THEY,

SUCH BIRDS TO SLAY,
THAT BRING THE FOG AND MIST!

THE FAIR BREEZE BLEW, THE WHITE FOAM FLEW,
THE FURROW FOLLOWED FREE;

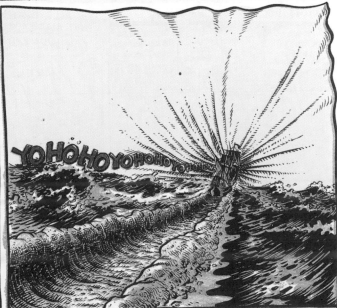

"THE RIME OF THE ANCIENT MARINER" SAMUEL TAYLOR COLERIDGE HUNT EMERSON

"THE RIME OF THE ANCIENT MARINER" SAMUEL TAYLOR COLERIDGE HUNT EMERSON

ALL IN A HOT AND COPPER SKY,
THE BLOODY SUN, AT NOON,
RIGHT UP ABOVE THE MAST DID STAND,
NO BIGGER THAN THE MOON...

DAY AFTER DAY, DAY AFTER DAY,
WE STUCK, NOR BREATH NOR MOTION...
AS IDLE AS A PAINTED SHIP
UPON A PAINTED OCEAN!

WATER, WATER, EVERYWHERE, AND ALL THE BOARDS DID SHRINK!

LOOK! THIS BOARD'S SHRUNK!

SO HAS THIS BOARD!

WATER...

...WATER, EVERYWHERE... NOR ANY DROP TO DRINK!

WATER SUPPLY
INVOICE
PAY £5000

"THE RIME OF THE ANCIENT MARINER" SAMUEL TAYLOR COLERIDGE HUNT EMERSON

"THE RIME OF THE ANCIENT MARINER" SAMUEL TAYLOR COLERIDGE HUNT EMERSON

AND SOME IN **DREAMS** ASSURÉD WERE OF THE **SPIRIT** THAT PLAGUED US SO...

NINE FATHOM DEEP HE HAD FOLLOWED US FROM THE LAND OF MIST AND SNOW!

NO! NO!

NO! NO!

AND EVERY TONGUE, THROUGH UTTER DROUGHT, WAS WITHERED AT THE ROOT; WE COULD NOT SPEAK, NO MORE THAN IF WE HAD BEEN CHOKED WITH SOOT!

AH! WELL A-DAY! WHAT EVIL LOOKS HAD I FROM OLD AND YOUNG!

AK! AK! AK! AK! AK!

INSTEAD OF THE **CROSS**...

...THE ALBATROSS...

...ABOUT MY NECK WAS HUNG!

"THE RIME OF THE ANCIENT MARINER" SAMUEL TAYLOR COLERIDGE HUNT EMERSON

"Auguries of Innocence"

William Blake

ART/ADAPTATION BY **Aidan Koch**

THROUGHOUT HIS WHOLE LIFE, FROM THE TIME he was a toddler in the early 1760s, William Blake had visions—talking to archangels and seeing God's face, angels in trees, and spirits of the dead (including his younger brother, Voltaire, a flea, and many, many others). He was also a social and political radical, supporting free love and violent revolution against tyranny.

He earned his living, barely, as an innovative, talented engraver and printer. This served him well with his own poetry, allowing him to self-publish books illustrated with his own stunning paintings, lettered by hand, and colored and printed in his own shop. (See *Jerusalem*, later in this volume, for a mind-blowing example.)

His most accessible, and most anthologized, poems come from *Songs of Innocence* and *Songs of Experience*: "The Chimney Sweeper," "The Lamb," "Holy Thursday," "The Little Girl Lost," "The Sick Rose," "London," "The Tyger" ("Tyger Tyger. burning bright, / In the forests of the night"). Most of the other work he published is prophetic, dense, and overtly visionary, and, being exceptionally hard to understand, isn't read as much.

Blake wrote the poem here, "Auguries of Innocence," in one of his notebooks, probably in 1803, well after the *Songs* books. He never published it, and it didn't see the light of day until thirty-six years after his 1827 death. The opening four lines are perhaps the most famous lines he wrote, presenting some of his mystical views in a shimmering, highly rhythmic little package. This quatrain is sometimes published as a stand-alone poem. The next two lines—"A Robin Red breast in a Cage / Puts all heaven in a Rage"—are fairly famous in their own right, but the rest of this somewhat lengthy poem is little-known. Aidan Koch applies her trademark checkerboard approach to the entire work, marking the first time that these words of Blake have been married with images.

Auguries of Innocence

TO SEE A WORLD IN A GRAIN OF SAND

AND A HEAVEN IN A WILD FLOWER ,

HOLD INFINITY IN THE PALM OF YOUR HAND AND ETERNITY IN AN HOUR.

A ROBIN RED BREAST IN A CAGE PUTS ALL HEAVEN IN A RAGE.

A DOVE HOUSE FILL'D WITH DOVES & PIGEONS SHUDDERS HELL THRO' ALL ITS REGIONS.

A DOG STARV'D AT HIS MASTER'S GATE PREDICTS THE RUIN OF THE STATE.

A HORSE MISUS'D UPON THE ROAD CALLS TO HEAVEN FOR HUMAN BLOOD.

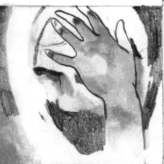

EACH OUTCRY OF THE HUNTED HARE A FIBRE FROM THE BRAIN DOES TEAR.

"AUGURIES OF INNOCENCE" WILLIAM BLAKE AIDAN KOCH

A SKYLARK WOUNDED
IN A WING,
A CHERUBIM DOES CEASE
TO SING.
THE GAME COCK CLIP'D
AND ARM'D FOR FIGHT
DOES THE RISING SUN
AFFRIGHT.
EVERY WOLF'S & LION'S
HOWL
RAISES FROM HELL A
HUMAN SOUL.
THE WILD DEER, WAND'RING
HERE AND THERE,
KEEP THE HUMAN SOUL
FROM CARE.
THE LAMB MISUS'D
BREEDS PUBLIC STRIFE
AND YET FORGIVES THE
BUTCHER'S KNIFE.

THE BAT THAT FLITS AT
CLOSE OF EVE
HAS LEFT THE BRAIN THAT
WON'T BELIEVE.
THE OWL THAT CALLS
UPON THE NIGHT
SPEAKS THE UNBELIEVER'S
FRIGHT.
HE WHO SHALL HURT THE
LITTLE WREN
SHALL NEVER BE BELOV'D
BY MEN.
HE WHO THE OX TO WRATH
HAS MOV'D
SHALL NEVER BE BY WOMAN
LOV'D.
THE WANTON BOY THAT
KILLS THE FLY
SHALL FEEL THE SPIDER'S
ENMITY.

HE WHO TORMENTS
THE CHAFER'S SPRITE
WEAVES A BOWER IN
ENDLESS NIGHT.
THE CATERPILLER ON
THE LEAF
REPEATS TO THEE THY
MOTHER'S GRIEF.

KILL NOT THE MOTH
NOR BUTTERFLY,
FOR THE LAST JUDGEMENT
DRAWETH NIGH.
HE WHO SHALL TRAIN
THE HORSE TO WAR
SHALL NEVER PASS
THE POLAR BAR.

THE BEGGAR'S DOG AND
WIDOW'S CAT,
FEED THEM AND THOU
WILT GROW FAT.
THE GNAT THAT SINGS HIS
SUMMER'S SONG
POISON GETS FROM
SLANDER'S TONGUE.
THE POISON OF THE SNAKE
AND NEWT
IS THE SWEAT OF ENVY'S
FOOT.
THE POISON OF THE
HONEY BEE
IS THE ARTIST'S JEALOUSY.
THE PRINCE'S ROBES AND
BEGGAR'S RAGS
ARE TOADSTOOLS ON THE
MISER'S BAGS.
A TRUTH IS TOLD WITH
BAD INTENT.
BEATS ALL THE LIES YOU
CAN INVENT.

IT IS RIGHT IT SHOULD
BE SO;
MAN WAS MADE FOR JOY
AND WOE;
AND WHEN THIS WE
RIGHTY KNOW
THRO' THE WORLD WE
SAFELY GO.
JOY AND WOE ARE
WOVEN FINE,
A CLOTHING FOR THE
SOUL DIVINE;
UNDER EVERY GRIEF & PINE
RUNS A JOY WITH SILKEN
TWINE.
THE BABE IS MORE THAN
SWADDLING BANDS;
THROUGHOUT ALL THESE
HUMAN LANDS
TOOLS WERE MADE, AND
BORN WERE HANDS,
EVERY FARMER
UNDERSTANDS.

EVERY TEAR
FROM EVERY EYE
BECOMES A BABE
IN ETERNITY;

THIS IS CAUGHT
BY FEMALES BRIGHT
AND RETURN'D
TO ITS OWN
DELIGHT.

THE BLEAT, THE BARK, BELLOW & ROAR
AND WAVES THAT BEAT ON HEAVEN'S SHORE.
THE BABE THAT WEEPS THE ROD BENEATH
WRITES REVENGE IN REALMS OF DEATH.
THE BEGGAR'S RAGS, FLUTTERING IN AIR,
DOES TO RAGS THE HEAVENS TEAR.
THE SOLDIER, ARM'D, WITH SWORD & GUN,
PALSIED STRIKES THE SUMMER'S SUN.
THE POOR MAN'S FARTHING IS WORTH MORE
THAN ALL THE GOLD ON AFRIC'S SHORE.
ONE MITE WRUNG FROM LABRER'S HANDS
SHALL BUY & SELL THE MISER'S LANDS:
OR, IF PROTECTED FROM ON HIGH,
DOES THAT WHOLE NATION SELL & BUY.

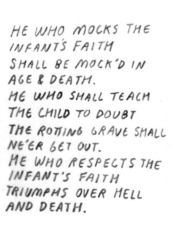

HE WHO MOCKS THE
INFANT'S FAITH
SHALL BE MOCK'D IN
AGE & DEATH.
HE WHO SHALL TEACH
THE CHILD TO DOUBT
THE ROTTING GRAVE SHALL
NE'ER GET OUT.
HE WHO RESPECTS THE
INFANT'S FAITH
TRIUMPHS OVER HELL
AND DEATH.

"AUGURIES OF INNOCENCE" WILLIAM BLAKE AIDAN KOCH

THE CHILD'S TOYS AND THE OLD MAN'S REASONS
ARE THE FRUITS OF THE TWO SEASONS.
THE QUESTIONER, WHO SITS SO SLY,
SHALL NEVER KNOW HOW TO REPLY.
HE WHO REPLIES TO WORDS OF DOUBT
DOTH PUT THE LIGHT OF KNOWLEDGE OUT.
THE STRONGEST POISON EVER KNOWN
CAME FROM CAESAR'S LAUREL CROWN.
NOUGHT CAN DEFORM THE HUMAN RACE
LIKE TO THE ARMOUR'S IRON BRACE.
WHEN GOLD & GEMS ADORN THE PLOW
TO PEACEFUL ARTS SHALL ENVY BOW.
A RIDDLE OR THE CRICKET'S CRY
IS TO DOUBT A FIT REPLY.
THE EMMET'S INCH AND EAGLE'S MILE
MAKE LAME PHILOSOPHY TO SMILE.

HE WHO DOUBTS
FROM WHAT HE SEES
WILL NE'ER BELIEVE,
DO WHAT YOU PLEASE.
IF THE SUN & MOON
SHOULD DOUBT,
THEY'D IMMEDIATELY
GO OUT.
TO BE IN A PASSION
YOU GOOD MAY DO,
BUT NO GOOD IF A
PASSION IS IN YOU.

THE WHORE & GAMBLER,
BY THE STATE
LICENC'D, BUILD THAT
NATION'S FATE.
THE HARLOT'S CRY FROM
STREET TO STREET
SHALL WEAVE OLD
ENGLAND'S WINDING SHEET.
THE WINNER'S SHOUT,
THE LOSER'S CURSE,
DANCE BEFORE DEAD
ENGLAND'S HEARSE.

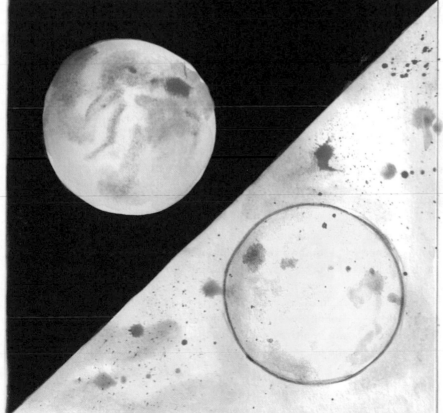

EVERY NIGHT & EVERY MORN
SOME TO MISERY ARE BORN.
EVERY MORN & EVERY NIGHT
SOME ARE BORN TO SWEET DELIGHT.
SOME ARE BORN TO SWEET DELIGHT,
SOME ARE BORN TO ENDLESS NIGHT.

WE ARE LED TO BELIEVE A LIE
WHEN WE SEE NOT THRO' THE EYE,
WHICH WAS BORN IN A NIGHT
TO PERISH IN A NIGHT
WHEN THE SOUL SLEPT IN BEAMS
OF LIGHT.

GOD APPEARS AND GOD IS LIGHT
TO THOSE POOR SOULS WHO DWELL
IN NIGHT,
BUT DOES A HUMAN FORM DISPLAY
TO THOSE WHO DWELL IN REALMS
OF DAY.

Pride and Prejudice

Jane Austen

ART/ADAPTATION BY **Huxley King**

DESIGN EDITOR: **Terrence Boyce**

DOES JANE AUSTEN NEED AN INTRODUCTION AT this point? We're firmly in the grip of Jane-mania, and it doesn't show signs of loosening. She herself would undoubtedly be surprised and probably upset. Most of her books sold fairly well while she was alive, but they were all published anonymously (at her urging)—attributed to "a Lady" or "the author of" her prior novels—and her name started appearing on them only after her death. So even though a lot of people read her books—and they received some favorable though brief reviews—she achieved no personal fame, which is exactly how she wanted it. And there was certainly no sign that she would be recognized as a great writer with all of her novels firmly in the canon.

She died young, aged forty-one, of a still-undetermined medical condition. The marble marker on her grave in Winchester Cathedral doesn't even mention that she was a writer, saying only that she was "the youngest daughter of the late Revd George Austen." Her novels continued to be read by a small number of admirers, but she was half-forgotten by the world at large until 1870, when, more than five decades after her death, her nephew published a fond, intimate family portrait entitled *A Memoir of Jane Austen.* The book ignited an intense interest in Austen and her works. The first wave of Jane-mania took off among the reading public, which couldn't get enough of *Sense and Sensibility*, *Pride and Prejudice*, *Emma*, and her other writings of women living in the strange confines of the lower-upper crust of Regency England. She also received a lot of critical attention at that time, but it was really in the early twentieth century that her literary reputation was cemented.

Huxley King and her husband, Terrence Boyce, a graphic designer for print and television, are longtime friends of mine. Huxley's immediately recognizable artwork is vibrant, contemporary, and erotically charged, yet her literary tastes—she's a voracious speed-reader—are almost entirely nineteenth century. I was eager to see them mix. Huxley says:

> The chance to draw Lizzy was entirely too good to pass up. Elizabeth Bennet has been my heroine since I was a young girl. She's an intelligent, witty, clever, and complex woman, much like Austen herself. I love all of Jane Austen's

work—her gently incisive satire is finely wrought—but *Pride and Prejudice* will always have a special place in my heart because of Lizzy. Besides, my two favorite things to draw are pretty girls and pretty clothes, and the Bennet sisters definitely fit the bill!

> I drew great inspiration from the classical obsession of the Georgian era. There's more than a hint of Greek statuary in the characters' faces, and the "architecture" of the pages features several intricate examples of Palladian-inspired columns, friezes, and arches.

> The creation of the piece was a truly collaborative process. I drew every element (patterns, figures, and frames) separately; they were compiled by my wonderful collaborator and design editor Terrence Boyce. This allowed several layers of patterns to be overlaid and used, for example, in the girls' dresses.

> My artwork is peculiarly pattern-heavy. While it makes for a very elaborate and interesting look, it presented one creative hurdle when making this piece. Jane Austen has a lot of dialogue! We soon realized that the enormous blocks of text, if put into a traditional speech bubble, would completely obscure a good portion of the background art.

Terrence explains how the unusual visual approach to dialogue came about:

> The treatment of the speech bubbles came about serendipitously—I was dropping-in Huxley's lettering line-by-line, and needed to make an edit. As I broke a word off from its line, I realized it looked like magnetic poetry text. I tried it out on a spread and really liked the effect. It keeps more of the artwork visible, and also allows for special emphasis in the way italics or bold type would typically be used.

In the portion of the novel adapted here, chapter 2, the Bennet sisters, all unmarried (the horror!), and their mother are in a tizzy over a wealthy, handsome bachelor who has moved into a nearby estate.

SOURCE

Ross, Josephine. *Jane Austen: A Companion*. New Brunswick, NJ: Rutgers University Press, 2003.

PRIDE AND PREJUDICE JANE AUSTEN HUXLEY KING WITH TERRENCE BOYCE

...THE REST OF THE EVENING WAS SPENT IN CONJECTURING HOW SOON HE WOULD RETURN MR. BENNET'S VISIT, AND DETERMINING WHEN THEY SHOULD ASK HIM TO DINNER.

"She Walks in Beauty"

George Gordon, Lord Byron

ART/ADAPTATION BY **David Lasky**

IT'S HARD TO GET ACROSS IN A SHORT SPACE THE larger-than-life figure of George Gordon, Lord Byron, the very archetype of the literary bad boy. One of his platoon of lovers, Lady Caroline Lamb, famously described him as, "Mad, bad, and dangerous to know." A *New York Times* review of one of his biographies offers a good summation of his infamies: "his compulsive love affairs with women and boys; his drinking and excess; the scandalous liaison with his half sister, Augusta (who may have borne him a child in 1814); the bizarre athletic feats; his exile in Italy and exotic death in 1824 at the age of thirty-six while trying to foment a revolution in Greece." The article takes note of

> . . . the mesmeric, even dizzying effect his body had on others. At a ball in London during the period of the scandal over his divorce from Annabella Milbanke, the militant prude whom he had married in 1815 in a disastrous attempt to cure himself of his own emotional excesses, a woman fainted at the sight of him; another warned her daughter, "Don't look at him, he is dangerous to look at." One-time lovers, like the louche Mrs. Wherry, cherished fetishistic mementos of his person—including black curling locks of his pubic hair—like magic talismans.

Byron's indoor pets included monkeys, peacocks, an eagle, and a crocodile. He carried two loaded sidearms with him at all times. What's a poet without pistols? It probably was a good idea, considering the public furor his daring poetry and dissolute life caused, plus there was no telling when a jealous husband might show up.

But beyond the wild life, there was the justly celebrated poetry: the world-weary *Childe Harold's Pilgrimage*, which made him famous overnight; the sexy, scandalous quasi-epic *Don Juan* ("What men call gallantry, and gods adultery, / Is much more common where the climate's sultry."); his much-anthologized "So, We'll Go No More a Roving," which he dashed off in a letter to a friend; and "She Walks in Beauty," his 1814 ode to his cousin's wife, Anne Horton Wilmot.

David Lasky is no stranger to graphically adapting literature. His minicomic condensing *Ulysses* into twelve pages is itself a classic (look for it in Volume 3), and his abstracted take on "The Raven" broke new ground. For this beautiful black and white ("dark and bright") adaptation, he incorporates portraits of fellow artists Sarah McIntyre and Molly Kiely, the first photograph of DNA, the Bride of Frankenstein, and other surprises.

SOURCES

Castle, Terry. "Mad, Bad and Dangerous to Know." *The New York Times*, April 13, 1997.

O'Brien, Edna. *Byron in Love: A Short Daring Life*. New York: W.W. Norton & Company, 2009.

She walks in beauty, like the night

Of cloudless climes and starry skies;

And all that's best of dark and bright

Meet in her aspect and her eyes:

Thus mellow'd to that tender light

Which heaven to gaudy day denies.

One shade more, one ray the less.

Had half impair'd the nameless grace

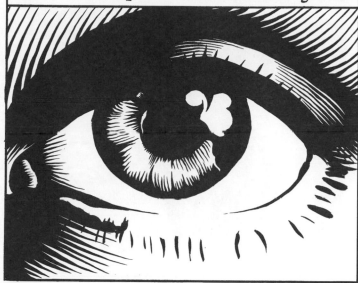

Which waves in every raven tress,

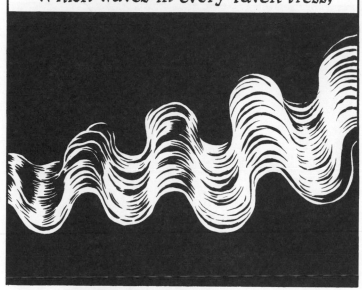

Or softly lightens o'er her face;

Where thoughts serenely sweet express

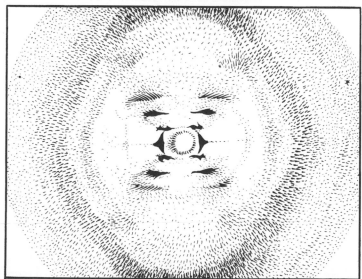

How pure, how dear their dwelling-place.

"SHE WALKS IN BEAUTY" GEORGE GORDON, LORD BYRON DAVID LASKY   29

And on that cheek, and o'er that brow,

So soft, so calm,

yet eloquent,

The smiles that win, the tints that glow,

But tell of days in goodness spent,

A mind at peace with all below,

A heart whose love is innocent!

She Walks in Beauty. Lord Byron, 1814. Adapted by David Lasky, 2012.

30 "SHE WALKS IN BEAUTY" GEORGE GORDON, LORD BYRON DAVID LASKY

"Ozymandias"

Percy Bysshe Shelley

ART/ADAPTATION BY **Anthony Ventura**

PERCY BYSSHE SHELLEY WAS A SOCIAL AND political radical who was thrown out of Oxford University in 1811 for his pamphlet "The Necessity of Atheism." He also espoused free love, vegetarianism, social justice, antiwar views, and nonviolent revolution. His second wife was *Frankenstein* author Mary Godwin, the daughter of the proto-anarchist writer William Godwin and Mary Wollstonecraft, author of the radical tract *A Vindication of the Rights of Woman* (covered in Volume 1). Like his brethren John Keats and Lord Byron, Shelley died young. Just short of his thirtieth birthday, he drowned while sailing in his schooner, and the circumstances are cloudy. Was it suicide, a "self-willed accident," an attempted robbery, a political hit, or simply the result of stormy weather? . . .

Among Shelley's surprisingly large body of work, which includes essays and fiction as well as some of the greatest poetry in the English language, is "To a Skylark," "Ode to the West Wind," *Prometheus Unbound*, and the anarchist-utopian *Queen Mab*:

> Look to thyself, priest, conqueror or prince!
> Whether thy trade is falsehood, and thy lusts
> Deep wallow in the earnings of the poor,
> With whom thy master was; or thou delight'st
> In numbering o'er the myriads of thy slain,
> All misery weighing nothing in the scale
> Against thy short-lived fame; or thou dost load
> With cowardice and crime the groaning land,
> A pomp-fed king. Look to thy wretched self!

"Ozymandias"—perhaps Shelley's most anthologized lyric poem (and the source for one of the central characters in Alan Moore's *The Watchmen*)—is in line with this angry, unimpressed view of rulers and kingdoms. You can almost hear Shelley laughing as he writes of a mighty, megalomaniacal pharaoh (Ramses II) whose vast empire has literally vanished into nothingness.

Anthony Ventura had used his talents as an illustrator and graphic designer to create engaging magazine-style spreads for contemporary Native American poems. I asked him to apply the same approach to some of the classics, including Shelley's mocking of earthly power.

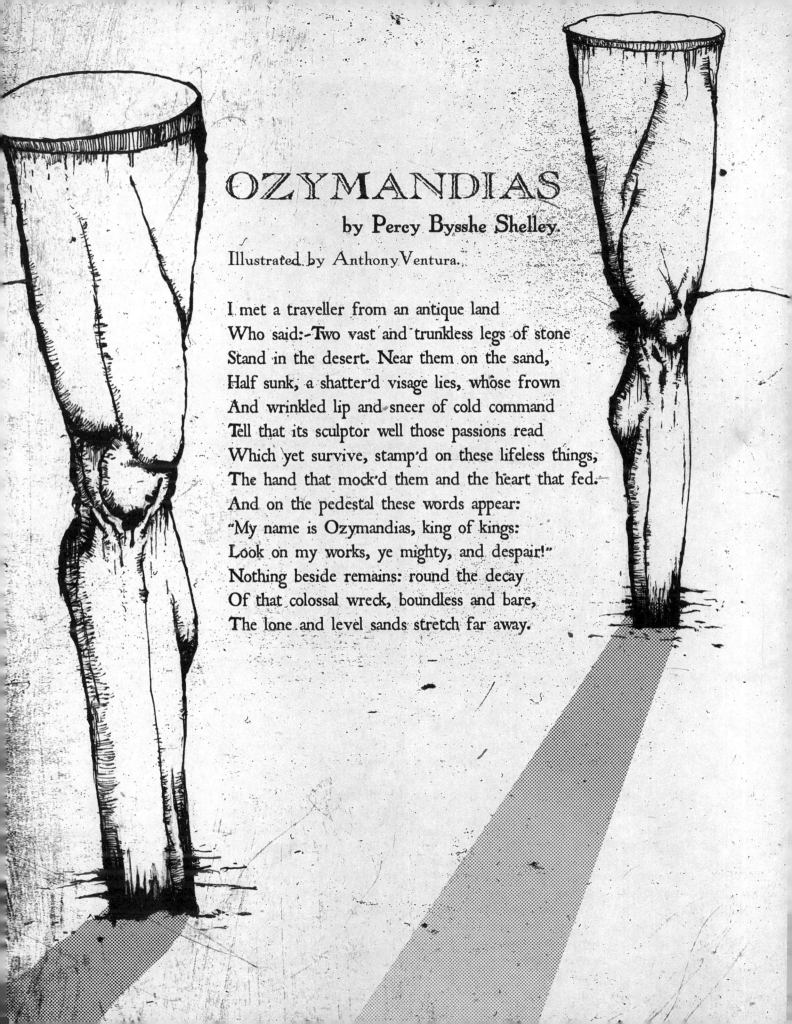

OZYMANDIAS
by Percy Bysshe Shelley.

Illustrated by Anthony Ventura.

I met a traveller from an antique land
Who said:—Two vast and trunkless legs of stone
Stand in the desert. Near them on the sand,
Half sunk, a shatter'd visage lies, whose frown
And wrinkled lip and sneer of cold command
Tell that its sculptor well those passions read
Which yet survive, stamp'd on these lifeless things,
The hand that mock'd them and the heart that fed.
And on the pedestal these words appear:
"My name is Ozymandias, king of kings:
Look on my works, ye mighty, and despair!"
Nothing beside remains: round the decay
Of that colossal wreck, boundless and bare,
The lone and level sands stretch far away.

"I Wandered Lonely as a Cloud"

William Wordsworth

ART/ADAPTATION BY **PMurphy**

WITH HIS CELEBRATIONS OF THE HEALING, redemptive power of nature and his straightforward style, William Wordsworth revolutionized poetry and essentially kick-started the Romantic movement in Britain. "I Wandered Lonely as a Cloud" is a perfect example of his approach, and it's become one of the most famous, most anthologized, and most taught poems in the English language.

The narrator unexpectedly came upon a beautiful field of daffodils, and the memory of it cheers and energizes him. The poem is based on an experience Wordsworth and his sister Dorothy had, in April 1802, while going for one of their many walks. At least two years later, Wordsworth wrote the poem, which was published in 1807 and heavily revised and expanded in 1815. His wife, Mary, wrote the two lines that Wordsworth considered the poem's best bit:

They flash upon that inward eye
Which is the bliss of solitude.

The poem isn't complicated. There are no nuances to speak of, no subtexts to tease out. There is some juicy stuff going on with "the inward eye," the comparison to stars and water, and the unusual "reverse personification" of the title/ first line, in which the narrator compares himself to a cloud, but it's still simple and charming. Like so many works of now-classic lit, "Daffodils" (as it's often called) was sliced to ribbons by critics and poets who sniffed at what they saw as a simplistic and sentimental poem.

While we know that William and Dorothy saw the expanse of daffodils by a large British lake, the poem itself doesn't specify a place. Artist PMurphy has therefore located it in a most unexpected spot, and applied what I want to call a delicious, candy-coated palette, creating a highly original take on a very familiar poem.

SOURCE

The Writer's Almanac with Garrison Keillor. National Public Radio, April 15, 2011.

"I WANDERED LONELY AS A CLOUD" WILLIAM WORDSWORTH PMURPHY   35

Continuous as the stars that shine & twinkle on the Milky Way, They stretched in never-ending line along the margin of a bay:

Ten thousand saw I at a glance, tossing their heads in sprightly dance.

The waves beside them danced; but they Out-did the sparkling waves in glee: A poet could not but be gay, in such a jocund company:

I gazed - and gazed - but little thought what wealth the show to me had brought.

For oft, when on my couch I lie In vacant or in pensive mood They flash upon that inward eye

Which is the bliss of solitude; And then my heart with pleasure fills And dances with the daffodils.

"O Solitude"

John Keats

ART/ADAPTATION BY **Hunt Emerson**

JOHN KEATS WAS THE LEAST WILD AND BAD-BOYISH of the second generation of British Romantics, though like his compatriots, he obeyed the unspoken dictum of dying young (at age twenty-five, after an ugly struggle with tuberculosis). Both his parents had died by the time he was fourteen, and he dealt with financial strife all his life, as brief as it was. He earned his medical license but never practiced, deciding to devote himself to writing poetry full-time, and if you've read many of my little introductions in this volume, you won't be surprised to learn that his now-revered work was either ignored or lambasted during his lifetime.

Of his brethren, he was the most concerned with the poetic process, the way the poet sees things. He famously wrote in a letter: "I am certain of nothing but the holiness of the Heart's affections and the truth of the imagination. What imagination seizes as Beauty must be truth." In another letter, he explained: ". . . at once it struck me what quality

went to form a Man of Achievement, especially in Literature, and which Shakespeare possessed so enormously—I mean Negative Capability, that is, when a man is capable of being in uncertainties, mysteries, doubts, without any irritable reaching after fact and reason . . ."

Keats is typically considered a finer poet than Byron or Shelley, with several of his works—including "To Autumn" and "Ode on a Grecian Urn"—numbered among the absolute best English-language poems in existence, sometimes referred to as flawless and perfect. On the following page we have his first published poem, "O Solitude," which ran in 1816 in a journal edited by Leigh Hunt (see "Rondeau" ["Jenny Kiss'd Me"] a little later in this volume). Hunt Emerson—"the dean of British cartoonists"—offers a humorous spin on Keats's maiden publication, which itself ends with a witty, unexpected twist.

Oh Solitude!

A SONNET BY John Keats

DRAWN BY HUNT EMERSON·

Frankenstein

Mary Shelley

ADAPTATION BY **Jason Cobley**

ART BY **Declan Shalvey**

IT'S FUNNY HOW MANY WORKS OF NINETEENTH- century literature have creation stories almost as famous as the writings themselves. In this case, Lord Byron was living on the shore of Lake Geneva in May 1816, having gone into self-imposed exile to escape public reaction to his affair with his half-sister (which was only the latest, though biggest, of the public scandals he touched off). Among his retinue was his physician, John Polidori, and they were joined by fellow Romantic poet Percy Bysshe Shelley; his lover and soon-to-be wife, the eighteen-year-old writer Mary Godwin Shelley; and Mary's stepsister, Claire Clairmont, lover to both Percy and Byron.

The weather was strangely dismal during the entire summer, resulting in a bad case of cabin fever, and one night after the group read ghost stories, Byron proposed a contest in which they'd all write horror stories. He and Percy wrote some fragments but soon lost interest. Mary couldn't figure out what to write until she had a profoundly disturbing waking dream—a reverie, a vision—of a scientist who uses corpse parts to make a being he animates with electricity. She wrote her story during the summer, and later expanded it to book length, including passages that we now know were written by Percy. *Frankenstein; or, The Modern Prometheus* was published in 1818, and a much-revised edition came out in 1831, the latter being the edition almost always published these days. (For his part, Polidori wrote "The Vampyre," generally considered the story that created the vampire literary genre.)

Just as Victor Frankenstein loosed his misunderstood creation upon the world, so Mary Shelley's own creation has been misunderstood. Frankenstein's monster is embedded in our cultural consciousness as a grunting, staggering, half-vegetative simpleton, mainly because this is the way he almost always has been portrayed in decades' worth of movies. Reading Shelley's novel is a shock. The creature—who was indeed cobbled together with corpse parts and given a jolt of lightning—is extraordinarily intelligent. Mensa material. He's eloquent and philosophical, thanks to finding a cache of classic literature from which he taught himself to read. Living in a hovel, he spies on a family in a cottage, learning about the love he's missing and will surely never have. Sensitive and caring, he becomes upset at having been rejected by his creator and by the humans he has so far encountered. The excerpt here is taken from a full-length graphic novel adapted by Jason Cobley, who has adapted other literary works for the UK's Classical Comics, with art by Declan Shalvey, who has drawn for Marvel and Vertigo. In it, we see what finally drives this internally lovely, externally hideous being over the edge. . . .

SOURCE

Mellor, Anne K. *Mary Shelley: Her Life, Her Fiction, Her Monsters.* New York: Routledge, 1999.

FRANKENSTEIN MARY SHELLEY JASON COBLEY AND DECLAN SHALVEY

CRACK!

IN A TRANSPORT OF FURY, HE DASHED ME TO THE GROUND. I COULD HAVE TORN HIM LIMB FROM LIMB. BUT MY HEART SUNK WITHIN ME AS WITH BITTER SICKNESS, AND I REFRAINED.

OVERCOME BY PAIN AND ANGUISH, I QUITTED THE COTTAGE, AND IN THE GENERAL TUMULT ESCAPED UNPERCEIVED TO MY HOVEL.

VOLUME II
CHAPTER VIII

MY PROTECTORS DEPARTED THE COTTAGE.

AS THE NIGHT ADVANCED, IN MY INSANITY OF RAGE AND REVENGE, I LIGHTED THE DRY BRANCH OF A TREE, AND THE COTTAGE WAS QUICKLY ENVELOPED BY THE FLAMES.

AND NOW, WITH THE WORLD BEFORE ME, WHITHER SHOULD I BEND MY STEPS?

I LEARNED FROM YOUR PAPERS THAT YOU WERE MY FATHER, MY CREATOR. YOU HAD MENTIONED GENEVA AS YOUR NATIVE TOWN;

AND TOWARDS THIS PLACE I RESOLVED TO PROCEED.

MY TRAVELS WERE LONG AND THE SUFFERINGS I ENDURED INTENSE. I GENERALLY RESTED DURING THE DAY AND TRAVELLED ONLY WHEN I WAS SECURED BY NIGHT FROM THE VIEW OF MAN.

ONE MORNING, HOWEVER, FINDING THAT MY PATH LAY THROUGH A DEEP WOOD, I VENTURED TO CONTINUE MY JOURNEY AFTER THE SUN HAD RISEN; THE SPRING DAY CHEERED ME.

I FELT EMOTIONS OF GENTLENESS AND PLEASURE REVIVE IN ME.

I HEARD THE SOUND OF VOICES, THAT INDUCED ME TO CONCEAL MYSELF. I WAS SCARCELY HID WHEN A YOUNG GIRL CAME RUNNING ALONG THE PRECIPITOUS SIDE OF THE RIVER.

SUDDENLY HER FOOT SLIPT, AND SHE FELL INTO THE RAPID STREAM!

I RUSHED FROM MY HIDING PLACE...

...AND WITH EXTREME LABOUR FROM THE FORCE OF THE CURRENT, SAVED HER AND DRAGGED HER TO SHORE.

SHE WAS SENSELESS, AND I ENDEAVOURED, BY EVERY MEANS IN MY POWER, TO RESTORE ANIMATION. I WAS SUDDENLY INTERRUPTED BY THE APPROACH OF A RUSTIC.

AFTER SOME WEEKS MY WOUND HEALED AND I CONTINUED MY JOURNEY. THE LABOURS I ENDURED WERE NO LONGER TO BE ALLEVIATED BY THE BRIGHT SUN; ALL JOY WAS BUT A MOCKERY WHICH INSULTED MY DESOLATE STATE. I WAS NOT MADE FOR THE ENJOYMENT OF PLEASURE.

IN TWO MONTHS I REACHED THE ENVIRONS OF GENEVA.

A SLIGHT SLEEP RELIEVED ME FROM THE PAIN OF REFLECTION...

...WHICH WAS DISTURBED BY THE APPROACH OF A BEAUTIFUL CHILD...

...RUNNING WITH THE SPORTIVENESS OF INFANCY.

AS I GAZED ON HIM, AN IDEA SEIZED ME THAT HE HAD LIVED TOO SHORT A TIME TO HAVE IMBIBED A HORROR OF DEFORMITY.

AAAHHH!

IF, THEREFORE, I COULD SEIZE HIM AND EDUCATE HIM AS MY COMPANION AND FRIEND, I SHOULD NOT BE SO DESOLATE IN THIS PEOPLED EARTH.

FRANKENSTEIN!

YOU BELONG THEN TO MY ENEMY - TO HIM TOWARDS WHOM I HAVE SWORN ETERNAL REVENGE!

YOU SHALL BE MY FIRST VICTIM!

THE CHILD STILL STRUGGLED, AND LOADED ME WITH EPITHETS WHICH CARRIED DESPAIR TO MY HEART; I GRASPED HIS THROAT TO SILENCE HIM...

...AND IN A MOMENT HE LAY DEAD AT MY FEET.

I TOO CAN CREATE DESOLATION! MY ENEMY IS NOT INVULNERABLE!

THIS DEATH WILL CARRY DESPAIR TO HIM, AND A THOUSAND OTHER MISERIES SHALL TORMENT AND DESTROY HIM!

AS I FIXED MY EYES ON THE CHILD, I SAW SOMETHING GLITTERING ON HIS BREAST. IT WAS A PORTRAIT OF A MOST LOVELY WOMAN.

I REMEMBERED THAT I WAS FOREVER DEPRIVED OF THE DELIGHTS THAT SUCH BEAUTIFUL CREATURES COULD BESTOW.

Fairy tales

The Brothers Grimm

ILLUSTRATIONS BY **S. Clay Wilson**

THE GERMAN LIBRARIANS, FOLKLORISTS, AND linguists Jacob and Wilhelm Grimm weren't looking to give generations of children around the world saccharine entertainment. As *National Geographic* explains, they were scholars on a mission:

> The stories collected by Jacob and Wilhelm Grimm in the early 1800s serve up life as generations of central Europeans knew it—capricious and often cruel. The two brothers, patriots determined to preserve Germanic folktales, were only accidental entertainers.
>
> Once they saw how the tales bewitched young readers, the Grimms, and editors aplenty after them, started "fixing" things. Tales gradually got softer, sweeter, and primly moral. Yet all the polishing never rubbed away the solid heart of the stories, now read and loved in more than 160 languages.

Because these so-called "fairy tales," in their original forms, are filled with all manner of violence, cruelty, dismemberment, horrible deaths, depravity, and grotesquerie, they actually provide the perfect source material for S. Clay Wilson, whose artwork has dealt with such themes for over forty years. Clay was part of the very first generation of underground comix artists—the San Franciscans of 1968 whose number include Robert Crumb and Gilbert Shelton—and he was the most extreme among them. His dense illustrations of motorcycle gangs, pirates, the Checkered Demon, and Ruby the Dyke simultaneously destroy so many taboos that they still haven't been equaled in their ferocity. Clay suffered traumatic brain injuries in November 2008—he was either attacked or fell outside of his house; he has no memory of the event—and has since stopped drawing.

In 2000, Clay drew illustrations for seven of the Brothers Grimm's tales, published as a small limited-edition book, *Wilson's Grimm*, by Word Play publications (operated by Malcolm Whyte, founder of the Cartoon Art Museum in San Francisco). In the following pages, you'll find "Little Snow White," "Hansel and Gretel," and "The Valiant Little Tailor." The text I include is from early English translations of the final 1857 edition of the Grimms' book *Kinder- und Hausmärchen (Children's and Household Tales)*. In one respect I have reverted "Snow White" and "Hansel and Gretel" to their original 1812 versions—in both tales, the wicked stepmother was actually the biological mother of the children.

"The Valiant Little Tailor"

ONE SUMMER'S morning a little tailor was sitting on his table by the window; he was in good spirits, and sewed with all his might. Then came a peasant woman down the street crying, "Good jams, cheap! Good jams, cheap!" This rang pleasantly in the tailor's ears; he stretched his delicate head out of the window, and called, "Come up here, dear woman; here you will get rid of your goods." The woman came up the three steps to the tailor with her heavy basket, and he made her unpack the whole of the pots for him. He inspected all of them, lifted them up, put his nose to them, and at length said, "The jam seems to me to be good, so weigh me out four ounces, dear woman, and if it is a quarter of a pound that is of no consequence." The woman who had hoped to find a good sale, gave him what he desired, but went away quite angry and grumbling. "Now, God bless the jam to my use," cried the little tailor, "and give me health and strength." So he brought the bread out of the cupboard, cut himself a piece right across the loaf, and spread the jam over it. "This won't taste bitter," said he, "but I will just finish the jacket before I take a bite." He laid the bread near him, sewed on, and in his joy, made bigger and bigger stitches.

In the meantime the smell of the sweet jam ascended so to the wall, where the flies were sitting in great numbers, that they were attracted and descended on it in hosts. "Hola! who invited you?" said the little tailor, and drove the unbidden guests away. The flies, however, who understood no German, would not be turned away, but came back again in ever-increasing companies. Then the little tailor at last lost all patience, and got a bit of cloth from the hole under his work-table, and saying, "Wait, and I will give it to you," struck it mercilessly on them. When he drew it away and counted, there lay before him no fewer than seven, dead and with legs stretched out. "Are you a fellow of that sort?" said he, and could not help admiring his own bravery. "The whole town shall know of this!" And the little tailor hastened to cut himself a girdle, stitched it, and embroidered on it in large letters, "Seven at one stroke!" "What, the town?" he continued, "The whole world shall hear of it!" And his heart wagged with joy like a lamb's tail. The tailor put on the girdle, and resolved to go forth into the world, because he thought his workshop was too small for his valor. Before he went away, he sought about in the house to see if there was anything which he could take with him; however, he found nothing but an old cheese, and that he put in his pocket. In front of the door he observed a bird which had caught itself in the thicket. It had to go into his pocket with the cheese.

Now he took to the road boldly, and as he was light and nimble, he felt no fatigue. The road led him up a mountain, and when he had reached the highest point of it, there sat a powerful giant looking about him quite comfortably. The little tailor went bravely up, spoke to him, and said, "Good day, comrade, so you are sitting there overlooking the wide-spread world! I am just on my way thither, and want to try my luck. Have you any inclination to go with me?" The giant looked contemptuously at the tailor, and said, "You ragamuffin! You miserable creature!"

"Oh, indeed?" answered the little tailor, and unbuttoned his coat, and showed the giant the girdle, "There may you read what kind of a man I am!" The giant read, "Seven at one stroke," and thought that they had been men whom the tailor had killed, and began to feel a little respect for the tiny fellow. Nevertheless, he wished to try him first, and took a stone in his hand and squeezed it together so that water dropped out of it. "Do that likewise," said the giant, "if you have strength?" "Is that all?" said the tailor, "that is child's play with us!" and put his hand into his pocket, brought out the soft cheese, and pressed it until the liquid ran out of it. "Faith," said he, "that was a little better, wasn't it?" The giant did not know what to say, and could not believe it of the little man.

Then the giant picked up a stone and threw it so high that the eye could scarcely follow it. "Now, little mite of a man, do that likewise." "Well thrown," said the tailor, "but after all the stone came down to earth again; I will throw you one which shall never come back at all." He put his hand into his pocket, took out the bird, and threw it into the air. The bird, delighted with its liberty, rose, flew away, and did not come back. "How does that shot please you, comrade?" asked the tailor. "You can certainly throw," said the giant, "but now we will see if you are able to carry anything properly." He took the little tailor to a mighty oak tree which lay there felled on the ground, and said, "If you are strong enough, help me to carry the tree out of the forest." "Readily," answered the little man; "take the trunk on your shoulders, and I will raise up the branches and twigs; after all, they are the heaviest." The giant took the trunk on his shoulder, but the tailor seated himself on a branch, and the giant who could not look round, had to carry away the whole tree, and the little tailor into the bargain: he behind, was quite merry and happy, and whistled the song, "Three tailors rode forth from the gate," as if carrying the tree were child's play. The giant, after he had dragged the heavy burden part of the way, could go no further, and cried, "Hark you, I shall have to let the tree fall!" The tailor sprang nimbly down, seized the tree with both arms as if he had been carrying it, and said to the giant, "You are such a great fellow, and yet can't even carry the tree!"

They went on together, and as they passed a cherry tree, the giant laid hold of the top of the tree where the ripest fruit was hanging, bent it down, gave it into the tailor's hand, and bade him eat. But the little tailor was much too weak to hold the tree, and when the giant let it go, it sprang back again, and the tailor was hurried into the air with it. When he had fallen down again without injury, the giant said, "What is this? Have you not strength enough to hold the weak twig?" "There is no lack of strength," answered the little tailor. "Do you think that could be anything to a man who has struck down seven at one blow? I leapt over the tree because the huntsmen are shooting down there in the thicket. Jump as I did, if you can do it." The giant made the attempt, but could not get over the tree, and remained hanging in the branches, so that in this also the tailor kept the upper hand.

The giant said, "If you are such a valiant fellow, come with me into our cavern and spend the night with us." The little tailor was willing, and followed him. When they went into the cave, other giants were sitting there by the fire, and each of them had a roasted sheep in his hand and was eating it. The little tailor looked round and thought, "It is much more spacious here than in my workshop." The giant showed him a bed, and said he was to lie down in it and sleep. The bed was, however, too big for the little tailor; he did not lie down in it, but crept into a corner. When it was midnight, and the giant thought that the little tailor was lying in a sound sleep, he got up, took a great iron bar, cut through the bed with one blow, and thought he had given the grasshopper his finishing stroke. With the earliest dawn the giants went into the forest, and had quite forgotten the little tailor, when all at once he walked up to them quite merrily and boldly. The giants were terrified, they were afraid that he would strike them all dead, and ran away in a great hurry.

The little tailor went onwards, always following his own pointed nose. After he had walked for a long time, he came to the court-yard of a royal palace, and as he felt weary, he lay down on the grass and fell asleep. While he lay there, the people came and inspected him on all sides, and read on his girdle, "Seven at one stroke." "Ah!" said they, "what does the great warrior here in the midst of peace? He must be a mighty lord." They went and announced him to the King, and gave it as their opinion that if war should break out, this would be a weighty and useful man who ought on no account to be allowed to depart. The counsel pleased the King, and he sent one of his courtiers to the little tailor to offer him military service when he awoke. The ambassador remained standing by the sleeper, waited until he stretched his limbs and opened his eyes, and then conveyed to him this proposal. "For this very reason have I come here," the tailor replied, "I am ready to enter the King's service." He was therefore honorably received, and a separate dwelling was assigned him.

The soldiers, however, were set against the little tailor, and wished him a thousand miles away. "What is to be the end of this?" they said among themselves. "If we quarrel with him, and he strikes about him, seven of us will fall at every blow; not one of us can stand against him." They came therefore to a decision, betook themselves in a body to the King, and begged for their dismissal. "We are not prepared," said they, "to stay with a man who kills seven at one stroke." The King was sorry that for the sake of one he should lose all his faithful servants, wished that he had never set eyes on the tailor, and would willingly have been rid of him again. But he did not venture to give him his dismissal, for he dreaded lest he should strike him and all his people dead, and place himself on the royal throne. He thought about it for a long time, and at last found good counsel. He sent to the little tailor and caused him to be informed that as he was such a great warrior, he had one request to make to him. In a forest of his country lived two giants, who caused great mischief with their robbing, murdering, ravaging, and burning, and no one could approach them without putting himself in danger of death. If the tailor conquered and killed these two giants, he would give him his only daughter to wife, and half of his kingdom as a dowry, likewise one hundred horsemen should go with him to assist him. "That would indeed be a fine thing for a man like me!" thought the little tailor. "One is not offered a beautiful princess and half a kingdom every day of one's life!" "Oh, yes," he replied, "I will soon subdue the giants, and do not require the help of the hundred horsemen to do it; he who can hit seven with one blow, has no need to be afraid of two."

The little tailor went forth, and the hundred horsemen followed him. When he came to the outskirts of the forest, he said to his followers, "Just stay waiting here; I alone will soon finish off the giants." Then he bounded into the forest and looked about right and left. After a while he perceived both giants. They lay sleeping under a tree, and snored so that the branches waved up and down. The little tailor, not idle, gathered

two pocketsful of stones, and with these climbed up the tree. When he was half-way up, he slipped down by a branch, until he sat just above the sleepers, and then let one stone after another fall on the breast of one of the giants. For a long time the giant felt nothing, but at last he awoke, pushed his comrade, and said, "Why are you knocking me?" "You must be dreaming," said the other; "I am not knocking you."

They laid themselves down to sleep again, and then the tailor threw a stone down on the second. "What is the meaning of this?" cried the other. "Why are you pelting me?" "I am not pelting you," answered the first, growling. They disputed about it for a time, but as they were weary they let the matter rest, and their eyes closed once more. The little tailor began his game again, picked out the biggest stone, and threw it with all his might on the breast of the first giant. "That is too bad!" cried he, and sprang up like a madman, and pushed his companion against the tree until it shook. The other paid him back in the same coin, and they got into such a rage that they tore up trees and belabored each other so long, that at last they both fell down dead on the ground at the same time. Then the little tailor leapt down. "It is a lucky thing," said he, "that they did not tear up the tree on which I was sitting, or I should have had to spring on to another like a squirrel; but we tailors are nimble."

He drew out his sword and gave each of them a couple of thrusts in the breast, and then went out to the horsemen and said, "The work is done; I have given both of them their finishing stroke, but it was hard work! They tore up trees in their sore need, and defended themselves with them, but all that is to no purpose when a man like myself comes, who can kill seven at one blow." "But are you not wounded?" asked the horsemen. "You need not concern yourself about that," answered the tailor. "They have not bent one hair of mine." The horsemen would not believe him, and rode into the forest; there they found the giants swimming in their blood, and all round lay the torn-up trees.

The little tailor demanded of the King the promised reward; he, however, repented of his promise, and again bethought himself how he could get rid of the hero. "Before you receive my daughter, and the half of my kingdom," said he to him, "you must perform one more heroic deed. In the forest roams a unicorn which does great harm, and you must catch it first." "I fear one unicorn still less than two giants. Seven at one blow is my kind of affair." He took a rope and an axe with him, went forth into the forest, and again bade those who were sent with him to wait outside. He had not to seek long. The unicorn soon came towards him, and rushed directly on the tailor, as if it would spit him on its horn without more ceremony. "Softly, softly; it can't be done as quickly as that," said he, and stood still and waited until the animal was quite close, and then sprang nimbly behind the tree. The unicorn ran against the tree with all its strength, and struck its horn so fast in the trunk that it had not strength enough to draw it out again, and thus it was caught. "Now, I have got the bird," said the tailor, and came out from behind the tree and put the rope round its neck, and then with his axe he hewed the horn out of the tree, and when all was ready he led the beast away and took it to the King.

The King still would not give him the promised reward, and made a third demand. Before the wedding the tailor was to catch him a wild boar that made great havoc in the forest, and the huntsmen should give him their help. "Willingly," said the tailor, "that is child's play!" He did not take the huntsmen with him into the forest, and they were well pleased that he did not, for the wild boar had several times received them in such a manner that they had no inclination to lie in wait for him. When the

"THE VALIANT LITTLE TAILOR" THE BROTHERS GRIMM S. CLAY WILSON

boar perceived the tailor, it ran on him with foaming mouth and whetted tusks, and was about to throw him to the ground, but the active hero sprang into a chapel which was near, and up to the window at once, and in one bound out again. The boar ran in after him, but the tailor ran round outside and shut the door behind it, and then the raging beast, which was much too heavy and awkward to leap out of the window, was caught. The little tailor called the huntsmen thither that they might see the prisoner with their own eyes.

The hero, however, went to the King, who was now, whether he liked it or not, obliged to keep his promise, and gave him his daughter and the half of his kingdom. Had he known that it was no warlike hero, but a little tailor who was standing before him, it would have gone to his heart still more than it did. The wedding was held with great magnificence and small joy, and out of a tailor a king was made.

After some time the young Queen heard her husband say in his dreams at night, "Boy, make me the doublet, and patch the pantaloons, or else I will rap the yard-measure over your ears." Then she discovered in what state of life the young lord had been born, and next morning complained of her wrongs to her father, and begged him to help her to get rid of her husband, who was nothing else but a tailor. The King

comforted her and said, "Leave your bedroom door open this night, and my servants shall stand outside, and when he has fallen asleep shall go in, bind him, and take him on board a ship which shall carry him into the wide world." The woman was satisfied with this; but the King's armor-bearer, who had heard all, was friendly with the young lord, and informed him of the whole plot. "I'll put a screw into that business," said the little tailor.

At night he went to bed with his wife at the usual time, and when she thought that he had fallen asleep, she got up, opened the door, and then lay down again. The little tailor, who was only pretending to be asleep, began to cry out in a clear voice, "Boy, make me the doublet and patch me the pantaloons, or I will rap the yard-measure over your ears. I smote seven at one blow. I killed two giants. I brought away one unicorn, and caught a wild boar, and am I to fear those who are standing outside the room?" When these men heard the tailor speaking thus, they were overcome by a great dread, and ran as if the wild huntsman were behind them, and none of them would venture anything further against him. So the little tailor was a king and remained one, to the end of his life. ✳

"Hansel and Gretel"

Hard by a great forest dwelt a poor wood-cutter with his wife and their two children. The boy was called Hansel and the girl Gretel. He had little to bite and to break, and once when great scarcity fell on the land, he could no longer procure daily bread. Now when he thought over this by night in his bed, and tossed about in his anxiety, he groaned and said to his wife, "What is to become of us? How are we to feed our poor children, when we no longer have anything even for ourselves?" "I'll tell you what, husband," answered the woman, "Early tomorrow morning we will take the children out into the forest to where it is the thickest, there we will light a fire for them, and give each of them one piece of bread more, and then we will go to our work and leave them alone. They will not find the way home again, and we shall be rid of them." "No, wife," said the man, "I will not do that; how can I bear to leave our children alone in the forest? The wild animals would soon come and tear them to pieces." "O, thou fool!" said she, "Then we must all four die of hunger; you may as well plane the planks for our coffins." She left him no peace until he consented. "But I feel very sorry for the poor children, all the same," said the man.

The two children had also not been able to sleep for hunger, and had heard what their mother had said to their father. Gretel wept bitter tears, and said to Hansel, "Now all is over with us." "Be quiet, Gretel," said Hansel, "do not distress thyself. I will soon find a way to help us." And when the old folks had fallen asleep, he got up, put on his little coat, opened the door below, and crept outside. The moon shone brightly, and the white pebbles which lay in front of the house glittered like real silver pennies. Hansel stooped and put as many of them in the little pocket of his coat as he could possibly get in. Then he went back and said to Gretel, "Be comforted, dear little sister, and sleep in peace, God will not forsake us," and he lay down again in his bed.

When day dawned, but before the sun had risen, the woman came and awoke the two children, saying, "Get up, you sluggards! We are going into the forest to fetch wood." She gave each a little piece of bread, and said, "There is something for your dinner, but do not eat it up before then, for you will get nothing else." Gretel took the bread under her apron, as Hansel had the stones in his pocket. Then they all set out together on the way to the forest. When they had walked a short time, Hansel stood still and peeped back at the house, and did so again and again. His father said, "Hansel, what are you looking at there and staying behind for? Mind what you're doing, and do not forget how to use your legs." "Ah, father," said Hansel, "I am looking at my little white cat, which is sitting up on the roof, and wants to say good-bye to me." The wife said, "Fool, that is not your little cat, that is the morning sun which is shining on the chimneys." Hansel, however, had not been looking back at the cat, but had been constantly throwing one of the white pebble-stones out of his pocket on the road.

When they had reached the middle of the forest, the father said, "Now, children, pile up some wood, and I will light a fire that you may not be cold." Hansel and Gretel gathered brushwood together, as high as a little hill. The brushwood was lighted, and when the flames were burning very high the woman said, "Now, children, lay yourselves down by the fire and rest. We will go into the forest and cut some wood. When we have done, we will come back and fetch you away."

Hansel and Gretel sat by the fire, and when noon came, each ate a little piece of bread, and as they heard the strokes of the wood-axe they believed that their father was near. It was, however, not the axe; it was a branch which he had fastened to a withered tree which the wind was blowing backwards and forwards. And as they had been sitting such a long time, their eyes shut with fatigue, and they fell fast asleep. When at last they awoke, it was already dark night. Gretel began to cry and said, "How are we to get out of the forest now?" But Hansel comforted her and said, "Just wait a little, until the moon has risen, and then we will soon find the way." And when the full moon had risen, Hansel took his little sister by the hand, and followed the pebbles which shone like newly-coined silver pieces, and showed them the way.

They walked the whole night long, and by break of day came once more to their father's house. They knocked at the door, and when the woman opened it and saw that it was Hansel and Gretel, she said, "You naughty children, why have you slept so long in the forest? We thought you were never coming back at all!" The father, however, rejoiced, for it had cut him to the heart to leave them behind alone.

Not long afterwards, there was once more great scarcity in all parts, and the children heard their mother saying at night to their father, "Everything is eaten again; we have one half loaf left, and after that there is an end. The children must go, we will take them farther into the wood, so that they will not find their way out again; there is no other means of saving ourselves!" The man's heart was heavy, and he thought, "It would be better for you to share the last mouthful with your children." The woman, however, would listen to nothing that he had to say, but scolded and reproached him. He who says A must say B, likewise, and as he had yielded the first time, he had to do so a second time also.

The children were, however, still awake and had heard the conversation. When the old folks were asleep, Hansel again got up, and wanted to go out and pick up pebbles, but the woman had locked the door, and Hansel could not get out. Nevertheless he comforted his little sister, and said, "Do not cry, Gretel. Go to sleep quietly. The good God will help us."

Early in the morning came the woman, and took the children out of their beds. Their bit of bread was given to them, but it was still smaller than the time before. On the way into the forest Hansel crumbled his in his pocket, and often stood still and threw a morsel on the ground. "Hansel, why do you stop and look round?" said the father; "Go on." "I am looking back at my little pigeon which is sitting on the roof, and wants to say good-bye to me," answered Hansel. "Simpleton!" said the woman. "That is not your little pigeon, that is the morning sun that is shining on the chimney." Hansel, however, little by little, threw all the crumbs on the path.

The woman led the children still deeper into the forest, where they had never in their lives been before. Then a great fire was again made, and the mother said, "Just sit there, you children, and when you are tired you may sleep a little; we are going into the forest to cut wood, and in the evening when we are done, we will come and fetch you away." When it was noon, Gretel shared her piece of bread with Hansel, who had scattered his by the way. Then they fell asleep and evening came and went, but no one came to the poor children. They did not awake until it was dark night, and Hansel comforted his little sister and said, "Just wait, Gretel, until the moon rises, and then we shall see the crumbs of bread which I have strewn about; they will show us our way home again." When the moon came they set out, but they found no crumbs, for the many thousands of birds which fly about in the woods and fields had picked them all up. Hansel said to Gretel, "We shall soon find the way," but they did not find it. They walked the whole night and all the next day too from morning till evening, but they did not get out of the forest, and were very hungry, for they had nothing to eat but two or three berries, which grew on the ground. And as they were so weary that their legs would carry them no longer, they lay down beneath a tree and fell asleep.

It was now three mornings since they had left their father's house. They began to walk again, but they always got deeper into the forest, and if help did not come soon, they must die of hunger and weariness. When it was mid-day, they saw a beautiful snow-white bird sitting on a bough, which sang so delightfully that they stood still and listened to it. And when it had finished its song, it spread its wings and flew away before them, and they followed it until they reached a little house, on the roof of which it alighted. And when they came quite up to little house they saw that it was built of bread and covered with cakes, but that the windows were of clear sugar. "We will set to work on that," said Hansel, "and have a good meal. I will eat a bit of the roof, and you, Gretel, can eat some of the window. It will taste sweet." Hansel reached up above, and broke off a little of the roof to try how it tasted, and Gretel leaned against the window and nibbled at the panes. Then a soft voice cried from the room:

"Nibble, nibble, gnaw,
Who is nibbling at my little house?"

The children answered:

"The wind, the wind,
The heaven-born wind,"

and went on eating without disturbing themselves. Hansel, who thought the roof tasted very nice, tore down a great piece of it, and Gretel pushed out the whole of one round window-pane, sat down, and enjoyed herself with it. Suddenly the door opened, and a very, very old woman, who supported herself on crutches, came creeping out. Hansel and Gretel were so terribly frightened that they let fall what they had in their hands. The old woman, however, nodded and said, "Oh, you dear children, who has brought you here? Do come in, and stay with me. No harm shall happen to you." She took them both by the hand, and led them into her little house. Then good food was set before them, milk and pancakes, with sugar, apples, and nuts. Afterwards two pretty little beds were covered with clean white linen, and Hansel and Gretel lay down in them, and thought they were in heaven.

The old woman had only pretended to be so kind; she was in reality a wicked witch, who lay in wait for children, and had only built the little bread house in order to entice them there. When a child fell into her power, she killed it, cooked and ate it, and that was a feast day with her. Witches have red eyes, and cannot see far, but they have a keen scent like the beasts, and are aware when human beings draw near. When Hansel and Gretel came into her neighborhood, she laughed maliciously, and said mockingly, "I have them; they shall not escape me again!"

Early in the morning before the children were awake, she was already up, and when she saw both of them sleeping and looking so pretty, with their plump red cheeks, she muttered to herself, "That will be a dainty mouthful!" Then she seized Hansel with her shriveled hand, carried him into a little stable, and shut him in with a grated door. He might scream as he liked; it was of no use. Then she went to Gretel, shook her till she awoke, and cried, "Get up, lazy thing, fetch some water, and cook something good for your brother; he is in the stable outside, and is to be made fat. When he is fat, I will eat him." Gretel began to weep bitterly, but it was all in vain; she was forced to do what the wicked witch ordered her.

And now the best food was cooked for poor Hansel, but Gretel got nothing but crab-shells. Every morning the woman crept to the little stable and cried, "Hansel, stretch out your finger that I may feel if thou wilt soon be fat." Hansel, however, stretched out a little bone to her, and the old woman, who had dim eyes, could not see it, and thought it was Hansel's finger, and was astonished that there was no way of fattening him. When four weeks had gone by, and Hansel still continued thin, she was seized with impatience and would not wait any longer, "Hola, Gretel," she cried to the girl, "be active, and bring some water. Let Hansel be fat or lean, tomorrow I will kill him, and cook him." Ah, how the poor little sister did lament when she had to fetch the water, and how her tears did flow down over her cheeks! "Dear God, do help us," she cried. "If the wild beasts in the forest had but devoured us, we should at any rate have died together." "Just keep your noise to yourself," said the old woman. "All that won't help you at all."

Early in the morning, Gretel had to go out and hang up the cauldron with the water, and light the fire. "We will bake first," said the old woman. "I have already heated the oven, and kneaded the dough." She pushed poor Gretel out to the oven, from which flames were already darting. "Creep in," said the witch, "and see if it is properly heated, so that we can shut the bread in." Once Gretel was inside, she intended to shut the oven and let her bake in it, and then she would eat her, too. But Gretel saw what she had in her mind, and said, "I do not know how I am to do it; how do you get in?" "Silly goose," said the old woman. "The door is big enough; just look, I can get in myself!" She crept up and thrust her head into the oven. Then Gretel gave her a push that drove her far into it, and shut the iron door, and fastened the bolt. Oh! Then she began to howl quite horribly, but Gretel ran away, and the godless witch was miserably burnt to death.

Gretel, however, ran like lightning to Hansel, opened his little stable, and cried, "Hansel, we are saved! The old witch is dead!" Then Hansel sprang out like a bird from its cage when the door is opened for it. How they did rejoice and embrace each other, and dance about and kiss each other! And as they had no longer any need to fear her, they went into the witch's house, and in every corner there stood chests full of pearls and jewels. "These are far better than pebbles!" said Hansel, and thrust into his pockets whatever could be got in, and Gretel said, "I, too, will take something home with me," and filled her pinafore full. "But now we will go away." said Hansel, "that we may get out of the witch's forest."

When they had walked for two hours, they came to a great piece of water. "We cannot get over," said Hansel, "I see no foot-plank and no bridge." "And no boat crosses either," answered Gretel, "but a white duck is swimming there; if I ask her, she will help us over." Then she cried:
"Little duck, little duck, do you see,

Hansel and Gretel are waiting for thee?
There's never a plank, or bridge in sight,
Take us across on your back so white."

The duck came to them, and Hansel seated himself on its back, and told his sister to sit by him. "No," replied Gretel, "that will be too heavy for the little duck; she shall take us across, one after the other." The good little duck did so, and when they were once safely across and had walked for a short time, the forest seemed to be more and more familiar to them, and at length they saw from afar their father's house. Then they began to run, rushed into the parlor, and threw themselves into their father's arms. The man had not known one happy hour since he had left the children in the forest; the woman, however, was dead. Gretel emptied her pinafore until pearls and precious stones ran about the room, and Hansel threw one handful after another out of his pocket to add to them. Then all anxiety was at an end, and they lived together in perfect happiness. ✳

Once upon a time in the middle of winter, when the flakes of snow were falling like feathers from the sky, a queen sat at a window sewing, and the frame of the window was made of black ebony. And whilst she was sewing and looking out of the window at the snow, she pricked her finger with the needle, and three drops of blood fell upon the snow. And the red looked pretty upon the white snow, and she thought to herself, "Would that I had a child as white as snow, as red as blood, and as black as the wood of the window-frame."

"Little Snow White"

Soon after that she had a little daughter, who was as white as snow, and as red as blood, and her hair was as black as ebony; and she was therefore called Little Snow White. The Queen was a beautiful woman, but proud and haughty, and she could not bear that any one else should surpass her in beauty. She had a wonderful looking-glass, and when she stood in front of it and looked at herself in it, and said—

"Looking-glass, Looking-glass, on the wall,
Who in this land is the fairest of all?"

the looking-glass answered—

"Thou, O Queen, art the fairest of all!"

Then she was satisfied, for she knew that the looking-glass spoke the truth.

But Snow White was growing up, and grew more and more beautiful; and when she was seven years old she was as beautiful as the day, and more beautiful than the Queen herself. And once when the Queen asked her looking-glass—

"Looking-glass, Looking-glass, on the wall,
Who in this land is the fairest of all?"

it answered—

"Thou art fairer than all who are here, Lady Queen."
But more beautiful still is Snow White, as I ween."

Then the Queen was shocked, and turned yellow and green with envy. From that hour, whenever she looked at Snow White, her heart heaved in her breast, she hated the girl so much.

And envy and pride grew higher and higher in her heart like a weed, so that she had no peace day or night. She called a huntsman, and said, "Take the child away into the forest; I will no longer have her in my sight. Kill her, and bring me back her heart as a token." The huntsman obeyed, and took her away; but when he had drawn his knife, and was about to pierce Snow White's innocent heart, she began to weep, and said, "Ah, dear huntsman, leave me my life! I will run away into the wild forest, and never come home again."

And as she was so beautiful the huntsman had pity on her and said, "Run away, then, you poor child." "The wild beasts will soon have devoured you," thought he, and yet it seemed as if a stone had been rolled from his heart since it was no longer needful for him to kill her. And as a young boar just then came running by he stabbed it, and cut out its heart and took it to the Queen as proof that the child was dead. The cook had to salt this, and the wicked Queen ate it, and thought she had eaten the heart of Snow White.

But now the poor child was all alone in the great forest, and so terrified that she looked at every leaf of every tree, and did not know what to do. Then she began to run, and ran over sharp stones and through thorns, and the wild beasts ran past her, but did her no harm.

She ran as long as her feet would go until it was almost evening; then she saw a little cottage and went into it to rest herself. Everything in the cottage was small, but neater and cleaner than can be told. There was a table on which was a white cover, and seven little plates, and on each plate a little spoon; moreover, there were seven little knives and forks, and seven little mugs. Against the wall stood seven little beds side by side, and covered with snow-white counterpanes.

Little Snow White was so hungry and thirsty that she ate some vegetables and bread from each plate and drank a drop of wine out of each mug, for she did not wish to take all from one only. Then, as she was so tired, she laid herself down on one of the little beds, but none of them suited her; one was too long, another too short, but at last she found that the seventh one was right, and so she remained in it, said a prayer and went to sleep.

When it was quite dark the owners of the cottage came back; they were seven dwarfs who dug and delved in the mountains for ore. They lit their seven candles, and as it was now light within the cottage they saw that some one had been there, for everything was not in the same order in which they had left it.

The first said, "Who has been sitting on my chair?"
The second, "Who has been eating off my plate?"
The third, "Who has been taking some of my bread?"
The fourth, "Who has been eating my vegetables?"
The fifth, "Who has been using my fork?"
The sixth, "Who has been cutting with my knife?"
The seventh, "Who has been drinking out of my mug?"
Then the first looked round and saw that there was a little hole on his bed, and he said, "Who has been getting into my bed?" The others came up and each called out, "Somebody has been lying in my bed too." But the seventh when he looked at his bed saw little Snow White, who was lying asleep therein. And he called the others, who came running up, and they cried out with astonishment, and brought their seven little candles and let the light fall on little Snow White. "Oh, heavens! oh, heavens!" cried they, "what a lovely child!" and they were so glad that they did not wake her up, but let her sleep on in the bed. And the seventh dwarf slept with his companions, one hour with each, and so got through the night.

When it was morning little Snow White awoke, and was frightened when she saw the seven dwarfs. But they were friendly and asked her what her name was. "My name is Snow White," she answered.

"How have you come to our house?" said the dwarfs. Then she told them that her mother had wished to have her killed, but that the huntsman had spared her life, and that she had run for the whole day, until at last she had found their dwelling. The dwarfs said, "If you will take care of our house, cook, make the beds, wash, sew, and knit, and if you will keep everything neat and clean, you can stay with us and you shall want for nothing." "Yes," said Snow White, "with all my heart," and she stayed with them. She kept the house in order for them; in the mornings they went to the mountains and looked for copper and gold, in the evenings they came back, and then their supper had to be ready. The girl was alone the whole day, so the good dwarfs warned her and said, "Beware of your mother; she will soon know that you are here; be sure to let no one come in."

But the Queen, believing that she had eaten Snow White's heart, could not but think that she was again the first and most beautiful of all; and she went to her looking-glass and said—

"Looking-glass, Looking-glass, on the wall,
Who in this land is the fairest of all?"

and the glass answered—

"Oh, Queen, thou art fairest of all I see,
But over the hills, where the seven dwarfs dwell,
Snow White is still alive and well,
And none is so fair as she."

Then she was astounded, for she knew that the looking-glass never spoke falsely, and she knew that the huntsman had betrayed her, and that little Snow White was still alive.

And so she thought and thought again how she might kill her, for so long as she was not the fairest in the whole land, envy let her have no rest. And when she had at last thought of something to do, she painted her face, and dressed herself like an old pedlar-woman, and no one could have known her. In this disguise she went over the seven mountains to the seven dwarfs, and knocked at the door and cried, "Pretty things to sell, very cheap, very cheap." Little Snow White looked out of the window and called out, "Good day, my good woman, what have you to sell?" "Good things, pretty things," she answered; "stay-laces of all colors," and she pulled out one which was woven of bright-colored silk. "I may let the worthy old woman in," thought Snow White, and she unbolted the door and bought the pretty laces. "Child," said the old woman, "what a fright you look; come, I will lace you properly for once." Snow White had no suspicion, but stood before her, and let herself be laced with the new laces. But the old woman laced so quickly and laced so tightly that Snow White lost her breath and fell down as if dead. "Now I am the most beautiful," said the Queen to herself, and ran away.

Not long afterwards, in the evening, the seven dwarfs came home, but how shocked they were when they saw their dear little Snow White lying on the ground, and that she neither stirred nor moved, and seemed to be dead. They lifted her up, and, as they saw that she was laced too tightly, they cut the laces; then she began to breathe a little, and after a while came to life again. When the dwarfs heard what had happened they said, "The old pedlar-woman was no one else than the wicked Queen; take care and let no one come in when we are not with you."

But the wicked woman when she had reached home went in front of the glass and asked—

"Looking-glass, Looking-glass, on the wall,
Who in this land is the fairest of all?"

and it answered as before—

"Oh, Queen, thou art fairest of all I see,
But over the hills, where the seven dwarfs dwell,
Snow White is still alive and well,
And none is so fair as she."

When she heard that, all her blood rushed to her heart with fear,
for she saw plainly that little Snow White was again alive. "But now,"
she said, "I will think of something that shall put an end to you," and
by the help of witchcraft, which she understood, she made a poisonous
comb. Then she disguised herself and took the shape of another old
woman. So she went over the seven mountains to the seven dwarfs,
knocked at the door, and cried, "Good things to sell, cheap, cheap!"
Little Snow White looked out and said, "Go away; I cannot let any
one come in." "I suppose you can look," said the old woman, and
pulled the poisonous comb out and held it up. It pleased the girl
so well that she let herself be beguiled, and opened the door. When
they had made a bargain the old woman said, "Now I will comb you
properly for once." Poor little Snow White had no suspicion, and let
the old woman do as she pleased, but hardly had she put the comb
in her hair than the poison in it took effect, and the girl fell down

senseless. "You paragon of beauty," said the wicked woman, "you are done for now," and she went away.

But fortunately it was almost evening, when the seven dwarfs came home. When they saw Snow White lying as if dead upon the ground they at once suspected the mother, and they looked and found the poisoned comb. Scarcely had they taken it out when Snow White came to herself, and told them what had happened. Then they warned her once more to be upon her guard and to open the door to no one.

The Queen, at home, went in front of the glass and said—

"Looking-glass, Looking-glass, on the wall,
Who in this land is the fairest of all?"

then it answered as before—

"Oh, Queen, thou art fairest of all I see,
But over the hills, where the seven dwarfs dwell,
Snow White is still alive and well,
And none is so fair as she."

When she heard the glass speak thus she trembled and shook with rage. "Snow White shall die," she cried, "even if it costs me my life!"

Thereupon she went into a quite secret, lonely room, where no one ever came, and there she made a very poisonous apple. Outside it looked pretty, white with a red cheek, so that every one who saw it longed for it; but whoever ate a piece of it must surely die.

When the apple was ready she painted her face, and dressed herself up as a country-woman, and so she went over the seven mountains to the seven dwarfs. She knocked at the door. Snow White put her head out of the window and said, "I cannot let any one in; the seven dwarfs have forbidden me." "It is all the same to me," answered the woman, "I shall soon get rid of my apples. There, I will give you one."

"No," said Snow White, "I dare not take anything." "Are you afraid of poison?" said the old woman; "look, I will cut the apple in two pieces; you eat the red cheek, and I will eat the white." The apple was so cunningly made that only the red cheek was poisoned. Snow White longed for the fine apple, and when she saw that the woman ate part of it she could resist no longer, and stretched out her hand and took the poisonous half. But hardly had she a bit of it in her mouth than she fell down dead. Then the Queen looked at her with a dreadful look, and laughed aloud and said, "White as snow, red as blood, black as ebony-wood! This time the dwarfs cannot wake you up again."

And when she asked of the Looking-glass at home—

"Looking-glass, Looking-glass, on the wall,
Who in this land is the fairest of all?"

it answered at last—

"Oh, Queen, in this land thou art fairest of all."

Then her envious heart had rest, so far as an envious heart can have rest.

The dwarfs, when they came home in the evening, found Snow White lying upon the ground; she breathed no longer and was dead.

They lifted her up, looked to see whether they could find anything poisonous, unlaced her, combed her hair, washed her with water and wine, but it was all of no use; the poor child was dead, and remained dead. They laid her upon a bier, and all seven of them sat round it and wept for her, and wept three days long.

Then they were going to bury her, but she still looked as if she were living, and still had her pretty red cheeks. They said, "We could not bury her in the dark ground," and they had a transparent coffin of glass made, so that she could be seen from all sides, and they laid her in it, and wrote her name upon it in golden letters, and that she was a king's daughter. Then they put the coffin out upon the mountain, and one of them always stayed by it and watched it. And birds came too, and wept for Snow White; first an owl, then a raven, and last a dove.

And now Snow White lay a long, long time in the coffin, and she did not change, but looked as if she were asleep; for she was as white as snow, as red as blood, and her hair was as black as ebony.

It happened, however, that a king's son came into the forest, and went to the dwarfs' house to spend the night. He saw the coffin on the mountain, and the beautiful Snow White within it, and read what was written upon it in golden letters. Then he said to the dwarfs, "Let me have the coffin, I will give you whatever you want for it." But the dwarfs answered, "We will not part with it for all the gold in the world." Then he said, "Let me have it as a gift, for I cannot live without seeing Snow White. I will honor and prize her as my dearest possession." As he spoke in this way the good dwarfs took pity upon him, and gave him the coffin.

And now the King's son had it carried away by his servants on their shoulders. And it happened that they stumbled over a tree-stump, and with the shock the poisonous piece of apple which Snow White had bitten off came out of her throat. And before long she opened her eyes, lifted up the lid of the coffin, sat up, and was once more alive. "Oh, heavens, where am I?" she cried. The King's son, full of joy, said, "You are with me," and told her what had happened, and said, "I love you more than everything in the world; come with me to my father's palace, you shall be my wife."

And Snow White was willing, and went with him, and their wedding was held with great show and splendor. But Snow White's wicked mother was also bidden to the feast. When she had arrayed herself in beautiful clothes she went before the Looking-glass, and said—

"Looking-glass, Looking-glass, on the wall,
Who in this land is the fairest of all?"

the glass answered—

"Oh, Queen, of all here the fairest art thou,
But the young Queen is fairer by far as I trow."

Then the wicked woman uttered a curse, and was so wretched, so utterly wretched, that she knew not what to do. At first she would not go to the wedding at all, but she had no peace, and must go to see the young Queen. And when she went in she knew Snow White; and she stood still with rage and fear, and could not stir. But iron slippers had already been put upon the fire, and they were brought in with tongs, and set before her. Then she was forced to put on the red-hot shoes, and dance until she dropped down dead. ✳

"How Six Made Good in the World"

The Brothers Grimm

ART/ADAPTATION BY **Shawn Cheng**

NOT ALL OF THE 200 OR SO FAIRY TALES IN THE Brothers Grimm's pioneering collection of 1812–1814, *Kinder- und Hausmärchen* (*Children's and Household Tales*), are familiar to us. "How Six Made Good in the World" is one of these lesser-known tales, but it's a peppy, rollicking action/ adventure featuring a knight and his unusual crew, each of whom has a very specific "superpower." I'll never understand how Disney has overlooked this gem. The action figures alone would rake in billions.

When Shawn Cheng expressed interest in adapting a fairy tale, he mentioned that his schedule permitted him to draw only three pages, which worked out extremely well. "How Six Made Good" has enough characters and action to fill a good ten pages, but the time/page constraint resulted in a beautifully dense, blazingly fast-paced work packed to the gills with Shawn's visual inventiveness. The original title of the tale in German is "*Sechse kommen durch die ganze Welt*," which is typically given a literal English translation: "[How] Six Men Got on in the World." Shawn elected to use a title that more accurately reflects the sense of the original.

"HOW SIX MADE GOOD IN THE WORLD" THE BROTHERS GRIMM SHAWN CHENG

"La Belle Dame Sans Merci"

John Keats

ART/ADAPTATION BY **Neil Cohn**

PART OF THE TRIUMVIRATE OF SECOND-GENERATION British Romantics, along with Shelley and Byron, John Keats had one of the most astonishing, high-level bursts of creative output the world has ever seen. Pretty much all of his greatest poetry was written in 1819, but beyond that, four of his six immortal odes ("Ode on a Grecian Urn," "Ode to a Nightingale," and so on) were written in a single month that year (May), and another was written immediately prior, in April. He had just turned twenty-four. The final ode, "To Autumn"—universally considered one of the finest poems ever written—was cranked out later that year in a *single day* (September 19). He also wrote his most famous longer poems that year, and just before writing the spring odes he "dashed off" his other most enduring short poem, "La Belle Dame Sans Merci." (What triggered this superhuman run of poetic brilliance? In fall of 1818, Keats had met the love of his life, Fanny Brawne, and in early April 1819 she moved next door to him. He would die of consumption less than two years later.)

"La Belle Dame Sans Merci" ("The Beautiful Woman Without Mercy/Pity") takes its name (but not its content) from an old French poem, and takes its form from the folk ballad. Buckets of ink have been spilled arguing about its interpretation. It seems to be about love lost, but is the fairy woman a femme fatale who crushes men's spirits for sport (as the title seems to strongly indicate), or is it a tale of star-cross'd lovers—human and fairy—who can't be together, as some lines hint? Or was Keats writing a metaphor about the poetic muse?

Neil Cohn studies, theorizes on, and writes about the linguistic aspects of comics and of visual language in general. He also draws comics, including two separate takes on "La Belle," approaching the poem, and its ending, in different ways. I chose to run the version that seems to stay more true to the poem and its bleak outcome. Not that I have anything against happy endings—I actually prefer them—but I don't see one in this poem, which, although written while Keats was deeply in love, also came about while he was tending to his dying, tubercular brother.

La Belle Dame Sans Merci

Adapted by Neil Cohn By John Keats APRIL 1819

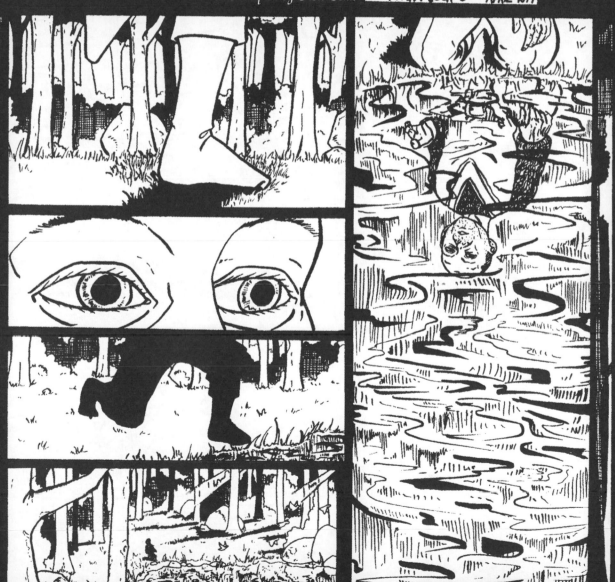

"LA BELLE DAME SANS MERCI" JOHN KEATS NEIL COHN

"I MET A LADY IN THE MEADS, FULL BEAUTIFUL, A FAERY'S CHILD,

HER HAIR WAS LONG, HER FOOT WAS LIGHT

AND HER EYES WERE WILD.

"LA BELLE DAME SANS MERCI" JOHN KEATS NEIL COHN

"LA BELLE DAME SANS MERCI" JOHN KEATS NEIL COHN

"LA BELLE DAME SANS MERCI" JOHN KEATS NEIL COHN

LA BELLE DAME SANS MERCI" JOHN KEATS NEIL COHN

"LA BELLE DAME SANS MERCI" JOHN KEATS NEIL COHN

Jerusalem: The Emanation of the Giant Albion

William Blake

ART AND LETTERING BY **William Blake**

BESIDES BEING A POET OF THE FIRST CALIBER, the mystic William Blake was also an extraordinary painter and printer. His "illuminated" books are jaw-dropping productions in which Blake handled every aspect: writing the poems, painting the images, hand-lettering the text, engraving the copper plates with a process he invented, coloring the plates, printing the pages, and binding the final books. The integration of words, images, and color is a wonder to behold. Blake's poems are now usually published as plain, typeset text, but seeing them in their original context adds immeasurably to their power.

Like much of his later work—book-length prophetic poems—*Jerusalem: The Emanation of the Giant Albion* is dense pretty much to the point of being impenetrable. The William Blake Archive explains:

> Blake's final and longest epic in illuminated printing constitutes a recapitulation and summation of his multiple interests, ranging from his own mythology to biblical history, from sexuality to epistemology, and from the Druids to Newton. The cast of characters is vast, but Los (the artist's imagination at work in the material world), Jerusalem and Albion (the female and male portions of divided humanity who must be reunited), the nature goddess Vala, and Jesus play major roles. The poem is divided into four chapters, each addressed

to a different audience: the Public, the Jews, the Deists, and the Christians. *Jerusalem* concludes with a vision of human consciousness in a postapocalyptic universe.

This work contains the famous line: "I must create a system, or be enslaved by another man's."

Jerusalem was published chapter by chapter from 1804 to 1820. When finished creating all 100 plates, Blake printed only one complete copy in color, and this one-of-a-kind work of art failed to find a buyer. Such was Blake's reception in his lifetime. (In 1999, a color printing of another of Blake's prophetic books, *The First Book of Urizen*—which is one-fourth the length of *Jerusalem*—sold at auction for $2.5 million. Five years later, a *single* hand-printed color drawing of his brought in $3.9 million. If only the destitute Blake could've received even a sliver of that fortune while he was alive. . . .)

The following images are photographs of the pages from that single color printing from Blake, now housed at Yale University's Center for British Art.

SOURCES

Website of The William Blake Archive, www.blakearchive.org.

Blake, William. *Jerusalem: The Illuminated Books, Volume One.* Princeton: Princeton University Press, 1998.

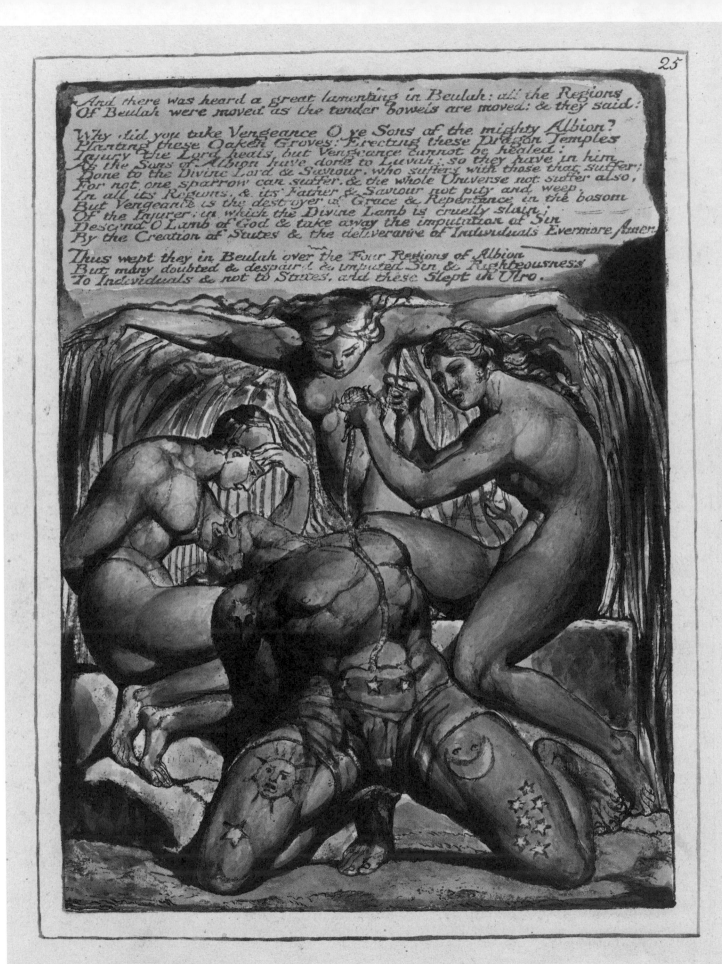

And there was heard a great lamenting in Beulah: all the Regions
Of Beulah were moved as the tender bowels are moved: & they said:

Why did you take Vengeance O ye Sons of the mighty Albion?
Planting these Oaken Groves: Erecting these Dragon Temples
Injury the Lord heals but Vengeance cannot be healed:
As the Sons of Albion have done to Luvah: so they have in him
Done to the Divine Lord & Saviour, who suffers with those that suffer:
For not one sparrow can suffer, & the whole Universe not suffer also,
In all its Regions, & its Father & Saviour not pity and weep.
But Vengeance is the destroyer of Grace & Repentance in the bosom
Of the Injurer: in which the Divine Lamb is cruelly slain:
Descend O Lamb of God & take away the imputation of Sin
By the Creation of States & the deliverance of Individuals Evermore Amen.

Thus wept they in Beulah over the Four Regions of Albion
But, many doubted & despair'd & imputed Sin & Righteousness
To Individuals & not to States, and these Slept in Ulro.

Leaning against the pillars. & his disease rose from his skirts
Upon the Precipice he stood ready to fall into Non-Entity.
Los was all astonishment & terror: he trembled sitting on the Stone
Of London: but the interiors of Albions fibres & nerves were hidden
From Los: astonishd he beheld only the petrified surfaces:
And saw his Furnaces in ruins. for Los is the Demon of the Furnaces;
He saw also the Four Points of Albion reversed inwards
He siezd his Hammer & Tongs, his iron Poker & his Bellows,
Upon the valleys of Middlesex, Shouting loud for aid Divine.

In stern defiance came from Albions bosom Hand, Hyle, Koban,
Gwantok, Peachy, Brereton, Slaid, Huttn, Skofeld, Kock, Kotope
Bowen.. Albions Sons: they bore him a golden couch into the porch
And on the Couch reposd his limbs trembling from the bloody field.
Rearing their Druid Patriarchal rocky Temples around his limbs.
(All things begin & end in Albions Ancient Druid Rocky Shore.)

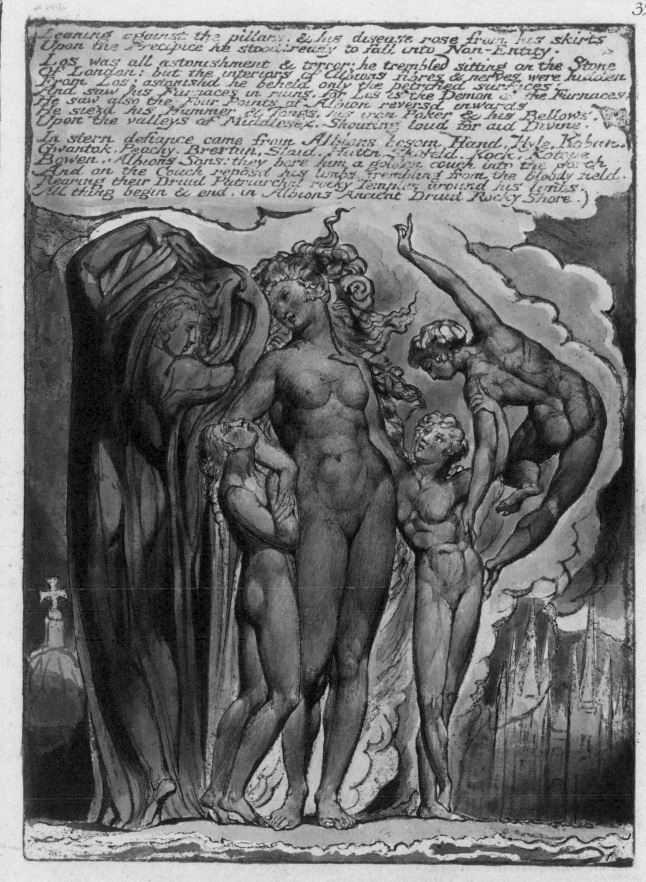

Bath who is Legions: he is the Seventh, the physician and
The poisoner: the best and worst in Heaven and Hell:
Whose Spectre first assimilated with Luvah in Albions mountains
A triple octave he took, to reduce Jerusalem to twelve
To cast Jerusalem forth upon the wilds to Poplar & Bow:
To Malden & Canterbury in the delights of cruelty: The Shuttles of death sing in the sky to Islington & Pancrass
Round Marybone to Tyburns River, weaving black melancholy as a net,
And despair as meshes closely wove over the west of London:
Where mild Jerusalem sought to repose in death & be no more.
She fled to Lambeths mild Vale and hid herself beneath
The Surrey Hills where Rephaim terminates: her Sons are siezd
For victims of sacrifice: but Jerusalem cannot be found! Hid
By the Daughters of Beulah: gently snatchd away: and hid in Beulah

There is a Grain of Sand in Lambeth that Satan cannot find
Nor can his Watch Fiends find it: tis translucent & has many Angles
But he who finds it will find Oothoons palace, for within
Opening into Beulah every angle is a lovely heaven
But should the Watch Fiends find it, they would call it Sin
And lay its Heavens & their inhabitants in blood of punishment
Here Jerusalem & Vala were hid in soft slumberous repose
Hid from the terrible East, shut up in the South & West.

The Twenty-eight trembled in Deaths dark caves, in cold despair
They kneeld around the Couch of Death in deep humiliation
And tortures of self condemnation while their Spectres ragd within
The Four Zoa's in terrible combustion clouded rage
Drinking the shuddering fears & loves of Albions Families
Destroying by selfish affections the things that they most admire
Drinking & eating, & pitying & weeping, as at a tragic scene.
The soul drinks murder & revenge, & applauds its own holiness

They saw Albion endeavouring to destroy their Emanations

Each Man is in
his Spectres power
Untill the arrival
of that hour,
When his Humanity
awake
And cast his Spectre
into the Lake

Bath. mild Physician of Eternity. mysterious power.
Whose springs are unsearchable & knowledge infinite.
Hereford. ancient Guardian of Wales. whose hands
Builded the mountain palaces of Eden. stupendous works!
Lincoln. Durham & Carlisle. Councellors of Los.
And Ely. Scribe of Los. whose pen no other hand
Dare touch: Oxford. immortal Bard! with eloquence
Divine he wept over Albion: speaking the words of God
In mild perswasion: bringing leaves of the Tree of Life.

Thou art in Error Albion. the Land of Ulro:
One Error not removd. will destroy a human Soul.
Repose in Beulahs night. till the Error is removd
Reason not on both sides. Repose upon our bosoms
Till the Plow of Jehovah. and the Harrow of Shaddai
Have passed over the Dead. to awake the Dead to Judgment.
But Albion turnd away refusing comfort.

Oxford trembled while he spoke. then Fainted in the arms
Of Norwich. Peterboro. Rochester. Chester awful. Worcester.
Litchfield. Saint Davids. Landaff. Asaph. Bangor. Soder:
Bowing their heads devoted: and the Furnaces of Los
Began to rage. thundering loud the storms began to roar
Upon the Furnaces. and loud the Furnaces rebellow beneath.

And these the Four in whom the twenty-four appeard four-fold:
Verulam. London. York. Edinburgh. mourning one towards another
Alas!——The time will come. when a mans worst enemies
Shall be those of his own house and family: in a Religion
Of Generation. to destroy by Sin and Atonement. happy Jerusalem.
The Bride and Wife of the Lamb. O God thou art Not an Avenger

Jerusalem
Chap 3

But Los, who is the Vehicular Form of strong Urthona
Wept vehemently over Albion where Thames currents spring
From the rivers of Beulah; pleasant river! soft, mild, parent stream
And the roots of Albions Tree enterd the Soul of Los
As he sat before his Furnaces clothed in sackcloth of hair
In gnawing pain dividing him from his Emanation;
Inclosing all the Children of Los time after time.
Their Giant forms condensing into Nations & Peoples & Tongues
Translucent the Furnaces, of Beryll & Emerald immortal:
And Seven-fold each within other, incomprehensible
To the Vegetated Mortal Eye's perverted & single vision
The Bellows are the Animal Lungs, the Hammers the Animal Heart
The Furnaces, the Stomach for Digestion; terrible their fury
Like seven burning heavens rangd from South to North

Here, on the banks of the Thames, Los builded Golgonooza,
Outside of the Gates of the Human Heart, beneath Beulah
In the midst of the rocks of the Altars of Albion. In fears
He builded it, in rage & in fury. It is the Spiritual Fourfold
London: continually building & continually decaying desolate!
In eternal labours: loud the Furnaes & loud the Anvils
Of Death thunder incessant around the flaming Couches of
The Twentyfour Friends of Albion and round the awful Four
For the protection of the Twelve Emanations of Albions Sons
The Mystic Union of the Emanation in the Lord; Because
Man divided from his Emanation is a dark Spectre
His Emanation is an ever-weeping melancholy Shadow
But she is made receptive of Generation thro' mercy
In the Potters Furnace, among the Funeral Urns of Beulah
From Surrey hills, thro' Italy and Greece, to Hinnoms vale.

All Human Forms identified even Tree Metal Earth & Stone. all
Human Forms identified living going forth & returning wearied
Into the Planetary lives of Years Months Days & Hours reposing
And then Awaking into his Bosom in the Life of Immortality.
And I heard the Name of their Emanations they are named Jerusalem

The End of The Song
of Jerusalem

The Confessions of Nat Turner

Nat Turner and Thomas R. Gray

ART/ADAPTATION BY **John Pierard**

THE HISTORY OF SLAVE REBELLIONS IN NORTH America is fairly well documented, although it remains little known beyond a subset of academic historians. Outside of the *Amistad* mutiny—made famous by a Spielberg movie—the best-known rebellion organized and carried out by slaves was led by Nat Turner in Virginia. Turner was extraordinarily intelligent and charismatic. He learned to read and write, then taught other slaves. He was a devout Christian—constantly praying, fasting, and preaching—who received visions his entire life. "I was ordained for some great purpose in the hands of the Almighty," he said in his *Confessions*.

Starting in 1828, Turner believed God was telling him to lead a violent rebellion against the white race in order to destroy slavery. He felt that a solar eclipse was the heavenly sign to get preparations under way, and the sun's odd coloring in mid-August 1831 was the final go-ahead. Turner and his band saw themselves as avenging angels of the Lord, with a duty to massacre as many white people as possible. They famously spared some poor white folk, but most families were killed en masse with axes and blunt instruments—old men, women, children . . . no one was spared. Babies were killed in their cradles. At the home of one large family, all ten children were decapitated. "'Twas my object to carry terror and devastation wherever we went," Turner said. Around sixty white people were murdered.

The rebellion/slaughter was put down in a little more than twenty-four hours, and all those who took part were immediately captured, except for Turner, who remained on the lam for more than two months. He was finally captured in a hole he had dug for himself and was brought to trial in, of all places, Jerusalem, Virginia. While awaiting trial, he freely, even proudly, told his story to a local lawyer, Thomas R. Gray, who published the conversations as a booklet in 1831, *The Confessions of Nat Turner* (which should not be confused with the 1967 Pulitzer Prize–winning novel of the exact same title, written by William Styron). A close analysis of *Confessions* confirms that, although Gray mingled his voice to a modest degree, it is primarily Turner's account.

Turner was tried and hanged, as were almost all of his conspirators. In the backlash to the events, around 200 black people were murdered by whites, and new repressive legislation was passed throughout the South.

Like an intriguing number of illustrators over the last 100+ years, John Pierard has illustrated both sexual material and children's books. He's also done work for Marvel and Graphic Classics. Here he takes up one of the most radical and disturbingly violent documents in the canon.

SOURCE

Greenberg, Kenneth S. *Nat Turner: A Slave Rebellion in History and Memory*. Oxford: Oxford University Press, 2003.

THE

CONFESSIONS

OF

NAT TURNER,

THE LEADER OF THE LATE

INSURRECTION IN SOUTHAMPTON, VA.

As fully and voluntarily made to

THOMAS R. GRAY,

SIR, YOU HAVE ASKED ME TO GIVE A HISTORY OF THE MOTIVES WHICH INDUCED ME TO UNDERTAKE THE LATE INSURRECTION, AS YOU CALL IT...THAT ENTHUSIASM, WHICH HAS TERMINATED SO FATALLY TO MANY, BOTH BLACK AND WHITE, AND FOR WHICH I AM ABOUT TO ATONE AT THE GALLOWS...

excerpted & illustrated by: J.W. Pierard

I SURELY WOULD BE A PROPHET, AS THE LORD HAD SHEWN ME THINGS THAT HAD HAPPENED BEFORE MY BIRTH...I HAD A VISION—AND I SAW WHITE SPIRITS AND BLACK SPIRITS ENGAGED IN A BATTLE, AND THE SUN WAS DARKENED—AND I HEARD A VOICE ROLLED IN THE HEAVENS AND BLOOD FLOWED IN STREAMS...

... I SALUTED THEM ON COMING UP, AND ASKED WILL HOW HE CAME THERE, AND HE ANSWERED, HIS LIFE WAS WORTH NO MORE THAN OTHERS, AND HIS LIBERTY WAS DEAR TO HIM. I ASKED HIM IF HE THOUGHT TO OBTAIN IT? HE SAID HE WOULD OR LOSE HIS LIFE...

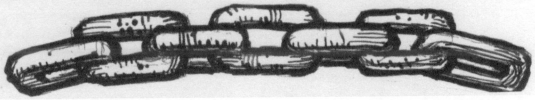

'TWAS MY OBJECT TO CARRY TERROR
AND DEVASTATION WHEREVER WE WENT...

KNOWING THEY WOULD BETRAY ME, I IMMEDIATELY LEFT MY HIDING PLACE, AND WAS PURSUED ALMOST INCESSANTLY UNTIL I WAS TAKEN A FORTNIGHT AFTERWARDS BY MR. BENJAMIN PHIPPS...ON DISCOVERING MY PLACE OF CONCEALMENT, HE COCKED HIS GUN AND AIMED AT ME...

"The Mortal Immortal"

Mary Shelley

ART/ADAPTATION BY **Lance Tooks**

IN GENERAL, MARY SHELLEY IS REGARDED AS A literary one-hit wonder. *Frankenstein* was a megahit indeed, embedding itself deeply, immovably, in our cultural consciousness for practically 200 years now (even if our culture's conception of the monster as a grunting simpleton is 100 percent wrong). But she wrote a lot more than that—six further novels, two books of travel writings, poems, plays, short biographies, a score of short stories, over 1,300 letters, and more. A handful of these works are fairly well-known among fans of early science fiction, since, like *Frankenstein*, they dealt with sci-fi themes (sometimes with supernatural elements) before that genre existed, more than fifty years before H. G. Wells and Jules Verne wrote their proto-sci-fi works. In her 1833 story, "The Mortal Immortal," an alchemist's apprentice discovers the downside of living forever.

Artist Lance Tooks has an immediately recognizable approach, a way of blending art with large amounts of text that effortlessly blurs the line between sequential comic and illustrated text. For this volume, he chose Shelley's story of an unhappy immortal, bringing the protagonist's long life to the present day.

The MORTAL IMMORTAL

Mary Shelley

THIS IS A MEMORABLE ANNIVERSARY FOR ME; ON IT I COMPLETE MY THREE HUNDRED AND TWENTY-THIRD YEAR!

adapted by **Lance Tooks**

"THE MORTAL IMMORTAL" MARY SHELLEY LANCE TOOKS

THE WANDERING JEW? -- CERTAINLY NOT. MORE THAN EIGHTEEN CENTURIES HAVE PASSED OVER HIS HEAD. IN COMPARISON WITH HIM, I AM A VERY YOUNG IMMORTAL.

AM I, THEN, IMMORTAL? THIS IS A QUESTION WHICH I HAVE ASKED MYSELF, BY DAY AND NIGHT, FOR NOW THREE HUNDRED AND THREE YEARS, AND YET CANNOT ANSWER IT. I DETECTED A GREY HAIR AMIDST MY BROWN LOCKS THIS VERY DAY -- THAT SURELY SIGNIFIES DECAY. YET IT MAY HAVE REMAINED CONCEALED THERE FOR THREE HUNDRED YEARS -- FOR SOME PERSONS HAVE BECOME ENTIRELY WHITE-HEADED BEFORE TWENTY YEARS OF AGE.

I WILL TELL MY STORY, AND MY READER SHALL JUDGE FOR ME. I WILL TELL MY STORY, AND SO CONTRIVE TO PASS SOME FEW HOURS OF A LONG ETERNITY, BECOME SO WEARISOME TO ME. FOR EVER! CAN IT BE? TO LIVE FOR EVER! I HAVE HEARD OF ENCHANTMENTS, IN WHICH THE VICTIMS WERE PLUNGED INTO A DEEP SLEEP, TO WAKE, AFTER A HUNDRED YEARS, AS FRESH AS EVER: I HAVE HEARD OF THE SEVEN SLEEPERS -- THUS TO BE IMMORTAL WOULD NOT BE SO BURDENSOME: BUT, OH! THE WEIGHT OF NEVER-ENDING TIME -- THE TEDIOUS PASSAGE OF THE STILL-SUCCEEDING HOURS! HOW HAPPY WAS THE FABLED NOURJAHAD! -- BUT TO MY TASK.

"THE MORTAL IMMORTAL" MARY SHELLEY LANCE TOOKS

ALL HAVE HEARD OF LEGENDARY CORNELIUS AGRIPPA, WHOSE APPRENTICE RAISED A FOUL FIEND DURING HIS MASTER'S ABSENCE AND WAS DESTROYED BY IT.

HIS SUBSEQUENT EXPERIMENTS FAILED, AS A SINGLE PAIR OF HANDS WAS INSUFFICIENT TO COMPLETE THEM.

THE DARK SPIRITS LAUGHED AT HIS INABILITY TO RETAIN A SINGLE MORTAL IN HIS SERVICE.

I WAS YOUNG, POOR, AND VERY MUCH IN LOVE. I HAD BEEN FOR ABOUT A YEAR THE PUPIL OF CORNELIUS, THOUGH I WAS ABSENT WHEN THE ACCIDENT TOOK PLACE. ON MY RETURN, MY FRIENDS IMPLORED ME NOT TO RETURN TO THE ALCHYMIST'S ABODE.

I TREMBLED AS I LISTENED TO THE DIRE TALE THEY TOLD; I REQUIRED NO SECOND WARNING; AND WHEN CORNELIUS CAME AND OFFERED ME A PURSE OF GOLD IF I WOULD REMAIN UNDER HIS ROOF, I FELT AS IF SATAN HIMSELF TEMPTED ME. I RAN OFF AS FAST AS MY KNEES WOULD PERMIT.

"THE MORTAL IMMORTAL" MARY SHELLEY LANCE TOOKS

I CANNOT RECALL THE HOUR WHEN I DID NOT LOVE BERTHA. WE WERE OF HUMBLE BIRTH, BUT EVERYTHING CHANGED UPON HER PARENTS' DEMISE. ADOPTED BY A RICH OLD WOMAN, BERTHA NOW WORE SILK AND I WAS TOO POOR TO MARRY.

I AM HONEST IF I AM POOR, WERE I NOT I WOULD SOON BE RICH.

YOU PRETEND TO LOVE, YET FEAR TO FACE THE DEVIL FOR LOVE'S SAKE.

THUS WAS I SHAMED INTO ACCEPTING THE ALCHYMIST'S OFFER.

POSSESSED NOW OF MONEY, I CONFESS TO NOT HAVING SEEN SO MUCH AS A CLOVEN HOOF. MOMENTS WITH BERTHA WERE STOLEN ONES, AS AGRIPPA'S DEMANDS UPON MY HOURS GREW.

HER HAUGHTY SPIRIT FIRED BY MY APPARENT NEGLECT, SHE BEGAN TO SPEND TIME IN THE COMPANY OF ALBERT HOFFER, A WEALTHY FOP FAVORED BY HER OLD PROTECTRESS.

"THE MORTAL IMMORTAL" MARY SHELLEY LANCE TOOKS

THE OLD PHILOSOPHER RETURNED TO HIS EFFORTS BEHIND CLOSED DOORS. I ENCOUNTERED A SMILING BERTHA IN TOWN, AND IT WAS QUITE TRUE THAT I NO LONGER LOVED HER-- I ADORED, WORSHIPPED, IDOLIZED HER!

SHE HAD ONLY THAT MORN BEEN PERSECUTED BY THE RICH HAG, OVER IMMEDIATE MARRIAGE WITH MY RIVAL. SHE NOW FELT REMORSE FOR HER TREATMENT OF ME, AND LONGED TO RETURN TO ME, REGARDLESS IF IT MEANT LIVING IN POVERTY.

I BECAME HER HUSBAND. I CEASED TO BE AGRIPPA'S SCHOLAR BUT CONTINUED AS HIS FRIEND. HIS ELIXER HAD NOT CURED ME OF LOVE, BUT HAD INSPIRED ME WITH COURAGE TO WIN MY BRIDE, AND I WAS GRATEFUL.

FIVE YEARS HENCE, I WAS CALLED TO THE MAGE'S DEATHBED. WE SPOKE OF THE NIGHT I'D BROKEN THE VESSEL, AND HE CLAIMED IT WAS TOO LATE NOW TO DO HIM ANY GOOD. WHEN I ASKED HIM HOW A CURE FOR LOVE COULD RESTORE HIS LIFE, HE ANSWERED WITH HIS LAST BREATH THAT IT WAS A CURE FOR ALL THINGS, AN ELIXER OF IMMORTALITY. TO DRINK WOULD BE TO LIVE FOREVER!

"THE MORTAL IMMORTAL" MARY SHELLEY LANCE TOOKS

I SURVEYED MYSELF IN A MIRROR. IT WAS TRUE! I FELT ASHAMED FOR DERIDING THE IDEA OF MY MASTER'S COMMAND OVER THE POWERS OF DARKNESS. I WAS LUCKY TO HAVE QUAFFED HEALTH AND GOOD SPIRITS...

...BUT SURELY LONGEVITY WAS NOT IMMORTALITY.

AFTER A FEW YEARS OF BLISS WITH MY BELOVED, I GREW TROUBLED. AS BERTHA BEGAN TO FADE, I APPEARED MORE LIKE HER SON. SHE BECAME JEALOUS, HER VIVACIOUS SPIRIT ALLIED TO ILL TEMPER. YET, I CHERISHED THE WIFE I HAD SOUGHT AND WON WITH SUCH PERFECT LOVE.

GREY HAIR IS PREFERABLE TO THE CHESTNUT HAIRS OF YOUTH, WINZY... THE REVERENCE AND RESPECT OF AGE IS SUPERIOR TO THE SLIGHT REGARD PAID CHILDREN.

BERTHA TURNED FIFTY AND OUR SITUATION BECAME INTOLER- ABLE.

I NO LONGER MINGLED WITH THE YOUNG, BUT MY HEART BOUNDED WITH THEM.

WE WERE SHUNNED BY ALL.

I FINALLY CONFESSED MY SECRET, AND OFFERED TO LEAVE HER, REGARDLESS OF MY LOVE FOR HER, SO THAT HER FRIENDS MIGHT RETURN. I WOULD NEVER DESERT HER IN AGE, BUT THAT HER HAPPINESS AND SAFETY REQUIRE IT.

"THE MORTAL IMMORTAL" MARY SHELLEY LANCE TOOKS

NO, WINZY, LET US LEAVE THIS PLACE TOGETHER. PERHAPS GOD WILL SEE FIT TO LIFT THIS CURSE FROM YOU.

I WILL BE YOUR TRUE, FAITHFUL HUSBAND AND DO MY DUTY BY YOU TILL THE LAST.

THE NEXT DAY WE PREPARED FOR OUR EMIGRATION, AND WITHOUT AN ADIEU TO ANYONE, TOOK OUR REFUGE IN FRANCE.

IT WAS CRUEL TO TRANSPORT HER AWAY FROM OUR NATIVE VILLAGE AND THE FRIENDS OF HER YOUTH, TO A NEW COUNTRY, NEW LANGUAGE, NEW CUSTOMS.

AWAY FROM ALL TELLTALE CHRONICLERS, SHE SOUGHT TO DECREASE OUR APPARENT DIFFERENCES BY A THOUSAND FEMININE ARTS-- ROUGE, YOUTHFUL DRESS, PLAYFUL MANNER. I COULD NOT BE ANGRY, DID I NOT MYSELF WEAR A MASK? WHY QUARREL WITH HERS BECAUSE IT WAS LESS SUCCESSFUL.

I GRIEVED AT THE REMEMBERENCE OF MY YOUTHFUL DARK-HAIRED GIRL, NOW A MINCING, SIMPERING OLD WOMAN.

HER JEALOUSY NEVER SLEPT.

SHE OBSESSIVELY PORED OVER MY FRAME FOR A WRINKLE OR GREY HAIR, DELUDED THAT SHE'D FOUND ONE.

I NEVER DARED ADDRESS ANOTHER WOMAN.

ONE BIRTHDAY, FANCYING THAT THE BELLE OF THE VILLAGE REGARDED ME WITH FAVORING EYES, SHE BROUGHT ME A GREY WIG.

HER CONSTANT DISCOURSE AMONG ACQUAINTANCES WAS, THAT ALTHOUGH I APPEARED YOUNG, THERE WAS A RUIN AT WORK WITHIN MY FRAME, THE WORST SYMPTOM BEING MY APPARENT HEALTH. MY YOUTH WAS A DISEASE, AND I OUGHT AT ALL TIMES TO PREPARE, IF NOT FOR A SUDDEN AND AWFUL DEATH, AT LEAST TO AWAKE SOME MORNING WHITE-HEADED AND BOWED DOWN IN ADVANCED YEARS.

"THE MORTAL IMMORTAL" MARY SHELLEY LANCE TOOKS

WHY DWELL ON THESE MINUTE CIRCUMSTANCES?

WE LIVED ON FOR MANY A YEAR. IT HAS EVER BEEN A CONSOLATION TO ME THAT I PERFORMED MY DUTY SCRUPULOUSLY TOWARDS HER.

SHE HAD BEEN MINE IN YOUTH, SHE WAS MINE IN AGE, AND AT LAST WHEN I HEAPED THE SOD OVER HER CORPSE, I WEPT AT THE LOSS OF ALL THAT REALLY BOUND ME TO HUMANITY.

DEATH! MYSTERIOUS ILL-VISAGED FRIEND OF WEAK HUMANITY! WHY ALONE OF ALL MORTALS HAVE YOU CAST ME FROM YOUR SHELTERING FOLD?

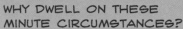

BERTHA MORTIMER WINSLOW
BELOVED WIFE
FOREVER YOUNG
1725 1801

OH, FOR THE PEACE OF THE GRAVE, THE SILENCE OF THE TOMB-- OH, THAT THOUGHT WOULD CEASE TO WORK IN MY BRAIN AND MY HEART WOULD BEAT NO MORE WITH SADNESS.

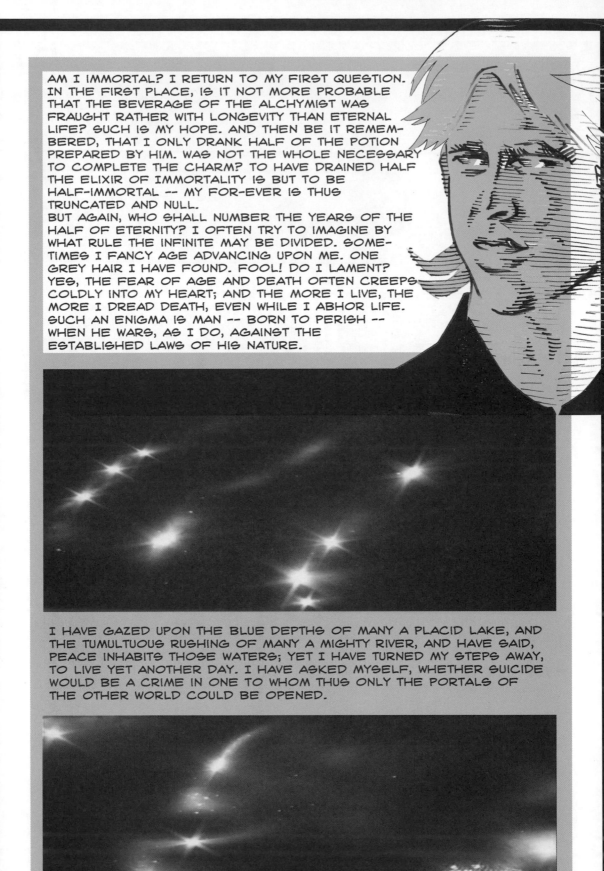

AM I IMMORTAL? I RETURN TO MY FIRST QUESTION. IN THE FIRST PLACE, IS IT NOT MORE PROBABLE THAT THE BEVERAGE OF THE ALCHYMIST WAS FRAUGHT RATHER WITH LONGEVITY THAN ETERNAL LIFE? SUCH IS MY HOPE. AND THEN BE IT REMEMBERED, THAT I ONLY DRANK HALF OF THE POTION PREPARED BY HIM. WAS NOT THE WHOLE NECESSARY TO COMPLETE THE CHARM? TO HAVE DRAINED HALF THE ELIXIR OF IMMORTALITY IS BUT TO BE HALF-IMMORTAL -- MY FOR-EVER IS THUS TRUNCATED AND NULL.

BUT AGAIN, WHO SHALL NUMBER THE YEARS OF THE HALF OF ETERNITY? I OFTEN TRY TO IMAGINE BY WHAT RULE THE INFINITE MAY BE DIVIDED. SOMETIMES I FANCY AGE ADVANCING UPON ME. ONE GREY HAIR I HAVE FOUND. FOOL! DO I LAMENT? YES, THE FEAR OF AGE AND DEATH OFTEN CREEPS COLDLY INTO MY HEART; AND THE MORE I LIVE, THE MORE I DREAD DEATH, EVEN WHILE I ABHOR LIFE. SUCH AN ENIGMA IS MAN -- BORN TO PERISH -- WHEN HE WARS, AS I DO, AGAINST THE ESTABLISHED LAWS OF HIS NATURE.

I HAVE GAZED UPON THE BLUE DEPTHS OF MANY A PLACID LAKE, AND THE TUMULTUOUS RUSHING OF MANY A MIGHTY RIVER, AND HAVE SAID, PEACE INHABITS THOSE WATERS; YET I HAVE TURNED MY STEPS AWAY, TO LIVE YET ANOTHER DAY. I HAVE ASKED MYSELF, WHETHER SUICIDE WOULD BE A CRIME IN ONE TO WHOM THUS ONLY THE PORTALS OF THE OTHER WORLD COULD BE OPENED.

SINCE THEN HOW MANY
HAVE BEEN MY CARES
AND WOES, HOW FEW
AND EMPTY MY ENJOY-
MENTS! I PAUSE HERE
IN MY HISTORY -- I WILL
PURSUE IT NO FURTHER.
A SAILOR WITHOUT
RUDDER OR COMPASS,
TOSSED ON A STORMY
SEA -- A TRAVELLER
LOST ON A WIDESPREAD
HEATH, WITHOUT
LANDMARK OR STONE
TO GUIDE HIM -- SUCH I
HAVE BEEN: MORE
LOST, MORE HOPELESS
THAN EITHER.
A NEARING SHIP, A
GLEAM FROM SOME
FAR COT, MAY SAVE
THEM; BUT I HAVE NO
BEACON EXCEPT THE
HOPE OF DEATH.

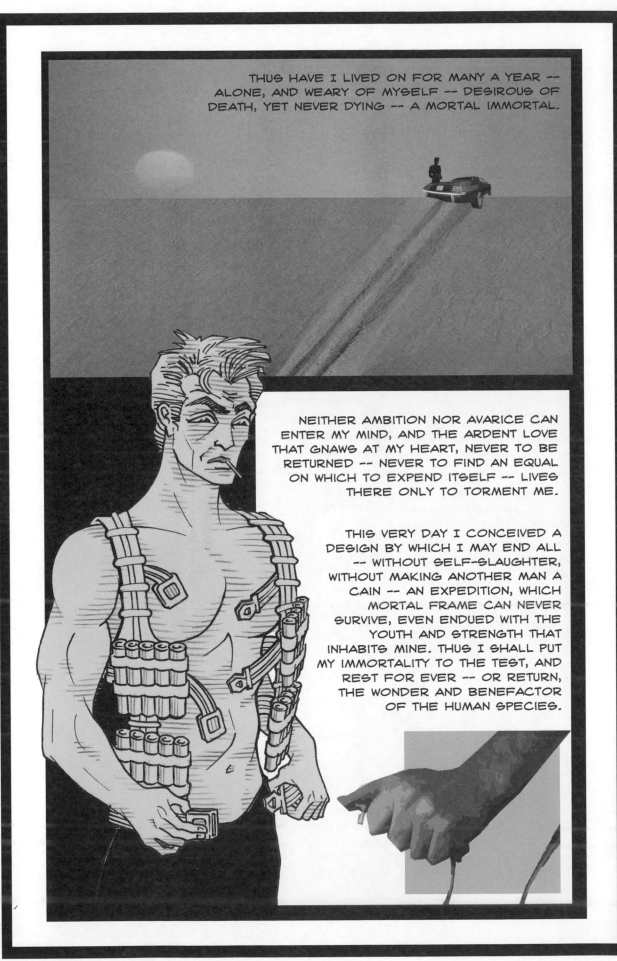

THUS HAVE I LIVED ON FOR MANY A YEAR -- ALONE, AND WEARY OF MYSELF -- DESIROUS OF DEATH, YET NEVER DYING -- A MORTAL IMMORTAL.

NEITHER AMBITION NOR AVARICE CAN ENTER MY MIND, AND THE ARDENT LOVE THAT GNAWS AT MY HEART, NEVER TO BE RETURNED -- NEVER TO FIND AN EQUAL ON WHICH TO EXPEND ITSELF -- LIVES THERE ONLY TO TORMENT ME.

THIS VERY DAY I CONCEIVED A DESIGN BY WHICH I MAY END ALL -- WITHOUT SELF-SLAUGHTER, WITHOUT MAKING ANOTHER MAN A CAIN -- AN EXPEDITION, WHICH MORTAL FRAME CAN NEVER SURVIVE, EVEN ENDUED WITH THE YOUTH AND STRENGTH THAT INHABITS MINE. THUS I SHALL PUT MY IMMORTALITY TO THE TEST, AND REST FOR EVER -- OR RETURN, THE WONDER AND BENEFACTOR OF THE HUMAN SPECIES.

"THE MORTAL IMMORTAL" MARY SHELLEY LANCE TOOKS

BEFORE I GO, A MISERABLE VANITY HAS CAUSED ME TO PEN THESE PAGES. I WOULD NOT DIE, AND LEAVE NO NAME BEHIND. THREE CENTURIES HAVE PASSED SINCE I QUAFFED THE FATAL BEVERAGE; ANOTHER YEAR SHALL NOT ELAPSE BEFORE, ENCOUNTERING GIGANTIC DANGERS -- WARRING WITH THE POWERS OF FROST IN THEIR HOME -- BESET BY FAMINE, TOIL, AND TEMPEST --

I YIELD THIS BODY, TOO TENACIOUS A CAGE FOR A SOUL WHICH THIRSTS FOR FREEDOM, TO THE DESTRUCTIVE ELEMENTS OF AIR AND WATER; OR, IF I SURVIVE, MY NAME SHALL BE RECORDED AS ONE OF THE MOST FAMOUS AMONG THE SONS OF MEN; AND, MY TASK ACHIEVED, I SHALL ADOPT MORE RESOLUTE MEANS, AND, BY SCATTERING AND ANNIHILATING THE ATOMS THAT COMPOSE MY FRAME, SET AT LIBERTY THE LIFE IMPRISONED WITHIN, AND SO CRUELLY PREVENTED FROM SOARING FROM THIS DIM EARTH TO A SPHERE M...

...MORE CONGENIAL TO ITS IMMORTAL ESSENCE.

Fairy tales

Hans Christian Andersen

ILLUSTRATIONS BY **S. Clay Wilson**

IN THEIR INTRODUCTION TO *THE STORIES OF HANS Christian Andersen: A New Translation from the Danish*, Diana Crone Frank and Jeffrey Frank write that "beyond Scandinavia, Andersen has generally been regarded not as a literary genius but as a quaint nineteenth-century writer of charming children's stories." This mischaracterization has two main sources—the dumbed-down translations of his work that have been appearing for well over 150 years and the almost entirely fictionalized Danny Kaye movie, *Hans Christian Andersen* (1952).

It turns out that Andersen's 168 children's tales are laced with irony and subtle humor, sociopolitical resonance, and occasional pessimism. In his homeland of Denmark, he is indeed considered a genius on a level with his contemporary, the philosopher Søren Kierkegaard (whose first published work, synchronistically, was a pamphlet attacking the early novels of Andersen). The Franks characterize him as "a major literary figure enclosed by a minor language." Harold Bloom even compares his writings to Tolstoy's later works for their aesthetic brilliance.

Andersen came from a colorful family that included "a grandfather who went mad, a grandmother who was jailed as a young woman for repeatedly having illegitimate chil-

dren, and an aunt who apparently ran a brothel in Copenhagen." He ceaselessly wrote novels, poems, plays, and fairy tales (it might be more accurate to simply call them stories for children). It was this final type of work that brought him international fame—he was constantly fêted by European royalty—and the admiration of the Brownings, Longfellow, and none other than Charles Dickens (the two became friends, and it's possible that Andersen was the only literary figure of the time whose fame eclipsed Dickens's).

Earlier in this volume, we saw illustrations of the Grimms' fairy tales by the untamable S. Clay Wilson, the most extreme of the first generation of underground comix artists. In another limited-edition volume for Word Play publications, Clay turned his attention to Andersen's tales, including the three presented here: "The Emperor's New Clothes" (1837), "The Nightingale" (1844), and the astoundingly morose "The Little Match Girl" (1846).

SOURCE

Frank, Diana Crone, and Jeffrey Frank. *The Stories of Hans Christian Andersen: A New Translation from the Danish*. New York: Houghton Mifflin Harcourt, 2003.

MANY YEARS ago, there was an Emperor who was so excessively fond of new clothes that he spent all his money in dress. He did not trouble himself in the least about his soldiers, nor did he care to go either to the theater or the chase, except for the opportunities then afforded him for displaying his new clothes. He had a different suit for each hour of the day. As of any other king or emperor, one is accustomed to say, "He is sitting in council." But it was always said of him, "The Emperor is sitting in his wardrobe."

"The Emperor's New Clothes"

Time passed merrily in the large town which was his capital; strangers arrived every day at the court. One day, two rogues, calling themselves weavers, made their appearance. They gave out that they knew how to weave stuffs of the most beautiful colors and elaborate patterns, the clothes manufactured from which would have the wonderful property of remaining invisible to everyone who was unfit for the office he held, or who was extraordinarily simple in character.

"These must, indeed, be splendid clothes!" thought the Emperor. "Had I such a suit, I might at once find out what men in my realms are unfit for their office, and also be able to distinguish the wise from the foolish! This stuff must be woven for me immediately." And he caused large sums of money to be given to both the weavers in order that they might begin their work directly.

So the two pretended weavers set up two looms, and affected to work very busily, though in reality they did nothing at all. They asked for the most delicate silk and the purest gold thread, put both into their own knapsacks, and then continued their pretended work at the empty looms until late at night.

"I should like to know how the weavers are getting on with my cloth," said the Emperor to himself, after some little time had elapsed. He was, however, rather embarrassed when he remembered that a simpleton, or one unfit for his office, would be unable to see the manufacture. To be sure, he thought he had nothing to risk in his own person, but yet, he would prefer sending somebody else, to bring him intelligence about the weavers and their work, before he troubled himself in the affair. All the people throughout the city had heard of the wonderful property the cloth was to possess; and all were anxious to learn how wise, or how ignorant, their neighbors might prove to be.

"I will send my faithful old minister to the weavers," said the Emperor at last, after some deliberation. "He will be best able to see how the cloth looks; for he is a man of sense, and no one can be more suitable for his office than he is."

So the faithful old minister went into the hall, where the knaves were working with all their might at their empty looms. "What can be the meaning of this?" thought the old man, opening his eyes very wide. "I cannot discover the least bit of thread on the looms." However, he did not express his thoughts aloud.

The impostors requested him very courteously to be so good as to come nearer their looms, and then asked him whether the design pleased him, and whether the colors were not very beautiful, at the same time pointing to the empty frames. The poor old minister looked and looked; he could not discover anything on the looms, for a very good reason, viz: there was nothing there. "What!" thought he again. "Is it possible that I am a simpleton? I have never thought so myself; and no one must know it now if I am so. Can it be that I am unfit for my office? No, that must not be said either. I will never confess that I could not see the stuff."

"Well, Sir Minister!" said one of the knaves, still pretending to work. "You do not say whether the stuff pleases you."

"Oh, it is excellent!" replied the old minister, looking at the loom through his spectacles. "This pattern, and the colors, yes, I will tell the Emperor without delay how very beautiful I think them."

"We shall be much obliged to you," said the impostors, and then they named the different colors and described the pattern of the pretended stuff. The old minister listened attentively to their words, in order that he might repeat them to the Emperor, and then the knaves asked for more silk and gold, saying that it was necessary to complete what they had begun. However, they put all that was given them into their knapsacks and continued to work with as much apparent diligence as before at their empty looms.

The Emperor now sent another officer of his court to see how the men were getting on, and to ascertain whether the cloth would soon be ready. It was just the same with this gentleman as with the minister; he surveyed the looms on all sides, but could see nothing at all but the empty frames.

"Does not the stuff appear as beautiful to you, as it did to my lord the minister?" asked the impostors of the Emperor's second ambassador, at the same time making the same gestures as before, and talking of the design and colors which were not there.

"I certainly am not stupid!" thought the messenger. "It must be that I am not fit for my good, profitable office! That is very odd; however, no one shall know anything about it." And accordingly he praised the stuff he could not see, and declared that he was delighted with both colors and patterns. "Indeed, please your Imperial Majesty," said he to his sovereign when he returned, "the cloth which the weavers are preparing is extraordinarily magnificent."

The whole city was talking of the splendid cloth which the Emperor had ordered to be woven at his own expense.

And now the Emperor himself wished to see the costly manufacture, while it was still in the loom. Accompanied by a select number of officers of the court, among whom were the two honest men who had already admired the cloth, he went to the crafty impostors, who, as soon as they were aware of the Emperor's approach, went on working more diligently than ever, although they still did not pass a single thread through the looms.

"Is not the work absolutely magnificent?" said the two officers of the crown, already mentioned. "If your Majesty will only be pleased to look at it! What a splendid design! What glorious colors!" And at the same time they pointed to the empty frames, for they imagined that everyone else could see this exquisite piece of workmanship.

"THE EMPEROR'S NEW CLOTHES" HANS CHRISTIAN ANDERSEN S. CLAY WILSON

"How is this?" said the Emperor to himself. "I can see nothing! This is indeed a terrible affair! Am I a simpleton, or am I unfit to be an Emperor? That would be the worst thing that could happen." Oh! The cloth is charming," said he, aloud. "It has my complete approbation." And he smiled most graciously, and looked closely at the empty looms, for on no account would he say that he could not see what two of the officers of his court had praised so much. All his retinue now strained their eyes, hoping to discover something on the looms, but they could see no more than the others; nevertheless, they all exclaimed, "Oh, how beautiful!" and advised his majesty to have some new clothes made from this splendid material, for the approaching procession. "Magnificent! Charming! Excellent!" resounded on all sides, and everyone was uncommonly gay. The Emperor shared in the general satisfaction, and presented the impostors with the ribbon of an order of knighthood, to be worn in their button-holes, and the title of "Gentlemen Weavers."

The rogues sat up the whole of the night before the day on which the procession was to take place, and had sixteen lights burning, so that everyone might see how anxious they were to finish the Emperor's new suit. They pretended to roll the cloth off the looms, cut the air with their scissors, and sewed with needles without any thread in them. "See!" cried they, at last. "The Emperor's new clothes are ready!"

And now the Emperor, with all the grandees of his court, came to the weavers, and the rogues raised their arms, as if in the act of holding something up, saying, "Here are your Majesty's trousers! Here is the scarf! Here is the mantle! The whole suit is as light as a cobweb; one might fancy one has nothing at all on, when dressed in it. That, however, is the great virtue of this delicate cloth."

"Yes indeed!" said all the courtiers, although not one of them could see anything of this exquisite manufacture.

"If your Imperial Majesty will be graciously pleased to take off your clothes, we will fit on the new suit, in front of the looking glass."

The Emperor was accordingly undressed, and the rogues pretended to array him in his new suit; the Emperor turning round, from side to side, before the looking glass.

"How splendid his Majesty looks in his new clothes, and how well they fit!" everyone cried out. "What a design! What colors! These are indeed royal robes!"

"The canopy which is to be borne over your Majesty, in the procession, is waiting," announced the chief master of the ceremonies.

"I am quite ready," answered the Emperor. "Do my new clothes fit well?" asked he, turning himself round again before the looking glass, in order that he might appear to be examining his handsome suit.

The lords of the bedchamber, who were to carry his Majesty's train, felt about on the ground, as if they were lifting up the ends of the mantle, and pretended to be carrying something, for they would by no means betray anything like simplicity or unfitness for their office.

So now the Emperor walked under his high canopy in the midst of the procession, through the streets of his capital, and all the people standing by, and those at the windows, cried out, "Oh! How beautiful are our Emperor's new clothes! What a magnificent train there is to the mantle; and how gracefully the scarf hangs!" In short, no one would allow that he could not see these much-admired clothes. Certainly, none of the Emperor's various suits had ever made so great an impression as these invisible ones.

"But the Emperor has nothing at all on!" said a little child.

"Listen to the voice of innocence!" exclaimed his father, and what the child had said was whispered from one to another.

"But he has nothing at all on!" at last cried out all the people.

The Emperor was vexed, for he knew that the people were right, but he thought the procession must go on now! And the lords of the bedchamber took greater pains than ever to appear holding up a train, although, in reality, there was no train to hold. *

"The Nightingale"

IN CHINA, as you know, the Emperor is a Chinaman, and all the folk he has about him are Chinamen too. It's many years ago now, but that is exactly the reason why it is worth while to listen to the story, before it's forgotten. The Emperor's palace was the most splendid in the world, wholly and entirely made of fine porcelain, very costly, but so brittle and risky to touch that one had to take very great care. In the garden the most extraordinary flowers were to be seen, and to the most magnificent of all little silver bells were tied, so that nobody might pass by without noticing the flower. Yes, everything was most carefully thought out in the Emperor's garden, and it extended so far that the gardener himself did not know the end of it. If you went on walking you came into a beautiful forest with tall trees and deep lakes. The forest went right down to the sea, which was blue and deep. Large ships could sail right in beneath the branches, and in the branches there lived a Nightingale, which sang so divinely that even the poor fisherman, who had so much else to think about, stopped and listened when he was out at night pulling up his fishing nets and happened to hear the Nightingale. "Lord, how pretty it is!" he said; but then he had to attend to his business and forgot the bird. Still, the next night when it sang again, and the fisherman came out here, he said once more: "Lord, how pretty it is!"

From all the countries in the world travelers came to the Emperor's city and were amazed at the palace and the garden; but when they came to hear the Nightingale, they all said: "After all, this is the best thing." And the travelers told of it when they got home, and clever people wrote many a book about the city, the palace, and the garden, but they did not overlook the Nightingale: it was put at the head of everything, and those who could make poetry wrote the loveliest poems all about the Nightingale in the forest by the deep lake.

The books went all over the world, and some of them came, once upon a time, to the Emperor, too. He was sitting in his golden chair reading and reading, and every minute he nodded his head, for it pleased him to hear the splendid description of the city and the palace and the garden. "Yet, the Nightingale is the best thing of all," was written there.

"What's this?" said the Emperor. "The Nightingale? Why, I know nothing whatever about it! Is there such a bird in my Empire—not to say in my garden? I never heard of it! This is what one can get by reading."

So he called his Marshal, who was of such high rank that when anyone inferior to him made bold to address him or ask him a question, he never made any reply but "P," which means nothing at all. "It appears that there is a most remarkable bird here, called a Nightingale," said the Emperor. "It is stated to be the very best thing in my vast realm! Why has no one ever told me anything about it?"

"I have never before heard it spoken of," said the Marshal; "it has never been presented at Court."

"I desire that it shall come here tonight and sing before me," said the Emperor. "Here is the whole world aware of what I possess, and I know nothing of it!"

"I have never before heard it spoken of," said the Marshal. "I must search for it, I must find it."

But where was it to be found? The Marshal ran up and down all the staircases, and through the halls and passages, but no one of all the people he met had heard tell of the Nightingale, and the Marshal ran back to the Emperor and said that it certainly must be an invention of the people who wrote books. "Your Imperial Majesty could never imagine the things people write; all manner of inventions, and something which is called the Black Art."

"But the book in which I read this," said the Emperor, "was sent to me by the high and mighty Emperor of Japan, so it cannot be an untruth. I will hear the Nightingale! It must be here tonight. It has my most exalted favor, and if it does not come, the whole court shall have its stomachs stamped upon when it has dined!"

"Tsing-pe!" said the Marshal; and ran again up and down all the staircases and through all the halls and passages, and half the court ran with him, for they did not at all wish to have their stomachs stamped upon. There was a hue and cry after this remarkable Nightingale, which was known to the whole world, but to nobody at the court.

At last they came on a poor little girl in the kitchen. She said: "O Lord, the Nightingale? I know it well; yes, indeed, how it can sing! Every evening I have leave to carry home leavings from the table to my poor sick mother. She lives down by the shore, and when I'm coming back and am tired and take a rest in the wood, I hear the Nightingale sing. The tears come in my eyes with it; it feels as if my mother was kissing me."

"Little kitchen girl," said the Marshal, "I will promise you a permanent position in the kitchen and leave to see the Emperor dine, if you can guide us to the Nightingale, for it is invited for this evening." So they all set out together for the wood where the Nightingale used to sing. Half the court was there. As they were making the best of their way along a cow began to low.

"Oh!" said the court pages. "Now we can hear it; it's a really remarkable power for such a small animal! I'm quite sure I've heard it before."

"No, that's the cows lowing," said the little kitchen girl. "We're a long way off the place yet."

Then the frogs began croaking in the pond.

"Lovely," said the Chinese master of the palace. "Now I hear her! It resembles small church bells."

"No, that's the frogs," said the little kitchen girl; "but I think we shall hear it very soon now."

Then the Nightingale began to sing.

"That's it," said the little girl. "Hark! Hark! And there it sits!" And she pointed to a little grey bird up among the branches. "Is it possible?" said the Marshal. "I could never have imagined it would be like that! And how very shabby it looks! It must certainly have lost its color at the sight of so many distinguished persons in its vicinity."

"Little Nightingale," the little kitchen girl called out aloud, "our gracious

Emperor very much wants you to sing to him."

"With the greatest of pleasure," said the Nightingale, and sang, so that it was a pure delight.

"It resembles glass bells," said the Marshal, "and look at its little throat, how it works it! It is most curious that we should never have heard it before! It will have a great success at court."

"Shall I sing once again for the Emperor?" said the Nightingale, who thought the Emperor was there too.

"My excellent little Nightingale," said the Marshal, "I have the great pleasure of being commanded to invite you to a court festival this evening, where you will enchant his exalted Imperial Grace with your charming song."

"It sounds best out in the green wood," said the Nightingale. But it gladly accompanied them when it heard that the Emperor asked for it.

At the palace there was a tremendous smartening up. The walls and floors, which were of porcelain, shone with the light of many thousands of golden lamps. The most beautiful flowers, which really could ring, were set about the windows. There was a running to and fro, and a draft of air, but that made all the bells ring till one couldn't hear one's own voice.

In the middle of the great hall where the Emperor sat, a golden perch was set up, and on it the Nightingale was to sit. The whole court was there, and the little kitchen girl had got permission to stand behind the door, seeing now she had the title of Actual Kitchenmaid. Everybody was in their best state attire, and everybody was looking at the little grey bird. The Emperor nodded to it.

And the Nightingale sang so beautifully that tears came into the Emperor's eyes; the tears ran down his cheeks, and then the Nightingale sang yet more delightfully, so that it went straight to his heart; and the Emperor was greatly pleased, and said that the Nightingale should have his golden slipper to wear on its neck. But the Nightingale thanked him and said it had already had reward enough.

"I have seen tears in the Emperor's eyes; that is to me the richest of treasures. An Emperor's tears have a marvelous power. God knows I am well paid." And it sang again with that sweet, divine voice.

"It is the most lovable coquetterie one can conceive," said the whole suite of ladies, and they put water in their mouths so as to gurgle when anyone spoke to them; they thought that they too were Nightingales. Yes, and the lackeys and chambermaids let it be understood that they also were satisfied, and that means a lot, for they are the most difficult people to suit. In fact, the Nightingale really did make a great success.

It was now to remain at court and have its own cage, and liberty to take exercise out of doors twice in the day time and once at night. It had twelve attendants, each of whom had a silken thread attached to its leg, which they held tight. There really was no satisfaction in these expeditions. The whole city talked of the remarkable bird, and when two people met, one of them would say nothing but "night," and the other said "gale." Whereupon they heaved a sigh and understood each other. Nay, more than eleven pork butchers' children were named after it, but not one of them had a note of music in its body.

One day there arrived a large parcel for the Emperor; on it was written, "Nightingale."

"Here now we have another book about our celebrated bird," said the Emperor, but it was not a book; it was a little machine that lay in a box—an artificial Nightingale made to resemble the live one, but all set with diamonds, rubies, and sapphires. As soon as ever the artificial bird was wound up, it could sing one of the strains the real one sang, and its tail moved up and down and glistened with silver and gold. Round its neck hung a little ribbon, and on it was written: "The Emperor of Japan's Nightingale is poor beside that of the Emperor of China."

"That is charming!" said everybody. And the man who had brought the artificial bird immediately received the title of Chief Imperial Bringer of Nightingales.

Now they must sing together; what a duet it will be!

So they had to sing together, but it wouldn't go right, for the real Nightingale sang in its own style, and the artificial bird went off into waltz-tunes.

"No blame attaches to it," said the bandmaster; "it keeps excellent time, and is entirely of my school." So the artificial bird was to sing alone. It made as great a success as the real one, and was, besides, far prettier to look at; it glittered like a bracelet or a brooch.

Three-and-thirty times over did it sing the self-same melody, and yet it was not tired. The people would have liked to hear it over again, but the Emperor said that now the live Nightingale should sing a little—but where was it? Nobody had noticed that it had flown out of the open window, away to its own green wood.

"But what is the meaning of this?" said the Emperor. And all the court people scolded, and said the Nightingale was a most ungrateful creature. "Still, we have the best bird, after all," they said, and the artificial bird had to sing again. It was the thirty-fourth time they had heard the same piece, but they didn't quite know it yet, for it was very difficult, and the bandmaster praised the bird in the highest terms, and assured them that it was superior to the real Nightingale, not only as regards the plumage and the many beautiful diamonds, but also internally.

"For observe, your lordships, and the Emperor above all, with the real Nightingale one can never calculate what will come next, but with the artificial bird all is definite; it is thus, and no otherwise. It can be accounted for; one can open it up and show the human contrivance, how the waltzes are set, how they go, and how one follows on another."

"Exactly what I think," said everybody; and the bandmaster got permission on the following Sunday to exhibit the bird to the people. They too should hear it sing, said the Emperor. And they did hear it, and were as delighted as if they had got drunk on tea (which is the genuine Chinese fashion), and everyone said "oh" and pointed the finger we call lick-pot up in the air and then nodded. But the poor fisherman, who had heard the real Nightingale, said: "It sings pretty enough, and it's like it too, but there's something wanting. I don't know what!"

The real Nightingale was exiled from the land and realm. The artificial bird had a place assigned it on a silk cushion close to the Emperor's bed. All the presents that had been made to it, gold and jewels, lay round it, and it had risen to the title of "High Imperial Nightingale Songster" and in precedence was Number One on the Left Hand Side, for the Emperor accounted that side to be the most distinguished on which the heart lay, and even an Emperor's heart is on the left side. And the bandmaster wrote five-and-twenty volumes on the subject of the artificial bird. The work was very learned and very long, full of the most difficult words in the Chinese language, and everyone said they had read it and understood it, for otherwise they would have been accounted stupid and would have had their stomachs stamped upon.

So things went on for a whole year. The Emperor, the court, and all the rest of the Chinese knew by heart every little cluck in the artificial bird's song, but precisely for that reason they liked it all the better: they could sing with it themselves, and so they did. The street-boys would sing "Zizizi! kluk, kluk, kluk!" and the Emperor sang too: in fact, it was admittedly exquisite.

But one evening, when the bird was singing its best and the Emperor was lying in bed listening to it, something went "snap" inside the bird. Whirr-rr! All the wheels whizzed round, and the music stopped. The Emperor jumped straight out of bed, and had his body physician summoned, but what use was that? They fetched the watchmaker, and after much talk and much examination, he got the bird into order after a fashion. But he said it must be most sparingly used, for it was very much worn in the bearings, and it was impossible to replace them so that you could be sure of the music. That was a sad affliction! Only once a year durst they let the bird sing, and even that was a severe strain. But thereupon the bandmaster made a short oration with plenty of difficult words, and said that it was just as good as before, and accordingly it was just as good as before.

Five years had now passed by, and a really great sorrow came upon the whole country, for at bottom they were very fond of their Emperor, and now he was ill, and, it was said, could not recover. A new Emperor was already chosen, and people stood outside in the streets and asked the Marshal how it went with their Emperor.

"P," said he, and shook his head.

Cold and pale lay the Emperor in his great stately bed; the whole court believed him dead, and every one of them ran off to pay their respects to the new Emperor. The servants of the bedchamber ran out to gossip about it, and the palace maids had a large coffee party. Everywhere, in all the halls and corridors, cloth was laid down so that footsteps should not be heard, and so everything was very, very quiet. But the Emperor was not yet dead; stiff and pale he lay there in the stately bed with the long velvet curtains and the heavy gold tassels. High up a window stood open, and the moon shone in upon the Emperor and the artificial bird.

The poor Emperor was hardly able to draw his breath; it seemed as if something was sitting on his chest. He opened his eyes, and then he saw that it was Death who was sitting on his breast, and had put on his golden crown, and was holding in one hand the gold sword of the Emperor, and in the other his splendid banner. And round about, in the folds of the great velvet bed curtains, strange faces pushed themselves out, some quite horrible, others divinely kind. There were all the Emperor's good and evil deeds, looking at him now that Death was seated upon his breast.

"Do you remember that?" whispered one after another. "Do you remember this?" And they told him of many things, so that the sweat broke out on his forehead. "I never knew of that," said the Emperor. "Music! Music! The great drum of China!" he called out, "that I may not hear all they are saying."

They went on, and Death nodded like a Chinaman at everything that was said.

"Music! Let me have music!" cried the Emperor. "You blessed little bird of gold, sing, do sing! I have given you gold and precious things. I myself hung my golden slipper about your neck! Sing, do sing!"

But the bird was silent; there was no one to wind it up, and without that it did not sing. But Death went on looking at the Emperor out of his great empty eye-holes, and everything was still, fearfully still.

At that instant there was heard, close by the window, the most lovely song. It was the little live Nightingale that was sitting on the branch outside. It had heard of its Emperor's need, and so had come to sing to him of comfort and hope: and as it sung, the forms became more and more shadowy. The blood coursed quicker and quicker through the Emperor's weak body, and Death himself listened and said: "Go on, little Nightingale! Go on."

"Yes, if you will give me the splendid gold sword! Yes, if you will give me the rich banner, and give me the Emperor's crown." And Death gave each of the treasures for a song, and the Nightingale still went on singing; and it sang of the quiet churchyard where the white roses grow, where the elder tree smells sweet, and where the fresh grass is moistened with the tears of those who are left. Then a yearning for his garden came upon Death, and he floated out of the window like a cold white mist.

"Thanks, thanks," said the Emperor, "you heavenly little bird, I know you now. I drove you out of my land and realm, and yet you have sung the foul sins away from my bed, and rid my heart of Death. How shall I repay you?"

"You have repaid me," said the Nightingale. "I drew tears from your eyes the first time I sang, and I shall never forget it. Those are the jewels that do the heart of the singer good. But sleep now, and become well and strong. I will sing to you."

"THE NIGHTINGALE" HANS CHRISTIAN ANDERSEN S. CLAY WILSON

And it sang, and the Emperor fell into a sweet sleep, a sleep that was kind and healing.

The sun was shining through the windows on him when he awoke, strengthened and whole. None of his attendants had come back yet, for they believed he was dead, but the Nightingale still sat there singing.

"You must always stay with me," said the Emperor. "You shall only sing when you like, and as for the artificial bird, I'll break it into a thousand bits."

"Don't do that," said the Nightingale. "It has done what good it could; keep it as before. I can't make any home at the palace, but do you let me come here when I like. Then I will sit at evening time on the branch there by this window and sing to you, to make you happy, and thoughtful too. I will sing about the happy and about those who suffer. I will sing of the evil and the good that is about you and is hidden from you. The little singing bird flies far and wide, to the poor fisherman, to the laborers' cottages, to everyone who is far removed from you and your court. I love your heart better than your crown; and yet the crown has about it a perfume of something holy. I will come, I will sing to you. But one thing you must promise me."

"Anything," said the Emperor, as he stood there in his imperial robes, which he had put on himself, and held the sword, heavy with gold, up against his heart.

"One thing I beg of you. Tell no one that you have a little bird that tells you everything. It will be better." And with that the Nightingale flew away.

The attendants came in to see their dead Emperor, and—well, there stood they, and the Emperor said: "Good morning." ✳

"The Little Match Girl"

MOST TERRIBLY cold it was; it snowed, and was nearly quite dark, and evening—the last evening of the year. In this cold and darkness there went along the street a poor little girl, bareheaded, and with naked feet. When she left home she had slippers on, it is true, but what was the good of that? They were very large slippers, which her mother had hitherto worn; so large were they the poor little thing lost them as she scuffled away across the street because of two carriages that rolled by dreadfully fast.

One slipper was nowhere to be found; the other had been laid hold of by an urchin, and off he ran with it. He thought it would do capitally for a cradle when he some day or other should have children himself. So the little maiden walked on with her tiny naked feet, which were quite red and blue from cold. She carried a quantity of matches in an old apron, and she held a bundle of them in her hand. Nobody had bought anything of her the whole livelong day; no one had given her a single farthing.

She crept along trembling with cold and hunger—a very picture of sorrow, the poor little thing!

The flakes of snow covered her long, fair hair, which fell in beautiful curls around her neck, but of that, of course, she never once now thought. From all the windows the candles were gleaming, and it smelt so deliciously of roast goose, for you know it was New Year's Eve. Yes, of that she thought.

In a corner formed by two houses, of which one advanced more than the other, she seated herself down and cowered together. Her little feet she had drawn close up to her, but she grew colder and colder, and to go home she did not venture, for she had not sold any matches and could not bring a farthing of money. From her father she would certainly get blows, and at home it was cold too, for above her she had only the roof, through which the wind whistled, even though the largest cracks were stopped up with straw and rags.

Her little hands were almost numbed with cold. Oh, a match might afford her a world of comfort, if she only dared take a single one out of the bundle, draw it against the wall, and warm her fingers by it. She drew one out. How it blazed, how it burnt! It was a warm, bright flame, like a candle, as she held her hands over it; it was a wonderful light. It seemed really to the little maiden as though she were sitting before a large iron stove, with burnished brass feet and a brass ornament at top. The fire burned with such blessed influence; it warmed so delightfully. The little girl had already stretched out her feet to warm them too, but—the small flame went out, the stove vanished. She had only the remains of the burnt-out match in her hand.

She rubbed another against the wall; it burned brightly, and where the light fell on the wall, there the wall became transparent like a veil, so that she could see into the room. On the table was spread a snow-white tablecloth; upon it was a splendid porcelain service, and the roast goose was steaming famously with its stuffing of apple and dried plums. And what was still more capital to behold was, the goose hopped down from the dish, reeled about on the floor with knife and fork in its breast, till it came up to the poor little girl; when—the match went out and nothing but the thick, cold, damp wall was left behind. She lighted another match. Now there she was sitting under the most magnificent Christmas tree; it was still larger, and more decorated than the one which she had seen through the glass door in the rich merchant's house.

Thousands of lights were burning on the green branches, and gaily-colored pictures, such as she had seen in the shop-windows, looked down upon her. The little maiden stretched out her hands towards them when—the match went out. The lights of the Christmas tree rose higher and higher; she saw them now as stars in heaven. One fell down and formed a long trail of fire.

"Someone is just dead!" said the little girl; for her old grandmother, the only person who had loved her, and who was now no more, had told her that when a star falls, a soul ascends to God.

She drew another match against the wall. It was again light, and in the luster there stood the old grandmother, so bright and radiant, so mild, and with such an expression of love.

"Grandmother!" cried the little one. "Oh, take me with you! You go away when the match burns out; you vanish like the warm stove, like the delicious roast goose, and like the magnificent Christmas tree!" And she rubbed the whole bundle of matches quickly against the wall, for she wanted to be quite sure of keeping her grandmother near her. And the matches gave such a brilliant light that it was brighter than at noon-day. Never formerly had the grandmother been so beautiful and so tall. She took the little maiden, on her arm, and both flew in brightness and in joy so high, so very high, and then above was neither cold, nor hunger, nor anxiety—they were with God.

But in the corner, at the cold hour of dawn, sat the poor girl, with rosy cheeks and with a smiling mouth, leaning against the wall—frozen to death on the last evening of the old year. Stiff and stark sat the child there with her matches, of which one bundle had been burnt. "She wanted to warm herself," people said. No one had the slightest suspicion of what beautiful things she had seen; no one even dreamed of the splendor in which, with her grandmother, she had entered on the joys of a new year. ✳

"THE LITTLE MATCH GIRL" HANS CHRISTIAN ANDERSEN S. CLAY WILSON   117

"Rondeau" ("Jenny Kiss'd Me")

Leigh Hunt

ART/ADAPTATION BY **Ellen Lindner**

JAMES HENRY LEIGH HUNT—BEST KNOWN AS SIM-
ply Leigh Hunt—was a core member of the British Romantic
movement, although his name isn't nearly as familiar as those
of his compatriots. Hunt wrote a lot of poetry, but his biggest
contributions were as editor of journals that published the
Romantics and other Victorian poets, including Tennyson
and Robert Browning, as an influential essayist and literary
critic, as a poetic influence on his good friend Percy Bysshe
Shelley, and as the guy who introduced Shelley and Keats.

His most enduring poem is the absolutely perfect little
gem published simply as "Rondeau" (which is a type of poem,
although this poem isn't a rondeau) but is almost always
referred to as "Jenny Kiss'd Me." Its brevity and the fact that
it's made up almost entirely of single-syllable words make
its power all the more amazing: we see that this unexpected
kiss is one of the high points of the narrator's life.

The poem was written about Jane Carlyle, known as
Jenny, the wife of towering Victorian writer-intellectual
Thomas Carlyle. Just why Mrs. Carlyle greeted him so
enthusiastically is unclear. I've read four explanations—
including that Hunt had recovered from life-threatening
flu, or that Jenny was severely impressed with one of
Hunt's poems—so this will likely remain one of literature's
many mysteries.

Ellen Lindner, who is contributing to each volume of *The
Graphic Canon*, here offers us a charming one-page take
on this little beauty, starring her then-next-door neighbor
Charlotte.

SOURCE

Roe, Nicholas. *Leigh Hunt: Life, Poetics, Politics*. New York:
Routledge, 2003.

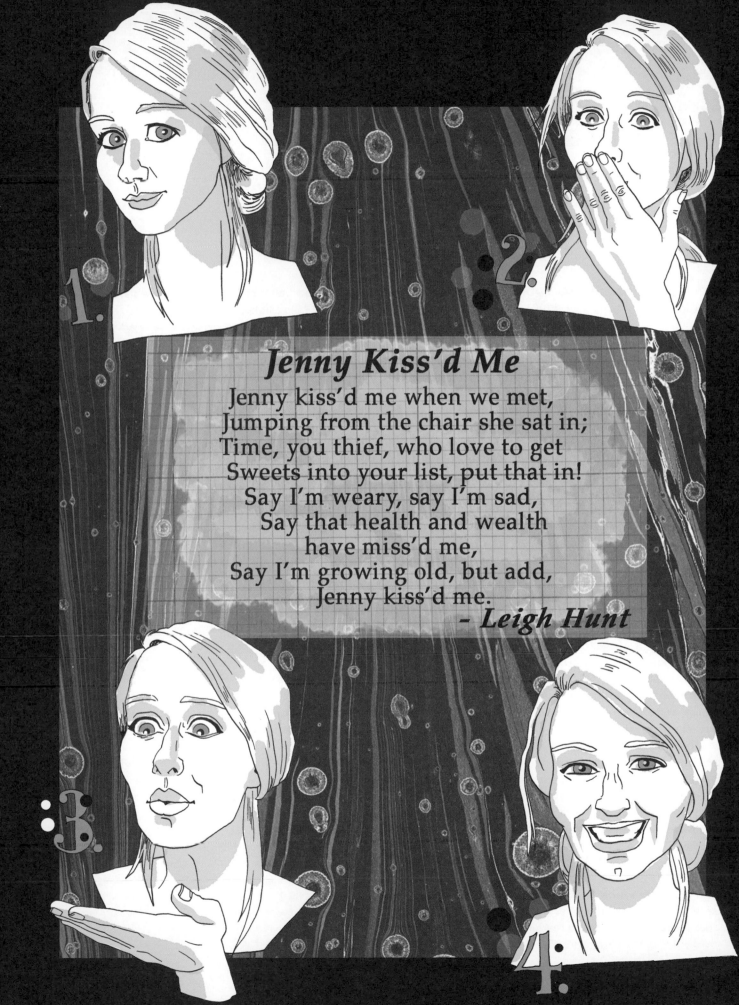

Jenny Kiss'd Me

Jenny kiss'd me when we met,
Jumping from the chair she sat in;
Time, you thief, who love to get
Sweets into your list, put that in!
Say I'm weary, say I'm sad,
Say that health and wealth
have miss'd me,
Say I'm growing old, but add,
Jenny kiss'd me.

- Leigh Hunt

Oliver Twist

Charles Dickens

ART/ADAPTATION BY **Kevin Dixon**

OFTEN CONSIDERED ENGLAND'S GREATEST NOVELIST, Charles Dickens wrote prolifically and enjoyed immense popularity during his lifetime. He was a celebrity, and in *Dickens and Popular Entertainment*, Paul Schlicke writes that his first trip to the US in 1842 "was rather like the Beatles going to New York more than a century later."

Dickens was obviously fascinated by life, by human beings, and his work is packed to bursting with memorable characters. Amazingly, his twenty novels—some of them humongous—have never gone out of print. His second novel, *Oliver Twist,* was his breakthrough work. Like many nineteenth-century novels, it was published in installments in a periodical; from February 1837 to April 1839 it appeared in *Bentley's Miscellany*. It proved so popular that before its magazine run had concluded, it had been published as a book, and no less than six theater productions had been staged. Young Queen Victoria, fewer than two years on the throne, called the novel "excessively interesting" in her diary, and was apparently taken aback by the squalor it describes.

This was as Dickens had intended. He meant for *Oliver Twist* to draw attention to horrid conditions of the poor and the plight of destitute and orphaned children, conditions he knew about first-hand. For a period of time when he was twelve, his parents and siblings were all in debtor's prison while he labored in inhuman conditions in a shoe-polish factory. He never stopped agitating for social and economic reform.

The portion adapted here is chapter 9. After being abused and neglected by a number of people in a small English town, Oliver—an orphan whose unmarried mother died in childbirth—walks seventy grueling miles to London. Just outside the metropolis, the severely weakened lad meets a jaunty boy his own age, known as the Artful Dodger, who says he knows a man in London who'll kindly give Oliver food and shelter. The naïve boy is taken to the dark lair of Fagin, the leader of a ring of young pickpockets, and one of the most memorable villains in literature (and source of endless controversy because he's Jewish, a fact that Dickens never lets the reader forget—he refers to Fagin as "the Jew" almost 300 times). Oliver is given a hearty meal and falls asleep.

We join him the next morning, when Fagin first threatens Oliver, thinking he had been spying on him. They're joined by the Artful Dodger and the mirthful Charley Bates, who have just come from boosting handkerchiefs and wallets. To keep Oliver ignorant of the situation, Fagin pretends that the boys have made these items, and Oliver believes him, much to the boys' amusement. The three play a "game" of pickpocketing. They're joined by two young women in Fagin's gang, Bet and Nancy, both presumably prostitutes. When the four of them leave, Fagin and Oliver play the game:

> "Is my handkerchief hanging out of my pocket, my dear?" said the Jew, stopping short.
>
> "Yes, sir," said Oliver.
>
> "See if you can take it out, without my feeling it; as you saw them do, when we were at play this morning."
>
> Oliver held up the bottom of the pocket with one hand, as he had seen the Dodger hold it, and drew the handkerchief lightly out of it with the other.
>
> "Is it gone?" cried the Jew.
>
> "Here it is, sir," said Oliver, showing it in his hand.
>
> "You're a clever boy, my dear," said the playful old gentleman, patting Oliver on the head approvingly. "I never saw a sharper lad. Here's a shilling for you. If you go on, in this way, you'll be the greatest man of the time."

Kevin Dixon—who gave us a faithful telling of *The Epic of Gilgamesh* in Volume 1—supplies a wordless take on this darkly humorous chapter from Dickens's quintessential novel.

SOURCES

Bloom, Harold, ed. *Bloom's Modern Critical Views: Charles Dickens* (updated ed.). New York: Chelsea House Publications, 2006.

Collins, Phillip, ed. *Charles Dickens: The Critical Heritage*. New York: Routledge, 2005.

Schlicke, Paul. *Dickens and Popular Entertainment*. Sydney, Australia: Allen & Unwin, 1988.

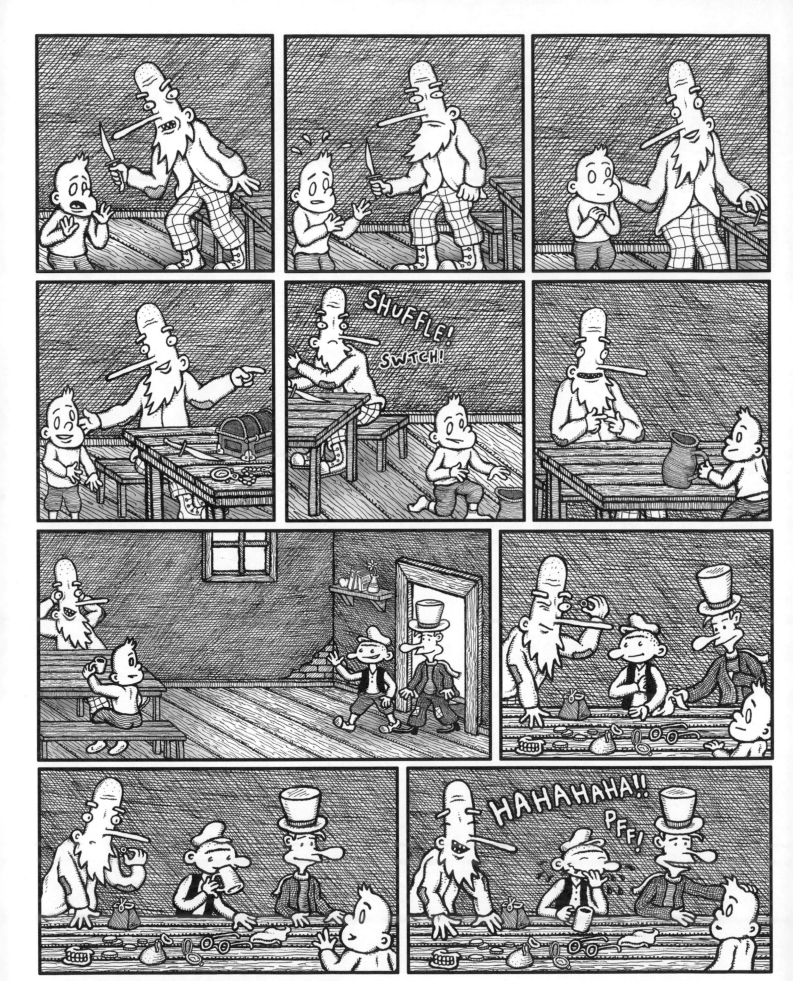

OLIVER TWIST CHARLES DICKENS KEVIN DIXON

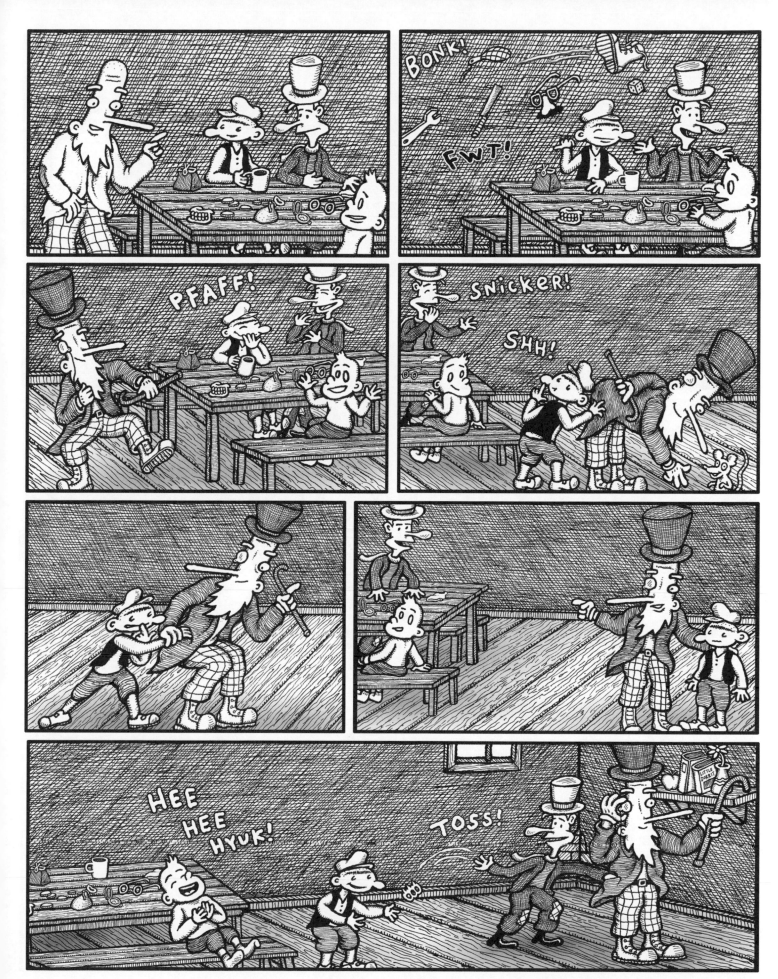

OLIVER TWIST CHARLES DICKENS KEVIN DIXON

"The Jumblies"

Edward Lear

ART/ADAPTATION BY **Hunt Emerson**

I FIND IT PLEASING THAT "NONSENSE" IS A RECOG-
nized, mainstream genre of literature, practiced by Lewis
Carroll, Ogden Nash, and even John Lennon. Though he
wasn't the originator of the form, Edward Lear is considered
the pioneer of nonsense, building his prose and highly rhythmic poems out of made-up words, non sequiturs, impossi-
bilities, contradictions, and the like. He is best known for his
limericks (a then-obscure form that he made popular) and
two somewhat longer poems: "The Owl and the Pussycat"
and "The Jumblies," both from his 1871 book, *Nonsense
Songs, Stories, Botany, and Alphabets.*

Lear was also a talented visual artist. His poems were
accompanied by his whimsical line drawings, and his paintings of wildlife and landscapes are rich and gorgeous. Hunt
Emerson, whom we met during "The Rime of the Ancient
Mariner," is himself a talented artist brimming with humor.
It's only natural that he sequentially adapted Lear's enduring rhyme about some very unusual mariners.

126

The JUMBLIES

THEY WENT TO SEA IN A SIEVE, THEY DID, IN A SIEVE THEY WENT TO SEA: IN SPITE OF ALL THEIR FRIENDS COULD SAY, ON A WINTER'S MORN, ON A STORMY DAY, IN A SIEVE THEY WENT TO SEA! AND WHEN THE SIEVE TURNED ROUND AND ROUND, AND EVERYONE CRIED,

YOU'LL ALL BE DROWNED!

THEY CALLED ALOUD, OUR SIEVE AIN'T BIG, BUT WE DON'T CARE A BUTTON! WE DON'T CARE A FIG! IN A SIEVE WE'LL GO TO SEA!

FAR AND FEW, FAR AND FEW, ARE THE LANDS WHERE THE JUMBLIES LIVE!

THEIR HEADS ARE GREEN, AND THEIR HANDS ARE BLUE, AND THEY WENT TO SEA IN A SIEVE!

THEY SAILED AWAY IN A SIEVE, THEY DID, IN A SIEVE THEY SAILED SO FAST, WITH ONLY A BEAUTIFUL PEA-GREEN VEIL TIED WITH A RIBAND BY WAY OF A SAIL, TO A SMALL TOBACCO-PIPE MAST;

AND EVERYONE SAID WHO SAW THEM GO, "OH WON'T THEY BE SOON UPSET, YOU KNOW! FOR THE SKY IS DARK, AND THE VOYAGE IS LONG, AND HAPPEN WHAT MAY, IT'S EXTREMELY WRONG IN A SIEVE TO SAIL SO FAST!"

THE WATER IT SOON CAME IN, IT DID- THE WATER IT SOON CAME IN;

Well, it is a sieve...

SO TO KEEP THEM DRY, THEY WRAPPED THEIR FEET IN A PINKY PAPER ALL FOLDED NEAT, AND THEY FASTENED IT DOWN WITH A PIN.

AND THEY PASSED THE NIGHT IN A CROCKERY-JAR, AND EACH OF THEM SAID,

HOW WISE WE ARE! THOUGH THE SKY BE DARK AND THE VOYAGE LONG, YET WE NEVER CAN THINK WE WERE RASH OR WRONG, WHILE ROUND IN OUR SIEVE WE SPIN!

Der Struwwelpeter

Heinrich Hoffmann

ILLUSTRATIONS AND LAYOUT BY **Sanya Glisic**

HOW DO YOU GET CHILDREN TO STOP SUCKING THEIR thumbs, hurting animals, playing with matches, and so on? You scare the living hell out of them, perhaps psychologically scarring them for life, of course! Not every one of the ten moralizing tales in *Der Struwwelpeter* is over the top, but the majority result in the death or disfigurement of the whippersnappers.

German doctor and psychiatrist Heinrich Hoffmann wrote and illustrated this imaginative monstrosity as a handmade book for his *three-year-old* son. He had it published anonymously in 1845, and it went on to become a classic of children's literature. For at least 100 years it was taken at face value. I know someone who remembers seeing it included in a 1950s collection of stories aimed at kids, which her parents bought for her. In recent years, it's been appreciated in a more ironic way, as in, "Can you believe this twisted book was given to generation after generation of kids?"

Sanya Glisic used *Der Struwwelpeter* to showcase her wide range of talents, creating a stunning limited-edition book from the ground up. She created the fantastic illustrations, laid out the type and design, printed each copy by hand-pulled silk-screening (each of the five colors was pulled separately for every page), and bound each book by hand. What you see here are scans of the hand-printed pages.

STRUWWELPETER

STORY BY HEINRICH HOFFMANN
ARTWORK BY SANYA GLISIC

THE STORY OF SHOCK-HEADED PETER

Just look at him! there he stands,

With his nasty hair and hands.

See! his nails are never cut;

They are grimed as black as soot;

And the sloven, I declare,

Never once has combed his hair;

Anything to me is sweeter

Than to see Shock-headed Peter.

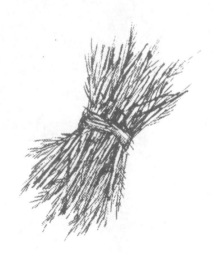

THE STORY OF THE INKY BOYS

As he had often done before,
The woolly-headed Black-a-moor
One nice fine summer's day went out
To see the shops, and walk about;
And, as he found it hot, poor fellow,
He took with him his green umbrella,
Then Edward, little noisy wag,
Ran out and laughed, and waved his flag;
And William came in jacket trim,
And brought his wooden hoop with him;
And Arthur, too, snatched up his toys
And joined the other naughty boys.
So, one and all set up a roar,
And laughed and hooted more and more,
And kept on singing,– only think! –
"Oh, Blacky, you're as black as ink!"

Now tall Agrippa lived close by ~
So tall, he almost touched the sky;
He had a mighty ink-stand, too,
In which a great goose-feather grew;
He called out in an angry tone
"Boys, leave the Black-a-moor alone!
For, if he tries with all his might,
He cannot change from black to white."

But, ah! they did not mind a bit
What great Agrippa said of it;
But went on laughing, as before,
And hooting at the Black-a-moor.

Then great Agrippa foams with rage
Look at him on this very page!
He seizes Arthur, seizes Ned,
Takes William by his little head;

And they may scream and kick and call,
Into the ink he dips them all;
Into the inkstand, one, two, three,
Till they are black as black can be.

See, there they are, and there they run!
The Black-a-moor enjoys the fun.
They have been made as black as crows,
Quite black all over, eyes and nose,
And legs, and arms, and heads, and toes,
And trousers, pinafores, and toys ~
The silly little inky boys!
Because they set up such a roar,
And teased the harmless Black-a-moor.

DER STRUWWELPETER HEINRICH HOFFMANN SANYA GLISIC

THE STORY OF THE MAN THAT WENT OUT SHOOTING

This is the man that shoots the hares;

This is the coat he always wears:

With game-bag, powder-horn, and gun

He's going out to have some fun.

He finds it hard, without a pair

Of spectacles, to shoot the hare.

The hare sits snug in leaves and grass,

And laughs to see the green man pass.

Now, as the sun grew very hot,

And he a heavy gun had got,

He lay down underneath a tree

And went to sleep, as you may see.

And, while he slept like any top,

The little hare came, hop, hop, hop,

Took gun and spectacles, and then

On her hind legs went off again.

The green man wakes and sees her place

The spectacles upon her face;

And now she's trying all she can

To shoot the sleepy, green-coat man.

He cries and screams and runs away;

The hare runs after him all day

And hears him call out everywhere:

"Help! Fire! Help! The Hare! The Hare!"

At last he stumbled at the well,

Head over ears, and in he fell.

The hare stopped short, took aim and, hark!

Bang went the gun – she missed her mark!

The poor man's wife was drinking up

Her coffee in her coffee-cup;

The gun shot cup and saucer through;

"Oh dear!" cried she; "what shall I do?"

There lived close by the cottage there

The hare's own child, the little hare;

And while she stood upon her toes,

The coffee fell and burned her nose.

"Oh dear!" she cried, with spoon in hand,

"Such fun I do not understand."

THE STORY OF LITTLE SUCK-A-THUMB

One day Mamma said "Conrad dear,

I must go out and leave you here.

But mind now, Conrad, what I say,

Don't suck your thumb while I'm away.

The great tall tailor always comes

To little boys who suck their thumbs;

And ere they dream what he's about,

He takes his great sharp scissors out,

And cuts their thumbs clean off – and then,

You know, they never grow again."

Mamma had scarcely turned her back,

The thumb was in, Alack! Alack!

The door flew open, in he ran,

The great, long, red-legged scissor-man.

Oh! children, see! the tailor's come

And caught out little Suck-a-Thumb.

Snip! Snap! Snip! the scissors go;

And Conrad cries out "Oh! Oh! Oh!"

Snip! Snap! Snip! They go so fast,

That both his thumbs are off at last.

Mamma comes home: there Conrad stands,

And looks quite sad, and shows his hands;

"Ah!" said Mamma, "I knew he'd come

To naughty little Suck-a-Thumb."

Poe montage

Edgar Allan Poe

ILLUSTRATION BY **Gris Grimly**

IS THERE ANY NINETEENTH-CENTURY WRITER WHO has more of a death grip on our culture than Edgar Allan Poe? More than 160 years after his death at age forty-one, the man and his works still permeate our consciousness. Even people who don't care for literature love Poe. And that might be part of the key. Academics are pretty unanimous in saying that his style isn't so amazing—he was not what would be called a great writer, in the sense of Melville or Dostoevsky. But the man knew how to get under our skin. What his writing lacks in finesse it makes up for in sheer dark power. Whether he's writing about a dismembered body hidden right under the floorboards, a man being sealed alive behind a brick wall, or a dead child-bride, he creeps us out.

Another sign of genius at work is how many paths he managed to blaze. He was obviously one of the pioneers of the genre of horror, but while he was at it he created the detective story and wrote proto-science fiction before H. G. Wells was a gleam in his parents' eyes. He's often credited as a major formulator of the short story in general, and he was an early practitioner of the literary hoax, presenting his short story "The Facts in the Case of M. Valdemar" as fact (he also wrote an entirely made-up newspaper article about a man who supposedly crossed the Atlantic in a propelled hot-air balloon). His literary criticism was much more lauded during his lifetime than his fiction or poems and influenced later critics.

Then there's his intriguingly dark personal life—orphaned by his mother and abandoned by his father; the depression, the alcoholism, the absinthe; the marriage to his thirteen-year-old first cousin when he was twenty-seven (she died at twenty-four from tuberculosis); the financial hardships, the uneven successes, and his bizarre, delirious death of an undetermined cause. No wonder literary critic Harold Bloom speaks of "the Poe cosmos, where you necessarily start out damned, doomed, and dismal."

Gris Grimly has achieved fame with artwork that's a blend of two-thirds macabre and one-third whimsy. He's birthed such demented children's books as *Sipping Spiders Through a Straw* and has created twisted takes on fairy tales and limericks. His illustrated versions of horror literature include two collections of Poe, "The Legend of Sleepy Hollow," and a full-length adaptation of the rarely read original version of *Frankenstein*. The following artwork was used as the wrap-around cover for his book *Edgar Allan Poe's Tales of Death and Dementia*. It's a montage of imagery from four stories: "The Tell-Tale Heart," "The Oblong Box," "The System of Dr. Tarr and Professor Fether" (which takes place in a mental asylum), and "The Facts in the Case of M. Valdemar" (about hypnotizing a man at the point of death).

SOURCE

Bloom, Harold, ed. *Bloom's Modern Critical Views: Edgar Allan Poe* (updated ed.). New York: Chelsea House Publications, 2006.

"The Raven"

Edgar Allan Poe

ART/ADAPTATION BY **Yien Yip**

I'VE ALWAYS ENJOYED POE'S POETRY EVEN MORE than his stories. I'm a sucker for the strong rhythms, musicality, repetition, and alliteration—the very qualities that produce a love-it-or-hate-it reaction. Martin Gardner summarizes the polarized feelings:

Poe's verse has always been admired by some and pilloried by others. Emerson called him "the jingle man," and Lowell wrote in his *Fable for Critics*:

Here comes Poe with his Raven, like Barnaby Rudge,
Three fifths of him genius, and two fifths sheer fudge.

On the other hand, W. B. Yeats considered him a "great lyric poet," and Elizabeth Barrett Browning praised "The Raven" in the following portion of a letter that Poe greatly prized:

Your *Raven* has produced a sensation, a "fit horror," here in England. Some of my friends are taken by the fear of it and some by the music. I hear of persons haunted by the "Nevermore," and one acquaintance of mine who has the misfortune of possessing "a bust of Pallas" never can bear to look at it in the twilight. I think you will like to be told that our great poet, Mr. Browning . . . was struck much by the rhythm of that poem.

Here, illustrator and textile artist Yien Yip presents an abridged version of Poe's immortal 108-line poem about a mysterious, one-word bird visiting a man grieving, then going insane, over his dead love, Lenore.

SOURCE

Gardner, Martin, ed. *Best Remembered Poems*. Mineola, NY: Dover Publications, 1992.

Once upon a midnight dreary, while I pondered, weak and weary,
Over many a quaint and curious volume of forgotten lore—

While I nodded, nearly napping, suddenly there came a tapping,
As of some one gently rapping, rapping at my chamber door.

"'Tis some visitor," I muttered, "tapping at my chamber door—
Only this, and nothing more."

Back into the chamber turning, all my soul within me burning,
Soon again I heard a tapping somewhat louder than before.
"Surely," said I, "surely that is something at my window lattice;
Let me see, then, what thereat is, and this mystery explore —
Let my heart be still a moment and this mystery explore; —

'Tis the wind and nothing more."

This I sat engaged in guessing, but no syllable expressing
To the fowl whose fiery eyes now burned into my bosom's core;

This and more I sat divining, with
my head at ease reclining
On the cushion's velvet lining that
the lamplight gloated o'er,

But whose velvet violet lining with the
lamplight gloating o'er,

She shall press, ah, nevermore!

"Prophet!" said I, "thing of evil – prophet still, if bird or devil! By that Heaven that bends above us – by that God we both adore – Tell this soul with sorrow laden if, within the distant Aidenn,

It shall clasp a sainted maiden whom the angels name Lenore –

Clasp a rare and radiant maiden whom the angels name Lenore."

Quoth the Raven, "Nevermore."

And the Raven, never flitting, still is sitting, still is sitting
On the pallid bust of Pallas just above my chamber door;

And his eyes have all the seeming of a
demon's that is dreaming,

And the lamplight o'er him streaming throws his
shadow on the floor;

And my soul from out that shadow that lies
floating on the floor

Shall be lifted – nevermore!

Works

Edgar Allan Poe

ILLUSTRATIONS BY **Maxon Crumb**

MAXON CRUMB IS THE YOUNGER BROTHER OF comics legend Robert Crumb, and he leads quite an interesting life of spiritual asceticism—practicing celibacy, eating a sparse diet, sometimes sleeping on a bed of nails, living in squalid conditions, meditating for hours in the lotus position, swallowing a purification cloth (a yogic practice that essentially amounts to flossing your entire digestive/eliminatory tract), paying off a karmic debt that his father incurred, and going into extended trance-like states when he creates art. He no longer begs on the street, able, since the hit documentary *Crumb*, to eke out a living through his artwork—which is wonderful indeed, because he has an artistic vision, a style unlike Robert's or anyone else's. The elongated, distorted figures, the prominent joints, the mask-like faces (that sometimes really are masks), the subtle energies made visible, the rectangular patterns, the stippling with dots of varying sizes—there's no mistaking a work by Maxon.

A lover of literature since childhood, he created a series of illustrations for Poe's work, published as a small, limited-run book, *Maxon's Poe*, by Word Play publications. In the pages that follow, you'll find one or more searing drawings for:

- "The Tell-Tale Heart"—the story of a murderer betrayed by his conscience—or is that heart really still beating?
- "The Pit and the Pendulum"—a nightmarish tale of torture
- "The Masque of the Red Death"—in which the aristocracy attempts to escape the plague
- "The Raven"—a grieving man and a mysterious bird in one of the most famous poems of all time
- "The Bells"—a joltingly auditory poem that looks at the progressively darker meanings of bells

SOURCE

Guthmann, Edward. "Still in the shadows, an artist in his own right." *San Francisco Chronicle*, October 3, 2006.

Art is long and Time is fleeting,
And our hearts, though stout and brave,
Still, like muffled drums, are beating
Funeral marches to the grave.
    —Longfellow.

"The Tell-Tale Heart"

TRUE!—nervous—very, very dreadfully nervous I had been, and am; but why will you say that I am mad? The disease had sharpened my senses—not destroyed—not dulled them. Above all was the sense of hearing acute. I heard all things in the heaven and in the earth. I heard many things in hell. How, then, am I mad? Hearken! and observe how healthily—how calmly I can tell you the whole story.

It is impossible to say how first the idea entered my brain; but once conceived, it haunted me day and night. Object there was none. Passion there was none. I loved the old man. He had never wronged me. He had never given me insult. For his gold I had no desire. I think it was his eye!—yes, it was this! One of his eyes resembled that of a vulture—a pale blue eye, with a film over it. Whenever it fell upon me, my blood ran cold; and so, by degrees—very gradually—I made up my mind to take the life of the old man, and thus rid myself of the eye forever.

Now this is the point. You fancy me mad. Madmen know nothing. But you should have seen me. You should have seen how wisely I proceeded—with what caution—with what foresight—with what dissimulation I went to work! I was never kinder to the old man than during the whole week before I killed him. And every night, about midnight, I turned the latch of his door and opened it—oh, so gently! And then, when I had made an opening sufficient for my head, I put in a dark lantern, all closed, closed, so that no light shone out, and then I thrust in my head. Oh, you would have laughed to see how cunningly I thrust it in! I moved it slowly—very, very slowly, so that I might not disturb the old man's sleep. It took me an hour to place my whole head within the opening so far that I could see him as he lay upon his bed. Ha!—would a madman have been so wise as this? And then, when my head was well in the room, I undid the lantern cautiously—oh, so cautiously—cautiously (for the hinges creaked)—I undid it just so much that a single thin ray fell upon the vulture eye. And this I did for seven long nights—every night just at midnight—but I found the eye always closed; and so it was impossible to do the work; for it was not the old man who vexed me, but his Evil Eye. And every morning, when the day broke, I went boldly into the chamber, and spoke courageously to him, calling him by name in a hearty tone, and inquiring how he has passed the night. So you see he would have been a very profound old man, indeed, to suspect that every night, just at twelve, I looked in upon him while he slept.

Upon the eighth night I was more than usually cautious in opening the door. A watch's minute hand moves more quickly than did mine. Never, before that night, had I felt the extent of my own powers—of my sagacity. I could scarcely contain my feelings of triumph. To think that there I was, opening the door, little by little, and he not even to dream of my secret deeds or thoughts. I fairly chuckled at the idea; and perhaps he heard me; for he moved on the bed suddenly, as if startled. Now you may think that I drew back—but no. His room was as black as pitch with the thick darkness, (for the shutters were close fastened, through fear of robbers,) and so I knew that he could not see the opening of the door, and I kept pushing it on steadily, steadily.

I had my head in, and was about to open the lantern, when my thumb slipped upon the tin fastening, and the old man sprang up in bed, crying out—"Who's there?"

I kept quite still and said nothing. For a whole hour I did not move a muscle, and in the meantime I did not hear him lie down. He was still sitting up in the bed, listening;—just as I have done, night after night, hearkening to the death-watches in the wall.

Presently I heard a slight groan, and I knew that it was the groan of mortal terror. It was not a groan of pain, or of grief—oh, no!—it was the low, stifled sound that arises from the bottom of the soul when overcharged with awe. I knew the sound well. Many a night, just at midnight, when all the world slept, it has welled up from my own bosom, deepening, with its dreadful echo, the terrors that distracted me. I say I knew it well. I knew what the old man felt, and pitied him, although I chuckled at heart. I knew that he had been lying awake ever since the first slight noise, when he had turned in the bed. His fears had been ever since growing upon him. He had been trying to fancy them causeless, but could not. He had been saying to himself—"It is nothing but the wind in the chimney—it is only a mouse crossing the floor," or "it is merely a cricket which has made a single chirp." Yes, he has been trying to comfort himself with these suppositions; but he had found all in vain. All in vain; because Death, in approaching him had stalked with his black shadow before him, and enveloped the victim. And it was the mournful influence of the unperceived shadow that caused him to feel—although he neither saw nor heard me—to feel the presence of my head within the room.

When I had waited a long time, very patiently, without hearing him lie down, I resolved to open a little—a very, very little crevice in the lantern. So I opened it—you cannot imagine how stealthily, stealthily—until, at length, a single dim ray, like the thread of the spider, shot from out the crevice and fell upon the vulture eye.

It was open—wide, wide open—and I grew furious as I gazed upon it. I saw it with perfect distinctness—all a dull blue, with a hideous veil over it that chilled the very marrow in my bones; but I could see nothing else of the old man's face or person: for I had directed the ray as if by instinct, precisely upon the damned spot.

And now—have I not told you that what you mistake for madness is but over acuteness of the senses?—now, I say, there came to my ears a low, dull, quick sound, such as a watch makes when enveloped in cotton. I knew that sound well, too. It was the beating of the old man's heart. It increased my fury, as the beating of a drum stimulates the soldier into courage.

But even yet I refrained and kept still. I scarcely breathed. I held the lantern motionless. I tried how steadily I could maintain the ray upon the eye. Meantime the hellish tattoo of the heart increased. It grew quicker and quicker, and louder and louder every instant. The old man's terror must have been extreme! It grew louder, I say, louder every moment!—do you mark me well? I have told you that I am nervous: —so I am. And now, at the dead hour of the night, amid the dreadful silence of that old house, so strange a noise as this excited me to uncontrollable terror. Yet, for some minutes longer I refrained and stood still. But the beating grew louder,

louder! I thought the heart must burst! And now a new anxiety seized me—the sound would be heard by a neighbor! The old man's hour had come! With a loud yell, I threw open the lantern and leaped into the room. He shrieked once—once only. In an instant I dragged him to the floor, and pulled the heavy bed over him. I then sat upon the bed and smiled gaily, to find the deed so far done. But, for many minutes, the heart beat on with a muffled sound. This, however, did not vex me; it would not be heard through the wall. At length it ceased. The old man was dead. I removed the bed and examined the corpse. Yes, he was stone, stone dead. I placed my hand upon the heart and held it there many minutes. There was no pulsation. He was stone dead. His eye would trouble me no more.

If still you think me mad, you will think so no longer when I describe

officers of the police. A shriek had been heard by a neighbor during the night; suspicion of foul play had been aroused; information had been lodged at the police office, and they (the officers) had been deputed to search the premises.

I smiled,—for what had I to fear? I bade the gentlemen welcome. The shriek, I said, was my own in a dream. The old man, I mentioned, was absent in the country. I took my visitors all over the house. I bade them search—search well. I led them, at length, to his chamber. I showed them his treasures, secure, undisturbed. In the enthusiasm of my confidence, I brought chairs into the room, and desired them here to rest from their fatigues; while I myself, in the wild audacity of my perfect triumph, placed my own seat upon the very spot beneath which reposed the corpse of the victim.

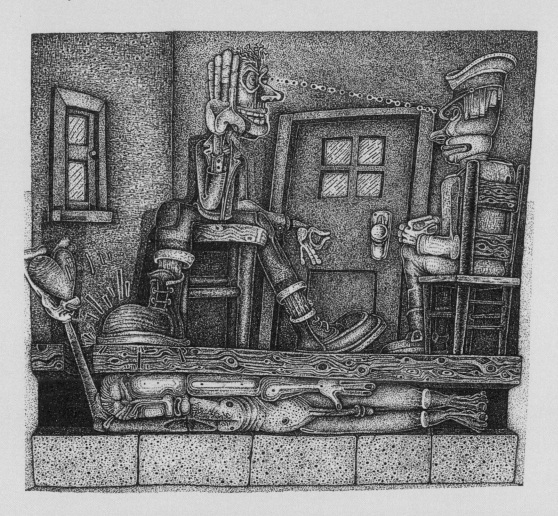

The officers were satisfied. My manner had convinced them. I was singularly at ease. They sat, and while I answered cheerily, they chatted of familiar things. But, ere long, I felt myself getting pale and wished them gone. My head ached, and I fancied a ringing in my ears: but still they sat and still chatted. The ringing became more distinct:—it continued and became more distinct: I talked more freely, to get rid of the feeling; but it continued and gained definiteness—until, at length, I found that the noise was not within my ears.

No doubt I now grew very pale;—but I talked more fluently, and with a heightened voice. Yet the sound increased—and what could I do? It was a low, dull, quick sound—much such a sound as a watch makes when enveloped in cotton. I gasped for breath—and yet the officers heard it not. I talked more quickly—more vehemently;—but the noise steadily increased. I arose, and argued about trifles, in a high key and with violent gesticulations; — but the noise steadily increased. Why would they not be gone? I paced the floor to and fro, with heavy strides, as if excited to

the wise precautions I took for the concealment of the body. The night waned, and I worked hastily, but in silence. First of all I dismembered the corpse. I cut off the head and the arms and the legs. I then took up three planks from the flooring of the chamber, and deposited all between the scantlings. I then replaced the boards so cleverly, so cunningly, that no human eye—not even his—could have detected anything wrong. There was nothing to wash out—no stain of any kind—no blood-spot whatever. I had been too wary for that. A tub had caught all—ha! ha!

When I had made an end of these labors, it was four o'clock—still dark as midnight. As the bell sounded the hour, there came a knocking at the street door. I went down to open it with a light heart,—for what had I now to fear? There entered three men, who introduced themselves, with perfect suavity, as

fury by the observations of the men;—but the noise steadily increased. Oh God! what could I do? I foamed—I raved—I swore! I swung the chair upon which I had been sitting, and grated it upon the boards, but the noise arose over all and continually increased. It grew louder—louder—louder! And still the men chatted pleasantly, and smiled. Was it possible they heard not? Almighty God!—no, no! They heard!—they suspected!—they knew!—they were making a mockery of my horror!—this I thought, and this I think. But anything was better than this agony! Anything was more tolerable than this derision! I could bear those hypocritical smiles no longer! I felt that I must scream or die!—and now—again!—hark! louder! louder! louder! louder!—

"Villains!" I shrieked, "dissemble no more! I admit the deed!—tear up the planks!—here, here!—it is the beating of his hideous heart!" ✳

"The Raven"

Once upon a midnight dreary, while I pondered, weak and weary,
Over many a quaint and curious volume of forgotten lore —
While I nodded, nearly napping, suddenly there came a tapping,
As of some one gently rapping, rapping at my chamber door.
"'Tis some visitor," I muttered, "tapping at my chamber door —
    Only this and nothing more."

Ah, distinctly I remember it was in the bleak December;
And each separate dying ember wrought its ghost upon the floor.
Eagerly I wished the morrow;—vainly I had sought to borrow
From my books surcease of sorrow—sorrow for the lost Lenore —
For the rare and radiant maiden whom the angels name Lenore —
    Nameless here for evermore.

And the silken, sad, uncertain rustling of each purple curtain
Thrilled me—filled me with fantastic terrors never felt before;
So that now, to still the beating of my heart, I stood repeating
"'Tis some visitor entreating entrance at my chamber door —
Some late visitor entreating entrance at my chamber door; —
    This it is and nothing more."

Presently my soul grew stronger; hesitating then no longer,
"Sir," said I, "or Madam, truly your forgiveness I implore;
But the fact is I was napping, and so gently you came rapping,
And so faintly you came tapping, tapping at my chamber door,
That I scarce was sure I heard you"—here I opened wide the door; ——
    Darkness there and nothing more.

Deep into that darkness peering, long I stood there wondering, fearing,
Doubting, dreaming dreams no mortal ever dared to dream before;
But the silence was unbroken, and the stillness gave no token,
And the only word there spoken was the whispered word, "Lenore?"
This I whispered, and an echo murmured back the word, "Lenore!" —
    Merely this and nothing more.

Back into the chamber turning, all my soul within me burning,
Soon again I heard a tapping somewhat louder than before.
"Surely," said I, "surely that is something at my window lattice;
Let me see, then, what thereat is, and this mystery explore —
Let my heart be still a moment and this mystery explore;—
    'Tis the wind and nothing more!"

Open here I flung the shutter, when, with many a flirt and flutter,
In there stepped a stately Raven of the saintly days of yore;
Not the least obeisance made he; not a minute stopped or stayed he;
But, with mien of lord or lady, perched above my chamber door —
Perched upon a bust of Pallas just above my chamber door —
    Perched, and sat, and nothing more.

Then this ebony bird beguiling my sad fancy into smiling,
By the grave and stern decorum of the countenance it wore,
"Though thy crest be shorn and shaven, thou," I said, "art sure no craven,
Ghastly grim and ancient Raven wandering from the Nightly shore —
Tell me what thy lordly name is on the Night's Plutonian shore!"
    Quoth the Raven "Nevermore."

Much I marvelled this ungainly fowl to hear discourse so plainly,
Though its answer little meaning—little relevancy bore;
For we cannot help agreeing that no living human being
Ever yet was blessed with seeing bird above his chamber door —
Bird or beast upon the sculptured bust above his chamber door,
    With such name as "Nevermore."

But the Raven, sitting lonely on the placid bust, spoke only
That one word, as if his soul in that one word he did outpour.
Nothing farther then he uttered—not a feather then he fluttered —
Till I scarcely more than muttered "Other friends have flown before —
On the morrow he will leave me, as my Hopes have flown before."
    Then the bird said "Nevermore."

Startled at the stillness broken by reply so aptly spoken,
"Doubtless," said I, "what it utters is its only stock and store
Caught from some unhappy master whom unmerciful Disaster
Followed fast and followed faster till his songs one burden bore —
Till the dirges of his Hope that melancholy burden bore
    Of 'Never—nevermore.'"

But the Raven still beguiling my sad fancy into smiling,
Straight I wheeled a cushioned seat in front of bird, and bust and door;
Then, upon the velvet sinking, I betook myself to linking
Fancy unto fancy, thinking what this ominous bird of yore —
What this grim, ungainly, ghastly, gaunt, and ominous bird of yore
    Meant in croaking "Nevermore."

This I sat engaged in guessing, but no syllable expressing
To the fowl whose fiery eyes now burned into my bosom's core;
This and more I sat divining, with my head at ease reclining
On the cushion's velvet lining that the lamp-light gloated o'er,
But whose velvet-violet lining with the lamp-light gloating o'er,
    She shall press, ah, nevermore!

Then, methought, the air grew denser, perfumed from an unseen censer
Swung by seraphim whose foot-falls tinkled on the tufted floor.
"Wretch," I cried, "thy God hath lent thee—by these angels he hath sent thee
Respite—respite and nepenthe, from thy memories of Lenore;
Quaff, oh quaff this kind nepenthe and forget this lost Lenore!"
    Quoth the Raven "Nevermore."

"Prophet!" said I, "thing of evil!—prophet still, if bird or devil! —
Whether Tempter sent, or whether tempest tossed thee here ashore,
Desolate yet all undaunted, on this desert land enchanted —
On this home by Horror haunted—tell me truly, I implore —
Is there—is there balm in Gilead?—tell me—tell me, I implore!"
    Quoth the Raven "Nevermore."

"Prophet!" said I, "thing of evil!—prophet still, if bird or devil!
By that Heaven that bends above us—by that God we both adore —
Tell this soul with sorrow laden if, within the distant Aidenn,
It shall clasp a sainted maiden whom the angels name Lenore —
Clasp a rare and radiant maiden whom the angels name Lenore."
    Quoth the Raven "Nevermore."

"Be that word our sign of parting, bird or fiend!" I shrieked, upstarting—
"Get thee back into the tempest and the Night's Plutonian shore!
Leave no black plume as a token of that lie thy soul hath spoken!
Leave my loneliness unbroken!—quit the bust above my door!
Take thy beak from out my heart, and take thy form from off my door!"
    Quoth the Raven "Nevermore."

And the Raven, never flitting, still is sitting, still is sitting
On the pallid bust of Pallas just above my chamber door;
And his eyes have all the seeming of a demon's that is dreaming,
And the lamp-light o'er him streaming throws his shadow on the floor;
And my soul from out that shadow that lies floating on the floor
    Shall be lifted—nevermore!

"The Bells"

Hear the sledges with the bells—
Silver bells!
What a world of merriment their melody foretells!
How they tinkle, tinkle, tinkle,
In the icy air of night!
While the stars that oversprinkle
All the heavens, seem to twinkle
With a crystalline delight;
Keeping time, time, time,
In a sort of Runic rhyme,
To the tintinnabulation that so musically wells
From the bells, bells, bells, bells,
Bells, bells, bells—
From the jingling and the tinkling of the bells.

II

Hear the mellow wedding-bells —
Golden bells!
What a world of happiness their harmony foretells!
Through the balmy air of night
How they ring out their delight!—
From the molten-golden notes,
And all in tune,
What a liquid ditty floats
To the turtle-dove that listens, while she gloats
On the moon!
Oh, from out the sounding cells,
What a gush of euphony voluminously wells!
How it swells!
How it dwells
On the Future!—how it tells
Of the rapture that impels
To the swinging and the ringing
Of the bells, bells, bells—
Of the bells, bells, bells, bells,
Bells, bells, bells—
To the rhyming and the chiming of the bells!

III

Hear the loud alarum bells—
Brazen bells!
What a tale of terror, now, their turbulency tells!
In the startled ear of night
How they scream out their affright!
Too much horrified to speak,
They can only shriek, shriek,

Out of tune,
In a clamorous appealing to the mercy of the fire,
In a mad expostulation with the deaf and frantic fire,
Leaping higher, higher, higher,
With a desperate desire,
And a resolute endeavor
Now—now to sit, or never,
By the side of the pale-faced moon.
Oh, the bells, bells, bells!
What a tale their terror tells
Of Despair!
How they clang, and clash, and roar!
What a horror they outpour
On the bosom of the palpitating air!
Yet the ear, it fully knows,
By the twanging
And the clanging,
How the danger ebbs and flows;
Yes, the ear distinctly tells,
In the jangling
And the wrangling,
How the danger sinks and swells,
By the sinking or the swelling in the anger of the bells—
Of the bells—
Of the bells, bells, bells, bells,
Bells, bells, bells—
In the clamour and the clangour of the bells!

IV

Hear the tolling of the bells—
Iron bells!
What a world of solemn thought their monody compels!
In the silence of the night,
How we shiver with affright
At the melancholy menace of their tone!
For every sound that floats
From the rust within their throats
Is a groan.
And the people—ah, the people—
They that dwell up in the steeple,
All alone,
And who, tolling, tolling, tolling,
In that muffled monotone,
Feel a glory in so rolling
On the human heart a stone—
They are neither man nor woman—

They are neither brute nor human—
They are Ghouls:—
And their king it is who tolls:—
And he rolls, rolls, rolls, rolls,
Rolls
A pæan from the bells!
And his merry bosom swells
With the pæan of the bells!
And he dances, and he yells;
Keeping time, time, time,
In a sort of Runic rhyme,
To the pæan of the bells—
Of the bells:—
Keeping time, time, time,

In a sort of Runic rhyme,
To the throbbing of the bells—
Of the bells, bells, bells—
To the sobbing of the bells:—
Keeping time, time, time,
As he knells, knells, knells,
In a happy Runic rhyme,
To the rolling of the bells—
Of the bells, bells, bells:—
To the tolling of the bells—
Of the bells, bells, bells, bells,
Bells, bells, bells—
To the moaning and the groaning of the bells.

156 "THE BELLS" EDGAR ALLAN POE MAXON CRUMB

"The Pit and the Pendulum"

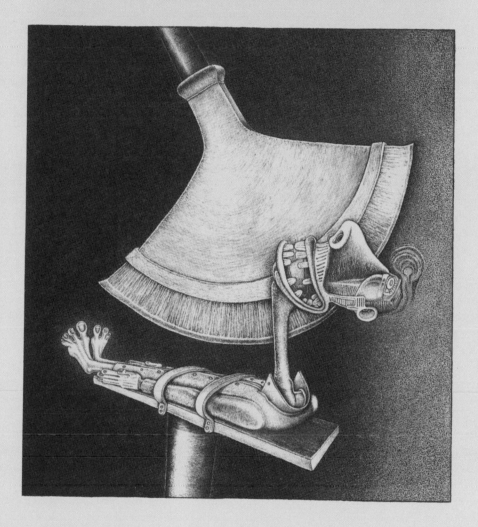

Impia tortorum longas hic turba furores
Sanguinis innocui, non satiata, aluit.
Sospite nunc patria, fracto nunc funeris antro,
Mors ubi dira fuit vita salusque patent.

[Quatrain composed for the gates of a market to be erected upon the site of the Jacobin Club House at Paris.]

I WAS SICK—sick unto death with that long agony; and when they at length unbound me, and I was permitted to sit, I felt that my senses were leaving me. The sentence—the dread sentence of death—was the last of distinct accentuation which reached my ears. After that, the sound of the inquisitorial voices seemed merged in one dreamy indeterminate hum. It conveyed to my soul the idea of revolution—perhaps from its associa-tion in fancy with the burr of a mill-wheel. This only for a brief period; for presently I heard no more. Yet, for a while, I saw; but with how terrible an exaggeration! I saw the lips of the black-robed judges. They appeared to me white—whiter than the sheet upon which I trace these words—and thin even to grotesqueness; thin with the intensity of their expression of firmness—of immoveable resolution—of stern contempt of human torture. I saw that the decrees of what to me was Fate, were still issuing from those lips. I saw them writhe with a deadly locution. I saw them fashion the syllables of my name; and I shuddered because no sound succeeded. I saw, too, for a few moments of delirious horror, the soft and nearly imperceptible waving of the sable draperies which enwrapped the walls of the apartment. And then my vision fell upon the seven tall candles upon the table. At first they wore the aspect of charity, and seemed white and slender angels who would save me; but then, all at once, there came a most deadly nausea over my spirit, and

I felt every fibre in my frame thrill as if I had touched the wire of a galvanic battery, while the angel forms became meaningless spectres, with heads of flame, and I saw that from them there would be no help. And then there stole into my fancy, like a rich musical note, the thought of what sweet rest there must be in the grave. The thought came gently and stealthily, and it seemed long before it attained full appreciation; but just as my spirit came at length properly to feel and entertain it, the figures of the judges vanished, as if magically, from before me; the tall candles sank into nothingness; their flames went out utterly; the blackness of darkness supervened; all sensations appeared swallowed up in a mad rushing descent as of the soul into Hades. Then silence, and stillness, and night were the universe.

I had swooned; but still will not say that all of consciousness was lost. What of it there remained I will not attempt to define, or even to describe; yet all was not lost. In the deepest slumber—no! In delirium—no! In a swoon—no! In death—no! even in the grave all is not lost. Else there is no immortality for man. Arousing from the most profound of slumbers, we break the gossamer web of some dream. Yet in a second afterward, (so frail may that web have been) we remember not that we have dreamed. In the return to life from the swoon there are two stages; first, that of the sense of mental or spiritual; secondly, that of the sense of physical, existence. It seems probable that if, upon reaching the second stage, we could recall the impressions of the first, we should find these impressions eloquent in memories of the gulf beyond. And that gulf is—what? How at least shall we distinguish its shadows from those of the tomb? But if the impressions of what I have termed the first stage, are not, at will, recalled, yet, after long interval, do they not come unbidden, while we marvel whence they come? He who has never swooned, is not he who finds strange palaces and wildly familiar faces in coals that glow; is not he who beholds floating in mid-air the sad visions that the many may not view; is not he who ponders over the perfume of some novel flower—is not he whose brain grows bewildered with the meaning of some musical cadence which has never before arrested his attention.

Amid frequent and thoughtful endeavors to remember; amid earnest struggles to regather some token of the state of seeming nothingness into which my soul had lapsed, there have been moments when I have dreamed of success; there have been brief, very brief periods when I have conjured up remembrances which the lucid reason of a later epoch assures me could have had reference only to that condition of seeming unconsciousness. These shadows of memory tell, indistinctly, of tall figures that lifted and bore me in silence down—down—still down—till a hideous dizziness oppressed me at the mere idea of the interminableness of the descent. They tell also of a vague horror at my heart, on account of that heart's unnatural stillness. Then comes a sense of sudden motionlessness throughout all things; as if those who bore me (a ghastly train!) had outrun, in their descent, the limits of the limitless, and paused from the wearisomeness of their toil. After this I call to mind flatness and dampness; and then all is madness—the madness of a memory which busies itself among forbidden things.

Very suddenly there came back to my soul motion and sound—the tumultuous motion of the heart, and, in my ears, the sound of its beating. Then a pause in which all is blank. Then again sound, and motion, and touch—a tingling sensation pervading my frame. Then the mere consciousness of existence, without thought—a condition which lasted long. Then, very suddenly, thought, and shuddering terror, and earnest endeavor to comprehend my true state. Then a strong desire to lapse into insensibility. Then a rushing revival of soul and a successful effort to move. And now a full memory of the trial, of the judges, of the sable draperies, of the sentence, of the sickness, of the swoon. Then entire forgetfulness of all that followed; of all that a later day and much earnestness of endeavor have enabled me vaguely to recall.

So far, I had not opened my eyes. I felt that I lay upon my back, unbound. I reached out my hand, and it fell heavily upon something damp and hard. There I suffered it to remain for many minutes, while I strove to imagine where and what I could be. I longed, yet dared not to employ my vision. I dreaded the first glance at objects around me. It was not that I feared to look upon things horrible, but that I grew aghast lest there should be nothing to see. At length, with a wild desperation at heart, I quickly unclosed my eyes. My worst thoughts, then, were confirmed. The blackness of eternal night encompassed me. I struggled for breath. The intensity of the darkness seemed to oppress and stifle me. The atmosphere was intolerably close. I still lay quietly, and made effort to exercise my reason. I brought to mind the inquisitorial proceedings, and attempted from that point to deduce my real condition. The sentence had passed; and it appeared to me that a very long interval of time had since elapsed. Yet not for a moment did I suppose myself actually dead. Such a supposition, notwithstanding what we read in fiction, is altogether inconsistent with real existence;—but where and in what state was I? The condemned to death, I knew, perished usually at the auto-da-fes, and one of these had been held on the very night of the day of my trial. Had I been remanded to my dungeon, to await the next sacrifice, which would not take place for many months? This I at once saw could not be. Victims had been in immediate demand. Moreover, my dungeon, as well as all the condemned cells at Toledo, had stone floors, and light was not altogether excluded.

A fearful idea now suddenly drove the blood in torrents upon my heart, and for a brief period, I once more relapsed into insensibility. Upon recovering, I at once started to my feet, trembling convulsively in every fibre. I thrust my arms wildly above and around me in all directions. I felt nothing; yet dreaded to move a step, lest I should be impeded by the walls of a tomb. Perspiration burst from every pore, and stood in cold big beads upon my forehead. The agony of suspense, grew at length intolerable, and I cautiously moved forward, with my arms extended, and my eyes straining from their sockets, in the hope of catching some faint ray of light. I proceeded for many paces; but still all was blackness and vacancy. I breathed more freely. It seemed evident that mine was not, at least, the most hideous of fates.

And now, as I still continued to step cautiously onward, there came thronging upon my recollection a thousand vague rumors of the horrors of Toledo. Of the dungeons there had been strange things narrated—fables I had always deemed them—but yet strange, and too ghastly to repeat, save in a whisper. Was I left to perish of starvation in this subterranean world of darkness; or what fate, perhaps even more fearful, awaited me? That the result would be death, and a death of more than customary bitterness, I knew too well the character of my judges to doubt. The mode and the hour were all that occupied or distracted me.

My outstretched hands at length encountered some solid obstruction. It was a wall, seemingly of stone masonry—very smooth, slimy, and cold. I followed it up; stepping with all the careful distrust with which certain antique narratives had inspired me. This process, however, afforded me no means of ascertaining the dimensions of my dungeon; as I might make its circuit, and return to the point whence I set out, without being aware of the fact; so perfectly uniform seemed the wall. I therefore sought the knife which had been in my pocket, when led into the inquisitorial chamber; but it was gone; my clothes had been exchanged for a wrapper of coarse serge. I had thought of forcing the blade in some minute crevice of the masonry, so as to identify my point of departure. The difficulty, nevertheless, was but trivial; although, in the disorder of my fancy, it seemed at first insuperable. I tore a part of the hem from the robe and placed the fragment at full length, and at right angles to the wall. In groping my way around the prison, I could not fail to encounter this rag upon completing the circuit. So, at least I thought: but I had not counted upon the extent of the dungeon, or upon my own weakness. The ground was moist and slippery. I staggered onward for some time, when I stumbled and fell. My excessive fatigue induced me to remain prostrate; and sleep soon overtook me as I lay.

Upon awaking, and stretching forth an arm, I found beside me a loaf and a pitcher with water. I was too much exhausted to reflect upon this circumstance, but ate and drank with avidity. Shortly afterward, I resumed my tour around the prison, and with much toil, came at last upon the fragment of the serge. Up to the period when I fell, I had counted fifty-two paces, and, upon resuming my walk, I had counted forty-eight more—when I arrived at the rag. There were in all, then, a hundred paces; and, admitting two paces to the yard, I presumed the dungeon to be fifty yards in circuit. I had met, however, with many angles in the wall, and thus I could form no guess at the shape of the vault; for vault I could not help supposing it to be.

I had little object—certainly no hope—in these researches; but a vague curiosity prompted me to continue them. Quitting the wall, I resolved to cross the area of the enclosure. At first, I proceeded with extreme caution, for the floor, although seemingly of solid material, was treacherous with slime. At length, however, I took courage, and did not hesitate to step firmly—endeavoring to cross in as direct a line as possible. I had advanced some ten or twelve paces in this manner, when the remnant of the torn hem of my robe became entangled between my legs. I stepped on it, and fell violently on my face.

In the confusion attending my fall, I did not immediately apprehend a somewhat startling circumstance, which yet, in a few seconds afterward, and while I still lay prostrate, arrested my attention. It was this: my chin rested upon the floor of the prison, but my lips, and the upper portion of my head, although seemingly at a less elevation than the chin, touched nothing. At the same time, my forehead seemed bathed in a clammy vapor, and the peculiar smell of decayed fungus arose to my nostrils. I put forward my arm, and shuddered to find that I had fallen at the very brink of a circular pit, whose extent, of course, I had no means of ascertaining at the moment. Groping about the masonry just below the margin, I succeeded in dislodging a small fragment, and let it fall into the abyss. For many seconds I hearkened to its reverberations as it dashed against the sides of the chasm in its descent: at length, there was a sullen plunge into water, succeeded by loud echoes. At the same moment, there came a sound resembling the quick opening, and as rapid closing of a door overhead, while a faint gleam of light flashed suddenly through the gloom, and as suddenly faded away.

I saw clearly the doom which had been prepared for me, and congratulated myself upon the timely accident by which I had escaped. Another step before my fall, and the world had seen me no more. And the death just avoided, was of that very character which I had regarded as fabulous and frivolous in the tales respecting the Inquisition. To the victims of its tyranny, there was the choice of death with its direst physical agonies, or death with its most hideous moral horrors. I had been reserved for the latter. By long suffering my nerves had been unstrung, until I trembled at the sound of my own voice, and had become in every respect a fitting subject for the species of torture which awaited me.

Shaking in every limb, I groped my way back to the wall—resolving there to perish rather than risk the terrors of the wells, of which my imagination now pictured many in various positions about the dungeon. In other conditions of mind, I might have had courage to end my misery at once, by a plunge into one of these abysses; but now I was the veriest of cowards. Neither could I forget what I had read of these pits—that the sudden extinction of life formed no part of their most horrible plan.

Agitation of spirit kept me awake for many long hours; but at length I again slumbered. Upon arousing, I found by my side, as before, a loaf and a pitcher of water. A burning thirst consumed me, and I emptied the vessel at a draught. It must have been drugged—for scarcely had I drunk, before I became irresistibly drowsy. A deep sleep fell upon me—a sleep like that of death. How long it lasted, of course, I know not; but when, once again, I unclosed my eyes, the objects around me were visible. By a wild, sulphurous lustre, the origin of which I could not at first determine, I was enabled to see the extent and aspect of the prison.

In its size I had been greatly mistaken. The whole circuit of its walls did not exceed twenty-five yards. For some minutes this fact occasioned me a world of vain trouble; vain indeed—for what could be of less importance, under the terrible circumstances which environed me, then the mere dimensions of my dungeon? But my soul took a wild interest in trifles, and I busied myself in endeavors to account for the error I had committed in my measurement. The truth at length flashed upon me. In my first attempt at exploration, I had counted fifty-two paces, up to the period when I fell: I must then have been within a pace or two of the fragment of serge; in fact, I had nearly performed the circuit of the vault. I then slept—and, upon awaking, I must have returned upon my steps—thus supposing the circuit nearly double what it actually was. My confusion of mind prevented me from observing that I began my tour with the wall to the left, and ended it with the wall to the right.

I had been deceived, too, in respect to the shape of the enclosure. In feeling my way, I had found many angles, and thus deduced an idea of great irregularity; so potent is the effect of total darkness upon one arousing from lethargy or sleep! The angles were simply those of a few slight depressions, or niches, at odd intervals. The general shape of the prison was square. What I had taken for masonry seemed now to be iron, or some other metal, in huge plates, whose sutures or joints occasioned the depression. The entire surface of this metallic enclosure was rudely daubed in all the hideous and repulsive devices to which the charnel superstition of the monks has given rise. The figures of fiends in aspects of menace, with skeleton forms, and other more really fearful images, overspread and disfigured the walls. I observed that the outlines of these monstrosities were sufficiently distinct, but that the colors seemed faded and blurred, as if from the effects of a damp atmosphere. I now noticed the floor, too, which was of stone. In the centre yawned the circular pit from whose jaws I had escaped; but it was the only one in the dungeon.

All this I saw indistinctly and by much effort—for my personal condition had been greatly changed during slumber. I now lay upon my back, and at full length, on a species of low framework of wood. To this I was securely bound by a long strap resembling a surcingle. It passed in many convolutions about my limbs and body, leaving at liberty only my head, and my left arm to such extent, that I could, by dint of much exertion, supply myself with food from an earthen dish which lay by my side on the floor. I saw, to my horror, that the pitcher had been removed. I say, to my horror—for I was consumed with intolerable thirst. This thirst it appeared to be the design of my persecutors to stimulate—for the food in the dish was meat pungently seasoned.

Looking upward, I surveyed the ceiling of my prison. It was some thirty or forty feet overhead, and constructed much as the side walls. In one of its panels a very singular figure riveted my whole attention. It was the painted figure of Time as he is commonly represented, save that, in lieu of a scythe, he held what, at a casual glance, I supposed to be the pictured image of a huge pendulum, such as we see on antique clocks. There was something, however, in the appearance of this machine which caused me to regard it more attentively. While I gazed directly upward at it, (for its position was immediately over my own,) I fancied that I saw it in motion. In an instant afterward the fancy was confirmed. Its sweep was brief, and of course slow. I watched it for some minutes, somewhat in fear, but more in wonder. Wearied at length with observing its dull movement, I turned my eyes upon the other objects in the cell.

A slight noise attracted my notice, and, looking to the floor, I saw several enormous rats traversing it. They had issued from the well, which lay just within view to my right. Even then, while I gazed, they came up in troops, hurriedly, with ravenous eyes, allured by the scent of the meat. From this it required much effort and attention to scare them away.

It might have been half an hour, perhaps even an hour, (for I could take but imperfect note of time) before I again cast my eyes upward. What I then saw, confounded and amazed me. The sweep of the pendulum had increased in extent by nearly a yard. As a natural consequence, its velocity was also much greater. But what mainly disturbed me, was the idea that it had perceptibly descended. I now observed—with what horror it is needless to say—that its nether extremity was formed of a crescent of glittering steel, about a foot in length from horn to horn; the horns upward, and the under edge evidently as keen as that of a razor. Like a razor also, it seemed massy and heavy, tapering from the edge into a solid and broad structure above. It was appended to a weighty rod of brass, and the whole hissed as it swung through the air.

I could no longer doubt the doom prepared for me by monkish ingenuity in torture. My cognizance of the pit had become known to the inquisitorial agents—the pit, whose horrors had been destined for so bold a recusant as myself—the pit, typical of hell, and regarded by rumor as the Ultima Thule of all their punishments. The plunge into this pit I had avoided by the merest of accidents, and I knew that surprise, or entrapment into torment, formed an important portion of all the grotesquerie of these dungeon deaths. Having failed to fall, it was no part of the demon plan to hurl me into the abyss; and thus (there being no alternative) a different and a milder destruction awaited me. Milder! I half smiled in my agony as I thought of such application of such a term.

What boots it to tell of the long, long hours of horror more than mortal, during which I counted the rushing oscillations of the steel! Inch by inch—line by line—with a descent only appreciable at intervals that seemed ages—down and still down it came! Days passed—it might have been that many days passed—ere it swept so closely over me as to fan me with its acrid breath. The odor of the sharp steel forced itself into my nostrils. I prayed—I wearied heaven with my prayer for its more speedy descent. I grew frantically mad, and struggled to force myself upward against the sweep of the fearful scimitar. And then I fell suddenly calm, and lay smiling at the glittering death, as a child at some rare bauble.

There was another interval of utter insensibility; it was brief; for, upon again lapsing into life, there had been no perceptible descent in the pendulum. But it might have been long—for I knew there were demons who took note of my swoon, and who could have arrested the vibration at pleasure. Upon my recovery, too, I felt very—oh, inexpressibly—sick and weak, as if through long inanition. Even amid the agonies of that period, the human nature craved food. With painful effort I outstretched my left arm as far as my bonds permitted, and took possession of the small remnant which had been spared me by the rats. As I put a portion of it within my lips, there rushed to my mind a half-formed thought of joy—of hope. Yet what business had I with hope? It was, as I say, a half-formed thought—man has many such, which are never completed. I felt that it was of joy—of hope; but I felt also that it had perished in its formation. In vain I struggled to perfect—to regain it. Long suffering had nearly annihilated all my ordinary powers of mind. I was an imbecile—an idiot.

The vibration of the pendulum was at right angles to my length. I saw that the crescent was designed to cross the region of the heart. It would fray the serge of my robe—it would return and repeat its operations—again—and again. Notwithstanding its terrifically wide sweep, (some thirty feet or more,) and the hissing vigor of its descent, sufficient to sunder these very walls of iron, still the fraying of my robe would be all that, for several minutes, it would accomplish. And at this thought I paused. I dared not go farther than this reflection. I dwelt upon it with a pertinacity of attention—as if, in so dwelling, I could arrest here the descent of the steel. I forced myself to ponder upon the sound of the crescent as it should pass across the garment—upon the peculiar thrilling sensation which the friction of cloth produces on the nerves. I pondered upon all this frivolity until my teeth were on edge.

Down—steadily down it crept. I took a frenzied pleasure in contrasting its downward with its lateral velocity. To the right—to the left—far and wide—with the shriek of a damned spirit! to my heart, with the stealthy pace of the tiger! I alternately laughed and howled, as the one or the other idea grew predominant.

Down—certainly, relentlessly down! It vibrated within three inches of my bosom! I struggled violently—furiously—to free my left arm. This was free only from the elbow to the hand. I could reach the latter, from the platter beside me, to my mouth, with great effort, but no farther. Could I have broken the fastenings above the elbow, I would have seized and attempted to arrest the pendulum. I might as well have attempted to arrest an avalanche!

Down—still unceasingly—still inevitably down! I gasped and struggled at each vibration. I shrunk convulsively at its every sweep. My eyes followed its outward or upward whirls with the eagerness of the most unmeaning despair; they closed themselves spasmodically at the descent, although death would have been a relief, oh, how unspeakable! Still I quivered in every nerve to think how slight a sinking of the machinery would precipitate that keen, glistening axe upon my bosom. It was hope that prompted the nerve to quiver—the frame to shrink. It was hope—the hope that triumphs on the rack—that whispers to the death-condemned even in the dungeons of the Inquisition.

I saw that some ten or twelve vibrations would bring the steel in actual contact with my robe—and with this observation there suddenly came over my spirit all the keen, collected calmness of despair. For the first time during many hours—or perhaps days—I thought. It now occurred to me, that the bandage, or surcingle, which enveloped me, was unique. I was tied by no separate cord. The first stroke of the razor-like crescent athwart any portion of the band, would so detach it that it might be unwound from my person by means of my left hand. But how fearful, in that case, the proximity of the steel! The result of the slightest struggle, how deadly! Was it likely, moreover, that the minions of the torturer had not foreseen and provided for this possibility? Was it probable that the bandage crossed my bosom in the track of the pendulum? Dreading to find my faint, and, as it seemed, my last hope frustrated, I so far elevated my head as to obtain a distinct view of my breast. The surcingle enveloped my limbs and body close in all directions—save in the path of the destroying crescent.

Scarcely had I dropped my head back into its original position, when there flashed upon my mind what I cannot better describe than as the unformed half of that idea of deliverance to which I have previously alluded, and of which a moiety only floated indeterminately through my brain when I raised food to my burning lips. The whole thought was now present—feeble, scarcely sane, scarcely definite—but still entire. I proceeded at once, with the nervous energy of despair, to attempt its execution.

For many hours the immediate vicinity of the low framework upon which I lay, had been literally swarming with rats. They were wild, bold, ravenous—their red eyes glaring upon me as if they waited but for motionlessness on my part to make me their prey. "To what food," I thought, "have they been accustomed in the well?"

They had devoured, in spite of all my efforts to prevent them, all but a small remnant of the contents of the dish. I had fallen into an habitual see-saw, or wave of the hand about the platter; and, at length, the unconscious uniformity of the movement deprived it of effect. In their voracity, the vermin frequently fastened their sharp fangs in my fingers. With the particles of the oily and spicy viand which now remained, I thoroughly rubbed the bandage wherever I could reach it; then, raising my hand from the floor, I lay breathlessly still.

At first, the ravenous animals were startled and terrified at the change—at the cessation of movement. They shrank alarmedly back; many sought the well. But this was only for a moment. I had not counted in vain upon their voracity. Observing that I remained without motion, one or two of the boldest leaped upon the fame-work, and smelt at the surcingle. This seemed the signal for a general rush. Forth from the well they hurried in fresh troops. They clung to the wood—they overran it, and leaped in hundreds upon my person. The measured movement of the pendulum disturbed them not at all. Avoiding its strokes, they busied themselves with the anointed bandage. They pressed—they swarmed upon me in ever accumulating heaps. They writhed upon my throat; their cold lips sought my own; I was half stifled by their thronging pressure; disgust, for which the world has no name, swelled my bosom, and chilled, with a heavy clamminess, my heart. Yet one minute, and I felt that the struggle would be over. Plainly I perceived the loosening of the bandage. I knew that in more than one place it must be already severed. With a more than human resolution I lay still.

Nor had I erred in my calculations—nor had I endured in vain. I at length felt that I was free. The surcingle hung in ribands from my body. But the stroke of the pendulum already pressed upon my bosom. It had divided the serge of the robe. It had cut through the linen beneath. Twice again it swung, and a sharp sense of pain shot through every nerve. But the moment of escape had arrived. At a wave of my hand my deliverers hurried tumultuously away. With a steady movement—cautious, sidelong, shrinking, and slow—I slid from the embrace of the bandage and beyond the reach of the scimitar. For the moment, at least, I was free.

Free!—and in the grasp of the Inquisition! I had scarcely stepped from my wooden bed of horror upon the stone floor of the prison, when the motion of the hellish machine ceased, and I beheld it drawn up, by some invisible force, through the ceiling. This was a lesson which I took desperately to heart. My every motion was undoubtedly watched. Free!—I had but escaped death in one form of agony, to be delivered unto worse than death in some other. With that thought I rolled my eyes nervously around on the barriers of iron that hemmed me in. Something unusual—some change which, at first, I could not appreciate distinctly—it was obvious, had taken place in the apartment. For many minutes of a dreamy and trembling abstraction, I busied myself in vain, unconnected conjecture.

During this period, I became aware, for the first time, of the origin of the sulphurous light which illumined the cell. It proceeded from a fissure, about half an inch in width, extending entirely around the prison at the base of the walls, which thus appeared, and were completely separated from the floor. I endeavored, but of course in vain, to look through the aperture.

As I arose from the attempt, the mystery of the alteration in the chamber broke at once upon my understanding. I have observed that, although the outlines of the figures upon the walls were sufficiently distinct, yet the colors seemed blurred and indefinite. These colors had now assumed, and were momentarily assuming, a startling and most intense brilliancy, that gave to the spectral and fiendish portraitures an aspect that might have thrilled even firmer nerves than my own. Demon eyes, of a wild and ghastly vivacity, glared upon me in a thousand directions, where none had been visible before, and gleamed with the lurid lustre of a fire that I could not force my imagination to regard as unreal.

Unreal!—Even while I breathed there came to my nostrils the breath of the vapor of heated iron! A suffocating odor pervaded the prison! A deeper glow settled each moment in the eyes that glared at my agonies! A richer tint of crimson diffused itself over the pictured horrors of blood. I panted! I gasped for breath! There could be no doubt of the design of my tormentors—oh! most unrelenting! oh! most demoniac of men! I shrank from the glowing metal to the centre of the cell. Amid the thought of the fiery destruction that impended, the idea of the coolness of the well came over my soul like balm. I rushed to its deadly brink. I threw my straining vision below. The glare from the enkindled roof illumined its inmost recesses. Yet, for a wild moment, did my spirit refuse to comprehend the meaning of what I saw. At length it forced—it wrestled its way into my soul—it burned itself in upon my shuddering reason. Oh! for a voice to speak!—oh! horror!—oh! any horror but this! With a shriek, I rushed from the margin, and buried my face in my hands—weeping bitterly.

The heat rapidly increased, and once again I looked up, shuddering as with a fit of the ague. There had been a second change in the cell—and now the change was obviously in the form. As before, it was in vain that I at first endeavored to appreciate or understand what was taking place. But not long was I left in doubt. The Inquisitorial vengeance had been hurried by my two-fold escape, and there was to be no more dallying with the King of Terrors. The room had been square. I saw that two of its iron angles were now acute—two, consequently, obtuse. The fearful difference quickly increased with a low rumbling or moaning sound. In an instant the apartment had shifted its form into that of a lozenge. But the alteration stopped not here—I neither hoped nor desired it to stop. I could have clasped the red walls to my bosom as a garment of eternal peace. "Death," I said, "any death but that of the pit!" Fool! might I have not known that into the pit it was the object of the burning iron to urge me? Could I resist its glow? or if even that, could I withstand its pressure? And now, flatter and flatter grew the lozenge, with a rapidity that left me no time for contemplation. Its centre, and of course, its greatest width, came just over the yawning gulf. I shrank back—but the closing walls pressed me resistlessly onward. At length for my seared and writhing body there was no longer an inch of foothold on the firm floor of the prison. I struggled no more, but the agony of my soul found vent in one loud, long, and final scream of despair. I felt that I tottered upon the brink—I averted my eyes —

There was a discordant hum of human voices! There was a loud blast as of many trumpets! There was a harsh grating as of a thousand thunders! The fiery walls rushed back! An outstretched arm caught my own as I fell, fainting, into the abyss. It was that of General Lasalle. The French army had entered Toledo. The Inquisition was in the hands of its enemies. ✳

THE "RED death" had long devastated the country. No pestilence had ever been so fatal, or so hideous. Blood was its Avatar and its seal—the redness and the horror of blood. There were sharp pains, and sudden dizziness, and then profuse bleeding at the pores, with dissolution. The scarlet stains upon the body and especially upon the face of the victim, were the pest ban which shut him out from the aid and from the sympathy of his fellow-men. And the whole seizure, progress and termination of the disease, were the incidents of half an hour.

"The Masque of the Red Death"

But the Prince Prospero was happy and dauntless and sagacious. When his dominions were half depopulated, he summoned to his presence a thousand hale and light-hearted friends from among the knights and dames of his court, and with these retired to the deep seclusion of one of his castellated abbeys. This was an extensive and magnificent structure, the creation of the prince's own eccentric yet august taste. A strong and lofty wall girdled it in. This wall had gates of iron. The courtiers, having entered, brought furnaces and massy hammers and welded the bolts. They resolved to leave means neither of ingress or egress to the sudden impulses of despair or of frenzy from within. The abbey was amply provisioned. With such precautions the courtiers might bid defiance to contagion. The external world could take care of itself. In the meantime it was folly to grieve, or to think. The prince had provided all the appliances of pleasure. There were buffoons, there were improvisatori, there were ballet-dancers, there were musicians, there was Beauty, there was wine. All these and security were within. Without was the "Red Death."

It was toward the close of the fifth or sixth month of his seclusion, and while the pestilence raged most furiously abroad, that the Prince Prospero entertained his thousand friends at a masked ball of the most unusual magnificence.

It was a voluptuous scene, that masquerade. But first let me tell of the rooms in which it was held. There were seven—an imperial suite. In many palaces, however, such suites form a long and straight vista, while the folding doors slide back nearly to the walls on either hand, so that the view of the whole extent is scarcely impeded. Here the case was very different; as might have been expected from the duke's love of the bizarre. The apartments were so irregularly disposed that the vision embraced but little more than one at a time. There was a sharp turn at every twenty or thirty yards, and at each turn a novel effect. To the right and left, in the middle of each wall, a tall and narrow Gothic window looked out upon a closed corridor which pursued the windings of the suite. These windows were of stained glass whose color varied in accordance with the prevailing hue of the decorations of the chamber into which it opened. That at the eastern extremity was hung, for example, in blue—and vividly blue were its windows. The second chamber was purple in its ornaments and tapestries, and here the panes were purple. The third was green throughout, and so were the casements. The fourth was furnished and lighted with orange—the fifth with white—the sixth with violet. The seventh apartment was closely shrouded in black velvet tapestries that hung all over the ceiling and down the walls, falling in heavy folds upon a carpet of the same material and hue. But in this chamber only, the color of the windows failed to correspond with the decorations. The panes here were scarlet—a deep blood color. Now in no one of the seven apartments was there any lamp or candelabrum, amid the profusion of golden ornaments that lay scattered to and fro or depended from the roof. There was no light of any kind emanating from lamp or candle within the suite of chambers. But in the corridors that followed the suite, there stood, opposite to each window, a heavy tripod, bearing a brazier of fire, that projected its rays through the tinted glass and so glaringly illumined the room. And thus were produced a multitude of gaudy and fantastic appearances. But in the western or black chamber the effect of the fire-light that streamed upon the dark hangings through the blood-tinted panes, was ghastly in the extreme, and produced so wild a look upon the countenances of those who entered, that there were few of the company bold enough to set foot within its precincts at all.

It was in this apartment, also, that there stood against the western wall, a gigantic clock of ebony. Its pendulum swung to and fro with a dull, heavy, monotonous clang; and when the minute-hand made the circuit of the face, and the hour was to be stricken, there came from the brazen lungs of the clock a sound which was clear and loud and deep and exceedingly musical, but of so peculiar a note and emphasis that, at each lapse of an hour, the musicians of the orchestra were constrained to pause, momentarily, in their performance, to harken to the sound; and thus the waltzers perforce ceased their evolutions; and there was a brief disconcert of the whole gay company; and, while the chimes of the clock yet rang, it was observed that the giddiest grew pale, and the more aged and sedate passed their hands over their brows as if in confused revery or meditation. But when the echoes had fully ceased, a light laughter at once pervaded the assembly; the musicians looked at each other and smiled as if at their own nervousness and folly, and made whispering vows, each to the other, that the next chiming of the clock should produce in them no similar emotion; and then, after the lapse of sixty minutes, (which embrace three thousand and six hundred seconds of the Time that flies,) there came yet another chiming of the clock, and then were the same disconcert and tremulousness and meditation as before.

But, in spite of these things, it was a gay and magnificent revel. The tastes of the duke were peculiar. He had a fine eye for colors and effects. He disregarded the decora of mere fashion. His plans were bold and fiery, and his conceptions glowed with barbaric lustre. There are some who would have thought him mad. His followers felt that he was not. It was necessary to hear and see and touch him to be sure that he was not.

He had directed, in great part, the moveable embellishments of the seven chambers, upon occasion of this great fete; and it was his own guiding taste which had given character to the masqueraders. Be sure they were grotesque. There were much glare and glitter and piquancy and phantasm—much of what has been since seen in "Hernani." There were arabesque figures with unsuited limbs and appoint-

ments. There were delirious fancies such as the madman fashions. There were much of the beautiful, much of the wanton, much of the bizarre, something of the terrible, and not a little of that which might have excited disgust. To and fro in the seven chambers there stalked, in fact, a multitude of dreams. And these—the dreams—writhed in and about, taking hue from the rooms, and causing the wild music of the orchestra to seem as the echo of their steps. And, anon, there strikes the ebony clock which stands in the hall of the velvet. And then, for a moment, all is still, and all is silent save the voice of the clock. The dreams are stiff-frozen as they stand. But the echoes of the chime die away—they have endured but an instant—and a light, half-subdued laughter floats after them as they depart. And now again the music swells, and the dreams live, and writhe to and fro more merrily than ever, taking hue from the many tinted windows through which stream the rays from the tripods. But to the chamber which lies most westwardly of the seven, there are now none of the maskers who venture; for the night is waning away; and there flows a ruddier light through the blood-colored panes; and the blackness of the sable drapery appals; and to him whose foot falls upon the sable carpet, there comes from the near clock of ebony a muffled peal more solemnly emphatic than any which reaches their ears who indulge in the more remote gaieties of the other apartments.

But these other apartments were densely crowded, and in them beat feverishly the heart of life. And the revel went whirlingly on, until at length there commenced the sounding of midnight upon the clock. And then the music ceased, as I have told; and the evolutions of the waltzers were quieted; and there was an uneasy cessation of all things as before. But now there were twelve strokes to be sounded by the bell of the clock; and thus it happened, perhaps that more of thought crept, with more of time, into the meditations of the thoughtful among those who revelled. And thus too, it happened, perhaps, that before the last echoes of the last chime had utterly sunk into silence, there were many individuals in the crowd who had found leisure to become aware of the presence of a masked figure which had arrested the attention of no single individual before. And the rumor of this new presence having spread itself whisperingly around, there arose at length from the whole company a buzz, or murmur, expressive of disapprobation and surprise—then, finally, of terror, of horror, and of disgust.

In an assembly of phantasms such as I have painted, it may well be supposed that no ordinary appearance could have excited such sensation. In truth the masquerade license of the night was nearly unlimited; but the figure in question had out-Heroded Herod, and gone beyond the bounds of even the prince's indefinite decorum. There are chords in the hearts of the most reckless which cannot be touched without emotion. Even with the utterly lost, to whom life and death are equally jests, there are matters of which no jest can be made. The whole company, indeed, seemed now deeply to feel that in the costume and bearing of the stranger neither wit nor propriety existed. The figure was tall and gaunt, and shrouded from head to foot in the habiliments of the grave. The mask which concealed the visage was made so nearly to resemble the countenance of a stiffened corpse that the closest scrutiny must have had difficulty in detecting the cheat. And yet all this might have been endured, if not approved, by the mad revellers around. But the mummer had gone so far as to assume the type of the Red Death. His vesture was dabbled in blood—and his broad brow, with all the features of the face, was besprinkled with the scarlet horror.

When the eyes of Prince Prospero fell upon this spectral image (which with a slow and solemn movement, as if more fully to sustain its role, stalked to and fro among the waltzers) he was seen to be convulsed, in the first moment with a strong shudder either of terror or distaste; but, in the next, his brow reddened with rage.

"Who dares?" he demanded hoarsely of the courtiers who stood near him—"who dares insult us with this blasphemous mockery? Seize him and unmask him—that we may know whom we have to hang at sunrise, from the battlements!"

It was in the eastern or blue chamber in which stood the Prince Prospero as he uttered these words. They rang throughout the seven rooms loudly and clearly—for the prince was a bold and robust man, and the music had become hushed at the waving of his hand.

It was in the blue room where stood the prince, with a group of pale courtiers by his side. At first, as he spoke, there was a slight rushing movement of this group in the direction of the intruder, who, at the moment was also near at hand, and now, with deliberate and stately step, made closer approach to the speaker. But from a certain nameless awe with which the mad assumptions of the mummer had inspired the whole party, there were found none who put forth hand to seize him; so that, unimpeded, he passed within a yard of the prince's person; and, while the vast assembly, as if with one impulse, shrank from the centres of the rooms to the walls, he made his way uninterruptedly, but with the same solemn and measured step which had distinguished him from the first, through the blue chamber to the purple—through the purple to the green—through the green to the orange—through this again to the white—and even thence to the violet, ere a decided movement had been made to arrest him. It was then, however, that the Prince Prospero, maddening with rage and the shame of his own momentary cowardice, rushed hurriedly through the six chambers, while none followed him on account of a deadly terror that had seized upon all. He bore aloft a drawn dagger, and had approached, in rapid impetuosity, to within three or four feet of the retreating figure, when the latter, having attained the extremity of the velvet apartment, turned suddenly and confronted his pursuer. There was a sharp cry—and the dagger dropped gleaming upon the sable carpet, upon which, instantly afterwards, fell prostrate in death the Prince Prospero. Then, summoning the wild courage of despair, a throng of the revellers at once threw themselves into the black apartment, and, seizing the mummer, whose tall figure stood erect and motionless within the shadow of the ebony clock, gasped in unutterable horror at finding the grave cerements and corpse-like mask which they handled with so violent a rudeness, untenanted by any tangible form.

And now was acknowledged the presence of the Red Death. He had come like a thief in the night. And one by one dropped the revellers in the blood-bedewed halls of their revel, and died each in the despairing posture of his fall. And the life of the ebony clock went out with that of the last of the gay. And the flames of the tripods expired. And Darkness and Decay and the Red Death held illimitable dominion over all. ✳

Jane Eyre

Charlotte Brontë

ART/ADAPTATION BY **Elizabeth Watasin**

IT'S ABSOLUTELY AMAZING WHEN YOU REFLECT on the fact that three sisters each wrote a classic work of literature. More than that, they did it *in the same year*. The year 1847 saw the publication of Charlotte Brontë's *Jane Eyre*, Emily Brontë's *Wuthering Heights*, and Anne Brontë's *Agnes Grey*. It's one of the most astounding creative achievements in history.

The three sisters and their brother, Branwell, started writing as children, concocting tales about elaborate worlds they had dreamed up. This continued through their teenage years and even beyond. Charlotte set about getting her poetry published, not giving up even when England's poet laureate brusquely advised her that writing is a man's business. In 1846, when the sisters were thirty (Charlotte), twenty-eight (Emily), and twenty-six (Anne), a small publisher put out a book containing poems written individually by each of them. In the landmark year that followed, Charlotte became the first to land a London publisher, who put out *Jane Eyre* a mere six weeks after receiving the manuscript. Published under an unusual male pseudonym, as each of their first novels would be, the story of an orphan who grows up to uncompromisingly make her way in the world was an immediate hit with readers and critics. English professor Elsie B. Michie writes that

the passionate voice of its first-person heroine took the Victorian literary world by storm. Contemporary reviewers called it "an extraordinary book," "unlike all that we have read," full of "originality and freshness." Readers loved it even more than critics: "the public taste seems to have outstripped its guides in appreciating the remarkable power which this book displays." An American journal characterized New England as suffering from "Jane Eyre fever." Queen Victoria wrote in her diaries that she stayed up till half past eleven reading to Prince Albert out of "that melancholy, interesting book, *Jane Eyre*." The energy that made Brontë's novel so compelling also meant it risked being unconventional, irreligious, improper, and revolutionary. One contemporary reviewer criticized it for "moral Jacobinism," a point expanded by Lady Eastlake, who described it as "pre-eminently an anti-Christian composition" that echoed "the tone of mind and thought which had overthrown authority and violated every code human and divine."

Elizabeth Watasin works with comics, illustration, prose, and animation (her film credits include *Beauty and the Beast*, *The Lion King*, and *Aladdin*). In the following pages, she has adapted most of chapter 8, which takes place at Lowood Boarding School, based on the nightmarish school that Charlotte and her sisters actually attended. Elizabeth explains:

I chose the Helen Burns, Jane Eyre, and Miss Temple scene because I was struck by how passionate Charlotte's language became in describing it. It went on thus for several passages and I didn't find a scene later that matched that intensity for that length. There were revelations before the event that could be tied in visually, and if I attempted surrealism I could bring a sense of stage and theater, hopefully, to the page. The language needed lettering, line, and color to match. It was only natural to attempt line and paint by hand, with its sense of accident and discovery.

SOURCE

Michie, Elsie B. *Charlotte Brontë's "Jane Eyre": A Casebook*. Oxford: Oxford University Press, 2006.

"Barbara," said she, "can you not bring a little more bread and butter? There is not enough for three." Barbara went out: she returned soon—— "Madam, Mrs. Harden says she has sent up the usual quantity."

Jane Eyre
by Charlotte Bronte

Mrs. Harden, be it observed, was the housekeeper: a woman after Mr. Brocklehurst's own heart, made up of equal parts of whalebone and iron.

"Oh, very well!" returned Miss Temple; "we must make it do, Barbara, I suppose." And as the girl withdrew she added, smiling, "Fortunately, I have it in my power to supply deficiencies for this once." Having invited Helen and me to approach the table, and placed before each of us a cup of tea with one delicious but thin morsel of toast, she got up, unlocked a drawer, and taking from it a parcel wrapped in paper, disclosed presently to our eyes a good—sized seed-cake.

forget Me not

"I meant to give each of you some of this to take wit you," said she, "but as there is so little toast, you must have it now," and she proceeded to cut slices with a generous hand. We feasted that evening as on nectar and ambrosia; and not the least delight of the entertainment was the smile of gratification with which our hostess regarded us, as we satisfied our famished appetites on the delicate fare she liberally supplied.

Tea over and the tray removed,
she again summoned us to the fire;
we sat one on each side of her,
and now a conversation followed
between her and Helen, which
it was indeed a privilege to be
admitted to hear.

Miss Temple had always something of serenity in her air, of state in her mien,
of refined propriety in her language, which precluded deviation into
the ardent, the excited, the eager: something which chastened
the pleasure of those who looked on her and listened to her, by a controlling
sense of awe; and such was my feeling now:
but as to Helen Burns, I was struck with wonder.

The refreshing meal, the brilliant fire, the presence and kindness of her beloved instructress,
or, perhaps, more than all these, something in her own unique mind, had roused her powers within her.
They woke, they kindled: first, they glowed in the bright tint of her cheek, which till this hour I had
never seen but pale and bloodless; then they shone in the liquid lustre of her eyes, which had suddenly acquired
a beauty more singular than that of Miss Temple's —a beauty neither of fine colour nor long eyelash,
nor pencilled brow, but of meaning, of movement, of radiance.

Then her soul sat on her lips, and language flowed, from what source I cannot tell. Has a girl of fourteen a heart large enough, vigorous enough, to hold the swelling spring of pure, full, fervid eloquence? Such was the characteristic of Helen's discourse on that, to me, memorable evening; her spirit seemed hastening to live within a very brief span as much as many live during a protracted existence.

They conversed of things I had never heard of; of nations and times past; of countries far away; of secrets of nature discovered or guessed at:

they spoke of books: how many they had read! What stores of knowledge they possessed! Then they seemed so familiar with French names and French authors: but my amazement reached its climax when Miss Temple asked Helen if she sometimes snatched a moment to recall the Latin her father had taught her, and taking a book from a shelf, bade her read and construe a page of Virgil; and Helen obeyed, my organ of veneration expanding at every sounding line.

She had scarcely finished ere
the bell announced
bedtime!

no delay could
be admitted;

Miss Temple embraced
us both, saying,
"God bless you,
my children!"

Helen she held a little longer than me: she let her go more reluctantly;
it was Helen her eye followed to the door; it was for her
she a second time breathed a sad sigh; for her she wiped a tear from her cheek.

On reaching the bedroom, we heard the voice of Miss Scatcherd: she was examining drawers;

she had just pulled out Helen Burns's, and when we entered Helen was greeted with a sharp reprimand, and told that tomorrow she should have half-a-dozen of untidily folded articles pinned to her shoulder.

"My things were indeed in shameful disorder," murmured Helen to me, in a low voice: "I intended to have arranged them, but I forgot."

Next morning, Miss Scatcherd wrote in conspicuous characters on a piece of pasteboard the word "Slattern,"

and bound it like a phylactery round Helen's large, mild, intelligent, and benign-looking forehead. She wore it till evening, patient, unresentful, regarding it as a deserved punishment. The moment Miss Scatcherd withdrew after afternoon school, I ran to Helen, tore it off, and thrust it into the fire:

the fury of which she was incapable had been burning in my soul all day, and tears, hot and large, had continually been scalding my cheek; for the spectacle of her sad resignation gave me an intolerable pain at the heart.

Elizabeth Watasin 2011

Wuthering Heights

Emily Brontë

ART/ADAPTATION BY **Tim Fish**

AS I MENTIONED IN THE INTRODUCTION TO *JANE Eyre*, the Brontë sisters pulled off one of the greatest artistic feats in history, with the near-simultaneous publication of three classic works of literature. But being in that family had its downsides. Not since the Romantics did so many writers die so young. Of the six Brontë siblings, not one lived to see the age of forty.

It really started with their mother, Maria, who died of cancer less than two years after Anne was born. The first two children—Maria Jr. and Elizabeth—died of tuberculosis within six weeks of each other, at ages eleven and ten. They contracted it at the horrible boarding school that most of the Brontë girls attended. The other four siblings made it to adulthood, but within a single eight-month period, brother Branwell and sisters Emily and Anne died. Charlotte made it longest, weeks away from turning thirty-nine, before succumbing—like all of them—to consumption. Their father, the Revered Patrick Brontë, lived to a ripe old age indeed, eighty-four, more than long enough to see his wife and all six of his children go to the grave.

During the banner year 1847, Charlotte was the first to find a London publisher. Soon after, Emily and Anne* found a different London publisher—an obscure and unscrupulous one—for their first novels. Unlike *Jane Eyre*, *Wuthering Heights* got mixed reviews, with lots of commentators shocked at the seething anger and cruelty dripping off its pages. Harold Bloom writes:

> *Wuthering Heights* is like nothing else in the language, though the closest work to it, the sister-book as it were, is Charlotte Brontë's *Jane Eyre*. Yet Charlotte rejected the affinity and regarded Heathcliff as a "mere demon." Heathcliff is much more than that; as a negative hero or hero-villain he has the sublimity of Captain Ahab in

Herman Melville's *Moby-Dick* and something even of the darkened splendor of Satan in Milton's *Paradise Lost*. Emily Brontë's implicit model for Heathcliff was the long poem *Manfred*, a self-portrait by Lord Byron in which the Romantic poet allows himself to absorb aspects of Milton's Satan.

Tim Fish originally proposed *Wuthering Heights* to Marvel for their Marvel Illustrated line of classic lit adaptations. (Like many other *Graphic Canon* artists—Rebecca Dart with *Paradise Lost*, Dame Darcy with the *Alice* books, Matt Kish with *Heart of Darkness*—Tim says that it's long been a dream of his to do this adaptation.) Marvel initially expressed interest, but the deal didn't pan out. I found out about this through Tim's blog, and approached him about doing a shorter adaptation. Luckily he agreed, and we now have this dynamic visual version of the first half of the novel, which famously focuses on the doomed love of stepsiblings Catherine and Heathcliff. (The second, less satisfying half of *Wuthering Heights* mainly concerns Catherine's daughter and Heathcliff's son.)

SOURCE

Bloom, Harold, ed. *Bloom's Guides: Emily Brontë's Wuthering Heights*. New York: Blooms Literary Criticism, 2008.

---

* I do want to offer an apology to Anne Brontë. Her novels *Agnes Grey* and *The Tenant of Wildfell Hall* are considered classics, but they generally get short shrift, not being as highly regarded as *Jane Eyre* and *Wuthering Heights*. Indeed, no one wanted to adapt any of Anne's work, a situation I hope will change in future volumes of *The Graphic Canon*.

"THREE YEARS LATER..."

WHO IS HERE TO VISIT, NELLY?

HEATHCLIFF, YOU MAY RECOLLECT HIM...

THE GYPSY?! THE PLOUGHBOY?

HUSH!

YOU CANNOT CALL HIM SUCH NAMES, SIR! SHE'D BE SADLY GRIEVED TO HEAR YOU!

EDGAR!

IT'S TRUE!!

HE'S BACK!

HEATHCLIFF IS BACK!!

YOU MUST RECEIVE HIM!

YOU MUST!

I'M AFRAID THE JOY IS TOO GREAT TO BE REAL!!!

CATHERINE, TRY TO BE GLAD WITHOUT BEING ABSURD!!

THE WHOLE HOUSE NEEDN'T WITNESS YOUR WELCOMING A RUNAWAY SERVANT AS A BROTHER!

" I WAS AMAZED TO SEE THE TRANSFORMATION IN HEATHCLIFF... HE HAD GROWN A TALL, ATHLETIC, WELL-FORMED MAN. HIS UPRIGHT CARRIAGE IMPLIED HE WAS IN THE ARMY. HIS COUNTENANCE WAS OLDER IN EXPRESSION AND IN DECISION THAN MR. LINTON'S. HIS MANNER SHOWED NO SIGN OF PAST DEGRADATION, BUT NEARLY OF GRACE. "

SIT DOWN, SIR.

HE IS SCARCELY MORE DEAR TO HER THAN HER DOG...

HOW CAN SHE LOVE IN HIM WHAT HE HAS NOT?!?

PREPARE HER TO SEE ME.

IF YOU DO NOT, I WILL GAIN ACCESS BY ANY MEANS POSSIBLE.

"I WAS NERVOUS HOW A VISIT FROM MR. HEATHCLIFF WOULD AFFECT MRS. LINTON... WHO WAS QUITE CHANGED DUE TO HER ILLNESS...'"

I.... HAVE A LETTER FOR YOU.

IT'S... FROM HEATH-CLIFF.

HE'S HERE, IN THE —

CATHY!

"SHE EXPLAINED:"

HINDLY HAD HOPED TO FIND HEATHCLIFF GRIEF-STRIKEN AND UNAWARE...

THEY FOUGHT...

"BUT ANY STRUGGLE WOULD BE TERRIBLY ONE-SIDED..."

"AS HINDLY WAS BARELY SOBER ENOUGH TO STAND, MOST DAYS..."

"EDGAR AND ISABELLA MADE AMENDS..."

"HE HELPED HER SETTLE IN LONDON..."

"WHERE SHE RAISED HER SON IN PEACE."

"NOT LONG AFTER, HINDLY EARNSHAW WAS FOUND DEAD."

"THE DOCTOR SAID HE DRANK HIMSELF TO DEATH..."

"MR. LINTON'S LAWYER CONFIRMED HINDLY HAD MORTGAGED HIS ENTIRE ESTATE TO FUND HIS GAMBLING..."

THE SOLE LENDER—

AND NOW OWNER OF WUTHERING HEIGHTS—

WAS MR. HEATHCLIFF!"

MR. LINTON HAS SENT ME FOR HIS WIFE'S NEPHEW!

OH?

I'VE DECIDED TO TRY MY HAND AT CHILD-REARING, NELLY.

LINTON WILL NOT REMOVE MY LITTLE WARD, LEST I RETRIEVE MY OWN...

The Scarlet Letter

Nathaniel Hawthorne

ILLUSTRATION BY **Ali J**

I'M GOING TO ASSUME THAT MOST EVERYONE IS familiar with this staple of high school English classes. Set in the Colonial era, when Boston was still a Puritan colony, it follows the travails of Hester Prynne, who has committed adultery while her husband is still in England. An illegitimate daughter has been born, and, after serving some time in jail, Hester is forced to wear the letter "A" (for "adulterer") embroidered in red. Her husband comes into town but keeps secret his relationship with Hester. Meanwhile, the baby's father turns out to be . . . well, if you don't remember from your school days, I won't spoil it for you.

Although the novel's plot may be familiar, the reason Hawthorne wrote his masterpiece may not be. He was broke. *The Scarlet Letter* is part of a tradition of literary classics written because their authors needed the money (see also: "The Rime of the Ancient Mariner," *Strange Case of Dr. Jekyll and Mr. Hyde*, and just about everything by John Keats). Hawthorne's favorite subject was the Puritans because, as it turns out, they were his ancestors, much to his chagrin. His relation to these hyperjudgmental, militant Calvinist prudes—including one of the judges at the Salem witch trials—bothered yet fascinated him, and he dealt with it on paper.

Speaking of paper, I love the way Australian artist Ali J incorporates a bit of collage, via cut newspaper or book pages, into her illustrations of women and girls. She wanted to do a portrait of Hester Prynne, who turned out intriguingly modern and stylish but with a retro-Puritan dress that hearkens back to the bad old days of mid-1600s New England.

SOURCE

Hawthorne, Nathaniel. *Ignatius Critical Editions: The Scarlet Letter.* Edited by Mary R. Reichardt. Introduction by Aaron Urbanczyk. San Francisco: Ignatius Press, 2009.

Moby-Dick

Herman Melville

ILLUSTRATIONS BY **Matt Kish**

THE PLOT OF *MOBY-DICK* IS EASY TO SUMMARIZE: A pissed-off captain is obsessed with chasing down and killing the whale that maimed him, even if it costs him and his crew their lives. And it is more or less possible to read the novel as a great adventure story peopled with some of the best characters in fiction. But on such a simple premise, Herman Melville—a writer of popular, easy-to-digest adventure stories based on his exotic travels—created one of the most complex works of art ever. *Moby-Dick* is almost universally regarded as the greatest American novel (the only other one seriously vying for that honor is *Adventures of Huckleberry Finn*). Like some kind of great whale, *Moby-Dick* swallowed and subsumed all kinds of literature that came before—sea tales, epic quests, the Old Testament, Shakespearean and ancient Greek tragedy, sermons, soliloquies, whaling manuals, operas, parodies, and on and on. But while the novel contains all of these elements and more, it isn't simply any one of them. It sprawls out almost endlessly, in all directions, never committing to any one approach, but still managing to cohere.

It's hard to explain in so many words, but it's as if *Moby-Dick* is a self-enclosed system, an entire universe that must be taken on its own terms. And no one really knew what to make of it. *Moby-Dick* did get some good reviews when it was first published in 1851, but it also got thrashed. And it didn't catch on with the reading public. It pretty much sank like the *Pequod*, almost entirely forgotten until the early twentieth century. It was around the time of World War I, with the rise of Modernism, that the literati realized, "Holy shit, this obscure sixty-five-year-old book is a masterpiece." Yale English professor Richard H. Brodhead writes:

> When qualities like discontinuous or fragmented form, symbolic structure, stylistic thickness, and antitraditional experiment were established as literary values, *Moby-Dick*'s peculiarities could be reinterpreted as marks of greatness, not incorrigibility.

In *Why Read Moby-Dick?*, Nathaniel Philbrick tells us the reaction of two masters of Modernism:

> In 1927, William Faulkner, who would later hang a framed print of Rockwell Kent's *Captain Ahab* in his living room in Oxford, Mississippi, claimed *Moby-Dick* was the one novel by another author that he wished he had written. In 1949, the ever-competitive Ernest Hemingway wrote to his publisher Charles Scribner that as he approached the end of his career, Melville was one of the handful of writers he was still trying to beat.

Matt Kish is a librarian by trade and is reluctant to call himself an artist, with all the cultural and psychological baggage/assumptions that label brings with it. He had been self-publishing his illustrations and photos for a decade, never making an attempt to reach a wide audience, when he very modestly started a monster of a project—to create an illustration for every page of *Moby-Dick*. Inspired by Zak Smith's earlier project to do the same thing for *Gravity's Rainbow*, Matt started a blog and, on August 4, 2009, wrote four sentences explaining what he was about to do, while posting the image for the novel's famous opening sentence, "Call me Ishmael."

Little did he realize that his project would draw the attention of *Moby-Dick* fans first, then a wide range of literature lovers, art fans, publishers, and the media. It became a phenomenon and led to the brick-like book *Moby-Dick in Pictures: One Drawing for Every Page*. Everyone, including myself, was intrigued by the labor-of-love quality of such an ambitious, obsessive project with an unforgiving daily schedule. The fact that Matt is a self-trained artist added to the allure. Then there was the art itself—nothing digital, everything hand-drawn, hand-painted, hand-collaged, with a range of approaches, media, and facets as wide as the novel itself. Many of the 552 pieces were on found paper—pages of other books, business forms, technical schematics. For the selection here, Matt and I agreed upon a small set of a dozen pieces that get across some of the many forms the art took, while telling a super-condensed version of the tale. (The page numbers on the following pages refer to the Signet Classics edition of *Moby-Dick*, which is the version that Matt used.)

SOURCES

Brodhead, Richard, ed. *New Essays on Moby-Dick, or The Whale*. New York: Columbia University Press, 1982.

Philbrick, Nathaniel. *Why Read Moby-Dick?* New York: Viking, 2011.

Call me Ishmael.

[page 1]

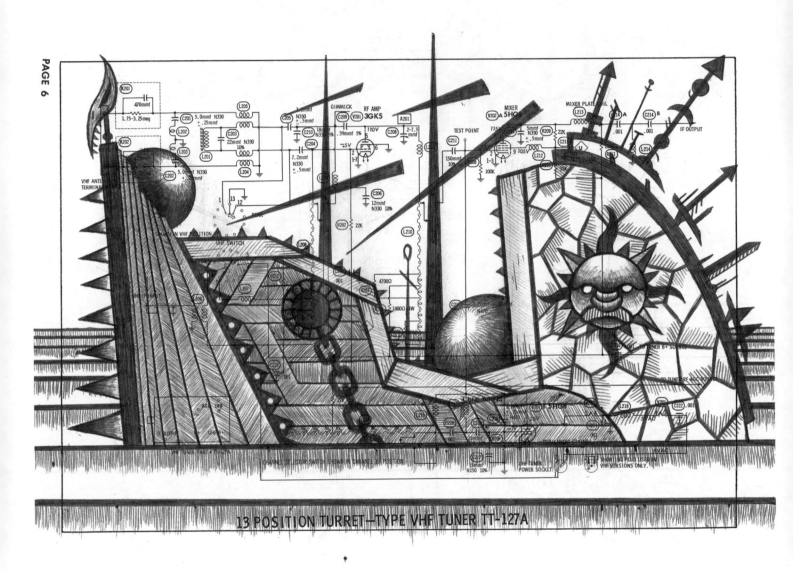

…take my word for it, you never saw such a rare old craft as this same rare old Pequod. She was a ship of the old school, rather small if anything; with an old fashioned claw-footed look about her.

[page 66]

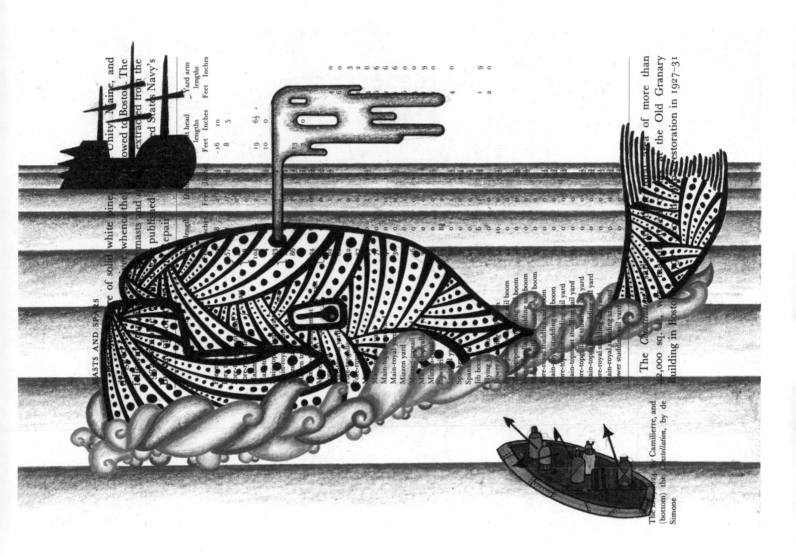

"I will have no man in my boat," said Starbuck, "who is not afraid of a whale."

[page 109]

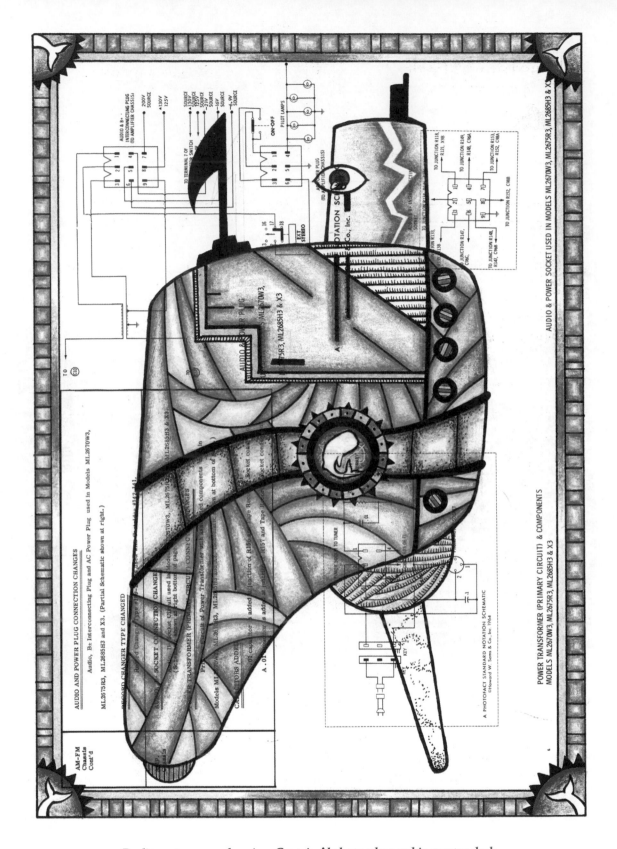

Reality outran apprehension; Captain Ahab stood upon his quarter-deck.

[page 117]

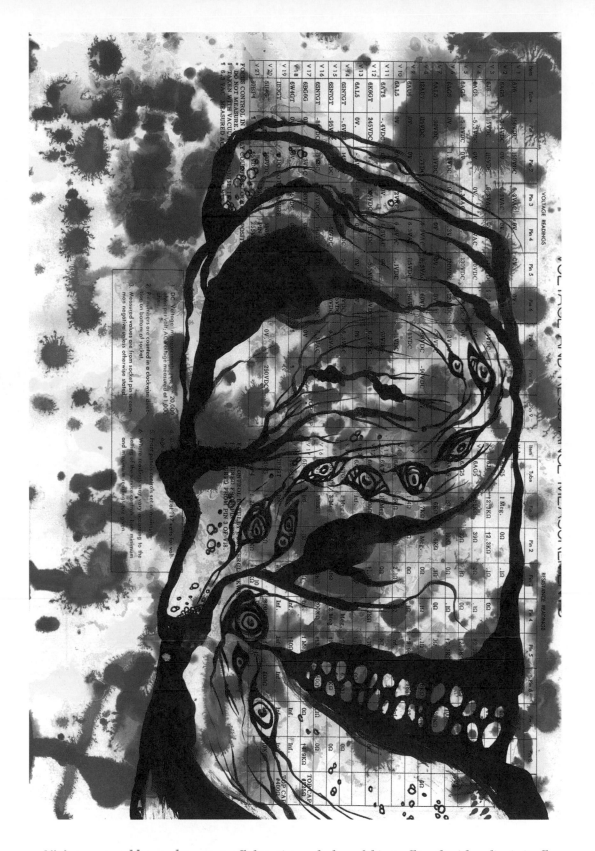

All that most maddens and torments; all that stirs up the lees of things; all truth with malice in it; all that cracks the sinews and cakes the brain; all the subtle demonisms of life and thought; all evil, to crazy Ahab, were visibly personified, and made practically assailable in Moby Dick.

[page 177]

Was it not so, O Don Miguel! thou Chilian whale, marked like an old
tortoise with mystic hieroglyphics upon the back!

[page 197]

Now, how had this noble rescue been accomplished? Why, diving after the slowly descending head, Queequeg with his keen sword had made side lunges near its bottom, so as to scuttle a large hole there; then dropping his sword, had thrust his long arm far inwards and upwards, and so hauled out our poor Tash by the head.

[page 333]

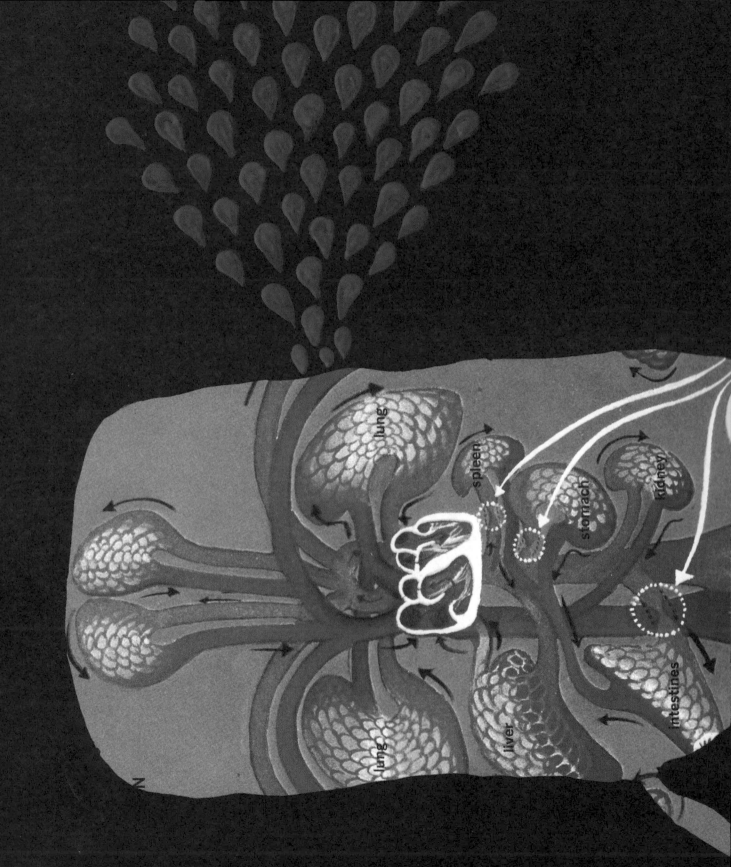

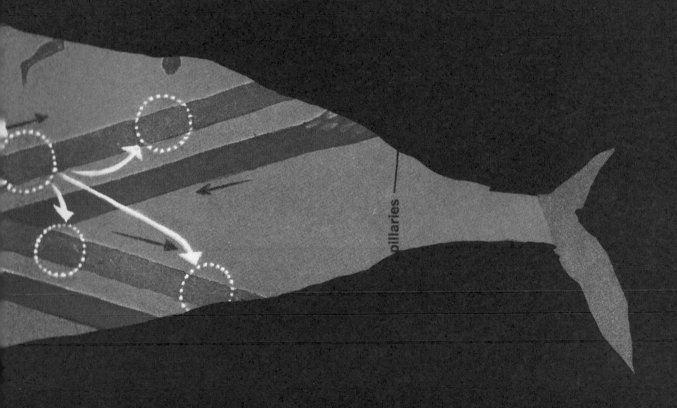

In most land animals there are certain valves or flood-gates in many of their veins, whereby when wounded, the blood is in some degree at least instantly shut off in certain directions. Not so with the whale; one of whose peculiarities it is, to have an entire nonvalvular structure of the blood-vessels, so that when pierced even by so small a point as a harpoon, a deadly drain is at once begun upon his whole arterial system . . .

[page 346]

. . . and let's finish it before the resurrection fellow comes a-calling with his horn for all legs, true or false . . .

[page 456]

"Look aloft!" cried Starbuck. "The St. Elmo's Lights (corpus sancti) corpusants! the corpusants!"

All the yard-arms were tipped with a pallid fire; and touched at each tri-pointed lightning-rod-end with three tapering white flames, each of the three tall masts was silently burning in that sulphurous air, like three gigantic wax tapers before an altar.

[page 484]

. . . Moby Dick bodily burst into view! For not by any calm and indolent spoutings; not by the peace-
able gush of that mystic fountain in his head, did the White Whale now reveal his vicinity; but by
the far more wondrous phenomenon of breaching. Rising with his utmost velocity from the furthest
depths, the Sperm Whale thus booms his entire bulk into the pure element of air, and piling up a
mountain of dazzling foam, shows his place to the distance of seven miles and more. In those moments,
the torn, enraged waves he shakes off, seem his mane; in some cases, this breaching is his act of defiance.

[page 534]

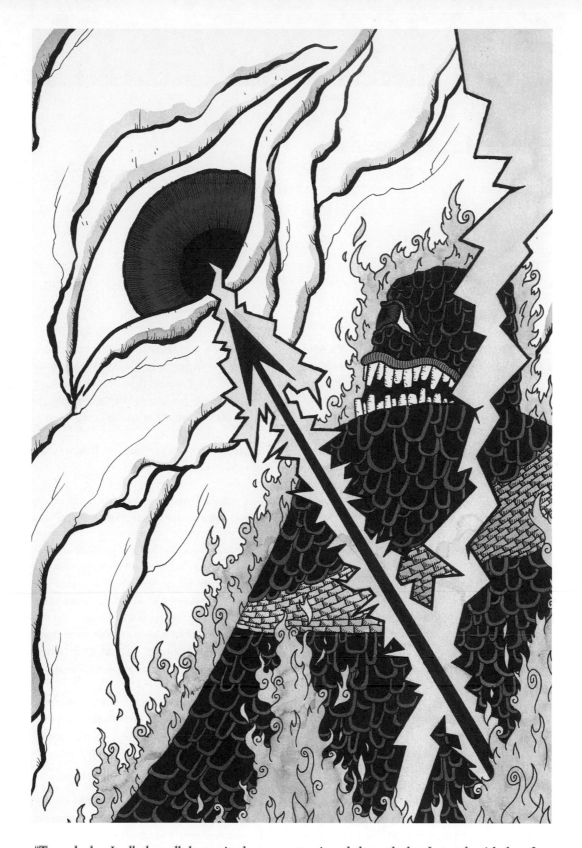

"Towards thee I roll, thou all-destroying but unconquering whale; to the last I grapple with thee; from hell's heart I stab at thee; for hate's sake I spit my last breath at thee. Sink all coffins and all hearses to one common pool! and since neither can be mine, let me then tow to pieces, while still chasing thee, though tied to thee, thou damned whale! Thus, I give up the spear!"

[page 550]

Walden

Henry David Thoreau

ART/ADAPTATION BY **John Porcellino**

ON JULY 4, 1845, ALMOST-TWENTY-EIGHT-YEAR-old Henry David Thoreau—Harvard graduate, experimental educator, surveyor, tax resister, writer for Ralph Waldo Emerson's transcendental journal *The Dial*—wanted to try an experiment in how to live. For a little over two years he settled into a bare-bones one-room house—which he built by himself—at Walden Pond, a mile and a half outside of Concord, Massachusetts. His much-quoted statement of purpose: "I went to the woods because I wished to live deliberately, to front only the essential facts of life, and see if I could not learn what it had to teach, and not, when I came to die, discover that I had not lived."

As he clearly and repeatedly discusses in *Walden*, he did not completely cut himself off from society, which seems to be the image nonreaders of the book have in mind. Usually once a week he walked into Concord to have some human contact. And he fairly regularly received visitors—strangers, townsfolk, friends—at the cabin, especially during springs and summers. But for the most part he was alone, living in an undeveloped area, and trying to singlehandedly meet all his own needs. He used some of his time to write about his experiences and thoughts, later turning these into *Walden*, which was published in 1854 and basically ignored until its greatness was recognized in the twentieth century.

Please excuse the cliché, but this is a book that changes people's lives. It's not just the joys of solitude that Thoreau describes, or his obvious love for individuals he does encounter, or his gorgeous descriptions of nature and its effects on the soul. It's also his thoughts on life, on society, on the human condition. It's his attempt to discover what really matters. *Walden* struggles with universal questions, and even though it was written by a twenty-something guy in New England more than a century and a half ago, it basically reads as if it were published this year. The critiques of capitalism and consumerism, the promotion of individualism and the inner self, the concern for the environment . . .

Every page bursts with brilliant quotations and self-contained passages, a few of which have become famous, most of which have not. It makes me suspect Thoreau was purposely filling his book with epigrams, sound bites for others to quote. Here's a sampling:

What a man thinks of himself, that it is which determines, or rather indicates, his fate.

The mass of men lead lives of quiet desperation. What is called resignation is confirmed desperation.

The greater part of what my neighbors call good I believe in my soul to be bad, and if I repent of anything, it is very likely to be my good behavior. What demon possessed me that I behaved so well? You may say the wisest thing you can, old man—you who have lived seventy years, not without honor of a kind—I hear an irresistible voice which invites me away from all that. One generation abandons the enterprises of another like stranded vessels.

Most of the luxuries, and many of the so-called comforts of life, are not only not indispensable, but positive hindrances to the elevation of mankind. With respect to luxuries and comforts, the wisest have ever lived a more simple and meager life than the poor.

But men labor under a mistake. The better part of the man is soon plowed into the soil for compost. By a seeming fate, commonly called necessity, they are employed, as it says in an old book, laying up treasures which moth and rust will corrupt and thieves break through and steal. It is a fool's life, as they will find when they get to the end of it, if not before.

There are a thousand hacking at the branches of evil to one who is striking at the root.

The winds which passed over my dwelling were such as sweep over the ridges of mountains, bearing the broken strains, or celestial parts only, of terrestrial music. The morning wind forever blows, the poem of creation is uninterrupted; but few are the ears that hear it. Olympus is but the outside of the earth everywhere.

I once had a sparrow alight upon my shoulder for a moment while I was hoeing in a village garden, and I felt that I was more distinguished by that circumstance than I should have been by any epaulet I could have worn.

It is something to be able to paint a particular picture, or to carve a statue, and so to make a few objects beautiful; but it is far more glorious to carve and paint the very atmosphere and medium through which we look, which morally we can do. To affect the quality of the day, that is the highest of arts. Every man is tasked to make his life, even in its details, worthy of the contemplation of his most elevated and critical hour.

Our life is frittered away by detail. An honest man has hardly need to count more than his ten fingers, or in extreme cases he may add his ten toes, and lump the rest. Simplicity, simplicity, simplicity! I say, let your affairs be as two or three, and not a hundred or a thousand; instead of a million count half a dozen, and keep your accounts on your thumb-nail. In the midst of this chopping sea of civilized life, such are the clouds and storms and quicksands and thousand-and-one items to be allowed for, that a man has to live, if he would not founder and go to the bottom and not make his port at all, by dead reckoning, and he must be a great calculator indeed who succeeds. Simplify, simplify.

Many a forenoon have I stolen away, preferring to spend thus the most valued part of the day; for I was rich, if not in money, in sunny hours and summer days, and spent them lavishly; nor do I regret that I did not waste more of them in the workshop or the teacher's desk.

I had no lock nor bolt but for the desk which held my papers, not even a nail to put over my latch or windows. I never fastened my door night or day, though I was to be absent several days; not even when the next fall I spent a fortnight in the woods of Maine. And yet my house was more respected than if it had been surrounded by a file of soldiers. The tired rambler could rest and warm himself by my fire, the literary amuse himself with the few books on my table, or the curious, by opening my closet door, see what was left of my dinner, and what prospect I had of a supper. Yet, though many people of every class came this way to the pond, I suffered no serious inconvenience from these sources, and I never missed anything but one small book, a volume of Homer, which perhaps was improperly gilded, and this I trust a soldier of our camp has found by this time. I am convinced, that if all men were to live as simply as I then did, thieving and robbery would be unknown. These take place only in communities where some have got more than is sufficient while others have not enough.

Creator of the long-running *King Cat* minicomic (73 issues and counting), John Porcellino is such a perfect match for Thoreau. Spare linework, chopped down to the absolute bone. Nothing unnecessary or wasteful, only what is absolutely needed to to get the point across. Simplicity, simplicity, simplicity! While studying at the Center for Cartoon Studies, he created a book-length adaptation of pieces from *Walden*—with a little material from Thoreau's extensive journals and his famous essay "On Civil Disobedience"—which was published by Hyperion. A nice, long chunk is excerpted here, including my favorite moment from *Walden*—Thoreau and the owl.

WALDEN HENRY DAVID THOREAU JOHN PORCELLINO

TO BE A PHILOSOPHER IS NOT MERELY TO HAVE SUBTLE THOUGHTS, NOR EVEN TO FOUND A SCHOOL, BUT TO SO LOVE WISDOM AS TO LIVE ACCORDING TO ITS DICTATES...

A LIFE OF SIMPLICITY, INDEPENDENCE, MAGNANIMITY, and TRUST.

IT IS TO SOLVE SOME OF THE PROBLEMS OF LIFE — NOT ONLY THEORETICALLY —

BUT PRACTICALLY...

MY PURPOSE IN GOING TO WALDEN POND WAS NOT TO LIVE CHEAPLY, NOR TO LIVE DEARLY THERE, BUT TO TRANSACT SOME PRIVATE BUSINESS WITH THE FEWEST OBSTACLES...

HOW TO GET MY LIVING HONESTLY, WITH FREEDOM LEFT FOR MY PROPER PURSUITS...

I LONG AGO LOST A HOUND, A BAY HORSE, and A TURTLE-DOVE...

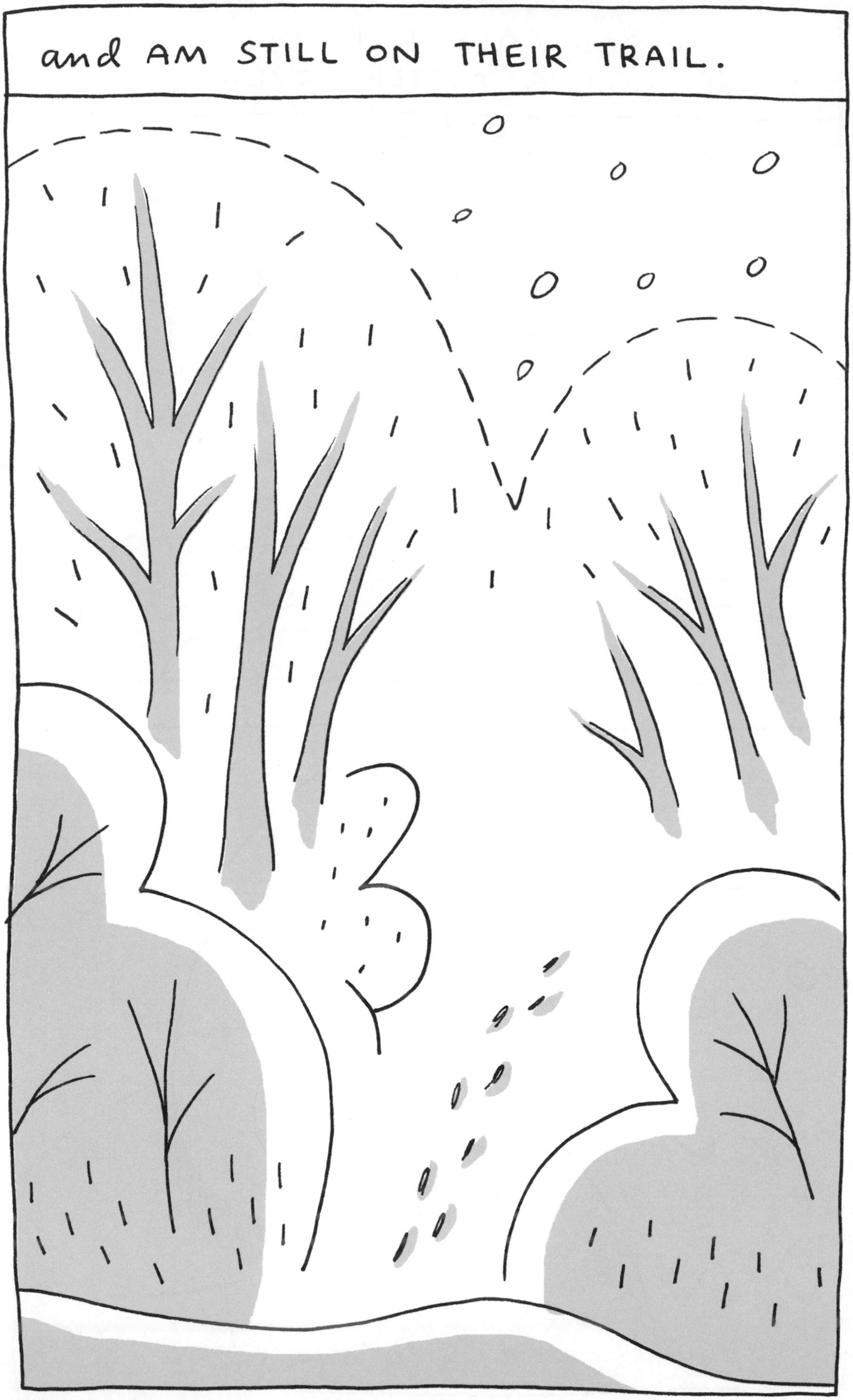
and AM STILL ON THEIR TRAIL.

CRONCH!

HOWEVER MEAN YOUR LIFE IS, MEET IT and LIVE IT...

... I AM CONVINCED, BOTH BY FAITH and EXPERIENCE, THAT TO MAINTAIN ONE'S SELF ON THIS EARTH IS NOT A HARDSHIP BUT A PASTIME, IF WE WILL LIVE SIMPLY and WISELY...

IF A MAN DOES NOT KEEP PACE WITH HIS COMPANIONS, PERHAPS IT IS BECAUSE HE HEARS A DIFFERENT DRUMMER...

LET HIM STEP TO THE MUSIC WHICH HE HEARS...

HOWEVER MEASURED OR FAR AWAY.

Leaves of Grass

Walt Whitman

ART/ADAPTATION BY **Tara Seibel**

IT'S HARD TO GET ACROSS WHAT AN ATOMIC BOMB Walt Whitman dropped on American literature and culture. Nobody had seen anything like it before. The long, loping lines of free verse. The riotous celebration of the body and all its functions, including the sexual and the excretory. The particular admiration for the male body. The whole-hearted embrace of democracy and the young country supposedly devoted to it. The devotion to the common people, the salt of the earth, the workers. The acceptance of death as nothing to fear, simply another part of life. The homegrown, full-scale mysticism. It was more than just a heady brew—it basically blew up poetry and rebuilt it from the ground up.

When *Leaves of Grass* first came out, it was a slim volume, a dozen poems and a preface taking up eighty-five pages. The first six poems were each titled "Leaves of Grass," and the second six were untitled. The long, first poem—later titled "Song of Myself"—opened with pure bravura:

> I celebrate myself,
> And what I assume you shall assume,
> For every atom belonging to me as good belongs to you.

Whitman had worked on and off as a teacher and in every position you could think of at a variety of New York newspapers—typesetter, editor, columnist, publisher. He had contributed some poems to newspapers when, in 1855, he paid for a Brooklyn printer to hand-crank 795 copies of *Leaves*. Hamilton professor Ivan Marki writes:

> Though no reliable records have survived, probably very few copies of the book were sold. A few reviews appeared, some of them discerning and sympathetic, but most of them somewhat bewildered by the new work and also offended by the sexual frankness of some of its passages. A small handful of unsigned reviews also appeared, which praised the volume in extravagant terms and in what must have appeared rather extravagant prose. These were written by the poet himself, who used his connections among the newspaper editors of New York to get them published. Apparently, they did not help sales much.

Someone who loved the book, though, was Ralph Waldo Emerson, who wrote a glowing letter to the newcomer. Whitman found a reluctant publisher for the next year's second edition, with twenty additional poems, titles for the original twelve, and revisions to "Song of Myself." The collection went through six or seven American editions (depending on how you count them), each time growing as Whitman added more poems, changed their order and grouping, and occasionally took some out, split or combined others, and always, always tinkered. The final, "death bed" edition of 1891–92 contains 293 poems. (Charting the changes among the editions is a cottage industry in academia.) By the time of this edition, Whitman was a living legend and *Leaves* was enshrined as the greatest American book of poems ever written.

Tara Seibel worked closely with legendary comics writer Harvey Pekar in the last part of his life, adapting several of his final works. Her art is often a total-package blend of spot illustrations, patterns, flourishes, hand-lettering, type, and layout and design. Here she applies her lovely approach to four short poems (in their entireties) from various editions of *Leaves of Grass*.

SOURCE

LeMaster, J. R., and Donald D. Kummings, eds. *Walt Whitman: An Encyclopedia.* New York: Garland Publishing, 1998. Selected entries reprinted on The Walt Whitman Archive (www.whitman-archive.org).

Beginners

How they are provided for upon the earth, (appearing at intervals,)
How dear and dreadful they are to the earth,
How they inure to themselves as much as to any what a paradox
appears their age,
How people respond to them, yet know them not,
How there is something relentless in their fate all times,
How all times mischoose the objects of their adulation and reward,
And how the same inexorable price must still be paid for the same
great purchase.

Leaves of grass by Walt Whitman artistic expression by Tara Seibel

When I read the Book

When I read the book, the biography famous,
And is this then (said I) what the author calls a man's life?
And so will some one when I am dead and gone write my life?
(As if any man really knew aught of my life,
Why even I myself I often think know little or nothing of my real l
Only a few hints, a few diffused faint clews and indirections
I seek for my own use to trace out here.)

To You

Stranger, if you passing meet me and desire to speak to me, why
should you not speak to me?
And why should I not speak to you?

Poets to Come

Poets to come! orators, singers, musicians to come!
Not to day is to justify me and answer what I am for,
But you, a new brood, native, athletic, continental, greater than
before known,
Arouse! for you must justify me.

I myself but write one or two indicative words for the future,
I but advance a moment only to wheel and hurry back in the darkness.

I am a man who, sauntering along without fully stopping, turns a
casual look upon you and then averts his face,
Leaving it to you to prove and define it,
Expecting the main things from you.

Leaves of Grass

Walt Whitman

ART/ADAPTATION BY **Dave Morice**

THROUGHOUT *LEAVES OF GRASS*, AND ESPECIALLY in his best-known, quintessential poem, "Song of Myself," Whitman (identifying himself as the poem's narrator) speaks of his all-encompassing nature. He is everything, all people, all of nature, "a kosmos." He is all industries, all activities, all religions, all things good and bad; he is you. "To me the converging objects of the universe perpetually flow." It sounds grandiose, but Whitman never forgets that he's also very human, "turbulent, fleshy, sensual." In the same line that he declares himself "a kosmos," he also calls himself "of Manhattan the son," a New York boy. And that's the point—*every* person is "a kosmos"; we each have everyone else within us. The entire universe flows through each of us. Elsewhere, Whitman wrote that this is indeed true of everyone, it's just that he is one of the few who is fully aware of it, who senses it. Of course, that's what being a mystic is all about: being directly in touch with that greater whole that is available to everyone, that includes everyone.

Anyway, Dave Morice decided to have a bit of fun with Whitman's grand vision. He casts Whitman as a super-hero—specifically, as a parody of Superman (Whit*man*) who also looks a tad like our culture's caricature of God—flying through the cosmos, punching out aliens, meeting an energy being, and so on. Dave is a pioneer in adapting literature—poetry, specifically—into comics. While there were efforts to turn classic prose into sequential art both before and after Dave's early work, he remains one of the very first to do this with poems. His self-published zine *Poetry Comics*, which had its main run from 1979 to 1982, not only broke new ground but created a body of work that has yet to be equaled.

As a writer, teacher, and adapter of poetry, Dave has an obvious love for Whitman's work, and his good-natured ribbing of Whitman also reveals a lot of the depth and expanse of the poet's vision. It starts off with famous lines from "Song of Myself," then quickly becomes a mash-up of bits from throughout *Leaves of Grass*. Other poems represented include "I Sing the Body Electric," "Salut au Monde!," and "Poem of the Road," with "Myself and Mine" supplying the closing lines.

WALT WHITMAN, A KOSMOS, OF MANHATTAN, THE SON,

TURBULENT, FLESHY, SENSUAL, EATING, DRINKING AND BREEDING,

NO SENTIMENTALIST, NO STANDER ABOVE MEN AND WOMEN OR APART FROM THEM,

?

NO MORE MODEST THAN IMMODEST,

!

UNSCREW THE LOCKS FROM THEIR DOORS! UNSCREW THE DOORS THEMSELVES FROM THEIR JAMBS!

FROM PAUMANOK STARTING I FLY LIKE A BIRD,

SPEEDING THROUGH SPACE,

SPEEDING THROUGH HEAVEN AND THE STARS,

SPEEDING AMID THE SEVEN SATELLITES AND THE BROAD RING, AND THE DIAMETER OF EIGHTY THOUSAND MILES,

SPEEDING WITH TAIL'D METEORS,

THROWING FIREBALLS LIKE THE REST,

I TREAD DAY AND NIGHT SUCH ROADS.

LEAVES OF GRASS WALT WHITMAN DAVE MORICE

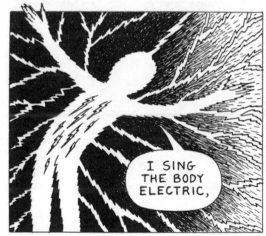

ANOTHER SELF, A DUPLICATE OF EVERYONE

SMARTLY ATTIRED, COUNTENANCE SMILING, FORM UPRIGHT,

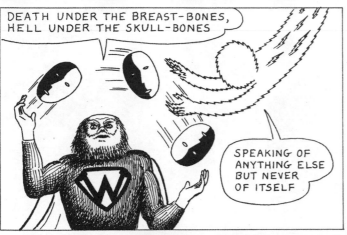

DEATH UNDER THE BREAST-BONES, HELL UNDER THE SKULL-BONES

SPEAKING OF ANYTHING ELSE BUT NEVER OF ITSELF

THEY GO! THEY GO!

I KNOW THAT THEY GO,

BUT I KNOW NOT WHERE THEY GO,

ALL PARTS AWAY FOR THE PROGRESS OF SOULS,

O TAKE MY HAND WALT WHITMAN!

WILL YOU SEEK AFAR OFF?

THE EARTH, THAT IS SUFFICIENT,

I DO NOT WANT THE CONSTELLATIONS ANY NEARER,

STILL HERE I CARRY MY OLD DELICIOUS BURDENS,

I SWEAR IT IS IMPOSSIBLE FOR ME TO GET RID OF THEM,

THE MAIN SHAPES ARISE, SHAPES OF DEMOCRACY TOTAL, RESULTS OF CENTURIES,

SHAPES BRACING THE EARTH

WHAT DO YOU SEE WALT WHITMAN?

I SEE A GREAT ROUND WONDER ROLLING THROUGH SPACE,

I SEE THE SHADED PART ON ONE SIDE WHERE THE SLEEPERS ARE SLEEPING, AND THE SUNLIT PART ON THE OTHER SIDE,

I SEE THE CITIES OF THE EARTH AND MAKE MYSELF AT RANDOM A PART OF THEM,

ARE YOU THE PRESIDENT?

THIS IS THE CITY

AND I AM ONE OF THE CITIZENS,

THE LITTLE PLENTIFUL MANNIKINS SKIPPING AROUND IN COLLARS AND TAIL'D COATS,

I AM AWARE WHO THEY ARE

I ACKNOWLEDGE THE DUPLICATES OF MYSELF, THE WEAKEST AND SHALLOWEST IS DEAREST WITH ME,

WHO ARE YOU?

AND WHAT ARE YOU SECRETLY GUILTY OF ALL YOUR LIFE?

END

226   LEAVES OF GRASS WALT WHITMAN DAVE MORICE

The Hasheesh Eater

Fitz Hugh Ludlow

ART/ADAPTATION BY **John Pierard**

THE CONFESSIONS OF AN ENGLISH OPIUM-EATER (1821) by Thomas de Quincey is the drug-taking narrative that enjoys the highest ranking in the literary canon. Trouble is, it's pretty boring and somehow manages to go its entire length with very few revealing descriptions of the effects of laudanum (a tincture of opium in alcohol, which had its heyday in the Victorian era). Thirty-five years after publication, it inspired Ivy League college student Fitz Hugh Ludlow to ingest ridiculously large doses of a potent cannabis extract being used for medical purposes (it was not, however, hashish) and write about his experiences in *The Hasheesh Eater*, which became enormously popular for a while after its 1857 publication. It's now recognized as an early classic of drug literature. In his introduction to an annotated edition of the book, David M. Gross writes:

> Not long after *The Hasheesh Eater* hit the shelves, the Gunjah Wallah Co. in New York began advertising "Hasheesh Candy". . . .
>
> John Hay, an adviser to President Lincoln who later became U.S. Secretary of State, remembered Brown University as the place "where I used to eat Hasheesh and dream dreams." And a classmate recalls that after reading Ludlow's book, Hay "must needs experiment with hasheesh a little, and see if it was such a marvelous stimulant to the imagination as Fitzhugh Ludlow affirmed. 'The night when Johnny Hay took hasheesh' marked an epoch for the dwellers in Hope College."

Within twenty-five years of the publication of *The Hasheesh Eater,* most major cities in the United States had private hashish parlors. And there was already controversy about the legality and morality of cannabis intoxication. In 1876, when tourists could stroll over to the Turkish exhibit at the Philadelphia Centennial Exposition and smoke hash pipes in a comfortable lounge, the *Illustrated Police News* would write about "The Secret Dissipation of New York Belles . . . a Hasheesh Hell on Fifth Avenue."

The Hasheesh Eater went through four editions in the late 1850s and early 1860s, each put out by Harper & Brothers. In 1903, another publishing house put [out] a reprint of the original edition—and the last complete edition until 1970.

Large portions of Ludlow's book were printed in occult, Beat, and counterculture periodicals through the decades.

John Pierard—who adapted *The Confessions of Nat Turner* earlier in this volume—now turns his attention to mind-altering substances (Jack London's alcohol-based autobiography, *John Barleycorn*, and Aldous Huxley's *The Doors of Perception* will follow in Volume 3). Ludlow's highly visual book presents numerous scenes ripe for visualization, and Pierard has given us many of the best.

SOURCE

Ludlow, Fitz Hugh. *The Annotated Hasheesh Eater.* Edited by David M. Gross. Seattle: CreateSpace, 2007.

THE HASHEESH EATER

FITZ HUGH LUDLOW

THE HASHEESH EATER:

BEING PASSAGES FROM THE LIFE OF A PYTHAGORIAN

"I WAS AWARE AT THE TIME THAT THE SYMBOLS BY WHICH I WAS TAUGHT WOULD BE MARROWLESS AND UNMEANING – THE BARE SHARD AND HUSK OF SYMBOLS..." – FITZ HUGH LUDLOW.

ADAPTED BY: J.W. PIERARD.

THE HASHEESH EATER FITZ HUGH LUDLOW JOHN PIERARD   229

I SPENT THE REMAINDER OF THE MORNING CONSULTING THE DISPENSATORY UNDER THE TITLE "CANNIBIS INDICA."

THE LITERATURE ONLY MOVED ME POWERFULLY TO CURIOSITY — I WAITED UNTIL MY FRIEND WAS OUT OF SIGHT, REMOVED A TEN-GRAIN WEIGHT PILL AND SWALLOWED IT,...

AFTER FOUR HOURS IT WAS CLEAR THAT THE DOSE HAD BEEN INSUFFICIENT,...

AFTER SEVERAL EXPERIMENTS OVER SEVERAL DAYS, I HAD COME TO THE CONCLUSION THAT I WAS UNSUSCEPTIBLE OF THE HASHEESH INFLUENCE, UNTIL ONE EVENING AT THE HOME OF AN INTIMATE FRIEND...

THE CLOCK STRUCK TEN!

HA! THE SUDDEN THRILL! VITAL FORCES SHOT THROUGH MY ENTIRE FRAME!

I DWELT IN A MARVELOUS INNER WORLD—NOW I WAS IN A GONDOLA SWEEPING THROUGH THE MOON-LIT LAGOONS OF VENICE—NOW MY SOUL CHANGED TO A VEGETABLE ESSENCE—THRILLED WITH STRANGE AND UNIMAGINED ECSTASY...

AWAKENING FOR PERHAPS THE 20th TIME, I RECOGNIZED MY SURROUNDINGS. A MUFFLED FIGURE STEPPED INTO THE PATH BEFORE ME...

HE ASKED ME TO WAIT WHILE THE SERVANT RETRIEVED A SEDATIVE. I GLANCED AT MY WATCH: 11:15. ALL WAS PERFECT SILENCE IN THE ROOM.

A SUBLIME MYSTERY BEGAN TO ENWRAP ME!

YEARS FLEW BY! I WAS A MOTE IN TIME AND SPACE!

WHEN AGAIN HE RETURNED I CONSULTED MY WATCH; 30 SECONDS HAD ELAPSED— MY GOD, I AM IN ETERNITY!

ACROSS THE FIRMAMENT A CHARIOT CAME LIKE LIGHTNING, FLASHING A GLORY OF INTENSE BRIGHTNESS— THE SABLE ANGEL TURNED AND RUSHED DOWNWARD INTO THE HORIZON — FROM AZRAEL I WAS SAVED.'

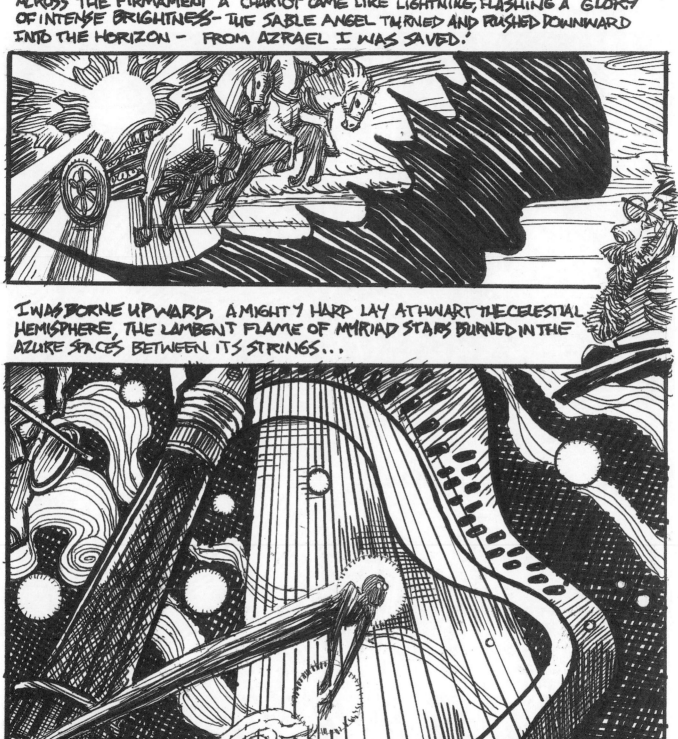

I WAS BORNE UPWARD, A MIGHTY HARP LAY ATHWART THE CELESTIAL HEMISPHERE, THE LAMBENT FLAME OF MYRIAD STARS BURNED IN THE AZURE SPACES BETWEEN ITS STRINGS...

I SWEPT THE HARP AND ALL HEAVEN THRILLED WITH AN UNUTTERABLE MUSIC.'

OVER MANY A MOUNTAIN RANGE, OVER PLAINS AND RIVERS, I HEARD WAFTED THE CRY OF MY HOUSEHOLD...

ABOVE ALL THE REST, A SISTER BITTERLY MOURNED FOR A BROTHER WHO WAS ABOUT TO DESCEND INTO HELL...

...."THERE IS INDEED SUCH A THING AS HELL," I SOLILOQUIZED, "FOR I HAVE SEEN IT! SHALL I BE SAVED?"

THE DREAD REGISTRAR SAT BEFORE ME, STRETCHED OUT TO ME THE GREAT VOLUME OF RECORD — I SCANNED THE PAGES — MY NAME WAS NOT THERE.'

UPON THE WALL APPEARED A CROSS — I EMBRACED HIS KNEES...

THAT SAD, SWEET FACE SMILED UPON ME, AND I SAW THAT MY UNSPOKEN PRAYER WAS GRANTED.

WHEN I AWOKE THE NEXT MORNING, I WAS FREE FROM ALL TRACES OF SUFFERING AS IF I HAD BEEN, ALL EVENING PREVIOUS, CRADLED IN A MOTHER'S ARMS.

On the Origin of Species

Charles Darwin

ADAPTATION BY **Michael Keller**

ART BY **Nicolle Rager Fuller**

SOME PIONEERING WORKS OF SCIENCE HAVE made their way into the overall literary canon. Starting in 1846, Charles Darwin—who had studied geology, marine biology, and some botany and entomology while at Cambridge, although he was actually in divinity school—devoted eight solid years to researching and writing a landmark four-volume work . . . on barnacles. This is not part of the canon. But his next book is.

After college, Darwin spent five years on the HMS *Beagle* expedition, mainly along the coast of South America, collecting loads of biological specimens on land and sea, which he sent back to England, making biological and geological observations, and chronicling the voyage in general. He wrote up much of this when he got home, always struggling with ill health, and in 1838 he came up with the theory of natural selection. At that point, the idea of evolution was already circulating—Darwin did not create it—but no one could satisfactorily explain how species changed, at least not without invoking God. Darwin believed that those individuals of a species less suited for a particular environment were likely to die before reproducing, while those better suited would reproduce and pass on those important traits to their offspring. Even this concept had some fuzzy forerunners— for one, Darwin's own grandfather, Erasmus Darwin, had proposed it kind of as a thought experiment—but Charles Darwin began amassing evidence for it. He wanted to build a solid case for it before publishing.

Twenty years went by. He wrote lots of other works, dealt with family issues, dissected barnacles. Then in the mail he received a short manuscript from a colleague, another natural- ist—Alfred Russel Wallace, fourteen years his junior—who had come up with essentially the same theory of natural selec- tion. Realizing he was about to get scooped, Darwin wrote his magnum opus and got it published within a year and half. When *On the Origin of Species* appeared in November 1859, it sold briskly and touched off massive scientific, cultural, and religious debates (that still haven't been resolved, as you might have noticed). Six editions were published in Darwin's lifetime, each one incorporating changes and additions as the author responded to criticisms and modified his own thinking (not always for the better, many believe).

In Charles Darwin's *On the Origin of Species: A Graphic Adaptation*, science writer Michael Keller presents the basics of *Origin* using Darwin's words from the final edition (by far the most commonly available of the six), as well as presenting the story of Darwin's research and travels, his writing of *Ori- gin*, and the reactions that it provoked. Science illustrator Nicolle Rager Fuller—whose work has been used by Duke University, the National Academy of Sciences, *Scientific American*, and MSNBC, among many others—supplies the art. The excerpt here is the crucial chapter 4, originally entitled "Natural Selection" and expanded to "Natural Selection; or The Survival of the Fittest" in the last two editions.

CHAPTER 4

NATURAL SELECTION; OR THE SURVIVAL OF THE FITTEST

HERE WE SEE THE VARIETY OF CHARACTERISTICS PRESENT IN ORGANISMS GIVES SOME A COMPETITIVE ADVANTAGE OVER OTHERS IN THE STRUGGLE TO SURVIVE. THE MOST FIT HAVE A BETTER CHANCE TO FLOURISH, MATE, AND REPRODUCE, PASSING ON THEIR SUCCESSFUL TRAITS TO FUTURE GENERATIONS.

ON THE ORIGIN OF SPECIES CHARLES DARWIN MICHAEL KELLER AND NICOLLE RAGER FULLER 239

Can it...be thought improbable, seeing that variations useful to man have undoubtedly occurred, that other variations useful in some way to each being in the great and complex battle of life, should occur in the course of many successive generations?

WHALE ANCESTORS

TIME

55 million years ago
PAKICETUS

52 million years ago
AMBULOCETUS

48 million years ago
RODHOCETUS

42 million years ago
DORUDON

37 million years ago
ODONTOCETES
(modern whales)

If such do occur, can we doubt (remembering that many more individuals are born than can possibly survive) that individuals having any advantage, however slight, over others, would have the best chance of surviving and of procreating their kind?

↑ MORE COMPETITION LESS FOOD

↓ LESS COMPETITION MORE FOOD

ON THE ORIGIN OF SPECIES CHARLES DARWIN MICHAEL KELLER AND NICOLLE RAGER FULLER

How fleeting are the wishes and efforts of man! How short his time! And consequently how poor will be his results, compared with those accumulated by Nature during whole geological periods!

As man can produce, and certainly has produced, a great result by his methodical and unconscious means of selection, what may not natural selection effect?

Man can act only on external and visible characters;

Nature, if I may be allowed to personify the natural preservation or survival of the fittest, cares nothing for appearances, except in so far as they are useful to any being.

She can act on every internal organ, on every shade of constitutional difference, on the whole machinery of life. Man selects only for his own good; Nature only for that of the being which she tends.

Can we wonder, then, that Nature's productions should be far "truer" in character than man's productions; that they should be infinitely better adapted to the most complex conditions of life, and should plainly bear the stamp of far higher workmanship?

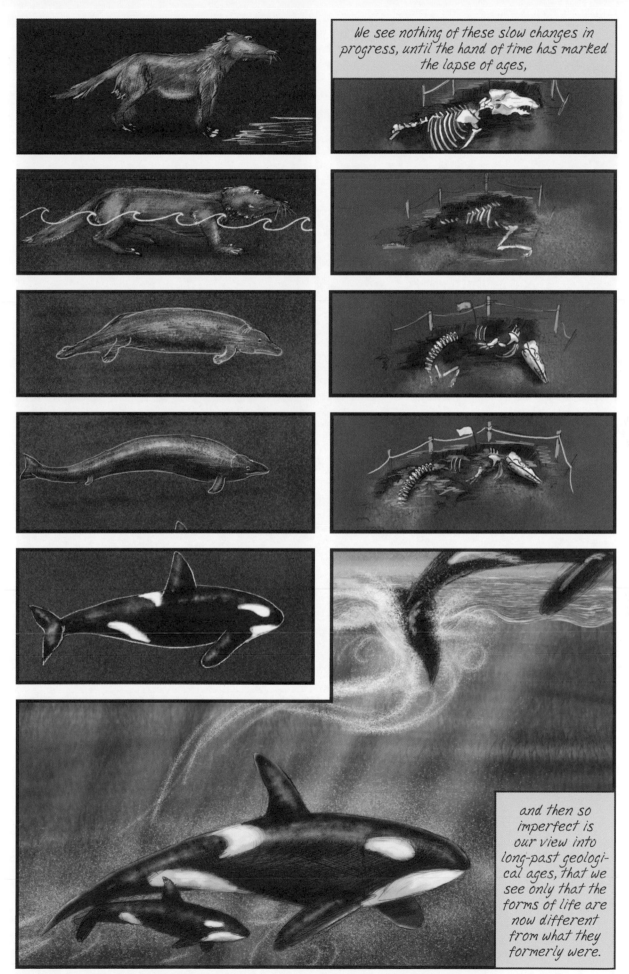

Although natural selection can act only through and for the good of each being, yet characters and structures, which we are apt to consider as of very trifling importance, may thus be acted on.

When we see leaf-eating insects green, and bark-feeders mottled-grey,

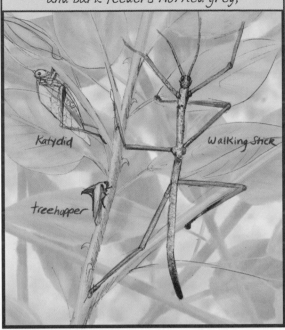

Katydid

Walking Stick

treehopper

the alpine ptarmigan white in winter, the red grouse the colour of heather, we must believe that these tints are of service to these birds and insects in preserving them from danger.

Grouse, if not destroyed at some period of their lives, would increase in countless numbers.

alpine ptarmigan
(Lagopus muta)
with winter coloring

Red grouse
(lagopus lagopus)

ON THE ORIGIN OF SPECIES CHARLES DARWIN MICHAEL KELLER AND NICOLLE RAGER FULLER

They are known to suffer largely from birds of prey,

and hawks are guided by eyesight to their prey.

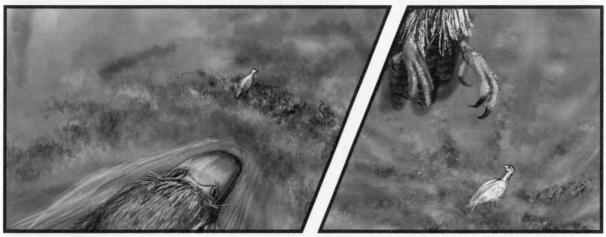

Hence natural selection might be effective in giving the proper colour to each kind of grouse, and in keeping that colour, when once acquired, true and constant.

Nor ought we to think that the occasional destruction of an animal of any particular colour would produce little effect.

ON THE ORIGIN OF SPECIES CHARLES DARWIN MICHAEL KELLER AND NICOLLE RAGER FULLER

SEXUAL SELECTION

This leads me to say a few words on what I have called Sexual Selection.

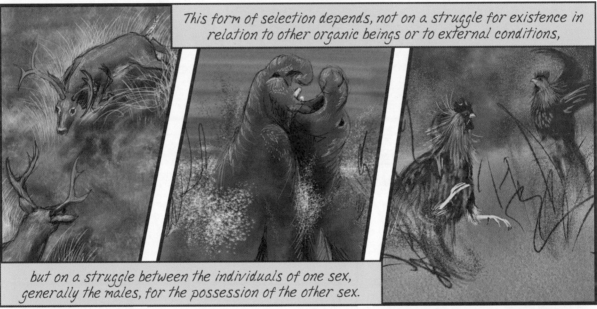

This form of selection depends, not on a struggle for existence in relation to other organic beings or to external conditions,

but on a struggle between the individuals of one sex, generally the males, for the possession of the other sex.

The result is not death to the unsuccessful competitor, but few or no offspring. Sexual selection is, therefore, less rigorous than natural selection. Generally, the most vigorous males, those which are best fitted for their places in nature, will leave most progeny.

GRANDFATHER

FATHER

SON

Sexual selection, by always allowing the victor to breed, might surely give indomitable courage, length to the spur, and strength to the wing to strike in the spurred leg

in nearly the same manner as does the brutal cockfighter by the careful selection of his best cocks.

The males of carnivorous animals are already well armed; though to them and to others, special means of defence may be given through means of sexual selection,

as the mane to the lion,

and the hooked jaw to the male salmon;

MANE MAY PROVIDE NECK PROTECTION FOR FIGHTING MALES.

A SEASONAL LOWER JAW GROWTH CALLED A KYPE MAY BE AN INDICATOR OF DOMINANCE IN MALE SALMON.

for the shield may be as important for victory, as the sword or spear.

ON THE ORIGIN OF SPECIES CHARLES DARWIN MICHAEL KELLER AND NICOLLE RAGER FULLER 247

Amongst birds, the contest is often of a more peaceful character....

The rock thrush of Guiana, birds of paradise, and some others, congregate;

and successive males display with the most elaborate care, and show off in the best manner, their gorgeous plumage.

They likewise perform strange antics before the females, which, standing by as spectators, at last choose the most attractive partner.

I can see no good reason to doubt that female birds, by selecting, during thousands of generations, the most melodious or beautiful males, according to their standard of beauty, might produce a marked effect.

ED. NOTE: ONE MATE CHOOSING ANOTHER IS NOW CALLED INTERSEXUAL SELECTION.

Thus it is, as I believe, that when the males and females of any animal have the same general habits of life, but differ in structure,

colour, or ornament, such differences have been mainly caused by sexual selection:

that is, by individual males having had, in successive generations, some slight advantage over other males,

in their weapons,

means of defence,

or charms, which they have transmitted to their male offspring alone.

I must here introduce a short digression.

What reason, it may be asked, is there for supposing—that two individuals ever concur in reproduction?

In the case of animals and plants with separated sexes, it is of course obvious that two individuals must always...unite for each birth.

FLOWER POLLINATION

With animals and plants a cross between different varieties gives vigour and fertility to the offspring.

On the other hand, close interbreeding diminishes vigour and fertility.

POSSIBLE RESULTS OF SELF-POLLINATION

BREEDING BETWEEN RELATED INDIVIDUALS

These facts alone incline me to believe that it is a general law of nature that no organic being fertilises itself for a perpetuity of generations; but that a cross with another individual is occasionally—perhaps at long intervals of time—indispensable.

We shall best understand the probable course of natural selection by taking the case of a country undergoing some slight physical change, for instance, of climate.

Species A

Species B

Species C

Arctic Climate

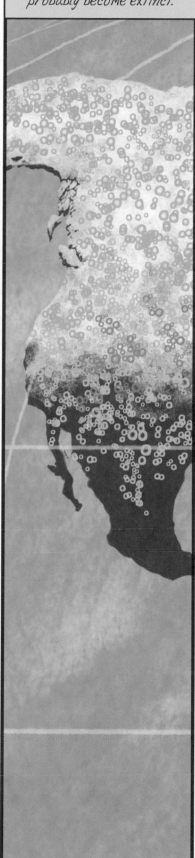

The proportional numbers of its inhabitants will almost immediately undergo a change, and some species will probably become extinct.

Species C Extinct

We may conclude, from what we have seen of the intimate and complex manner in which the inhabitants of each country are bound together, that any change in the numerical proportions of the inhabitants, independently of the change of climate itself, would seriously affect the other.

ON THE ORIGIN OF SPECIES CHARLES DARWIN MICHAEL KELLER AND NICOLLE RAGER FULLER

Though Nature grants long periods of time for the work of natural selection, she does not grant an indefinite period,

THE EXTINCT WOODLAND MUSK OX, BOOTHERIUM BOMBIFRONS, RANGED ACROSS MUCH OF NORTH AMERICA'S GRASSLANDS WITH MASTODONS AND GIANT BEAVERS. IT BECAME EXTINCT 10,000 YEARS AGO AT THE END OF THE LAST ICE AGE DUE TO CHANGING CLIMATE AND COMPETITION FROM BISON AND ITS RELATIVE, THE TUNDRA MUSK OX.

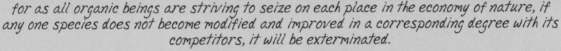

for as all organic beings are striving to seize on each place in the economy of nature, if any one species does not become modified and improved in a corresponding degree with its competitors, it will be exterminated.

THE TUNDRA MUSK OX OF TODAY, OVIBOS MOSCHATUS, IS SMALLER THAN ITS ICE AGE RELATIVES, BUT STILL SURVIVES IN THE NORTHERN TUNDRA OF THE ARCTIC.

ANOTHER RELATIVE OF THE MUSK OX, THE BIGHORN SHEEP, OVIS CANADENSIS, STILL THRIVES TODAY IN MOUNTAINOUS AREAS OF NORTH AMERICA.

Unless favourable variations be inherited by some at least of the offspring, nothing can be effected by natural selection.

Isolation also is an important element in the modification of species through natural selection.

For within a confined area, with some place in the natural polity not perfectly occupied, all the individuals varying in the right direction, though in different degrees, will tend to be preserved.

PINUS PONDEROSA

But if the area be large, its several districts will almost certainly present different conditions of life.

NORTH AMERICA PINE TREE DISTRIBUTION

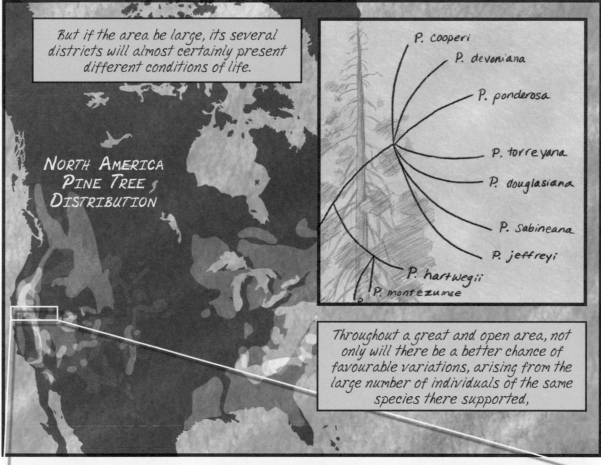

P. cooperi
P. devoniana
P. ponderosa
P. torreyana
P. douglasiana
P. sabineana
P. jeffreyi
P. hartwegii
P. montezumae

Throughout a great and open area, not only will there be a better chance of favourable variations, arising from the large number of individuals of the same species there supported,

but the conditions of life are much more complex from the large number of already existing species; and if some of these many species become modified and improved, others will have to be improved in a corresponding degree, or they will be exterminated.

Sugar Pine (Pinus lambertiana)

Ponderosa Pine (Pinus ponderosa)

Pinyon Pine (Pinus monophylla)

Knobcone Pine (Pinus attenuata) grows in mild climates. Poor soil

Coast, windy, poor soil mild temperature

Mountainous cold winters, moderate moisture

mountainous dry, cold winters

dry, hot, exposed high desert + scrub

ON THE ORIGIN OF SPECIES CHARLES DARWIN MICHAEL KELLER AND NICOLLE RAGER FULLER   253

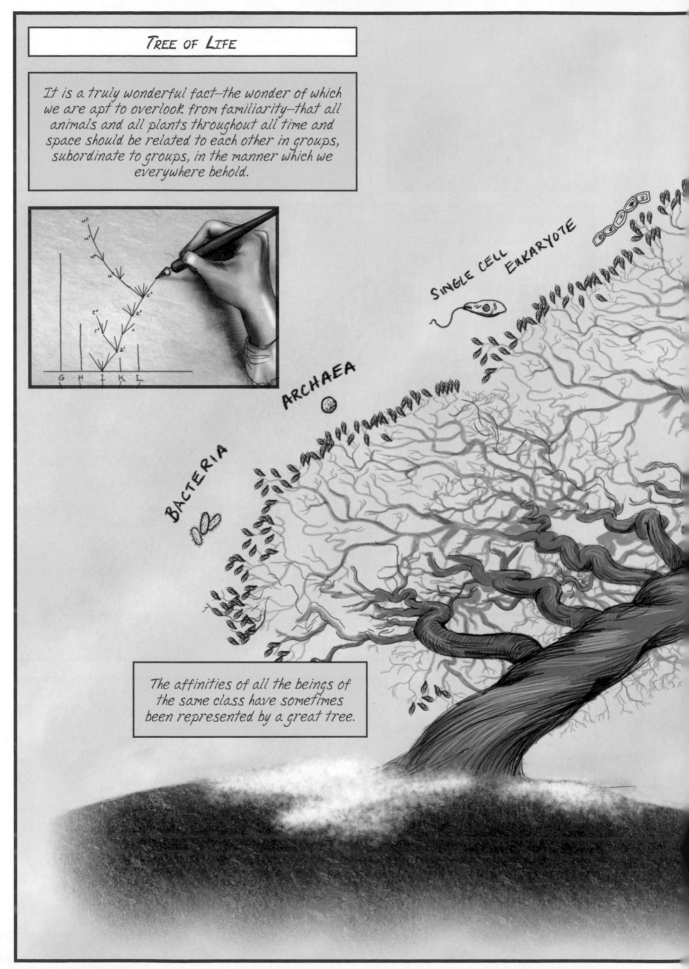

TREE OF LIFE

It is a truly wonderful fact—the wonder of which we are apt to overlook from familiarity—that all animals and all plants throughout all time and space should be related to each other in groups, subordinate to groups, in the manner which we everywhere behold.

The affinities of all the beings of the same class have sometimes been represented by a great tree.

SINGLE CELL EUKARYOTE

ARCHAEA

BACTERIA

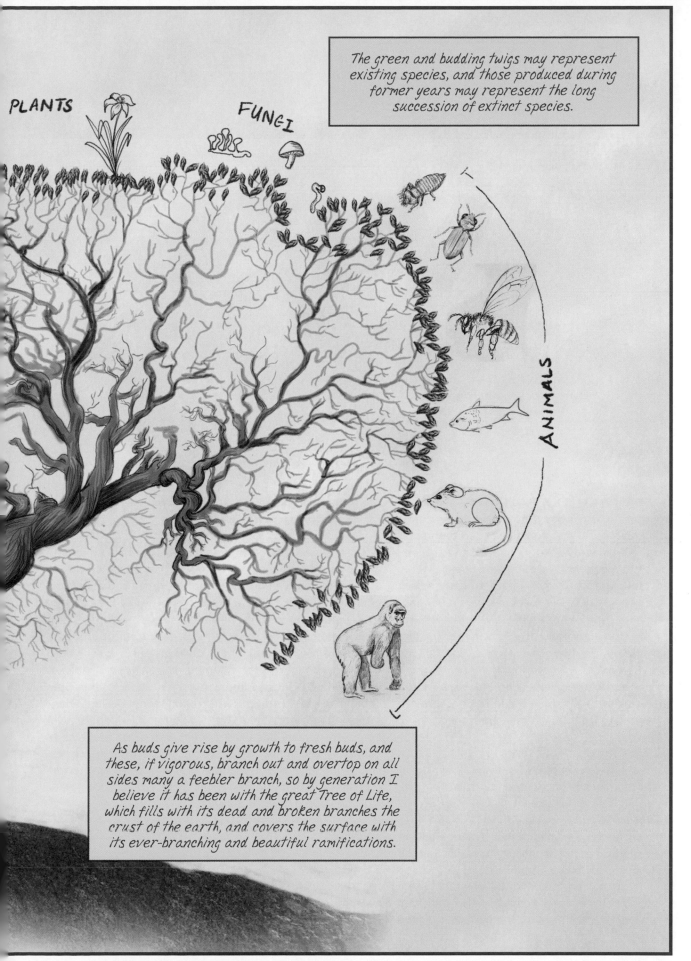

PLANTS

FUNGI

ANIMALS

The green and budding twigs may represent existing species, and those produced during former years may represent the long succession of extinct species.

As buds give rise by growth to fresh buds, and these, if vigorous, branch out and overtop on all sides many a feebler branch, so by generation I believe it has been with the great Tree of Life, which fills with its dead and broken branches the crust of the earth, and covers the surface with its ever-branching and beautiful ramifications.

"The Message from Mount Misery"

Frederick Douglass

ART/ADAPTATION BY **Seth Tobocman**

AS YOU'LL SEE FROM THE FOLLOWING PIECE, Frederick Douglass was a slave who stood up to a particularly brutal master and eventually escaped to lifelong freedom. While still a slave, he taught himself, then others, to read. Soon after becoming free, he was unexpectedly asked to give a talk at an antislavery gathering and found that he had a gift for oration. His speeches were legendary for their power, and a number of them are considered classics. (Likewise, his first autobiography, *Narrative of the Life of Frederick Douglass, an American Slave*, is a part of the literary canon. It's typically regarded as one of the three greatest American autobiographies, along with Mark Twain's and Benjamin Franklin's.) Historian David B. Chesebrough wrote of the reaction to Douglass's first major speech, given in August 1841:

> When [famed anti-slavery leader William Lloyd] Garrison followed Douglass to the platform to deliver his own speech, referring back to that oration that had just mesmerized the audience, Garrison declared that "Patrick Henry, of revolutionary fame, never made a speech more eloquent in the cause of liberty than the one we have just listened to from the lips of that hunted fugitive."
>
> A correspondent, who attended the event, reported: "One recently from the house of bondage, spoke with great power. Flinty hearts were pierced, and cold ones melted by its eloquence. Our best pleaders for the slave held their breath for fear of interrupting him."

On August 3, 1857, Douglass gave a speech in Canandaigua, New York, focusing on the 1833 law by which Britain abolished slavery in the West Indies. He praised many acts of slave resistance that are now forgotten. In the midst of these specifics, though, he made some blindingly powerful statements on the nature of freedom, oppression, and struggle in general. These portions of his speech have become probably the most famous words he ever spoke or wrote, and it is these still-incendiary statements that Seth Tobocman has illustrated. Seth is a founder of the legendary, radical magazine *World War 3 Illustrated*, which for over twenty-five years has used comics and other graphics to illuminate and fight political, social, and economic oppression around the world. His collection of Reagan-era artwork is a classic with a title that itself is classic: *You Don't Have to Fuck People Over to Survive*.

SOURCES

Chesebrough, David B. *Frederick Douglass: Oratory from Slavery*. Westport, CT: Greenwood Publishing Group, 1998.

"(1857) Frederick Douglass, 'If There Is No Struggle, There Is No Progress.'" BlackPast.org website.

POWER

HE WAS BORN A SLAVE.

AT THE AGE OF 16, HIS OWNER SENT HIM TO "MOUNT MISERY" THE PLANTATION OF EDWARD COVEY, A PROFESSIONAL "NEGRO-BREAKER". *

✱ Today, Mount Misery is the Summer house of former Defense Secretary Donald Rumsfeld.

"THE MESSAGE FROM MOUNT MISERY" FREDERICK DOUGLASS SETH TOBOCMAN

"THE MESSAGE FROM MOUNT MISERY" FREDERICK DOUGLASS SETH TOBOCMAN

FREDERICK DOUGLASS ESCAPED SLAVERY

TO BECOME ONE OF AMERICA'S GREATEST ORATORS.

SHORTLY BEFORE THE CIVIL WAR HE GAVE THIS PROPHETIC SPEECH:✱

THE GENERAL SENTIMENT OF MANKIND IS THAT A MAN WHO WILL NOT FIGHT FOR HIMSELF, WHEN HE HAS THE MEANS OF DOING SO, IS NOT WORTH BEING FOUGHT FOR BY OTHERS. AND THIS SENTIMENT IS JUST.

FOR A MAN WHO DOES NOT VALUE FREEDOM FOR HIMSELF WILL NEVER VALUE IT FOR OTHERS, OR PUT HIMSELF TO ANY INCONVENIENCE TO GAIN IT FOR OTHERS.

SUCH A MAN, THE WORLD SAYS, MAY LIE DOWN UNTIL HE HAS SENSE ENOUGH TO STAND UP. IT IS USELESS AND CRUEL TO PUT A MAN ON HIS LEGS IF THE NEXT MOMENT HIS HEAD IS TO BE BROUGHT AGAINST A CURBSTONE.

✱ Excerpted here. The original speech is longer.

"THE MESSAGE FROM MOUNT MISERY" FREDERICK DOUGLASS SETH TOBOCMAN

"THE MESSAGE FROM MOUNT MISERY" FREDERICK DOUGLASS SETH TOBOCMAN

THEY WANT THE OCEAN

WITHOUT THE AWFUL ROAR OF ITS MANY WATERS. THIS STRUGGLE MAY BE A MORAL ONE, OR IT MAY BE A PHYSICAL ONE,

AND IT MAY BE BOTH MORAL AND PHYSICAL,

BUT IT MUST BE A STRUGGLE.

"THE MESSAGE FROM MOUNT MISERY" FREDERICK DOUGLASS SETH TOBOCMAN

FIND OUT JUST WHAT ANY PEOPLE WILL QUIETLY SUBMIT TO AND YOU HAVE FOUND OUT THE EXACT MEASURE OF INJUSTICE AND WRONG WHICH SHALL BE HEAPED UPON THEM,

AND THESE WILL CONTINUE UNTIL THEY ARE RESISTED WITH EITHER WORDS OR BLOWS OR BOTH. THE LIMITS OF TYRANTS ARE PRESCRIBED BY THE ENDURANCE OF THOSE THEY OPPRESS.

POWER CONCEDES NOTHING WITHOUT A DEMAND. IT NEVER HAS AND IT NEVER WILL.

"THE MESSAGE FROM MOUNT MISERY" FREDERICK DOUGLASS SETH TOBOCMAN   263

IN LIGHT OF THESE IDEAS, NEGROES WILL BE HUNTED AT THE NORTH AND HELD AND FLOGGED AT THE SOUTH SO LONG AS THEY SUBMIT TO THOSE DEVILISH OUTRAGES AND MAKE NO RESISTANCE EITHER MORAL OR PHYSICAL.

MEN MAY NOT GET ALL THEY PAY FOR IN THIS WORLD, BUT THEY MUST CERTAINLY PAY FOR ALL THEY GET.

IF EVER WE GET FREE FROM THE OPPRESSION AND WRONGS HEAPED UPON US, WE MUST PAY FOR THEIR REMOVAL, BY LABOR,

BY SUFFERING, BY SACRIFICE, AND IF NEEDS BE, BY OUR LIVES AND THE LIVES OF OTHERS.

Illustrated by Seth Tobocman　　　　　　**Dedicated to the memory of Michael Shenker**

　"THE MESSAGE FROM MOUNT MISERY" FREDERICK DOUGLASS SETH TOBOCMAN

Les Misérables

Victor Hugo

ART/ADAPTATION BY **Tara Seibel**

LES MISÉRABLES (THE MISERABLE, THE WRETCHED) is a sprawling, almost-2,000-page novel (in the original French) about romantic and familial love, crime and punishment, poverty and revolution, and, well, sewers. Victor Hugo is the recognized grandpappy of French literature, but it wasn't always so. His introduction of Romanticism infuriated the neoclassical establishment, and Paris intellectuals were literally divided into pro-Hugo and anti-Hugo camps. Adam Gopnik of *The New Yorker* writes that during performances of Hugo's 1830 play *Hernani*: "There were literally fistfights in the audience between Romantics and conservatives." Literature is dangerous business, people.

And that's typically the case with new movements in literature and art—the present order resents and strenuously resists the new approach by these snot-nosed upstarts. Then the upstarts become the new order. So it was with Hugo, who, immediately after *Hernani*, began his literary (and political) ascendancy, becoming recognized as one of France's greatest poets and getting elected to the National Assembly. He had to abandon the writing of *Les Misérables* during his political career, but when the winds shifted and he went into exile, he finished the novel and sold it to the highest-bidding publisher, a Belgian house, which launched an international publicity campaign. After having to write so often about classic literary works that tanked when they were first released, it's a pleasure to say that *Les Misérables* was a huge success that upset the authorities and was embraced by the masses. Gopnik writes:

> In Paris, booksellers sold every copy in the three days. Factory workers were reported to have pooled their money to buy shared copies. Conservatives denounced a book that presented a criminal as a hero. Pope Pius IX placed *Les Misérables* on the Church's Index of proscribed books, and copies were publicly burned in Spain. In Paris and all around the world, *Les Misérables* solidified Hugo's reputation as the champion of the poor and the enemy of tyranny. The novel was devoured by everyone from Tolstoy and Dostoevsky to soldiers on both sides of the American Civil War.

Tara Seibel took on this humongous work and created something extraordinary that's neither fish nor fowl. The blend of small illustrations, decorative motifs, beautiful colors, text, and design makes each page a treasure. The way the type runs to the edges, sometimes hidden behind other elements and occasionally almost lost in the background, is a daring choice that makes the type very much an element of the art. But if you read the text—which is purposely not always easy or possible—you see that Tara chose some of the most key bits of this giant book, and they do indeed tell the story.

It probably helps to know the basics of the narrative, though, which is that Jean Valjean has just gotten out of prison after serving nineteen years for stealing a loaf of bread. In the town of Digne, he is given shelter by a bishop, and when Valjean steals his silverware, the bishop tells the police that it was a gift. Valjean straightens out and in another town he changes his name to Monsieur Madeleine and starts a factory. We then meet another main character, Fantine, a young girl with an illegitimate daughter, whom she leaves in the paid care of the Thénardier family. Little Cosette is tormented and used as a slave while her mother gets a job in Valjean/Madeleine's factory. Fantine's past is discovered, and she's fired from her job, forcing her into prostitution. She's arrested by another main character, Inspector Javert, and Valjean intercedes on her behalf. She's very sick and asks that Cosette be brought to her before she dies. Valjean wants to help, but he gets in hot water when his conscience compels him to admit *his* secret past to the authorities. He escapes Javert's clutches, Fantine dies, and Valjean buys Cosette's freedom, becoming her devoted caretaker. The two live on the lam in Paris for years. Then we meet Marius, a broke law student and budding radical who falls in love with Cosette when he sees her in the park. We are now about midway through the novel, and this is where Tara's adaptation ends.

SOURCE

Hugo, Victor. *Les Misérables.* Translated by Julie Rose. Introduction by Adam Gopnik. New York: Modern Library, 2009.

A graphic Adaptation: Les Misérables

Victor Hugo's

by Tara Seibel

In 1815, M. Charles Francois Bienvenu Myriel was Bishop of Digne. He was an old man of about seventy-five years of age; he had occupied the see of Digne since 1806. Although this detail has no connection whatever with the real substance of what we are about to relate, it will not be useless, if merely for the sake of exactness in all points, to mention here the various rumors and remarks which had been in circulation about him from the very moment when he arrived in the diocese. True or false, that which is said of men often occupies as important a place in their lives, and above all in their destinies, as that which they do. M. Myriel was the son of a councillor of the parliament of Aix; hence he belonged to the nobility of the bar. It was said that his father, destining him to be the heir of his own post, had married him at a very early age, eighteen or twenty, in accordance with a custom which is rather widely prevalent in parliamentary families. In spite of this marriage, however, it was said that Charles Myriel created a great deal of talk. He was well formed, though rather short in stature, elegant, graceful, intelligent; the whole of the first portion of his life had been devoted to the world and to gallantry.

The Bishop did not omit his pastoral visits because he had converted his carriage into alms. The diocese of Digne is a fatiguing one. There are very few plains and a great many mountains; hardly any roads, as we have just seen; thirty two curacies, forty one vicarships, and two hundred and eighty five auxiliary chapels. To visit all these is quite a task. The Bishop managed to do it. He went on foot when it was in the neighborhood, in a tilbury when it was on the plain, and on a donkey in the mountains. When the trip was too ... One day he arrived ... mounted on an ass ... not permit him ... town came to receive him at the ... dismount from his ass, with scar... were laughing around him. "Mons... Messieurs, citizens, I perceive ... apparent in a poor priest ... Jesus Christ. I have done so from necessity ... and not from vanity." In the course of these trips he was kind and indulgent, and talked rather than preached. He never went far in search of his arguments

His conversation was gay and affable. He put himself on a level with the two old women who had passed their lives beside him. When he laughed, it was the laugh of a schoolboy. Madame Magloire liked to call him Your Grace [Votre Grandeur]. One day he rose from his armchair, and went to his library in search of a book. This book was on one of the upper shelves. As the ... could not reach it. "Mada... [grandeur] does ... one of his dista... rarely allowed ... an opportunity ... what she ...sign... had numerous ... whom her sons ... to receive from ... the second was ... eldest was to ... succee... accustomed ... listen in silen... boasts. On one occasion, however, he appeared ... ore thoughtful than usual, while Madame de Lo was relating once again the details of all these inheritances and all these "expectations." She interrupted herself

The private life of M. Myriel was filled with the same thoughts as his public life. The voluntary poverty in which the Bishop of Digne would have been a solemn and charming sight for any one who could have viewed it close at hand. Like all old men, and like the majority of thinkers, he slept little. This brief slumber was profound. In the morning he meditated for an hour, then he said his mass, either at the cathedral or in his own house. His mass said, he broke his fast on rye bread dipped in the milk of his own cows. Then he set to work.

A Bishop is a very busy man: he must every day receive the secretary of the bishopric, who is generally a canon, and nearly every day his vicars general. He has congregations to reprove, privileges to grant, a whole ecclesiastical library to examine, prayer books, diocesan catechisms, books of hours, etc., charges to write, sermons to authorize, cures and mayors to reconcile, a clerical correspondence, administrative correspondence; on one side the State, on the other Holy See; and a thousand matters of business. What time was left to him, after these thousand details of business, and his offices and his breviary, he bestowed first on the necessitous, the sick, and the afflicted; the sick, and the necessitous, he devoted to work. Sometimes he dug in his garden; again, he read or wrote. He had but one word inally, the rumor one day spread through the town that a sort of young shepherd, who served the member of the Convention in his hovel, had in quest of a doctor; that the old wretch was dying, that paralysis was gaining on him, and that he would not live over night. "Thank God!" some added. The Bishop took his staff, put on his cloak, on account threadbare cassock and because of the evening breeze which w was setting, and had almost reached the lived at the excommunicate his staff, he recognized the over a ditch, leaped a hedge, boughs, entered a neglected padd of boldness, and suddenly, at behind lofty brambles, he caug low hut, poor, small, and clean, Near the door, in an old wheel here was a white-haired m stood a young boy, th jar of milk. While the Bishop was the old man spoke: "Thank you," he said, "I need nothing." And his smile quitted the sun to rest upon the child.

Thanks for the food and bed.

The Bishop, on his side, although he generally restrained his curiosity which, in his opinion, bordered on a fault, could not refrain from examining the member of the Convention with an attention which, as it did not have its course in sympathy, would have served his conscience a matter of reproach, in connection with any other man. A member of Convention produced on him somewhat the effect of being outside the of the law, even of the law of charity. G⸺ body almost upright, his voice vibrating, was one of th⸺ ⸺arians who form the subject of astonishment to the physic⸺ ⸺tion had many of these men, proportioned to the ⸺ ⸺man one was conscious of a man put to the proc⸺ ⸺ he preserved all the gestures of he⸺ ⸺rm tone, in the robust movement of ⸺ng calculated to disconcert death. Az⸺ the sepulchre, would have turned back, a⸺ ⸺ mistaken the door. G⸺ seemed to be dying bec⸺ there was freedom in his agony. His legs alone w⸺ ⸺there tha the shadows held him fast. His feet wer⸺ ⸺t his head survived with all the power of life, and ⸺ ⸺ight. G⸺, at this solemn moment, resembled the king i⸺ ⸺e of the Orient was flesh above and marble below.

he member of the Convention resumed:

So far as Louis XVI was concerned, I said 'no.' I did not think that I had the right to kill a man, but I felt it my duty to exterminate evil. I voted the end of the tyrant, that is to say, the end of prostitution for woman, the end of slavery for man, the end of night for the child. In voting for the Republic, I voted for that. I voted for fraternity, concord, the dawn. I have aided in the overthrow of prejudices and errors. The crumbling away of prejudices and errors causes light. We have caused the fall of the old world, and the old world, that vase of miseries, has become, through its upsetting upon the human race, an urn of joy." "Mixed joy," said the Bishop.

"Ah, Monsieur Priest, you love not the crudities of the true. Christ loved them. He seized a rod and cleared out the Temple. His scourge, full of lightnings, was a harsh speaker of truths. When he cried, 'Sinite parvulos,' he made no disbetween the little children. It would not have embarrasseg together the Dauphin of Barabbas and the Dauphin of Hence, Monsieur, is its own crown. Innocence has no nIt is as august in rags as in fleurs de lys."

"That is true," saidthe Bishop in a low voice.

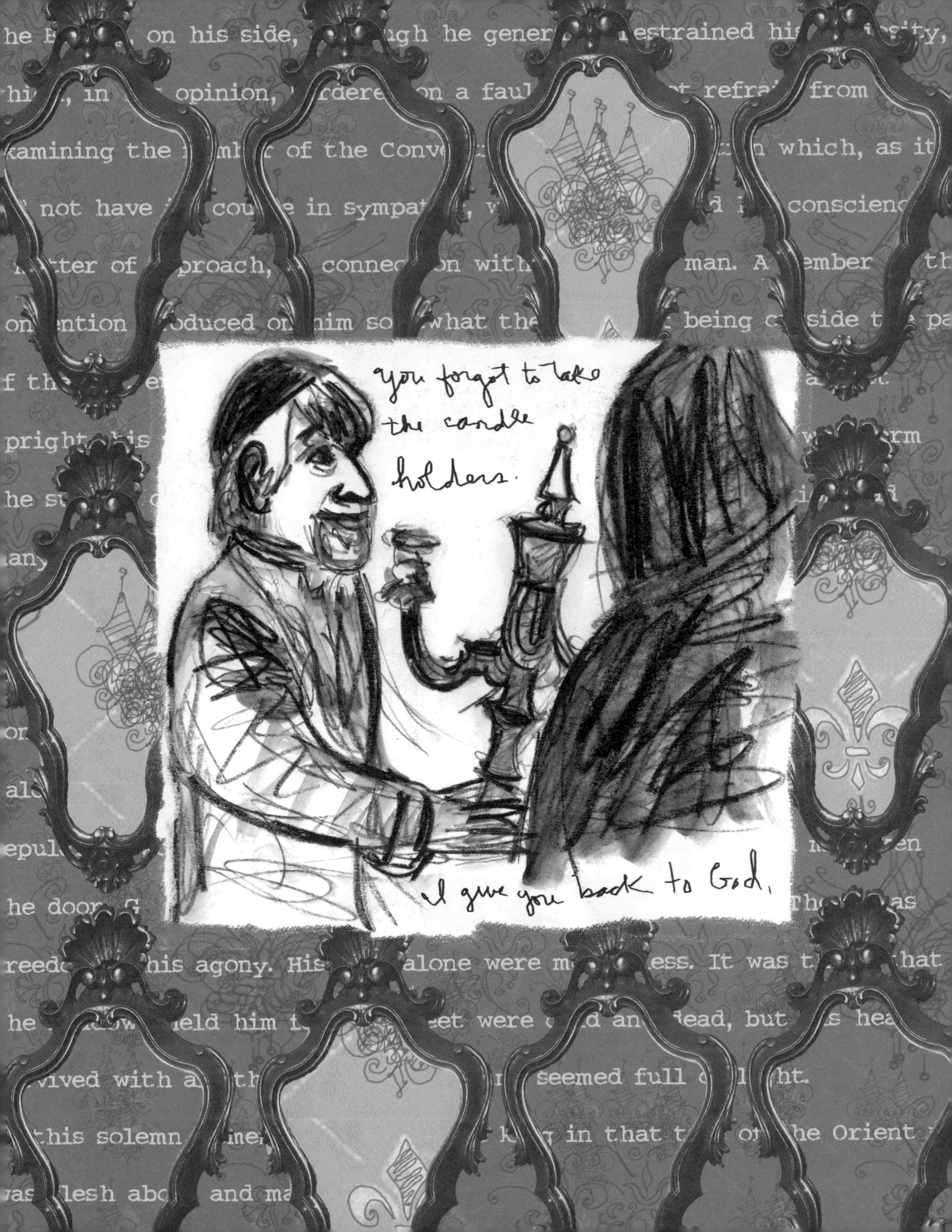
you forgot to take
the candle
holders.
I give you back to God.

Yes, sir, the people have been suffering a long while. And hold! that is not all, either; why have you just questioned me and talked to me about Louis XVII? I know you not. Ever since I have been in these parts I have dwelt in this enclosure alone, never setting foot outside, seeing no one but that child who helps me. Your name has reached me in a confused manner, it is true, and very badly pronounced, I must admit; but that signifies nothing: clever men have so many ways of imposing on that honest goodman, the people. By the way, I did not hear the sound of your carriage; you have left it yonder, behind the coppice at the fork of the roads, no doubt. I do not know you, I tell you. You have told me that you are the Bishop; but that affords me no information as to your moral personality. In short, I repeat my question. Who are you? You are a bishop; that is to say, a prince of the church, one of those men who are encrusted with heraldic bearings and revenues, and who have fat prebends

...ey were of those dwarfed natures which, if a dull fire chances to

...arm them up, easily become monstrous. There was in the woman a

...ubstratum of the brute, and in the man the material for a blackguard

...usceptible, in the highest degree, of that sort of hideous progress

...hich is accomplished in the direc...

...ouls which are continually retre...

...etrograding in life rather than ad...

...gment their deformity growing i...

...nd more impregnated with an ever a...

...man possessed such souls.

...henardier, in particular, was troub...

...e can only look at some men to...

...hey are dark in both directions...

...hreatening in front. There is something of the unknown about them.

...ne can no more answer for what they have done than for what they

...ill do. The shadow which they bear in their glance denounces them.

...ly merely hearing them utter a word or seeing them make a

...esture, one obtains a glimpse of sombre secrets in their

...ast and of sombre mysteries in their future.

It was at the epoch when the ancient classical romance which, after

having been Clelie, was no long___ ___thing but Lodoiska, still noble,

but ever more and more vulgar, h___ing fallen from Mademoiselle de

Scuderi to Ma___e Bournon ___larm___ and ___om Madam___ ___afayette to

Madame Bart___y H___t, was s___ the lov___ hear___ of the

portresses o___ ___is aflame, and ___en rav___ ___ sub___ to some

extent. Mad___e ___ar___ as ___tu___ ___g___ ___ead this

sort of book___ ___ ___v ___ ___em. ___ ___ ___ ___t brains sh___

given her, wh___, ___ ___ ___ la___ ___ort of pensive

attitude tow___ ___ ___ ___ ___mp ___ ___ain d___t, a ruffian

lettered to th___ ___ ___ma___ ___ ___at one and th___

same time, but___ ___ ___ ___ ___ ___ given to the

perusal of Piga___ ___ ___ ___ wh___ ___us ___x," as he said

in his jargon ___ ___ght, ___ ___igat___ ___ ___ ___is ___ was twelve or

fifteen years ___ ___nger ___an he ___as. La___ ___ whe___ ___ ___ir, arranged

in a romanti___ ___y drooping fash___n, b___ ___ ___ gri___ ___ ___hen the

Magaera be___ ___ ___ ___ ___ Thenardie___

but a coarse, vicious woman, ___ ___ ___led in stupid romances. Now

one cannot read nonsense with impunity. The result was that her

eldest daughter was named Eponine; as for the younger, the poor litt___

came near being called Gulnare; I know not to what diversion, effect___

hanks to the traveller's fifty s... rancs, Thenardier had been able

o avoid a protest and to hono... ...ature. On the following month

hey were again in need of ...oney. The wom... took Cosette's outfit to

...aris, and pawned it at the p...nbroker's ... sixty francs. As soon

...s that sum was spent, the The...rdiers ...rew accustomed to look on the

...ttle girl merely as a child wh... ...h... were caring for out of charity,

...nd they treated her accordingly. ... she had no longer any clothes,

...ressed her in the cast off pet... coats ...d chemises of the Thenardier

...rats; that is to say, in rags. ...ey fed ...er on what all the rest

...ad left ...a little better th... ...the dog, a ...ttle worse than the cat.

...oreover, the cat and the d... were her h...itual table companions;

...osette ate with them under t... ...rom a wooden bowl similar to

...heirs.

It is sad to think that the love of a mother can possess villainous aspects. Little as was the space occupied by Cosette, it seemed to her as though it were taken from her own, and that that little child diminished the air which her daughters breathed. This woman, like many women of her sort, had a load of caresses and a burden of blows and injuries to dispense each day. If she had not had Cosette, it is certain that her daughters, idolized as they were, would have received the whole of it; but the stranger did them the service to divert the blows to herself. received nothing but caresses. Cosette could not make a motion which did not draw down upon her head a heavy shower of violent blows and unmerited chastisement. The sweet, feeble being, who should not have understood anything of this world or of God, incessantly punished, scolded, ill used, beaten, and seeing beside her two little creatures like herself, who lived in a ray of dawn!

A year passed; then another. People in the village said:

"Those Thenardiers are good people.They are not rich, and yet they are bringing up a poor child who was abandoned on their hands!"

They thought that Cosette's mother had forgotten her.

In the meanwhile, Thenardier, having learned, it is impossible to say by what obscure means, that the child was probably a bastard, and that the mother could not acknowledge it, exacted fifteen francs a month, sayingthat "the creature" was growing and "eating," and threatening to sendher away. "Let her not bother me," he exclaimed, "or I'll fire her brat right into the middle of her secrets. I must have an increase." The mother paid the fifteen francs.

From year to year the child grew, and so did her wretchedness.

As long as Cosette was little, she was the scape goat of the two other children; as soon as she began to develop a little, that is to say, before she was even five years old, she became the servant of the household.

Fantine

injustice had made her peevish, and misery had made her ugly.

Nothing remained to her except her beautiful eyes, which inspired

pain, because, large as they were, it seemed as though one beheld in

them a stilllarger amount of sadness. It was a heart breaking thing

to see this poor child, not yet six years old, shivering in the winter

in her old rags of linen, full of holes, sweeping the street before

daylight, with an enormous broom in her tiny red hands,

and a tear in her great eyes.

She was called the Lark in the neighborhood. The populace, who are

fond of these figures of speech, had taken a fancy to bestow this

name on this trembling, frightened, and shivering little creature, no

bigger than a bird, who was awake every morning before any one else

in the house or the village, and was always in the street or the

fields before daybreak. Only the little lark never sang.

THE HISTORY OF A PROGRESS IN BLACK GLASS TRINKETS

And in the meantime, what had become of that mother who according to the people at Montfermeil, seemed to have abandoned her child?

Where was she? What was she doing?

After leaving her little Cosette with the Thenardiers, she had continued her journey, and had reached M. sur M.

This, it will be remembered, was in 1818.

Fantine had quitted her province ten years before. M. sur M. had changed its aspect. While Fantine had been slowly descending from wretchedness to wretchedness, her native town had prospered.

About two years previously one of those industrial facts which are the grand events of small districts had taken place.

This detail is important, and we regard it as useful to develop it at length; we should almost say, to underline it.

MADELEINE. He was a man about fifty years of age, who had a preoccupied air, and who was good. That was all that could be said about him. Thanks to the rapid progress of the industry which he had so admirably re constructed, M. sur M. had become a rather important centre of trade. Spain, which consumes a good deal of black made enormous purchases there each year. M. sur M. almost rivalled London and Berlin in this branch of commerce. Father Madeleine's profits were such, that at the end of the second year he was able to erect a large factory, in which there were two vast workrooms, one for the men, and the other for women. Any one who was hungry could present himself there, and was sure of finding employment and bread. Father Madeleine required of the men good will, of the women pure morals, and of all, probity. He had separated the work rooms in order to separate the sexes, and so that the women and girls might remain discreet. On this point he was inflexible. It was the only thing in which he was in a manner intolerant. He was all the more firmly set on this severity, since M. sur M., being a garrison town, opportunities for corruption abounded. However, his coming had been a boon, and his presence was a godsend.

Nevertheless, in 1819 a rumor one morning circulated through the town to the effect that, on the representations of the prefect and in consideration of the services rendered by him to the country, Father Madeleine was to be appointed by the King, mayor of M. sur M. Those who had pronounced this new comer to be "an ambitious fellow," seized with delight on this opportunity which all men desire, to exclaim, "There! what did we say!" All M. sur M. was in an uproar. The rumor was well founded. Several days later the appointment appeared in the Moniteur. On the following day Father Madeleine refused.

antine was seized with a fit of trembling.

My child!" she cried, "to go and fetch my child! She is not here, hen! Answer me, sister; where is Cosette? I want my child! Monsieur Iadeleine! Monsieur le Maire!" Javert stamped his foot.

le stared intently at Fantine, and added, once more taking into his rasp Jean Valjean's cravat, shirt and collar:

antine raised herself in bed with a bound, supporting herself on her tiffened arms and on both hands: she gazed at Jean Valjean, she gazed t Javert, she gazed at the nun, she opened her mouth as though to peak; a rattle proceeded from the depths of her throat, her teeth hattered; she stretched out her arms in her agony, opening her ands convulsively, and fumbling about her like a drowning erson; then suddenly fell back on her pillow. Her head struck the ead board of the bed and fell forwards on her breast, with gaping outh and staring, sightless eyes.

he was dead.

Jean Valjean turned his back on him and walked in the dark.

Sadness, uneasiness, anxiety, depression, this fresh misfortune of being forced to flee by night, to seek a chance refuge in Paris for Cosette and himself, the necessity of regulating his pace to the pace of the child all this, without his being aware of it, had altered Jean Valjean's walk, and impressed on his bearing such senility, that the police themselves, incarnate in the person of Javert, might, and did in fact, make a mistake. The impossibility of approaching too close, his costume of an emigre preceptor, the declaration of Thenardier which made a grandfather of him, and, finally, the belief in his death in prison, added still further to the uncertainty which gathered thick in Javert's mind.

So Fantine was buried in the free corner of the cemetery which belongs to anybody and everybody, and where the poor are lost. Fortunately, God knows where to find the soul again. Fantine was laid in the shade, among the first bones that came to hand; she was subjected to the promiscuousness of ashes. She was thrown into the public grave. Her grave resembled her bed.

Cosette crawled out of the sort of hole in which she had hidden herself. The Thenardier resumed: "Mademoiselle Dog lack name, go and water that horse." "But, M——," said Cosette, feebly, "there is no water." The Thenardier threw the street door wide open: "Well, go and get some, then." Cosette dropped her head and went for an empty bucket which stood near the chimney corner. This bucket was bigger than she was, and the child could have set down in it at her ease.

The Thenardier returned to her stove, and tasted what was in the stewpan, with a wooden spoon, grumbling the while: "There's plenty in the spring. There never was such a malicious creature as that. I think I should have done better to strain my onions." Then she rummaged in a drawer which contained sous, pepper, and shallots.

"See here, Mam'selle Toad," she said, "on your way back, you will get a big loaf from the baker. Here's a fifteen sou piece."

The child had laid her head on a stone and fallen asleep.

He sat down beside her and began to think. Little by little, as he

gazed at her, he grew calm and regained possession of his

freedom of mind. He clearly perceived this truth, the foundation of

his life henceforth, that so long as she was there, so long as he had

her near him, he should need nothing except for her, he should fear

nothing except for her. He was not even conscious that he was very

cold, since he had taken off his coat to cover her.

If the tape was pulled, and someone heard a voice very near at

hand, which made one start, "Who is there?" the voice demanded.

It was a woman's voice, a gentle voice, so gentle that it was mournful.

Here, again, there was a magical word which it was necessary to know.

If one did not know it, the voice ceased, the wall became silent once

more, as though the terrified obscurity of the sepulchre had been

on the other side of it. If one knew the password, the voice

resumed, "Enter on the right."

For Cosette laughed now.

Cosette's face had even undergone a change, to a certain extent. The gloom had disappeared from it. A smile is the same as sunshine; it banishes winter from the human countenance.

Paris is always showing its teeth; when it is not scolding it is laughing. Such is Paris. The smoke of its roofs forms the ideas of the universe. A heap of mud and stone, if you will, but, above all, a moral being. It is more than great, it is immense. Why? Because it is daring. To dare; that is the price of progress.

h!" murmured Marius, "how beautiful you are! I dare not look at you. is all over with me when I contemplate you. You are a grace. know not what is the matter with me. The hem of your gown, when e tip of your shoe peeps from beneath, upsets me. And then, what enchanted gleam when you open your thought even but a little! u talk astonishingly good sense. It seems to me at times that you re a dream. Speak, I listen, I admire. Oh Cosette! how strange it is d how charming! I am really beside myself. You are adorable, ademoiselle. I study your feet with the icroscope and your soul with the elescope."

"Because I Could Not Stop for Death"

Emily Dickinson

ART/ADAPTATION BY **Dame Darcy**

THE WORLD WAS NOT READY FOR EMILY DICKINSON. Her short, dash-filled, profound, highly elliptical (at times, some would say, obtuse) poems were from another universe than the verses coming from her Victorian brethren. "Tell the truth," she famously said, "but tell it slant." It was too slant for anyone to comprehend at the time. Less than a dozen of her poems were published while she was alive, all but one running in newspapers, and not a single one of them ran with attribution. Even then the editors "normalized" her punctuation and phrasing in an attempt to turn her into a garden-variety Victorian poet.

Essayist and cultural commentator Cristina Nehring put it as well and as fiercely as anyone could:

> Dickinson's editor friends failed with superhuman regularity to see that they were dealing with the most original and intense poetic talent of their period—and a great number of other periods as well. Her poems went almost uniformly unpublished in her lifetime—not entirely, as is sometimes thought, because of her seclusion and unwillingness to show her work—but as much for the resilient stupidity of her literary allies. There was hardly a moment in her adult life that she was not vigorously exchanging poems and letters with a man who might have published her verse as easily as he tied his shoes in the morning.

It's still astonishing to realize that one of the most amazing bodies of work ever produced by a poet simply sat in a trunk during that poet's lifetime. After Dickinson's death in 1886, her younger sister found her hand-bound notebooks, brimming with poems. They began to get published—in altered form—starting four years later, and despite their popularity, no one bothered to publish the poems as Dickinson wrote them until the 1950s.

"Because I Could Not Stop for Death" (which, like almost all of Dickinson's poems, is actually untitled) is one of her most famous works. Like a large percentage of her poetry, it concerns death, presenting one amazing image after another as the narrator is picked up in a carriage driven by the Grim Reaper. The legendary Dame Darcy—illustrator, animator, painter, doll-maker, musician, among her other hats—is the perfect pairing for Dickinson. Both of them often deal with the darkness but never get wrapped up in it, never get nihilistic. Notice that Darcy has transformed Dickinson's grave into a fairy house. . . .

SOURCE

Nehring, Cristina. *A Vindication of Love: Reclaiming Romance for the Twenty-first Century.* New York: HarperCollins, 2009.

Website of the Emily Dickinson Museum, Amherst, MA (www.emilydickinsonmuseum.org).

Because I Could Not Stop For Death ~ by: Emily Dickinson
Illustrations by: Dame Darcy

Because I could not stop for Death, He kindly stopped for me; The carriage held but just ourselves

And Immortality

We slowly drove, he knew no haste, And I had put away My labor and my

leisure too for his "civility.

We passed the school where children played, their lessons scarcely done; We passed the feilds of gazing grain We passed the setting sun...

"I Taste a Liquor Never Brewed"

Emily Dickinson

ART/ADAPTATION BY **Diana Evans**

HERE WE SEE ANOTHER MAJOR FACET OF EMILY Dickinson's work. She wrote about death and dying an awful lot (see the previous "Because I Could Not Stop for Death"), but she also wrote bright, beautiful hymns to nature. "I Taste a Liquor Never Brewed" buzzes with phrases capturing the intoxication that the outdoors induces. The poem's narrator is a "debauchee of dew." The clear, wide-open skies are "inns of molten blue." Butterflies drink "drams" of nectar from flowers. It's one of the greatest celebrations of nature ever written, without an ounce of darkness or irony. The ecstatic mood is reflected beautifully in this saturated adaptation by Diana Evans, who often illustrates children's books.

Given Dickinson's masterful range, it's no wonder that Harold Bloom, preeminent literature professor and champion of the Western canon, has marveled at her "astonishing cognitive originality, surpassed only by Shakespeare, among the poets," with "a mind so original and powerful that we scarcely have begun, even now, to catch up with her."

SOURCE

Bloom, Harold, ed. *Bloom's Modern Critical Reviews: Emily Dickinson* (new ed.). New York: Chelsea House Publications, 2008.

I taste a liquor never brewed,
From tankards scooped in pearl;
Not all the vats upon the Rhine
Yield such an alcohol!

Inebriate of air am I,
And debauchee of dew,
Reeling, through endless summer days,
From inns of molten blue.

When landlords turn the drunken bee
Out of the foxglove's door,
When butterflies renounce their drams,
I shall but drink the more!

Till seraphs swing their snowy hats,
And saints to windows run,
To see the little tippler
Leaning against the sun!

- Emily Dickinson

Letter to George Sand

Gustave Flaubert

ART/ADAPTATION BY **Corinne Mucha**

LETTERS ARE A SOMEWHAT OVERLOOKED PART of the literary canon. Sure, they almost always weren't intended for publication, but they get published anyway because, really, anytime you have the greatest writers in history putting pen to paper, you're going to get something worth reading. Robert Browning and Elizabeth Barrett wrote 573 love letters to each other. D. H. Lawrence wrote 5,500 letters. Emily Dickinson is thought to have written 10,000 letters, of which 10 percent survive and have been published. Samuel Beckett wrote a staggering 15,000 letters over the course of his life, and Voltaire penned over 20,000. Mark Twain wrote at least 11,000. Marcel Proust's collected letters take up twenty-one volumes, and that doesn't include all of them. *The Letters of Ernest Hemingway* is projected to be at least sixteen volumes by the time it's completed in the 2030s. (All of which is enough to make you wonder how these writers, and others like them, had the time to write their prose, plays, and poetry, not to mention leading full lives, as Voltaire and Hemingway did.)

Gustave Flaubert, one of France's greatest writers, is known as a consummate stylist, obsessed with crafting the perfect phrase, the perfect sentence, the perfect paragraph. . . . His *Madame Bovary* is a masterpiece of world literature (although many people—and this included the author himself—consider *The Temptation of Saint Anthony* his greatest work). Flaubert wrote around 3,500 letters that have been published—plus many others that have been lost—and he lavished much care upon them, resulting in a number of missives that are considered first-rate works of literature. This is especially true of his youthful love letters to the poet Louise Colet and his later correspondence with George Sand—the pen name of French novelist and playwright Amantine Dupin, who not only took a male pseudonym but also dressed in men's clothes and smoked in public. Their full exchange was published in 1884 and remains a classic.

In one surprising letter to Sand (apparently written in September 1866), Flaubert not only expresses his belief in reincarnation but goes on to enumerate his previous lives. Philadelphia artist Corinne Mucha takes us through the ages with her charming style.

DEAR MASTER

an excerpt from a letter from Gustave Flaubert to George Sand ~ drawn by CORINNE MUCHA

FLAUBERT
(1821 - 1880)

ONE oF France's Greatest writers, FAMOUS FOR HIS MASTERPIECE, MADAME BOVARY,—

MADAME BOVARY

WAS ALSO A LETTER WRITER.

Dear pen pal, scribble scribble

FOR 12 years he exchanged letters with another famous French novelist, George Sand,

A.K.A. AMANTINE DUPIN, (1804 - 1876)

wearer of men's clothing, cigar smoker, famous for her love affairs as well as her prose.

At the time of their correspondence, both were past the wildness of youth. Flaubert was a grumpy hermit of 40. Sand, 17 years his senior, was enjoying a settled, less saucy, period of her life.

They were not natural allies, and often disagreed. Even their basic views of art contrasted greatly. To her, art was a means of salvation, an expression of love and idealism. To him, it was an escape, and a way to critique society.

Despite their differences, he treated her with utmost respect, addressing her as "dear master" in his letters. She treated him like a mother, offering sympathy and wisdom.

Together, they helped one another grow old.

LA POSTE

But what does growing old matter, if your spirit lives on forever? In one letter, Flaubert offered Sand his fantastical view of other lives.

I don't experience, as you do, the feeling of a life which is beginning, the stupefaction of a newly commenced existence.

IT SEEMS TO ME, ON THE CONTRARY, that I have ALWAYS Lived!

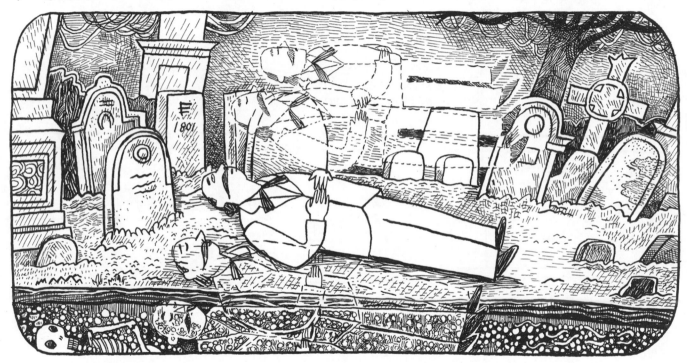

And I possess memories which go back to the pharoahs.

I see myself clearly, at different ages of history, practicing different professions, and in many sorts of fortune.

My present personality is the result of my lost personalities.

I have been a boatman on the Nile.

a Leno in Rome, at the time of the Punic Wars,

a Greek rhetorician in Subura, where I was devoured by insects.

LETTER TO GEORGE SAND GUSTAVE FLAUBERT CORINNE MUCHA

I died during the Crusade from having eaten too many grapes on the Syrian shore.

I have been a pirate, monk, mountebank, and coachman!

PERHAPS EVEN....

AN EMPEROR OF THE EAST!

MANY THINGS would be explained if we could know our real genealogy

For since the elements which make a man are limited, should not the same combinations reproduce themselves?

Alice's Adventures in Wonderland
and Through the Looking-Glass

Lewis Carroll

ART/ADAPTATION BY **Dame Darcy**

AT THE BEGINNING OF THE VOLUME, I WROTE that "Kubla Khan" has the most famous creation story in literature, but that honor is at least shared, if not surpassed, by *Alice's Adventures in Wonderland*. On July 4, 1862, Charles Dodgson—a graduate student and lecturer in mathematics at Christ Church College at the University of Oxford—went on a rowing expedition with the three daughters of Henry Liddell, the dean of Christ Church. The middle girl, Alice, then ten years old, asked Dodgson to tell them a story as they floated along the Thames, and, as he had before, he regaled them with tales of a girl named Alice who fell down a rabbit hole and ended up in a strange place.

Alice asked him to write down these stories, and after some delay, Dodgson did. Before giving Alice the handwritten manuscript—*Alice's Adventures under Ground*, which he himself illustrated—Dodgson showed it to his friend George MacDonald, a writer of fantasy and fairy tales. MacDonald's children went nuts for it, which spurred Dodgson to show it to the publisher Macmillan. Dodgson presented Alice with the manuscript in November 1864, and the following year Macmillan published a greatly expanded version (almost twice the original length) called *Alice's Adventures in Wonderland*, under Dodgson's pen name, Lewis Carroll. It was an immediate, overwhelming success. Six years later, he followed up with *Through the Looking-Glass, and What Alice Found There,* a darker, more sophisticated novel of Alice's further adventures. They are the works of "children's literature" that have by far the highest ranking in the overall literary canon.

A large part of what makes them so amazing—besides being works of sheer bravado of the imagination—is that they can be read on many levels, interpreted many ways. Some critics have pointed out that until the *Alice* novels, all books for children were meant to teach the kiddies a lesson and were filled with heavy-handed moralizing and instructions for proper behavior. The *Alice* books were the first to dispense with this didactic approach and actually *take the side of the children*. Wonderland is the ridiculous adult world, filled with nutty characters who do things that don't make any sense because, well, that's just the way that things are done. Alice is puzzled and frazzled by these idiotic rules and rituals and by the grown-ups (human and animal) who unquestioningly engage in them.

But wait. Maybe Wonderland is a joyfully bizarre, anarchic world, and Alice is simply a stick in the mud who can't abide such nonsense. Or, in a similar vein, perhaps Wonderland is the outer reaches of the British Empire, and the characters are the natives with their age-old customs. Alice is the epitome of the uptight, close-minded Victorian Brit who gasps and "my word!"s when exposed to such uncivilized behavior. Or is it a drug text describing altered states? The hookah, the tea party, the mushroom that changes your size. . . . Is it a political satire? Did Dodgson mean for any of this to be in there?

It's hard to overstate the cultural effects of the *Alice* books, the way they've saturated our collective conscious. Have there ever been two books that have presented more characters that are now household names? The White Rabbit, the Cheshire Cat, the Mad Hatter, Tweedledee and Tweedledum, the Queen of Hearts, the Dormouse, the Mock Turtle, Humpty Dumpty, the Jabberwock, Alice herself . . .

It's also impossible to overstate the fuel that the books have provided for artists. Without a doubt, no other works of fiction have led to more visual art. Dodgson illustrated his original manuscript; legendary *Punch* cartoonist Sir John Tenniel created the immortal illustrations for the two novels; hundreds of illustrated editions have since been published; famous artists who have interpreted Alice include Max Ernst, René Magritte, Salvador Dalí, Ralph Steadman, Nan Goldin, Pierre & Gilles, and Annie Leibovitz; even now, around 150 years later, the Web is chockablock with artists of all professional levels offering their visions of Wonderland.

Dame Darcy is a fixture of underground comics. Her long-lived comic *Meatcake*—which she began self-publishing two decades ago and is still going strong as a Fantagraphics title—can be seen as a darker, more menacing version of Wonderland. Her immediately recognizable visual style illustrates a Victorian world of humor and gruesome horror, romance and dismemberment, sprites and fairy tales, dolls and mermaids, serial killers and Siamese twins. One month before I approached her about contributing to *The Graphic Canon*, the Dame—who is also a musician, doll-maker, and animator—gave an interview in which she was asked to describe her dream project. She replied: to create an illustrated version of the *Alice* books. Here she presents a sixteen-page tour-de-force (publishers take note—she's eager to do a full-length version). If you've ever seen Darcy (just Google her for photos), you'll notice a distinct similarity between artist and subject. . . .

A bright idea came into Alices head. "Is that the reason so many tea-things are put out here?" She asked.

"Yes, thats it," said the Hatter with a sigh: "its always tea time, and we've no time to wash the things between whiles."

"Then you keep moving round, I suppose?" Said Alice. "Exactly so," said the Hatter: as the things get used up."

"But what happens when you come to the beginning again?" Alice ventured to ask. "Suppose we change the subject," the March Hare interrupted yawning. "I'm tired of this. I vote the young lady tells us a story."

"I'm afraid I don't know one," said Alice, rather alarmed at the proposal.

"Then the Dormouse shall!" They both cried.

"wake up and they pinched it on both sides at once.

"Tell us a story!" said the March Hare. "Yes, please do!" pleaded Alice.

"Once upon a time there were three little sisters," the Dormouse began in a great hurry; and
Dame Darcy

their names were Elsie, Lacie, and Tillie; and they lived at the bottom of a well—"

"what did they live on?" Said Alice, who always took a great interest in questions of eating and drinking.

A large rose-tree stood near the entrance of the garden: the roses growing on it were white, but there were three gardeners at it, busily painting them red.

Alice thought this a very curious thing, and she went nearer to watch them, and, just as she came up to them, she heard one of them say "Look now Five!"

"Don't go splashing paint on me like that!"

"you'd better not talk," said Five "I heard the queen say yesterday you deserved to be beheaded!"

"Would you tell me please." said Alice a little timidly, "Why you are painting those roses?"

"Why, the fact is, you see, miss, this here ought to have been a red-rose tree, and we put a white one in by mistake; and if the Queen was to find it out...

Dame Darcy

We should all have our heads cut off, you know.

ALICE

thought she had never seen such a curious croquet ground in her life: it was all ridges and furrows the croquet balls were live hedgehogs, and the mallets live flamingoes, and the soldiers had to double themselves up and stand on their hands and feet, to make the arches. The chief difficulty found at first was managing her flamingo: she succeeded in getting its body tucked away under her arm,

With its legs hanging down, but generally just as she had got its neck

nicely straightened out, and was going to give the hedgehog a blow with its head, it would twist itself round and look up in her face, with such a puzzled expression that she could not help bursting out laughing.

And when she had got its head down and was going to begin again it was very provoking to find that the hedgehog had

Dame Darcy

unrolled itself and was in the act of crawling away.

ALICE'S ADVENTURES LEWIS CARROLL DAME DARCY

The Lion and the Unicorn were fighting for the crown
the lion beat the unicorn all around the town
some gave them white bread and some gave them brown
and some gave them plum~cake and drummed them out of town.

"Jabberwocky"

Lewis Carroll

ART/ADAPTATION BY **Eran Cantrell**

CHARLES DODGSON (A.K.A. LEWIS CARROLL) started his writing career with satirical and love poetry, and he included over a dozen original poems—including lullabies, nursery rhymes, and song lyrics—in the *Alice* books. Of them, "Jabberwocky" has gone on to become a stand-alone classic, much-anthologized and often adapted, illustrated, and even filmed by Terry Gilliam.

It occurs very early in *Through the Looking-Glass*, when Alice has first stepped through the mirror to the room on the other side. She finds a book with odd writing, which she realizes is English in reverse, so she holds it up to the mirror and reads this self-contained adventure about a boy slaying the fearsome Jabberwock with his vorpal blade.

Carroll might have written it as a parody of heroic Anglo Saxon poems; it's easy to see it as a twisted take on *Beowulf*.

The poem is an absolute masterpiece of nonsense, filled to the brim with made-up words that still manage to convey meaning and mood. *Frabjuous* seems to be a mash-up of *fabulous* and *joyous*, while Carroll later wrote that *frumious* is a combination of *furious* and *fuming*. One of the words, *chortle*, has entered common English usage.

Calgary artist Eran Cantrell created a series of gorgeous silhouetted images for the poem, then designed and self-published a book of them. I was beamish when she allowed us to include them in *The Graphic Canon*.

'Twas brillig, and the slithy toves

Did gyre and gimble in the wabe;

All mimsy were the borogoves,

And the mome raths outgrabe.

"Beware the Jabberwock, my son!

The jaws that bite, the claws that catch!

Beware the Jubjub bird, and shun

The frumious Bandersnatch!"

He took his vorpal sword in hand:

Long time the manxome foe he sought—

"JABBERWOCKY" LEWIS CARROLL **ERAN CANTRELL**

So rested he by the Tumtum tree,

And stood awhile in thought.

And as in uffish thought he stood,

The Jabberwock, with eyes of flame,

"JABBERWOCKY" LEWIS CARROLL ERAN CANTRELL

Came whiffling through the tulgey wood,

And burbled as it came!

One, two!

One, two!

and through and through

The vorpal blade went snicker-snack!

He left it dead,

and with its head

He went galumphing back.

"And hast thou slain the Jabberwock?

Come to my arms, my beamish boy!

O frabjous day! Callooh! Callay!"

He chortled in his joy.

"JABBERWOCKY" LEWIS CARROLL ERAN CANTRELL

Twas brillig, and the slithy toves
Did gyre and gimble in the wabe;
All mimsy were the borogoves,
And the mome raths outgrabe.

THE END.

In case of Jabberwocky,
break glass.

"JABBERWOCKY" LEWIS CARROLL ERAN CANTRELL

Alice gallery

ILLUSTRATIONS BY **various artists**

THE ALICE BOOKS FIRE THE ARTISTIC IMAGINATION like no other works. Several anthologies have been published just to collect representative samples from the hundreds upon hundreds of illustrators, painters, photographers, collage artists, animators, and others who have visualized these mesmerizing characters. As I collected material and approached artists for *The Graphic Canon*, I was struck by the number who had already delved into Wonderland and Looking-Glass Land, and I couldn't resist putting together a gallery. Sir John Tenniel's officially sanctioned illustrations for the original editions still have a death-grip on our mental images of the characters and scenes, but they're just one person's conception. Let's see what else Charles Dodgson (a.k.a. Lewis Carroll) hath wrought.

The gallery opens with *We're All Mad Here* by Raphaëlle Vimont, a clever silhouettes-within-silhouettes image that yields more motifs from the *Alice* books the longer you look at it. It originally ran in the French magazine *Peau de Lapin*.

Who says that Alice has to be blonde? Or that the Mad Hatter has to have two eyes, for that matter? In *Alice and Mad*, Bill Carman—painting like an old-school Surrealist—radically reimagines these two at the tea party.

And speaking of making Alice brunette, why hasn't anyone modeled the Alice of the books on *the* Alice herself, Alice Liddell? Legendary underground comix artist Kim Deitch corrected this oversight when he illustrated a complete edition of *Alice's Adventures under Ground,* the original, rarely reprinted story that Carroll wrote for his little muse. (He then expanded it to nearly twice the length and titled it *Alice's Adventures in Wonderland*.) Two of those illustrations are here: 1) Alice getting bored while sitting next to her sister, who's reading a book, on the riverbank and 2) the mouse telling his tale after everyone gets soaked in Alice's pool of tears.

John Coulthart created two calendars of psychedelic collages based on the *Alice* books. As he puts it: "The 1860s collide with the 1960s in lurid efflorescence!" *A Mad Tea Party* is here in rainbow-hued glory. The blazing *The Wasp in a Wig* illustrates an episode that Carroll dropped from *Through the Looking-Glass* at the insistence of Tenniel. (It remained unknown and unpublished until 1977.)

May Ann Licudine, working in the Philippines, knows a thing or two about bright, beautiful colors. She was invited by Nucleus, a fantastic gallery in Alhambra, California, to take part in their show "Curiouser and Curiouser: An Exhibit Inspired by 'Alice in Wonderland.'" One of her pieces, *I see you, Cheshire*, is a gorgeous riot of Easter egg colors with all kinds of surprises, including Christmas ornaments hanging from the Cheshire Cat's tree and a number of heart-shaped objects with a chessboard pattern on the outside and watermelon on the inside. *Young Queen of Hearts* is an arresting portrait done in graphite. *The Hole in Alice's World* presents a swirling, fluttering vision of Alice's plunge into Wonderland, with a nod to M. C. Escher.

Caterpillar Concept by Swedish illustrator and concept artist Andrea Femerstrand offers a subtly unsettling vision of Wonderland's popular, hookah-smoking denizen.

Straight out of Kiev and now in the Bay area, Olga Lopata imagines the Caterpillar in a totally different way—in a candy-colored, somewhat flattened scheme, with a placid expression and the multiple arms of a Hindu deity.

Continuing to show Alice's worldwide appeal, *Alice and White Rabbit* from Lithuania-based artist Natalie Shau presents a more, um, mature, sophisticated version of our heroine, bathed in a beautiful blue sheen.

In *Mr. White Rabbit*, Emerson Tung gives us a startlingly different take on the furry creature and his timepiece. Emerson explains: "Because he was late all the time, the Queen decided that she had the last straw with him, and chained him to the royal timepiece as a punishment of irony. Now that he has to drag it around he's even more late than ever."

Peter Kuper, known for his searing sociopolitical artwork, got to do dozens of illustrations for a recent Mexican edition of the *Alice* books. The Queen of Hearts, fond of ordering executions ("Off with their heads!"), looks a lot like a certain former US vice president and oil baron, who was known to have heart problems. The other image here is for a scene I'd never before seen illustrated, from chapter 3 of *Through the Looking-Glass*:

"[W]hy, what *are* those creatures, making honey down there? They can't be bees—nobody ever saw bees a mile off you know—" and for some minutes she stood silent, watching one of them that was bustling about among the flowers, poking its proboscis into them, "just as if it was a regular bee," thought Alice.

However, this was anything but a regular bee: in fact, it was an elephant—as Alice soon found out, though the idea quite took her breath away at first. "And what enormous flowers they must be!" was her next idea. "Something like cottages with the roofs taken off, and stalks put to

them—and what quantities of honey they must make! I think I'll go down and—no, I won't go *just* yet."

Having grown up in a family business that made toys by hand—essentially a Santa's workshop come to life—it is fitting that John Ottinger took part in "What Is the Use of a Book Without Pictures," a multi-artist effort to create an illustration for every single *paragraph* of the Alice books. John introduces a steampunk element with a humongous robo Mad Hatter wearing a truly epic hat.

David W. Tripp also took part in the project, creating a highly stylized, consistent vision across more than seventy illustrations. The sinuousness of the female characters, including Alice, is at its peak in *Alice Paragraph 162*. Alice is in the kitchen with the starkly inky Duchess and her baby when the cook inexplicably begins throwing pans and dishes. In *Alice Paragraph 276*, the Queen of Hearts is starting the famous croquet game, with flamingo mallets and hedgehogs as the balls. In the book, her soldiers are literally giant playing cards with hands and feet at the corners. In Tripp's hands, they're jackbooted thugs, complete with spiked helmets, gas masks, and fascist uniforms bearing their number and suit.

Meanwhile, our man in Paris, Christopher Panzner, metic-ulously rendered Alice and the Caterpillar in pen and ink, bringing a stunning Art Nouveau style to *Alice's Adventures in Wonderland (Paragraph 108)*.

Working exclusively in acrylics, Gothic/fairy painter Jasmine Becket-Griffith has done over forty astonishingly inventive portraits of Alice, whom she often portrays as a big-eyed waif. One subset of this series reimagines Alice in the works of the masters, including van Eyck and Dalí. In *Alice and the Bosch Monsters* our girl is surrounded by a different set of mad characters coming from Hieronymus Bosch's otherworldly masterpiece, *The Garden of Earthly Delights* (circa 1500).

Surprisingly, the Alice books don't contain any descriptions of Alice's appearance. And although Alice is named after Carroll's young friend, he later confirmed that his character isn't meant to *be* Alice Liddell (as is obvious from the books' official illustrations, in which Tenniel used a blonde girl as the model). So why can't Alice be black? And more to the point, why in the world, after 150+ years, hasn't anybody portrayed Alice as being of African descent? Molly Kiely fills in this blind spot with her pioneering *Alice and Humpty*. And while she was questioning the hue of the main character's skin, Molly also broke new ground with Humpty Dumpty, envisioning him as a mottled blue robin's egg.

ALICE GALLERY FROM ALICE'S ADVENTURES UNDER GROUND KIM DEITCH

ALICE GALLERY YOUNG QUEEN OF HEARTS MAY ANN LICUDINE

ALICE GALLERY CATERPILLAR CONCEPT ANDREA FEMERSTRAND

ALICE GALLERY ALICE AND WHITE RABBIT NATALIE SHAU

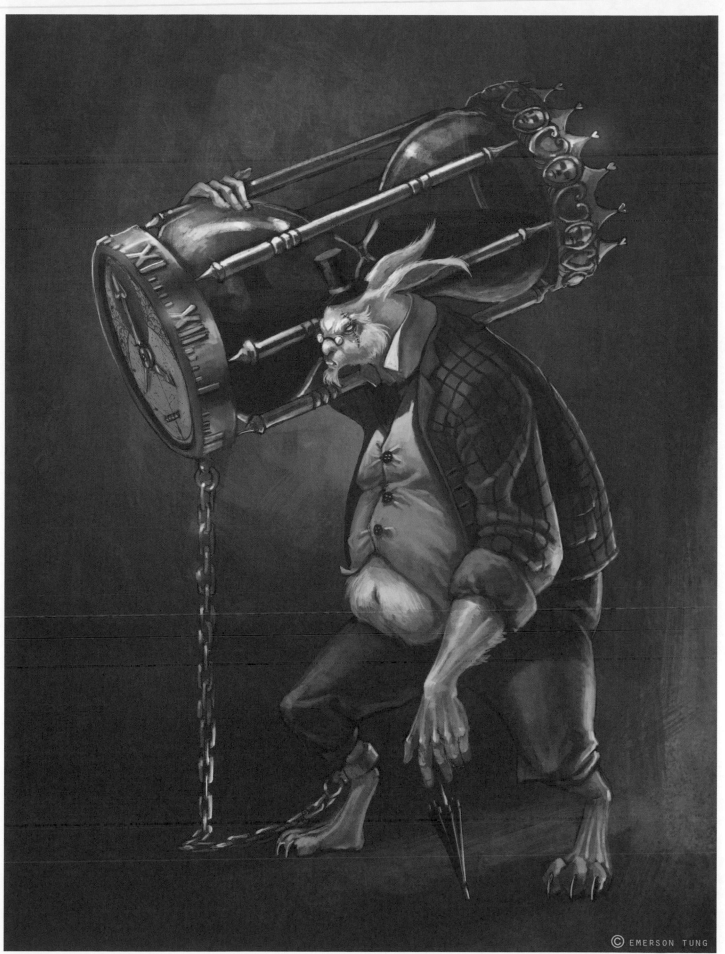

ALICE GALLERY MR. WHITE RABBIT EMERSON TUNG 349

ALICE GALLERY FROM A TRAVÉS DEL ESPEJO Y LO QUE ALICIA ENCONTRÓ ALLÍ PETER KUPER

ALICE GALLERY ALICE PARAGRAPH 276 DAVID W. TRIPP

ALICE GALLERY ALICE'S ADVENTURES IN WONDERLAND (PARAGRAPH 108) CHRISTOPHER PANZNER

ALICE GALLERY ALICE AND THE BOSCH MONSTERS JASMINE BECKET-GRIFFITH

If he smiled much more the ends of his mouth might meet behind...

Crime and Punishment

Fyodor Dostoevsky

ART/ADAPTATION BY **Kako**

TRAINED AS A MILITARY ENGINEER, FYODOR Dostoevsky instead turned to writing as a career, leading to a life filled with long stretches of poverty, during which he wouldn't eat for days at a time. His predilection for gambling didn't help either. His first short novel, *Poor Folk*, was a well-received success, but his subsequent short novels and short stories bombed for years afterward.

Dostoevsky was always concerned with the plight of the commoners and with social justice, and he joined some of the revolutionary groups/communes of his day. In 1849 he was arrested, along with the rest of the radical but fairly tame Petrashevsky Circle (basically a reading group, not a collection of armed revolutionaries), on suspicion of trying to foment the overthrow of Tsarist rule. The group was to be executed by firing squad. They were divided into threes, with Dostoevsky in the second group. As the first trio was tied to posts, and the guns were aimed, the execution was halted. It had, in fact, been a mock execution, never meant to kill, just to terrorize its victims. Instead the group was sent to Siberia, and Dostoevsky served four years of hard labor in the most squalid, inhumane conditions imaginable. Hours after the mock execution, Dosty wrote in a letter to his brother:

> When I look back on my past and think how much time I wasted on nothing, how much time has been lost in futilities, errors, laziness, incapacity to live; how little I appreciated it, how many times I sinned against my heart and soul—then my heart bleeds. Life is a gift, life is happiness, every minute can be an eternity of happiness!

Upon his release, Dostoevsky began to write a series of masterpieces, including *Notes from the Underground*, *The Idiot*, *Crime and Punishment*, and *The Brothers Karam-*azov. By the time of his death, he was recognized as a great writer, and he now ranks next to Tolstoy at the top of the formidable Russian literary pantheon.

Crime and Punishment tells the story of a Russian student, Raskolnikov, a young radical who holds the fashionable idea that an intellectually superior man doesn't need to cling to common notions of morality. He decides to kill his pawnbroker, a contemptible, loathsome old lady he believes adds nothing to society. He'll then take the money she's hidden away and use it to help people. He convinces himself that this isn't really a crime and that he'll remain emotionally detached and reasonable. Raskolnikov has a dream about a childhood incident in which he witnessed a horse get beaten to death by its owner, which disturbed him greatly. It's almost enough to make him call off his plan . . . but not quite.

The next night, he bludgeons the old lady to death. While trying to find her money, Raskolnikov is discovered by her sister, whom he also kills. He finds it's not so easy to stay detached and struggles with his conscience for the rest of the novel. Meanwhile, a police investigator suspects him, making the novel also work as a high-end detective story. Dostoevsky was about a century ahead of his time in his acute perceptions of human psychology.

The Brazilian artist Kako—regularly featured in the world's most prestigious illustration compendiums and with a client list that includes DC and Vertigo, Nike, and Sony—gives us an epic, hallucinatory four-spread vision of the pivotal murder scene, blended with Raskolnikov's violent dream from the previous night.

SOURCE

Frank, Joseph. *Dostoevsky: A Writer in His Time.* Princeton: Princeton University Press, 2010.

IT IS NOT SERIOUS AT ALL.

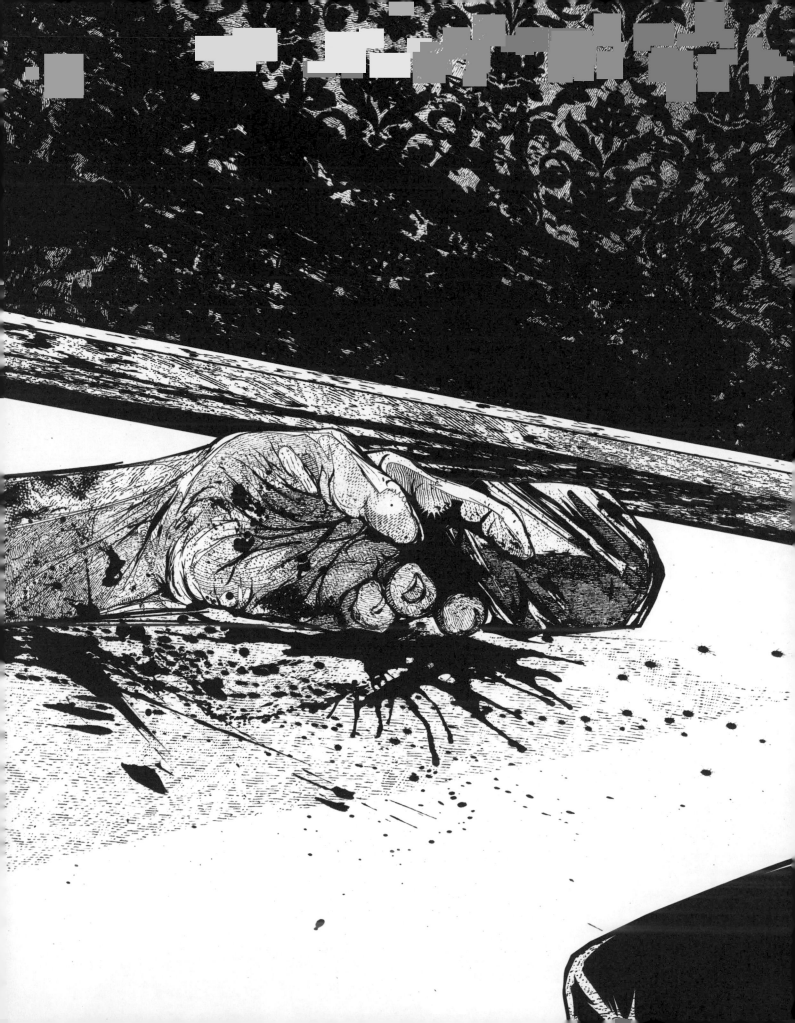

YES, MAYBE IT IS A PLAYTHING!

Venus in Furs

Leopold von Sacher-Masoch

ART/ADAPTATION BY **Molly Kiely**

AUSTRIAN HISTORIAN, DECORATED SOLDIER, AND author Leopold von Sacher-Masoch had a prolific and fairly successful writing career. By far his best-known work—especially outside the German language, in which he wrote—is the 1870 novella *Venus in Furs*. It was part of *Love*, the first volume of stories he wrote for an unfinished epic series of books, *The Legacy of Cain*.

Venus tells the story of a man who slowly convinces a woman to sexually dominate and abuse him. It's based firmly on Sacher-Masoch's own predilections. Among other practices, he had his wives and lovers flay him with whips studded with nails (an implement of his own devising), and he encouraged them to cheat on him. His name was famously used by nineteenth-century sexologist Richard von Krafft-Ebing to coin the word *masochism*, the enjoyment of receiving pain and humiliation.

Molly Kiely's oeuvre includes a wide range of media and

subjects, but she made her mark in the 1990s as one of a vanishingly small number of women creating erotic comics. She has adapted works for all three volumes of *The Graphic Canon*, and here she turns to a classic of erotica that—like the Marquis de Sade's major novels and *Fanny Hill* by John Cleland—has gained entry into the fringes of the literary canon. She says:

> *Venus in Furs* has the reputation of being a spicy, lurid tale of a thigh-booted dominatrix—and, indeed, there are some very hot passages here and there—but mostly it's a bittersweet, intelligently written ode to one man's aesthetic obsession with creating his ideal mate. I hope this overlooked aspect of the novel comes through in my adaptation—but there's some hot stuff in it, too.

SOURCE

Ellis, Havelock. *Studies in the Psychology of Sex, Volume 3* (2nd ed.). 1913.

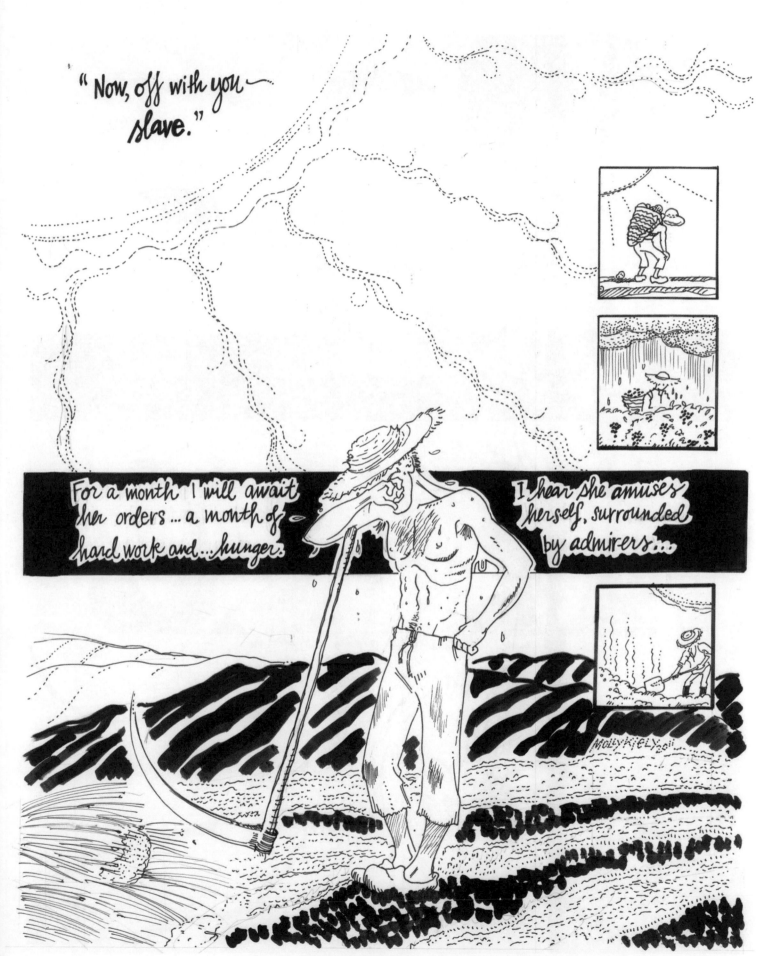

VENUS IN FURS LEOPOLD VON SACHER-MASOCH MOLLY KIELY   373

"The Drunken Boat"

Arthur Rimbaud

ART/ADAPTATION BY **Julian Peters**

IF THE ROMANTICS AND THE BRONTËS TAUGHT US anything by their examples, it's that nothing cements your literary reputation better than writing astounding work, then dying young. But Arthur Rimbaud did something that in some ways is even more intriguing. In his teens, he wrote blindingly brilliant poetry unlike anything else the world has ever seen. Legend has it that Victor Hugo called him "an infant Shakespeare." Then, at age twenty, Rimbaud simply walked away. He quit writing poetry—quit writing anything at all for publication—and became a globe-trotting colonial trader, gun-runner, and soldier who ended up deserting.

A small-town farmboy in the French countryside, Rimbaud was a rebel who showed a gift for writing at a very early age. When he was sixteen, he wrote a now-famous passage in a letter to the teacher who had encouraged his love of writing and literature:

> I'm now making myself as scummy as I can. Why? I want to be a poet, and I'm working at turning myself into a *Seer*. You won't understand any of this, and I'm almost incapable of explaining it to you. The idea is to reach the unknown by the derangement of *all the senses*. It involves enormous suffering, but one must be strong and be a born poet. And I've realized that I am a poet. It's really not my fault.

Also at the tender age of sixteen, Rimbaud wrote a letter to the renowned French poet Paul Verlaine, whom he admired, enclosing several of his own poems. The elder poet insisted the lad come to Paris and live with him and his wife. Verlaine and Rimbaud became lovers—one of the most notorious couples in literary history. Rimbaud was uncouth, arrogant, cruel, and obnoxious. (Writer and critic Edmond Goncourt wrote of Rimbaud in his journal: "That man was perversity incarnate.") Their extraordinarily dysfunctional, volatile relationship finally ended when, in a drunken, suicidal, armed rage, Verlaine shot the boy-poet in the wrist. Rimbaud called the cops, and Verlaine ended up doing two years hard labor.

Returning home, Rimbaud wrote *A Season in Hell*, a nine-part prose poem with bits of verse, which is generally considered his long-form masterpiece. Biographer Graham Robb writes that the work "is without precedent. Even *post*-cedents are hard to find. Fifty years before *Ulysses* and *The Waste Land*, Rimbaud, at the age of eighteen, has invented a linguistic world that can happily be explored for years like the scrapyard of a civilization."

Rimbaud then wrote a series of short, individual prose poems published as *Illuminations*. And then, for reasons we'll probably never know, he gave up poetry. He refused to discuss his writings for the rest of his life, referring to them as "ridiculous" and "disgusting" when asked about them. He died at age thirty-seven, in 1891, from cancer.

Rimbaud's most admired short poem is "The Drunken Boat," written when he was sixteen. He brought it with him to Paris, wowing the literati by passing around handwritten copies at soirees. Writing in *The New Yorker*, Daniel Mendelsohn explains:

> The poem is characterized by a formal correctness (it's composed of twenty-five rhymed quatrains of alexandrines, the classic French six-beat line) placed in the service of a destabilizing fantasy—a dream of liberation from correct form. It ostensibly describes the downstream journey of a vessel that has lost its haulers, its rudder, its anchor, wandering to and fro and witnessing bizarre sights en route to nowhere in particular. ("Huge serpents, vermin-plagued, drop down into the mire / With black effluvium from the contorted trees!") But as you make your way through the poem, each stanza seeming at once to latch tightly on to the last and yet move further into imaginative space, it seems to expand into a parable about life and art in which loss of control—of the boat, of the poem itself, of what we think "meaning" in a poem might be—becomes the key to a kind of spiritual and aesthetic redemption.

As all-around genius Paul Valéry noted: "Before Rimbaud all literature was written in the language of common sense." Montreal artist Julian Peters, who works in the tradition of *fumetti* (photocomics), explains his approach to this adaptation:

> I generally sought to capture whatever images most readily popped into my head when reading each stanza. I also looked to a lot of late-nineteenth-century/early twentieth-century symbolist painting for ideas on how this transfer from a mental picture to a concrete one could be more elegantly accomplished. This visual frame of reference is by no means accidental, of course, as "The Drunken Boat" is considered one of the key works that ushered in the symbolist era in literature, which in turn led, a decade or so later, to symbolist painting and sculpture. For this reason it can be said that Rimbaud, the most visual of poets, is also one of the poets who has had the most influence on the development of the visual arts.

SOURCES

Mendelsohn, Daniel. "Rebel Rebel: Arthur Rimbaud's Brief Career." *The New Yorker*, August 28, 2011.

Robb, Graham. *Rimbaud: A Biography*. New York: W.W. Norton & Company, 2001.

White, Edmund. *Rimbaud: The Double Life of a Rebel*. New York: Atlas & Co. Publishers, 2008.

ARTHUR RIMBAUD

DRAWINGS BY
JULIAN PETERS

THE DRUNKEN BOAT

AS I SLID DOWN IMPASSABLE RIVER NARROWS,
I FELT THE CURRENTS LIFT ME, TAKE ME THROUGH.
SWINGING FROM PAINTED STAKES, SHOT FULL OF ARROWS,
THE TARGETS FOR WHOOPING REDSKINS, HUNG MY CREW.

BUT I DID NOT CARE FOR CREWS OF WATER-GUIDES,
BEARERS OF BRITISH COTTON, FLEMISH GRAIN,
AND WHEN THE RACKET WITH THESE TOWS-MEN DIED,
THE RIVERS LET ME SLIDE AT WILL AGAIN.

SO IN THE SLAPPINGS OF THE SURF I SAILED
DEAF AS A CHILD'S BRAIN, HOLLOW TO THE BRINE.
PERHAPS PENINSULAS UNMOORED ARE HAILED
WITH SOME SUCH HURLY-BURLY AS WAS MINE.

KIND STORMS POURED OUT THEIR MISCHIEF ON MY HEAD.
WITHOUT THE SILLY EYES OF LANTERN GUIDES
OVER ETERNAL ROCKINGS OF THE DEAD
AND LIGHTER THAN A CORK, I DANCED THE TIDES.

TENDER AS THE FLESH OF APPLES TO A CHILD
GREEN SPRAY SHOT UP INTO MY SHELL OF PINE,
SPLIT HELM AND GRAPPLING HOOK, AND, UNDEFILED,
WASHED ME IN STAINS OF VOMITINGS AND WINE.

AND I HAVE SINCE BATHED IN THE MILK AND RHYMES
OF THE POEM SEA, INFUSED WITH STARS AROUND,
DEVOURED THE GLAUCOUS WATERS WHERE SOMETIMES
A MAN'S RAPT BODY DRIFTS BY, PENSIVE, DROWNED;

WHERE CRUSTING THE BLUE WITH SIMULTANEOUS FIRES
AND RHYTHMS LIKE THE RUTILENCE ABOVE,
STRONGER THAN WHISKEY, VASTER THAN YOUR LYRES,
FERMENT THE TAWNY-BITTER REDS OF LOVE!

"THE DRUNKEN BOAT" ARTHUR RIMBAUD JULIAN PETERS

I KNOW SKIES SPLIT BY LIGHTNING, CLOUDS OF THORN THAT SEEM AS SOFT AS EVENING SCENERY, EXALTED AS A RACE OF DOVES, THE DAWN, AND I HAVE SEEN WHAT MEN BELIEVE THEY SEE.

I SAW THE LOW SUN MASKED WITH TRAGIC RAGE LIGHT UP LONG VIOLET-CLOTTED WOUNDS, BESTOW SPENT FIRE AND PATHOS, AN ACTOR ON A STAGE, AND WAVES WITH DOVECOTE SHUDDERINGS AT THE SHOW.

I DREAMED THE NIGHT GREEN THROUGH A DAZZLING SWARM OF WHITE FLAKES; OF THE OCEAN'S GENTLE BUSS; FIERCE-CIRCULATING SAPS; THE BLUE ALARM OF SINGING STARS, THE BIRDS OF PHOSPHORUS.

FOR MONTHS I FOLLOWED THE MAD ROCKWARD BEAT OF THE SURF IN ORDER TO MARVEL WHEN SUAVE IN CALMS AT HOW THE VIRGIN'S LUMINOUS FEET COULD MUZZLE ALL THAT PANTING DRIVE OF WAVE.

"THE DRUNKEN BOAT" ARTHUR RIMBAUD JULIAN PETERS

I TOUCHED, DO YOU HEAR? ON FLORIDAS THAT SANG, HEAPED HIGH WITH FLOWERS AND SKINS OF MEN AND EYES OF PANTHERS, WHERE THE BURNISHED RAINBOWS HANG LIKE REINS OF SEA-GREEN SHEEP FROM COPPER SKIES...

I PASSED ENORMOUS NETS; I WATCHED A WHOLE LEVIATHAN ROTTING; VIOLENT INSTANCES OF CRASHINGS AMONG CALMS. I KNEW THE ROLE PLAYED BY ABYSSES AGAINST DISTANCES.

GLACIERS, SILVER SUNS, AND BLOODIED SKIES, STRANDINGS IN VALLEYS YELLOW WITH DISEASE WHERE GIANT SERPENTS, EATEN AWAY BY FLIES, FALL WITH BLACK PERFUMES FROM THE TWISTED TREES!

HOW BOYS WOULD HAVE ADMIRED MY GIANT TANK OF GOLD DORADOES, THE FISH THAT LEAPING, SINGS! THE FOAM OF FLOWERS BLESSED ME WHEN I SANK, AND SWEET WINDS BORE ME WHEN I NEEDED WINGS.

"THE DRUNKEN BOAT" ARTHUR RIMBAUD JULIAN PETERS

AT TIMES, A MARTYR WEARY OF ZONES AND POLES,
THE SEA, WHOSE SOBBING MADE MY BUFFETS DEAR,
LIFTED SHADOW-BLOOMS IN YELLOW SHOALS;
AND LIKE A WOMAN KNEELING, I FELL THERE,

UNTIL AN ISLAND HEAPED MY SIDES AGAIN
WITH THE QUARRELS AND DUNG OF BLOND-EYED
[BIRDS; SUCH SIGNS
OF INTIMACY, I FLED. I SAILED. DROWNED MEN,
DESCENDING TO SLEEP BACKWARDS CROSSED MY LINES...

BUT I, BOAT LOCKED FAST BETWEEN RIVER-LIPS,
FLUNG BY THE TEMPEST INTO BIRDLESS ZONE,
I WHOM NO MONITORS, NO HANSA SHIPS
COULD FISH UP, WATER DRUNKEN, CARCASS GONE,

FREE, FUMING, STUDDED IN THE PURPLE MIST,
BORING THE RUDDY WALL THAT POETS KNEW
AND CLIMBED ACROSS THE SHELVES OF AMETHYST
FOR JAMS OF SUN AND SNOT-BLUE OF THE BLUE.

"THE DRUNKEN BOAT" ARTHUR RIMBAUD JULIAN PETERS   381

I WHO RAN SPOTTED WITH ELECTRIC RINGS,
MAD PLANK, WHILE BLACK SEA-HORSES SWEPT ME BY,
WHEN MARINE SKIES WERE SCORCHED AND BLEEDING THINGS
UNDER THE BLUDGEONINGS OF RED JULY!

LET EUROPE'S MEDITERRANEANS FLOAT OR FAIL!
I WANT OF HER WATERS ONE COLD POOL, SOON TO DRY,
ON WHICH AT TWILIGHT A SAD CHILD MIGHT SAIL
A BOAT AS FRAIL AS A MAY BUTTERFLY.

I CAN NO LONGER BATHING IN YOUR RAGS,
O WAVES, RAISE UP THE WASH OF CHANNEL TRIPS,

NOR CROSS THE OLD UNFRIENDLY PRIDE OF FLAGS,

NOR SWIM IN THE HORRID EYES OF PRISON SHIPS!

"THE DRUNKEN BOAT" ARTHUR RIMBAUD JULIAN PETERS

Middlemarch

George Eliot

ART/ADAPTATION BY **Megan Kelso**

MARY ANNE EVANS—WHO WROTE UNDER THE male pseudonym George Eliot in order to be taken seriously—was considered England's greatest novelist next to Dickens, and after his death, she took the crown. *The Mill on the Floss*, *Silas Marner*, and her other five novels still rank high, and *Middlemarch* is the crowning jewel. With an epic sweep, it covers the interlocking lives of many residents of a small, fictional English town, with great psychological insight, a realistic view of marriage, an unsparing look at how the choices we make affect us, and lots of ideas about the roles that art, science, religion, and occupation play in our lives.

CUNY English professor Felicia Bonaparte makes the case that Evans was one of the most intelligent, most learned novelists in history:

> She could speak with authority on history, music, art, theology, anthropology, philosophy, sociology, psychology, and any number of other subjects; she was an excellent mathematician and had a love of all the sciences, especially physics, geology, chemistry, and astronomy; entomology and biology, the pursuits she assigns in the novel to the vicar Mr. Farebrother and the physician Tertius Lydgate, were of particular interest to her; literature was her deepest love, the literature of many countries, and having made

herself proficient, by the end of her life, in eight tongues (English, French, Italian, German, Spanish, Hebrew, Latin, and Greek), she knew a good deal of Western literature in its original languages.

> Most of this she taught herself. Women were rarely, in those days, given a serious education . . .

One of the wittiest writers about literature, Jack Murnighan, says: "There are smart novels, there are smarter novels, then there's *Middlemarch*."

Comics artist Megan Kelso drew the comic strip *Watergate Sue* for the *New York Times Magazine* and won the Xeric Award for her minicomic *Girl Hero*. She has a clean, spare style that uses so very few lines to convey tremendous emotion and expression. In this adaptation of chapters 19 through 21, I'm still trying figure out how—with such minimalism—Dorothea can be so beautiful and her much older, nonpassionate husband, Casaubon, can be so ugly.

SOURCES

Eliot, George. *Middlemarch*. Introduction by Felicia Bonaparte. Oxford: Oxford University Press, 2008.

Murnighan, Jack. *Beowulf on the Beach*. New York: Three Rivers Press, 2009.

George Eliot's

MIDDLEMARCH

an excerpt adapted by Megan Kelso

Dorothea

Will Ladislaw

Edward Casaubon

Adolf Naumann

MIDDLEMARCH GEORGE ELIOT MEGAN KELSO   387

MIDDLEMARCH GEORGE ELIOT MEGAN KELSO

MIDDLEMARCH GEORGE ELIOT MEGAN KELSO

The Hunting of the Snark

Lewis Carroll

ART/ADAPTATION BY **Mahendra Singh**

OXFORD MATH PROFESSOR AND ANGLICAN DEACON Charles Dodgson (a.k.a. Lewis Carroll) had megahits on his hands with *Alice's Adventures in Wonderland* (1865) and its sequel, *Through the Looking-Glass* (1871). Five years later, Macmillan published his long nonsense poem *The Hunting of the Snark*, which is typically regarded as his other main contribution to literature. It tells of a quest over sea and land for a creature known as the Snark, whose very nature remains a mystery throughout the tale.

In the first of its eight sections (called "Fits"), we're introduced to the ten-member crew, which includes the Baker, the Bellman, the Butcher, and

> There was also a Beaver, that paced on the deck,
> Or would sit making lace in the bow:
> And had often (the Bellman said) saved them from wreck,
> Though none of the sailors knew how.

In the Second Fit—the portion excerpted here—we're shown the minimalist map brought by the Bellman, who—after they make landfall—schools the crew on five quite unusual characteristics of Snarks.

Mahendra Singh's highly lauded graphic adaptation of the entire mock-epic poem was published in 2010 by the redoubtable Melville House. Singh uses a collage approach that bears a resemblance to Max Ernst's famous collage novels of the 1930s. In fact, Singh channels the Surrealists and Dadaists in his visual approach, making the interesting connection that Dodgson could be considered a forerunner of Ernst, Breton, Dalí, Man Ray, et al. . . . a proto-Surrealist. There are truckloads of references, allusions, visual puns, optical delusions, and other shenanigans going on in these panels. The Bellman is portrayed as a literal birdbrain, with his head as a cage containing a bird sculpture by Romanian sculptor Constantin Brâncusi; the rest of the crew—equally birdbrained for listening to the Bellman—are shown as avians as portrayed by Surrealists Hans Arp and Joan Miró.

Freud makes an appearance early on in this fit, probably because of the role the unconscious plays in the works of Dodgson and the Surrealists. Nietzsche, Van Gogh, Dalí's melting watches, and Magritte's cloth-wrapped heads all show up, as does Sir John Tenniel, the illustrator of the *Alice* books, who used himself as the model for the White Knight in *Through the Looking-Glass*, so we also get an indirect appearance by an *Alice* character. Meanings within meanings . . .

Fit the Second
THE BELLMAN'S SPEECH

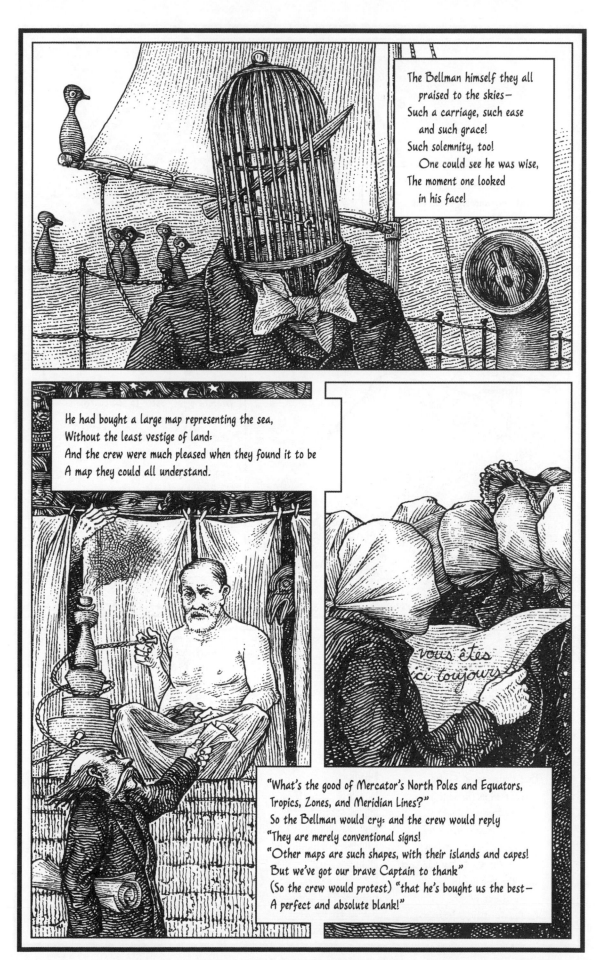

This was charming, no doubt:
   but they shortly found out
That the Captain they trusted so well
Had only one notion for
   crossing the ocean,
And that was to tingle his bell.

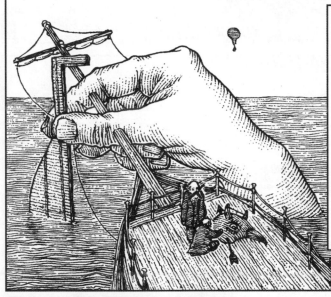

He was thoughtful and grave—
   but the orders he gave
Were enough to bewilder a crew.
When he cried "Steer to starboard,
   but keep her head larboard!"
What on earth was the
   helmsman to do?
Then the bowsprit got mixed
   with the rudder sometimes:
A thing, as the Bellman remarked,
That frequently happens
   in tropical climes,
When a vessel is, so to speak, "snarked."

But the principal failing
   occurred in the sailing,
And the Bellman,
   perplexed and distressed,
Said he *had* hoped, at least,
   when the wind blew due East,
That the ship would *not*
   travel due West!

But the danger was past—they had landed at last,
With their boxes, portmanteaus, and bags:
Yet at first sight the crew were not pleased with the view,
Which consisted of chasms and crags.

"We have sailed many weeks,
    we have sailed many days,
(Seven days to the week I allow),
But a Snark, on the which we
    might lovingly gaze,
We have never beheld till now!
"Come, listen, my men,
    while I tell you again
The five unmistakable marks
By which you may know,
    wheresoever you go,
The warranted genuine Snarks.

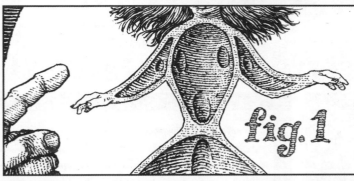

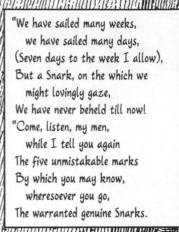

fig. 1

"Let us take them in order.
    The first is the taste,
Which is meager and hollow, but crisp:
Like a coat that is rather too
    tight in the waist,
With a flavour of Will-o-the-wisp.

"Its habit of getting up late you'll agree
That it carries too far, when I say
That it frequently breakfasts at five-o'clock tea,
And dines on the following day.

fig. 2

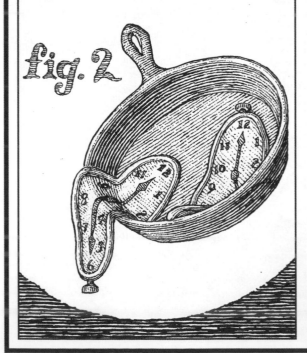

fig. 3

"The third is its slowness in taking a jest.
Should you happen to venture on one,
It will sigh like a thing that is deeply distressed:
And it always looks grave at a pun.

"The fourth is its fondness for bathing-machines,
Which it constantly carries about,
And believes that they add to the beauty of scenes—
A sentiment open to doubt.

"The fifth is ambition. It next will be right
To describe each particular batch:
Distinguishing those that have feathers, and bite,
From those that have whiskers, and scratch.

"For, although common Snarks do no manner of harm,
Yet, I feel it my duty to say,
Some are Boojums—" The Bellman broke off in alarm,
For the Baker had fainted away.

Anna Karenina

Leo Tolstoy

ART/ADAPTATION BY **Ellen Lindner**

WHAT DO YOU DO AFTER YOU'VE WRITTEN *WAR and Peace*—a sweeping colossus involving five families and 130 characters—a novel for the ages, and one that becomes synonymous with sprawl, with epic grandeur, with sheer bulk? You scale things back, maybe write a tragic romance with a small number of main characters, focus on family life. But being Tolstoy, the godfather of Russian literature, you begin it with one of the greatest opening lines in literature: "Happy families are all alike; every unhappy family is unhappy in its own way." Your perfected writing style and more intimate scope of events means you create what many other towering writers—Dostoevsky, Nabokov, Faulkner—consider a flawless work, the greatest novel ever. Yet you use the romance as a springboard to much more, a penetrating look at love in a variety of forms, at marriage and adultery, at children and parents, at life and death, and at a whole bunch of social, political, and cultural issues. In the introduction to their landmark translation of the novel, Richard Pevear and Larissa Volokhonsky write:

> *Anna Karenina* is a tissue of polemics on all the issues then being discussed in the aristocratic salons and the newspapers, with Konstantin Levin acting as spokesman for his creator. There are arguments with the aristocracy as well as with the nihilists on the "woman question" [i.e., the role of women in society]; . . . with the landowners and peasants on questions of farm management; with advocates of old and new forms of political representation—local councils, provincial elections among the nobility—and of such judicial institutions as open courts and rural justices of the peace; with new ideas about the education of children and of peasants; with the new movements in art and music; with such recent fashions among the aristocracy as spiritualism, table-turning, pietism and non-Church mysticism, but also with the "official" Church, its teachings and practices; with corrupt and ineffective bureaucrats, lawyers, capitalists foreign and domestic; with proponents of the "Eastern question" and supporters of the volunteers who went to aid the Serbs and Montenegrins in their war with the Turks (Tolstoy's handling of this issue was so hot that his publisher refused to print the final part of the novel, and Tolstoy had to bring it out in a separate edition at his own expense).

But even with all this commentary woven in, *Anna Karenina* never loses its soul as a tragic love story. More than a few readers through the decades have been moved to tears over Anna's fate.

Ellen Lindner brings a fresh, crisp look to this aristocratic world, adapting chapters 22 and 23 of Book One, which take place at a Moscow society ball, full of ritual and artifice. Princess Kitty has just rejected a marriage proposal from a man who loves her because she's sure that hunky Count Vronsky will propose to her that night. But oh, Vronsky met Kitty's sister-in-law, the married Anna Karenina, two days earlier, and here she is at the ball. . . .

SOURCE

Tolstoy, Leo. *Anna Karenina: A Novel in Eight Parts*. Translated by Richard Pevear and Larissa Volokhonsky. New York: Penguin Books, 2001.

ANNA KARENINA LEO TOLSTOY ELLEN LINDNER

That he did not ask her for the mazurka when they were dancing the quadrille did not disturb her. She was sure that they would dance the mazurka together as they had at previous balls.

Sorry~ already spoken for!

But while dancing the last quadrille with one of the youthful bores it would not do to refuse, she happened to be vis-à-vis with Vronsky and Anna.

She noticed that Anna was elated with success~ a feeling Kitty knew well. She also saw that Anna was intoxicated with the rapture she produced.

Kitty knew that feeling and knew its symptoms, and recognized them in Anna. She saw that quivering light flashing in her eyes, the smile of happiness and elation that involuntarily curled her lips, the exactitude and lightness of her movements.

I know that look!

She's happy to be admired by someone special.

Isn't Ivan Ivanovitch SO absurd when he speaks French?

And did you see the Eletsky girl? She's married so badly!

And that one- could it be HIM?

And Vronsky~ his face had an expression she'd never seen before. They discussed mutual friends, carrying on a seemingly meaningless conversation, but to Kitty it seemed that each word they said decided their fate and hers.

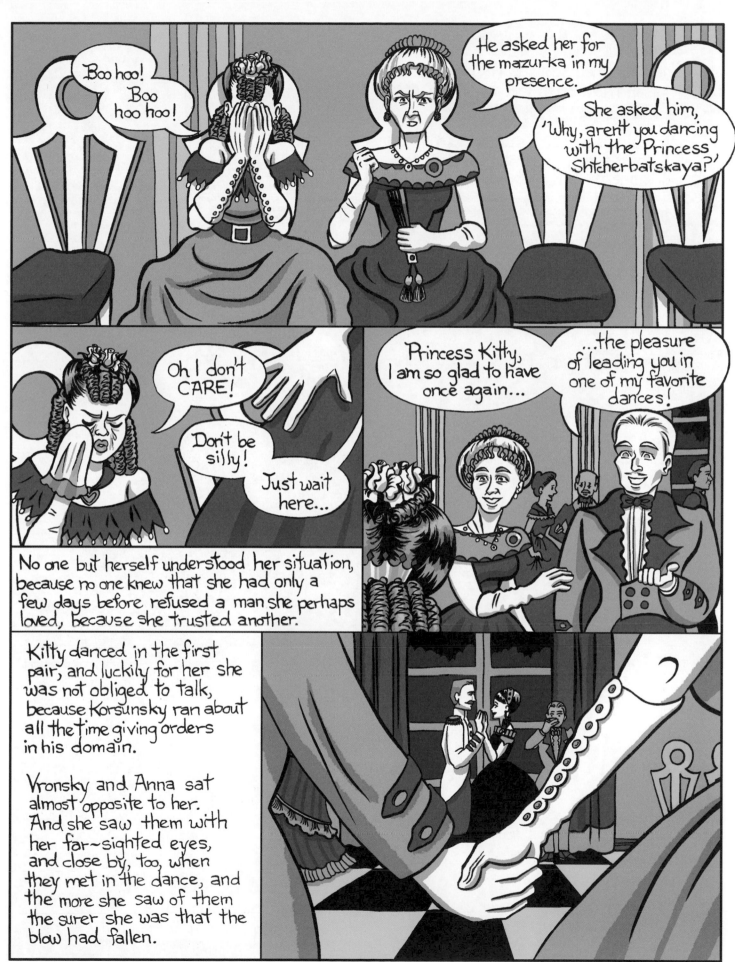

Adventures of Huckleberry Finn

Mark Twain

ART/ADAPTATION BY **J. Ben Moss**

IN 1876, MARK TWAIN—A.K.A. SAMUEL CLEMENS, America's funniest, folksiest titan of literature—wrote *The Adventures of Tom Sawyer*, a now-classic tale of a Midwestern, middle-class scallywag's shenanigans. Eight years later he did something altogether different for the sequel. He gave us the great American novel. (Only *Moby-Dick* is considered a rival for that title.) Ernest Hemingway declared: "All modern American literature comes from one book by Mark Twain called 'Huckleberry Finn.' . . . [I]t's the best book we've had. All American writing comes from that. There was nothing before. There has been nothing as good since."

The story of Tom Sawyer's buddy, Huck Finn, the vagrant, motherless son of an abusive alcoholic, deals with issues of race, socioeconomic class, conscience, and morality that were only hinted at in the prior book. Huck and the slave Jim take to the mighty Mississippi River together, both looking to escape—Huck from his father, Jim from his slave master, who wants to sell him. Part epic aquatic adventure (shades of *The Odyssey*), part road novel (a wet precursor of *On the Road*), part escape thriller, and part comedy, it features a protagonist who wrestles with his conscience like no one in literature outside of Raskolnikov in *Crime and Punishment*.

Huck likes Jim and recognizes him as a fellow human being, but Huck's culture has taught him that Jim isn't a human being—he's a piece of property, and helping him escape is theft. Huck vacillates between the two outlooks. He considers turning in Jim along the way. The crisis of conscience reaches its climax in chapter 16, the portion adapted here.

Down in Shreveport, Louisiana, overlooking the Red River (the last major tributary to the Mississippi), J. Ben Moss paints, illustrates, draws comics, and designs T-shirts, among other things. He perfectly captures the feel of that lone raft on the Mississippi at night, integrating Twain's pitch-perfect use of dialects that were previously unseen in literature. Now, *Adventures of Huckleberry Finn* has been graphically adapted in full several times, but each time the language has been bowdlerized, no doubt to avoid the fate of the novel itself, which is still routinely banned in classrooms and school libraries. Specifically, Twain's notorious use of the N-word—which appears almost 200 times—is erased. But that's how people of that time and place spoke, and that's the way Twain wrote it, so I asked Ben to leave the language alone. This marks the first time I know of that Twain's masterpiece has been faithfully adapted.

SOURCE

Twain, Mark. *The Annotated Huckleberry Finn*. Edited and annotated by Michael Patrick Hearn. New York: W.W. Norton & Company, 2001.

It hadn't ever come
home to me before,
what this thing was
that I was doing.

But now it did;
and it stayed with me, and
scorched me more and more.

I got to feeling
so mean and so
miserable I most
wished I was dead.

Every time Jim danced
around and says,

Dah's
Cairo!

it went through
me like a shot.

It most froze me to hear such talk.

He wouldn't ever dared to talk such talk in his life before.

Just see what a difference it made in him the minute
he judged he was about free.

It was according to the old saying,
'Give a nigger an inch and he'll take an ell.'

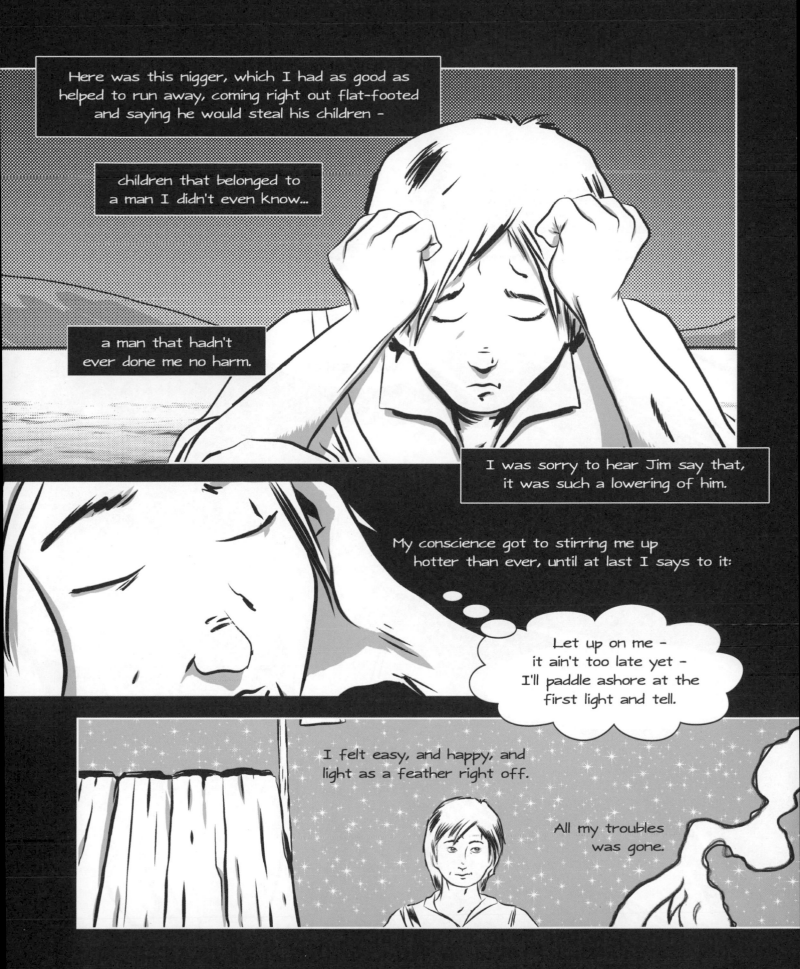

He jumped and got the canoe ready...

and put his old coat in the bottom for me to set on...

...and give me the paddle.

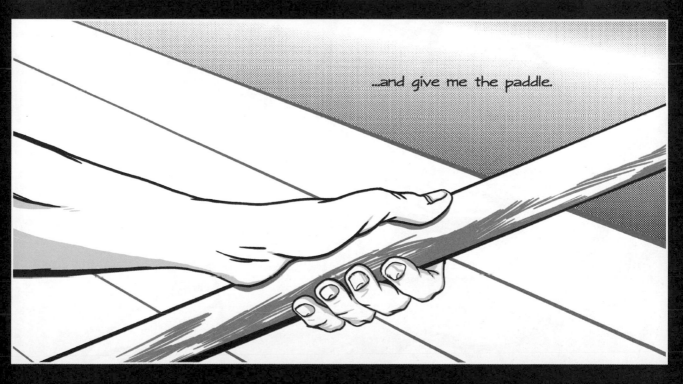

I was paddling off, all in a sweat to tell on him; but when he says this, it seemed to take the tuck all out of me.

I went along slow then, and I warn't right down certain whether I was glad I started or whether I warn't.

Dah you goes, de ole true Huck.

De on'y white genlman dat ever kep' his promise to ole Jim.

Well, I just felt sick.

I *got* to do it— I can't get *out* of it.

Right then, along comes a skiff with two men in it, with guns.

They stopped and I stopped.

What's that, yonder?

A piece of raft.

Do you belong on it?

Yes, sir.

Any men on it?

Only one, sir.

Thus Spake Zarathustra

Friedrich Nietzsche

ADAPTATION BY **Laurence Gane**

ART BY **Piero**

IN HIS CLASSIC BIOGRAPHY, *NIETZSCHE: PHILOSOPHER, Psychologist, Antichrist*, Walter Kaufmann summed up the nineteenth-century German wild man: "Nietzsche became a myth even before he died in 1900, and today his ideas are overgrown and obscured by rank fiction. Divergent evaluations, of course, are not uncommon; but in Nietzsche's case there is not even basic agreement about what he stood for: his admirers are as much at odds about this as his critics."

The Stanford Encyclopedia of Philosophy gives it a shot, though:

> He was interested in the enhancement of individual and cultural health, and believed in life, creativity, power, and the realities of the world we live in, rather than those situated in a world beyond. Central to his philosophy is the idea of "life-affirmation," which involves an honest questioning of all doctrines that drain life's expansive energies, however socially prevalent those views might be.

As Nietzsche wrote in *Thus Spake Zarathustra*: "I tell you: one must still have chaos in one, to give birth to a dancing star. I tell you: ye have still chaos in you."

His writings were mostly ignored during his lifetime, although he did finally catch on at the exact moment that he went irreversibly insane, at the beginning of 1889. *Thus Spake*

Zarathustra was one of an astounding string of major works that Nietzsche cranked out during his final decade of sanity, which includes, among others: *The Gay Science, Beyond Good and Evil, On the Genealogy of Morals, Twilight of the Idols, The Anti-Christ,* and *Ecce Homo* (the last three were completed in a single year, 1888). This is all the more impressive when you realize that Nietzsche was leading a nomadic existence this entire time, staying in cities across Europe, never for more than a few months in any one. He was stateless, having renounced his German citizenship but not becoming a citizen of any other country.

The following pages summarize and excerpt *Zarathustra*. They come from the book *Introducing Nietzsche*—written by Laurence Gane and illustrated by Piero—part of Icon Books' series of spirited graphic guides to philosophers and schools of philosophy, with the occasional heavy-hitter from science, literature, or religion.

SOURCES

Kaufmann, Walter. *Nietzsche: Philosopher, Psychologist, Antichrist.* Princeton: Princeton University Press, 1975.

Wicks, Robert. "Friedrich Nietzsche." In *The Stanford Encyclopedia of Philosophy*. Edited by Edward N. Zalta. Stanford: Stanford University, 2011. http://plato.stanford.edu/entries/nietzsche/.

Thus Spake Zarathustra

In February 1883, Nietzsche's own *furor philosophicus* reached new heights when, at Rapallo in Italy where he had spent the winter, he wrote the first part of his best-known work, *Thus Spake Zarathustra,* in just ten days.

His intense loneliness, following the Lou Andreas-Salomé affair, is clearly reflected in the character of Zarathustra.

He has a messianic quality, yet rejects those who approach him as disciples. At the end of part four, completed two years later, Zarathustra speaks only to himself.

The title of the book refers to the Sanskrit *Iti vuttakam*, "Thus spake the Holy One". **Zarathustra** or **Zoroaster** (c. 628–551 BC) was a prophet who founded Zendavesta, the religion of Persia before Islam, which survives today in India among the Parsee.

Zarathustra must now raise his voice not for metaphysics but in the name of the earth, the body, and most of all the Superman.

The Oracle Speaks

The book is a new departure: the anguished outpourings of a being who has arrived at the edge of human affairs. "One must speak with thunder and heavenly fireworks to feeble and dormant senses!" Zarathustra is an extraordinary blend of mystical insight, poetry, yearnings and intuitions.

Truly, a return of the Dionysian spirit! Later, in his autobiography *Ecce Homo* (1888), Nietzsche speaks of his experience of writing *Zarathustra*. "If one had the slightest trace of superstition left in one, it would be hard to deny the idea that one is the incarnation, mouthpiece and medium of almighty powers."

Indeed, it is the work of a poet rather than a philosopher. Although *Zarathustra* is very far from being a philosophical treatise, we can identify three main teachings in it.

1. *The Superman*

2. *The Will to Power*

3. *Eternal Recurrence*

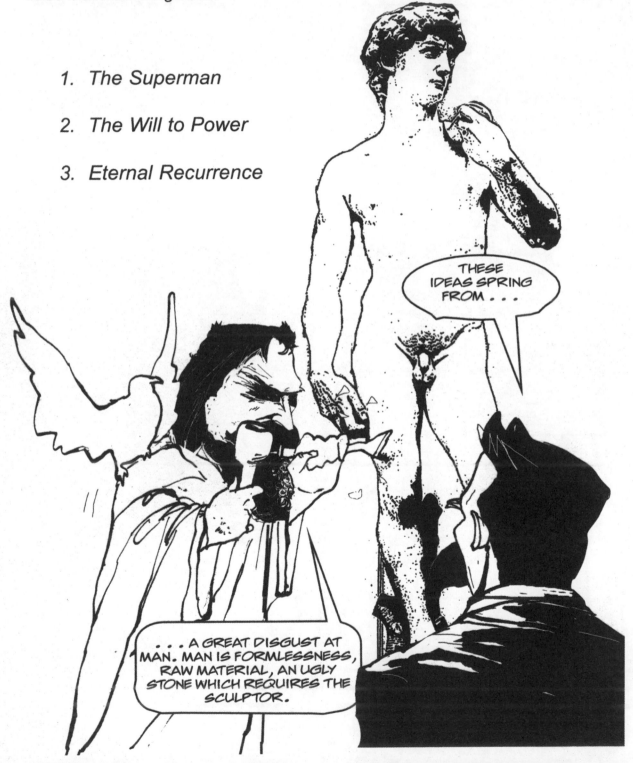

THESE IDEAS SPRING FROM . . .

. . . A GREAT DISGUST AT MAN. MAN IS FORMLESSNESS, RAW MATERIAL, AN UGLY STONE WHICH REQUIRES THE SCULPTOR.

It is Zarathustra's task to diagnose present ills and provide direction for a better future.

Although Zarathustra's teachings are the essence of the book, much of the text is devoted to a relentless psychological dissection of modern man, the emptiness of his values and beliefs. This is a picture of a nihilistic, anti-life society which promotes the mediocre and mistrusts originality.

Zarathustra sees around him a general malaise.

Indifference to life (nihilism).

Hypocrisy in morals (and religion).

Fear of the unknown.

On Nihilism

Too much information causes indigestion of the spirit. If we travel far down this road, we shall "choke on our own reason". It is the road to **nihilism**. True knowledge must be **useful** for the projects of human action.

On Virtuous Hypocrisy

The belief of "the virtuous" is a form of hypocrisy. When people say "virtue is necessary", they are really saying "the police is necessary", for what they crave is a quiet, orderly and safe society, where they will be well looked after.

Even worse, they expect a **reward** from their God for being virtuous. Is this a love of virtue?

"The sick and perishing – it was they who despised the body and the earth, and invented the heavenly world and the redeeming blood-drops: but even those sweet sad poisons they borrowed from the body and the earth!" Would the raptures of "heavenly transport" be possible *without a body*?

On Fear

"For today the petty people [the masses] have become lord and master; they preach submission and acquiescence and prudence and diligence and consideration . . ."

Behind this lies a fear of doing, risking and seeking one's own fate. A fear of wanting too much and facing failure.

This modern fear of pain and of suffering shows only that we have not suffered _enough_. All knowledge requires a price.

What is "The Superman"?

Nietzsche's ideas on the evolution of quality prepare the way for the often misunderstood doctrine of the Superman (*Ubermensch* or "over-man"). The term occurs in the work of the Greek satirist **Lucian** (c. 120–180 AD) as *hyperanthropos,* and in part one of *Faust* by **J.W. von Goethe** (1749–1832). It is usually understood in evolutionary terms – an inevitable development towards new life-forms.

We can make an ironic comparison with the Christian project of overcoming one's human weaknesses in the quest for salvation of the soul. But in the first pages of the book we are already reminded: "Could it be possible! This old saint in his forest has not yet heard that **God is dead**."

Only the most ambitious project can fill the void left by the death of God – the Superman is the only possible justification left to us.

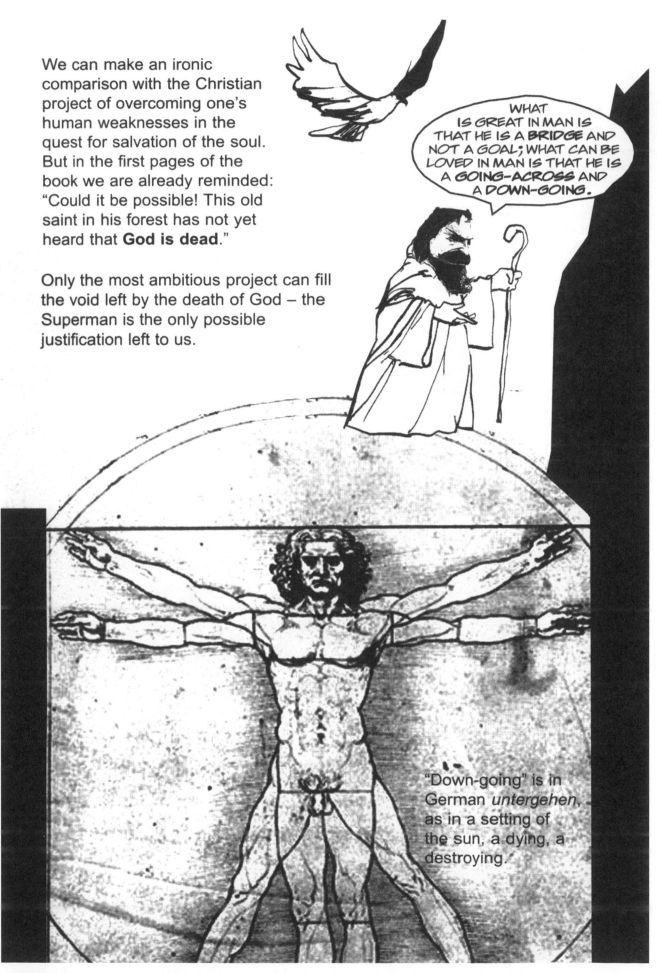

WHAT IS GREAT IN MAN IS THAT HE IS A **BRIDGE** AND NOT A GOAL; WHAT CAN BE LOVED IN MAN IS THAT HE IS A **GOING-ACROSS** AND A **DOWN-GOING**.

"Down-going" is in German *untergehen*, as in a setting of the sun, a dying, a destroying.

Later, in *The Genealogy of Morals*, Nietzsche will connect the Superman with the "noble" spirit who lives and wills in opposition to the common people who "ask very little of life". Zarathustra has contempt for the ordinary man who "makes everything small. His race is as inexterminable as the flea." Yet to accuse Zarathustra of inhumanity is to miss the point.

A Human or Post-Human Future?

Zarathustra's recurring fear is that the time is not right for his teachings: "The mob could become master, and all time be drowned in shallow waters." The doctrine of the Superman is perhaps as frightening to us today as it was in 1883. If so, then the shopkeepers shall inherit the earth!

THEY CRUCIFY HIM WHO WRITES NEW VALUES ON NEW LAW-TABLES, THEY SACRIFICE THE FUTURE TO THEMSELVES – THEY CRUCIFY THE WHOLE HUMAN FUTURE!

And thus, we the people (you and I?) will hold on to our happiness, our comforts and our gods. A weariness of spirit afflicts us, "a poor ignorant weariness, which no longer wants even to want: that created all gods and afterworlds".

The Will to Power

Clearly, the challenge of the Superman requires an attitude of mind which Nietzsche found lacking in his own culture. Such an attitude requires an extraordinary level of courage. Zarathustra calls this **the Will to Power**. Nietzsche had encountered this idea in Schopenhauer.

Any creature that deliberately risks its life for any reason is denying the "will to live". In such a situation, that creature shows something more fundamental still – the Will to Power.

Superficially, the idea of the Will to Power suggests a crude principle –
the victory of the strongest. But fundamentally, it is a psychological
principle of human behaviour that every being seeks to extend its
sphere of action and influence: to consolidate itself.

In the section "Of Self-Overcoming", Zarathustra says: "The will of the
weaker persuades it to serve the stronger; its will wants to be master
over those weaker still: this delight alone it is unwilling to forgo."

The greater the will, the higher the stakes, and even the weakest can
"steal by secret paths into the castle and even into the heart of the more
powerful – and steal their power".

Self-Obedience

Strength of will can overcome the greatest power of arms, yet the hardest overcoming will be the **overcoming of itself**: "He who cannot obey himself will be commanded."

. . . COMMANDING IS MORE DIFFICULT THAN OBEYING . . . FOR THE COMMANDER BEARS THE BURDEN OF ALL WHO OBEY, AND THAT BURDEN CAN EASILY CRUSH HIM.

Difficult also because the Will to Power must find within itself its **own** reasons for what it does, not those of another. No wonder Nietzsche calls this philosophy "strenuous" – for together with the total responsibility for every action goes the requirement of creating one's own **value** for that action.

The Free Spirit

Clearly, the higher man or "free spirit" who can totally embody the Will to Power is a being not yet seen, although Nietzsche contends that certain historical individuals do approach that ideal – Julius Caesar, Goethe, Napoleon.

Critics usually see in these doctrines the picture of a selfish, egotistical, unscrupulous and self-serving individual. But Nietzsche will not allow this as counting against his position.

AT THE RISK OF DISPLEASING INNOCENT EARS, I SUBMIT THAT EGOISM BELONGS TO THE ESSENCE OF A NOBLE SOUL . . . AND HAS ITS BASIS IN THE PRIMARY LAW OF THINGS.

Concerning the accusation of "self-serving", he might reply, "Who else should we wish to serve, if not ourselves?" Here, as elsewhere, we see his old opponent Christian ethics (our ethics?) under the microscope.

The Circle of Time

Zarathustra's third doctrine – the eternal recurrence of things – shows a more human (rather than superhuman) side to his character, since it offers a metaphysical solace to our feelings of abandonment at the loss of our gods.

In "Of the Vision and the Riddle", Zarathustra describes two roads.

The portal is inscribed "The Moment". An eternity lies behind him, and an eternity yet again lies before him; an unending chain of events in which he is inextricably involved.

A Pessimistic Consolation

If "eternal recurrence" offers us the promise of an eternity, it is not one with a "happy ending" – for it offers no ending at all. Like the punishment of Sisyphus in the Greek myth, we are condemned to a terrible repetition of events for all eternity. This lack of purpose or ending – a form of meaninglessness which echoes the "endless desiring" in Schopenhauer's philosophy – adds a pessimistic undertone to Zarathustra's otherwise joyful preachings.

Here again we find an emphasis on "the moment" – on our present **action** and **will** – and whatever follows is tied to this for all eternity.

BUT WHERE SCHOPENHAUER PREACHES RESIGNATION, I TEACH DEFIANCE, FOR THE SUPERMAN AND THE WILL TO POWER ARE PRIMARILY *LIFE-AFFIRMING* DOCTRINES.

Strange Case of Dr. Jekyll and Mr. Hyde

Robert Louis Stevenson

ADAPTATION BY **Danusia Schejbal**

ART BY **Andrzej Klimowski**

THE "PENNY DREADFULS" OR "SHILLING SHOCK-ers" of the Victorian era were cheaply printed, lurid, sensationalistic works of fiction that the public ate up like candy. Robert Louis Stevenson—who had already written the popular adventure novel *Treasure Island*—was a fan of the penny dreadfuls. Being in dire financial straits at the time—"bankruptcy at my heels," he wrote to his wife—he decided to write one, filled with the requisite murder, mystery, and Gothic creepiness. "For two days I went about racking my brains for a plot of any sort," he later wrote. Then his long-standing fascination with the idea of hidden aspects of ourselves led to a nightmare in which he saw three scenes that would lead to his story of a basically normal man who transforms into a violent, uncontrollable fiend.

Stevenson cranked out this novella of over 30,000 words in *three days*. But his wife thought he hadn't really gotten past the sensationalism, to the allegory right under the surface, so he burned the manuscript. Then he rewrote it in another three days. Stevenson had been sickly and weak since he was a child, and at this point in his life he was, to use a Victorianism, an invalid. That he managed to write around 70,000 words—two versions of a now-classic work of literature—in a six-day-and-night marathon is astonishing. It's led to conjecture that this burst was fueled by cocaine, which was then all the rage in medical journals and papers, being dispensed by doctors, lauded by Sigmund Freud, and apparently used by Stevenson's fellow Scottish writer, Arthur Conan Doyle. There's no direct evidence that Stevenson was using blow, but we know that he took morphine. And then there's the intriguing way in which Dr. Jekyll turns into Mr. Hyde: he ingests a chemical concoction he created in the lab.

At any rate, Stevenson then spent at least a month polishing the manuscript, and it was published at the beginning of 1886. In three months, 6,000 copies had been sold in the US, and in six months, 40,000 had been sold in Britain. Professor Katherine Lineman writes that

the tale has never been out of print, and its popularity has been worldwide. More than eighty translations have appeared, in at least thirty different languages. Since its

publication, the tale has generated an ongoing stream of critical commentary and garnered tributes from writers as various as Henry James, Gerard Manley Hopkins, Vladimir Nabokov, John Fowles, Jorge Luis Borges, Stephen King, Joyce Carol Oates, and Italo Calvino.

Several things account for its appeal and its literary reputation. It completely works simply as a penny dreadful, as a creepy, suspenseful murder/blackmail mystery with a quasi-supernatural element. Also, Stevenson hit a deep nerve with his tale of two personalities, of the unhinged demon-spawn that seems to exist in even the most respectable of us. But the reason it works as literature—in addition to the superior quality of the writing—is that the author worked in so much nuance and ambiguity. Despite the general take on the book's plot, Dr. Jekyll is not entirely nice and wonderful (as we see by the fact that he first relished becoming the unaccountable Hyde), and Mr. Hyde has a bit of good and decency in him still. The relationship between them is complex—they are not polar opposites but overlapping aspects of the same person. Furthering the book's depth, the puzzle-like narrative is told in many ways, in several voices. And the moral of the story, if any, is wide open for debate.

Now a professor at the Royal College of Art in London, Polish artist Andrzej Klimowski has won many awards for his work over the last four-plus decades, which includes posters for film, theater, and opera, books covers, animation, and newspaper illustration for the *Guardian*. Danusia Schejbal creates art in such diverse media as paintings, movie posters, and theater props and costumes. In this excerpt from their full-length adaptation of *Strange Case of Dr. Jekyll and Mr. Hyde*, it's apparent that they perfectly captured the darkness of this dreadful tale.

SOURCES

Stevenson, Robert Louis. *Strange Case of Dr. Jekyll and Mr. Hyde: A Norton Critical Edition*. Edited by Katherine Linehan. New York: W.W. Norton & Company, 2003.

Streatfeild, Dominic. *Cocaine: An Unauthorized Biography*. New York: Picador, 2003.

I immediately bought a particular salt from a chemist. Then one fateful night I mixed the elements, watched them boil and smoke...

... plucked up courage and drank the potion.

DR. JEKYLL AND MR. HYDE ROBERT LOUIS STEVENSON DANUSIA SCHEJBAL AND ANDRZEJ KLIMOWSKI 449

DR. JEKYLL AND MR. HYDE ROBERT LOUIS STEVENSON DANUSIA SCHEJBAL AND ANDRZEJ KLIMOWSKI

DR. JEKYLL AND MR. HYDE ROBERT LOUIS STEVENSON DANUSIA SCHEJBAL AND ANDRZEJ KLIMOWSKI

It was nearly morning~

~The inmates of my house were fast asleep, and I was determined to take the risk in my new shape and go to my bedroom.

DR. JEKYLL AND MR. HYDE ROBERT LOUIS STEVENSON DANUSIA SCHEJBAL AND ANDRZEJ KLIMOWSKI **453**

... I saw for the first time
EDWARD HYDE

I felt no repugnance ~
I knew I was wicked,
ten times more wicked,
and that thought both
braced and delighted me.

DR. JEKYLL AND MR. HYDE ROBERT LOUIS STEVENSON DANUSIA SCHEJBAL AND ANDRZEJ KLIMOWSKI

DR. JEKYLL AND MR. HYDE ROBERT LOUIS STEVENSON DANUSIA SCHEJBAL AND ANDRZEJ KLIMOWSKI

Back in my cabinet I again prepared and drank the cup...

DR. JEKYLL AND MR. HYDE ROBERT LOUIS STEVENSON DANUSIA SCHEJBAL AND ANDRZEJ KLIMOWSKI

DR. JEKYLL AND MR. HYDE ROBERT LOUIS STEVENSON DANUSIA SCHEJBAL AND ANDRZEJ KLIMOWSKI 457

...returned as Henry Jekyll. That night I reached the fatal crossroads. Had I approached my discovery in a more noble spirit I would have come forth an angel instead of a fiend. From now on I had two characters.

One was wholly evil, the other was still the old Henry Jekyll.

DR. JEKYLL AND MR. HYDE ROBERT LOUIS STEVENSON DANUSIA SCHEJBAL AND ANDRZEJ KLIMOWSKI

DR. JEKYLL AND MR. HYDE ROBERT LOUIS STEVENSON DANUSIA SCHEJBAL AND ANDRZEJ KLIMOWSKI

At the other house I told my servants that a Mr. Hyde was to have complete freedom in my home. I then drew up a will, so that if anything happened to me as Dr. Jekyll, I could still enter as Hyde without any financial loss.

For years, men have hired assassins to carry out their crimes ~ I was the first that ever did so for pleasure. I could escape into my laboratory, mix and swallow the draught, and whatever Hyde had done would vanish; for in his place would be Henry Jekyll.

The pleasures that I looked for in my disguise were, as I have said, undignified...

... but in Edward Hyde's hands they were monstrous. Henry Jekyll was appalled at Hyde's acts. It was Hyde after all, and Hyde alone, that was guilty. Where it was possible Jekyll would try and undo the evil done by Hyde and so his conscience slept.

"An Occurrence at Owl Creek Bridge"

Ambrose Bierce

ART/ADAPTATION BY **Sandy Jimenez**

AMBROSE "BITTER" BIERCE WAS A DECORATED AND wounded Union soldier in the US Civil War; a journalist who exposed political corruption; a writer of stories primarily in the genres of war, horror/weird, proto-science fiction, and tall tales; and one of the most famous Americans (along with Amelia Earhart, Jimmy Hoffa, and Judge Joseph Crater) to simply disappear.

His cynical, misanthropic tendencies are in their most concentrated form in *The Devil's Dictionary*, a book-length collection of biting definitions:

AIR, n. A nutritious substance supplied by a bountiful Providence for the fattening of the poor.

FRIENDLESS, adj. Having no favors to bestow. Destitute of fortune. Addicted to utterance of truth and common sense.

PLUNDER, v. To take the property of another without observing the decent and customary reticences of theft.

Bierce's most enduring short story is "An Occurrence at Owl Creek Bridge" (1890), which famously opens *in medias res* (that is, in the middle of the action), with unadorned, declarative sentences that feel like a forerunner of Hemingway's style:

A man stood upon a railroad bridge in northern Alabama, looking down into the swift water twenty feet below. The man's hands were behind his back, the wrists bound with a cord. A rope closely encircled his neck.

In his last collection of essays, Kurt Vonnegut singled out "Occurrence" as "the greatest American short story."

Sandy Jimenez—creator of the "Shit House Poet" stories, appearing for over twenty years in *World War 3 Illustrated*—explains his approach to adapting one of the masterworks of short fiction:

I decided early on that if I was going to use the structure of a comic book's gutters and panels, I was not going to edit and recompose Bierce's prose with excerpts out of respect for the story. I instead tried to recreate the images I saw in my own mind that Bierce's writing had inspired, and do a wordless adaptation.

By far the toughest things to communicate without words were the shifts in time within the story; there is a lengthy flashback (a term that didn't exist in the pre-cinema nineteenth century) within what is presumably the past event of the story itself.

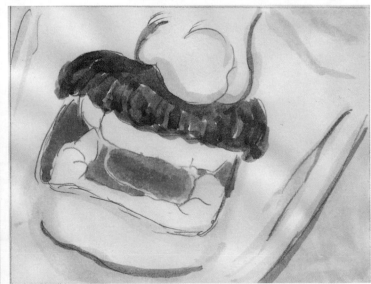

"AN OCCURRENCE AT OWL CREEK BRIDGE" AMBROSE BIERCE SANDY JIMENEZ

"AN OCCURRENCE AT OWL CREEK BRIDGE" AMBROSE BIERCE SANDY JIMENEZ

"AN OCCURRENCE AT OWL CREEK BRIDGE" AMBROSE BIERCE SANDY JIMENEZ

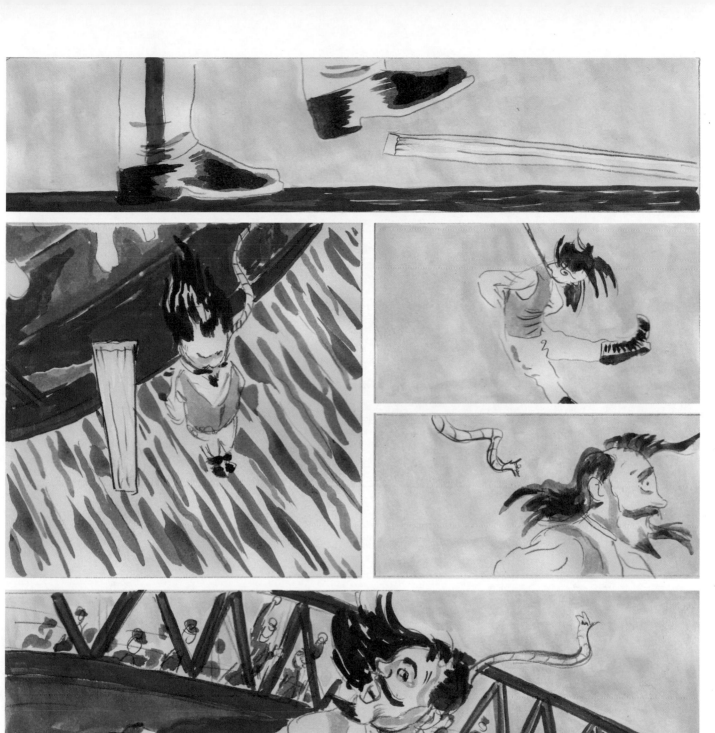

"AN OCCURRENCE AT OWL CREEK BRIDGE" AMBROSE BIERCE SANDY JIMENEZ   467

"AN OCCURRENCE AT OWL CREEK BRIDGE" AMBROSE BIERCE SANDY JIMENEZ

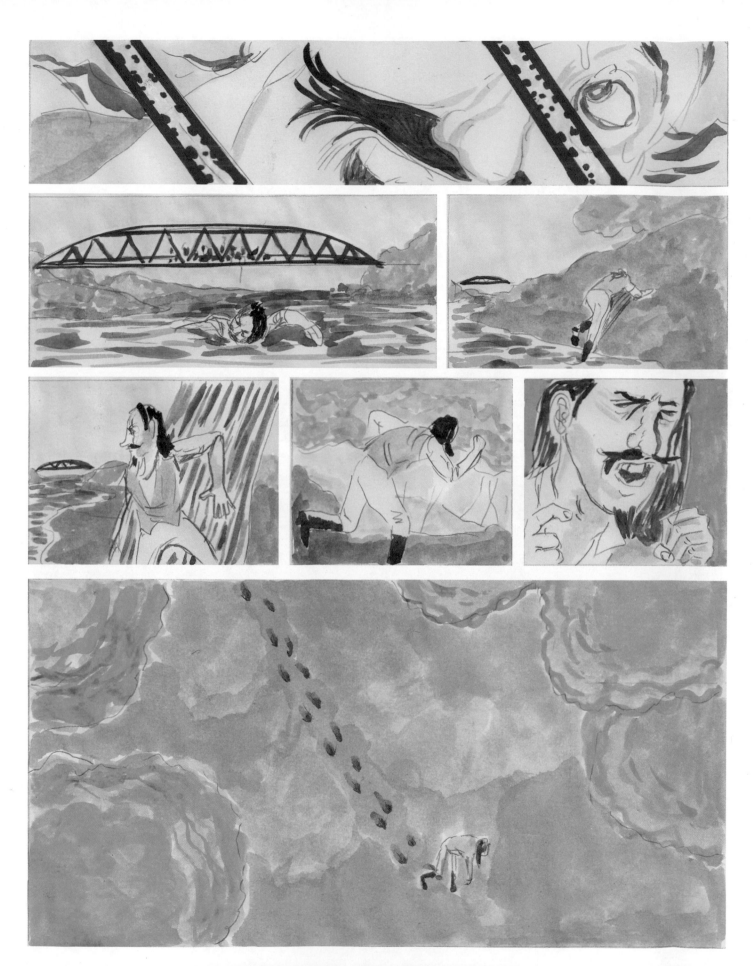

"AN OCCURRENCE AT OWL CREEK BRIDGE" AMBROSE BIERCE SANDY JIMENEZ

"AN OCCURRENCE AT OWL CREEK BRIDGE" AMBROSE BIERCE SANDY JIMENEZ 471

"AN OCCURRENCE AT OWL CREEK BRIDGE" AMBROSE BIERCE SANDY JIMENEZ

The Picture of Dorian Gray

Oscar Wilde

ART/ADAPTATION BY **John Coulthart**

OSCAR WILDE IS A LARGER-THAN-LIFE FIGURE—A decadent dandy, a witty aesthete, the toast of the literary and theater scenes of *fin de siècle* Paris and London, an almost-out gay man who became a martyr for sexual freedom.

Wilde had published some journalism, reviews, fairy tales, mystery stories, and essays on aestheticism—his classic plays were yet to come—when his first (and only) novel, *The Picture of Dorian Gray*, was published in a highly regarded literary journal in 1890. It famously tells the story of a dashing young man who gets to keep his physical beauty while a portrait of him ages hideously, as it reflects not only the march of time but also the selfish, libertine life he leads. The protagonist is obviously bisexual, and while nothing explicit is described, the homoeroticism is hard to miss. Even though the journal's editor cut some of the most daring passages, *Dorian Gray* was predictably savaged as immoral and obscene. When published as a stand-alone book the following year, it was greatly expanded while simultaneously being further tamed by Wilde's own hand. (It wasn't until 2011 that the original version, as Wilde first wrote it, was published.)

At the height of his fame, in 1895, things suddenly fell apart. One of Wilde's consorts—his main squeeze, actually—was the much younger Lord Alfred Douglas. This hellion's father, the Marquess of Queensberry, publicly accused Wilde of being a "somdomite" [*sic*]. In a very ill-advised move, Wilde sued him for libel; Queensberry defended himself by proving that Wilde was a promiscuous lover of men, leading to his arrest. During his trial for gross indecency, *The New Yorker* explains, "the opposing attorneys read aloud from 'Dorian Gray,' calling it a 'sodomitical book.' Wilde went to prison not because he loved young men but because he flaunted that love, and 'Dorian Gray' became the chief exhibit of his shamelessness."

Wilde was sentenced to two years of hard labor in a brutal prison; the experience destroyed his health, leading to his death in abject poverty at age forty-six in 1900, three years after his release.

Artist John Coulthart came to my attention in the 1990s, with his intricate pen-and-ink work for the notorious series of comics revolving around the character Lord Horror, put out by Manchester's untamed press, Savoy. His masterful attention to detail, old-school techniques, and frequent references to Decadent, Symbolist, and Modernist literature and art made him seem like an artist from some past golden age transported to our time. In recent years, John has turned his attention to collage, with the same exquisite results. For *The Graphic Canon*, he has adapted one of his favorite literary works as a series of ten full-page collages filled with hidden significances and connections. He reveals some of them:

> The portrait itself is a painting by John Singer Sargent of illustrator W. Graham Robertson, who not only knew Wilde but was also friends with Robert de Montesquiou, Huymans' model for Des Esseintes in *À Rebours*, the Decadent novel that greatly influenced *The Picture of Dorian Gray*. The framed picture of the two young men on the "invert" page is of two of Wilde's rent boy acquaintances. The street scene near the end is Gustave Doré's depiction of the real Bluegate Fields.

The text that you see in the collages is taken from scans of a first edition of *The Picture of Dorian Gray*.

SOURCE

Ross, Alex. "Deceptive Picture: How Oscar Wilde Painted Over 'Dorian Gray.'" *The New Yorker,* August 8, 2011.

THE PICTVRE OF DORIAN·GRAY· BY OSCAR WILDE

DESIGNS BY JOHN COVLTHART

"Tell me more about Mr. Dorian Gray. How often do you see him?"

"Every day. I couldn't be happy if I didn't see him every day. He is absolutely necessary to me."

"How extraordinary! I thought you would never care for anything but your art."

"He is all my art to me now," said the painter, gravely.

THE PICTURE OF DORIAN GRAY OSCAR WILDE JOHN COULTHART

"Ah! realize your youth while you have it. Don't squander the gold of your days, listening to the tedious, trying to improve the hopeless failure, or giving away your life to the ignorant, the common, and the vulgar. These are the sickly aims, the false ideals, of our age. Live! Live the wonderful life that is in you!"

"We degenerate into hideous puppets, haunted by the memory of the passions of which we were too much afraid, and the exquisite temptations that we had not the courage to yield to. Youth! Youth! There is absolutely nothing in the world but youth!"

Dorian Gray listened, open-eyed and wondering.

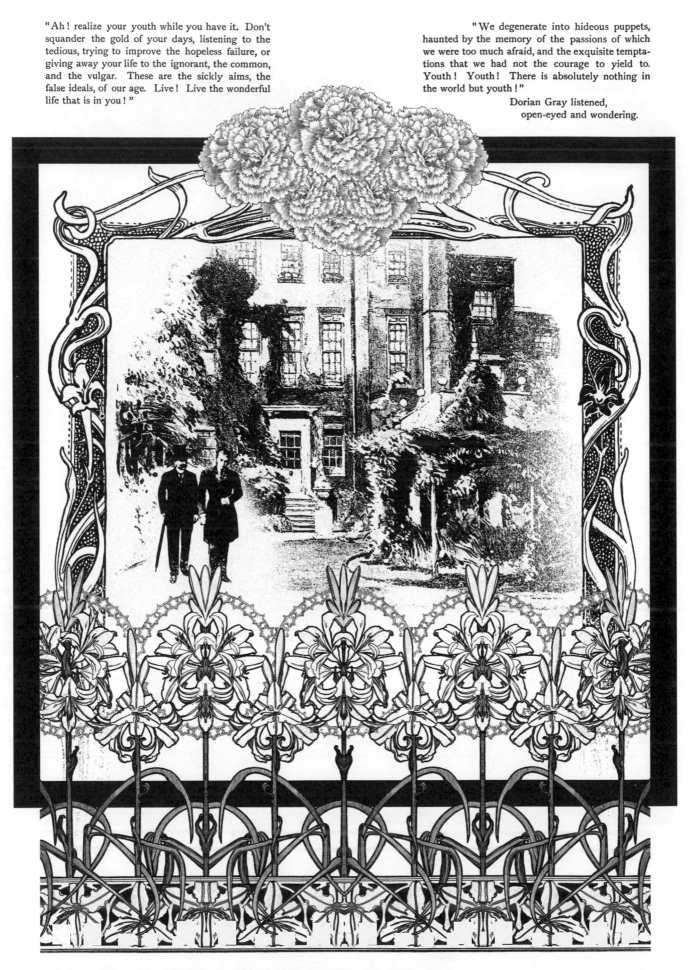

"Who are you in love with?"
    asked Lord Henry, after a pause.
"With an actress," said Dorian Gray, blushing.
Lord Henry shrugged his shoulders. "That is
a rather commonplace *début*."

"You would not say so if you saw her, Harry."
"Who is she?"
"Her name is Sibyl Vane."

Lord Henry walked across the room, and, sitting down by Dorian Gray, took both his hands in his own, and held them tightly. "Dorian," he said, "my letter—don't be frightened—was to tell you that Sibyl Vane is dead."

THE PICTURE OF DORIAN GRAY OSCAR WILDE JOHN COULTHART

For these treasures, and everything that he collected in his lovely house, were to be to him means of forgetfulness, modes by which he could escape, for a season, from the fear that seemed to him at times to be almost too great to be borne.

THE PICTURE OF DORIAN GRAY OSCAR WILDE JOHN COULTHART 479

"Why is your friendship so fatal to young men? There was that wretched boy in the Guards who committed suicide. You were his great friend. There was Sir Henry Ashton, who had to leave England, with a tarnished name. You and he were inseparable.

"What about Adrian Singleton, and his dreadful end? What about Lord Kent's only son, and his career? I met his father yesterday in St. James's Street. He seemed broken with shame and sorrow. What about the young Duke of Perth? What sort of life has he got now?"

"There was nothing evil in it, nothing shameful. You were to me such an ideal as I shall never meet again. This is the face of a satyr."

"It is the face of my soul."

"Christ! what a thing I must have worshipped! It has the eyes of a devil."

"Each of us has Heaven and Hell in him, Basil," cried Dorian, with a wild gesture of despair.

Dorian Gray glanced at the picture, and suddenly an uncontrollable feeling of hatred for Basil Hallward came over him, as though it had been suggested to him by the image on the canvas, whispered into his ear by those grinning lips.

FURTHER READING
JORDYN OSTROFF

"KUBLA KHAN" AND "THE RIME OF THE ANCIENT MARINER"

Along with his best friend forever and fellow poet, William Wordsworth, Samuel Taylor Coleridge is known to have sounded the starting pistol of English Romanticism at the turn of the nineteenth century. Although heavy opium use contributed to a somewhat early death, Coleridge was prolific enough during his lifetime to fill several hundred pages with radical new poetry and criticism. William Keach's *The Complete Poems* (Penguin Classics, 1997) covers the writer's entire body of poetry, and includes comprehensive notes and an introduction. For a more conveniently sized (and priced) volume, you might try *Selected Poetry*, which major Coleridge scholar H. J. Jackson edited for Oxford World's Classics; it's still got all the major poems, like "The Rime of the Ancient Mariner" and "Kubla Khan." But Coleridge was a genius in prose, too, so it's worth checking out the other Coleridge volume from Oxford World's Classics, also a Jackson-edited edition, *Samuel Taylor Coleridge: The Major Works*, which presents the meat of the writer's poetry alongside the full text of his most significant critical work, *Biographia Literaria*, and a selection of letters, notebooks, and marginalia. But if you really can't get enough Coleridge, you'll probably want to invest a hefty chunk of cash (as well as time and physical strength) into Princeton University Press's *Collected Works of Samuel Taylor Coleridge*, which comprises all of Coleridge's known writings—prose, verse, notebooks, and letters—into twenty-three clothbound volumes, each with a slew of notes. Several volumes are now out of print, so you'll have to be truly dedicated to all things Coleridge if you hope to acquire a complete set.

"AUGURIES OF INNOCENCE" AND *JERUSALEM: THE EMANATION OF THE GIANT ALBION*

In his own lifetime, William Blake was often declared mad for his radical, idiosyncratic views and mystical visions. Today, he is considered one of the most expressive, talented—and, sadly—under-read literary and visual artists of the Romantic period. Despite his artistic talent, Blake had a rather impenetrable scrawl. Luckily, we've got scholar David V. Erdman, who used far-out technology like infrared and microphotography to decipher the writer's handwriting for Anchor's *The Complete Poetry & Prose of William Blake*. First published in 1965, it is still lauded as the best available edition of Blake's work, and includes the full text of *Jerusalem: The Emanation of the Giant Albion*, Blake's last and greatest prophetic book. Anchor's revised edition (1988) even includes critical commentary by the god of English-language literature, Harold Bloom. Norton's second critical edition, *Blake's Poetry and Designs*, is even more star-studded; it features various commentaries from Samuel Taylor Coleridge, Allen Ginsberg, Northrop Frye, and others, as well as color images from Blake's illuminated poems and extensive contextual documentation. Blake actually illuminated many of his own texts, and his famously difficult prophetic books are particularly notable for their engravings. You can take a gander at the breathtaking images of this "apocalyptic humanist" (as Harold Bloom calls him) in *William Blake: The Complete Illuminated Books* (Thames & Hudson, 2001) and *William Blake's Divine Comedy Illustrations: 102 Full-Color Plates* (Dover Fine Art, 2008).

"I WANDERED LONELY AS A CLOUD"

William Wordsworth may be known for his sympathy for the average man's "common speech," but his own verse is anything but common; it is profound, beautifully reflective, and deeply indebted to nature. Together with his bosom buddy Samuel Taylor Coleridge, Wordsworth published *Lyrical Ballads* in 1798, launching English-language Romanticism. Today's lovers of romance and the natural world continue to take dreamy solace in poems like "I Wandered Lonely as a Cloud" (one of Wordsworth's most famous, also known as "The Daffodils") in a myriad of collections. *William Wordsworth: The Major Works*, edited by Stephen Gill for Oxford World's Classics, has all the most important prose and poetry, and very thorough notes. True Wordsworth devotees may need to invest more heavily—perhaps in *The Cambridge Companion to Wordsworth* (2003), also edited by Stephen Gill, and containing essays on all aspects of the poet's life, by the crème de la crème of Wordsworth scholars. To truly set the man in context, though, the dedicated reader should leaf through Duncan Wu's *Romanticism: An Anthology*; Wiley-Blackwell's brand new fourth edition of this truly essential anthology is updated to include notes, explanatory material, and the latest in scholarly findings.

PRIDE AND PREJUDICE

Well before zombies walked the grounds of Meryton (*Pride and Prejudice and Zombies*, by Seth Grahame-Smith, Quirk Books, 2009), Jane Austen's *Pride and Prejudice* was spawning sequels, prequels, TV miniseries, movies, sci-fi adaptations, Japanese comic books, and even Bollywood musicals. But before the commercial frenzy surrounding the Bennet sisters and their boy troubles ever began, readers got their Mr. Darcy fix straight from the novel itself. Though the novel was not published in the United States till 1832, the Norton Critical Edition (2000)—edited by Donald Gray and including essays, letters, and early writings by Jane Austen herself—contains the original 1813 text, rather than the 1923 version that most modern publications include. *The Annotated Pride and Prejudice* (Anchor Books, 2007) is indeed thoroughly annotated by David M. Shapard. As befits a novel that is as much concerned with image and decorum as with content and passion, many of these editions are truly gorgeous: acclaimed fashion illustrator Ruben Toledo designed the 2009 Penguin Classics Deluxe Edition; Nancy Butler and Hugo Petrus wrote and illustrated a 2010 graphic adaptation for Marvel; and Patricia Meyer Spacks's 2010 annotated edition for Harvard University Press contains lovely period illustrations. But for those days when you really just need a dose of Darcy in your living room, pick your poison—BBC's Colin Firth and Jennifer Ehle (1995) or Focus Features's Matthew Macfadyen and Keira Knightley (2005)—and zone out with a sigh: "It is a truth universally acknowledged, that a single man in a possession of a good fortune, must be in want of a wife. . . ."

"SHE WALKS IN BEAUTY"

Beautiful and preening, manic-depressive, and prone to extremes in eating, exercise, and emotion, Lord Byron was a celebrity even in his own day in the early nineteenth century. His wife coined the term "Byromania" to refer to the hubbub of attention surrounding him. Today's Byromaniacs need look no further than the classic vampire to find traces of their hero in popular culture—Bram Stoker's decadent, seductive, and dangerous Dracula is in fact based on Byron himself. Byron may have died tragically early, but his literary output was still enormous. Jerome J. McGann's *Lord Byron: The Major Works* (Oxford World's Classics, 2008) is a correspondingly enormous volume, incorporating a selection of letters and journal entries into the comprehensive collection. For those seeking a more thorough explanation of Byron's gorgeous verse, there is *Selected Poems* (Penguin Classics, 2006), which actually includes Byron's own notes for each poem directly alongside the text, and Alice Levine's *Byron's Poetry and Prose* (Norton Critical Editions, 2009), which organizes the poet's writing into chronological clusters and includes critical essays from a number of major Byron scholars. Of course, at least some of Byron's appeal lies in the swirling rumors of sodomy and incest, his fervent and multitudinous love affairs, and his heroic early death in support of the Greek movement for independence. For more on his swashbuckling, passionate life, readers should check out *Byron: Child of Passion, Fool of Fame* (Vintage, 2000) by noted biographer Benita Eisler.

"O SOLITUDE" AND "LA BELLE DAME SANS MERCI"

John Keats, a seminal figure of English Romanticism, was not popular during his own very brief, agonized lifetime, but by the end of the nineteenth century, his sensual odes had become an integral part of English literature. "O Solitude" was published in *The Examiner* in 1816, becoming the first of his poems to appear in print. Keats did in fact know solitude well: he watched family and friends succumb to tuberculosis one by one in damp London apartments. If you're feeling a bit lonely yourself, you can find catharsis in "O Solitude" and other poems like "La Belle Dame Sans Merci," in John Barnard's *John Keats: Selected Poetry* (Penguin Classics, 2007) or Jeffrey N. Cox's *Keats's Poetry and Prose* (Norton Critical Editions, 2008), which includes critical apparatus via a full stable of Keats scholars. The definitive Keats volume, though, is *Complete Poems*, first published by Belknap Press at Harvard in 1978. Containing useful explanatory notes from editor Jack Stillinger and a new introduction speculating on Keats's life and genius, this edition has endured numerous printings and remains in print today.

"OZYMANDIAS"

The theme of nineteenth-century Romantic poet Percy Bysshe Shelley's "Ozymandias" might be the inevitable fall of leaders and their empires, but Shelley's own lyric literary empire is still going strong. "Ozymandias" was first published in 1818 as part of a competition with Shelley's friend Horace Smith, who also published a poem on the subject. Since then, it has inspired short fiction, songs, computer games, and television programs, including a scene in *Monty Python's Flying Circus*. The poem itself appears alongside the best of Romantic poetry in Duncan Wu's *Romanticism: An Anthology* (fourth edition, Wiley-Blackwell, 2012). It also appears in Norton's second critical edition, *Shelley's Poetry and Prose*, edited by Shelley

scholars Neil Fraistat and Donald H. Reiman and with criticism by Harold Bloom, among illustrious others. The Oxford World's Classics *Percy Bysshe Shelley: The Major Works* is also excellent, and even more affordable despite the fact that it is the fullest one-volume English-language selection. If you simply must know everything there is to know about this uncompromisingly idealistic poet, check out James Bieri's definitive *Percy Bysshe Shelley: A Biography* (Johns Hopkins University Press, 2008). Of course, behind every great man is a great woman, and in this case that woman was exceptional: Shelley's wife, author Mary Shelley.

FRANKENSTEIN

Mary Shelley's *Frankenstein; or, The Modern Prometheus*, a brooding, gothic novel in which a hubristic scientist endows a mangled, cobbled-together corpse with the spark of life, remains frighteningly relevant in today's world of far-out, dangerous science. Shelley first published *Frankenstein* anonymously in England in 1818, and then published a significantly revised (and less controversial) edition in 1831. Readers can find the revised text in Bedford/St. Martin's Case Studies in Contemporary Criticism edition (2000), along with critical essays analyzing the novel from contemporary psychoanalytic, feminist, and cultural perspectives. The original 1818 text, which some scholars argue remains truer to the spirit of the story, can be found in J. Paul Hunter's Norton Critical Edition (the best-selling student edition on the market), which includes a slew of useful contextual essays, maps, illustrations, and annotations. The Oxford World's Classics edition, edited by Marilyn Butler, also contains the 1818 text, and it sets the novel in the context of the radical science of its time. And, it's way cheaper. But for the cheapest, simplest edition, check out the Barnes and Noble Classics Edition (2005), which is under five dollars and still has a great intro by NYU professor Karen Karbiener. In *The Original Frankenstein* (Vintage, 2009), Charles E. Robinson presents Mary's very first draft of the story, from 1816, and a longer draft from the next year, in which we can see the numerous changes that Percy made, including writing some segments himself. *Frankenstein* has also inspired dozens of theatrical and cinematic adaptations, including Universal's 1931 film with Boris Karloff as a pitiable Frankenstein, the 1935 sequel *The Bride of Frankenstein*, and the looser (and lewder) 1973 musical adaptation, *The Rocky Horror Picture Show*. For a lavish examination of the mark Frankenstein has made on stage, screen, Halloween costumes, and even politics and science, see *Frankenstein: A Cultural History* by Susan Tyler Hitchcock (W.W. Norton and Company, 2007).

FAIRY TALES BY THE BROTHERS GRIMM

Brothers Jacob and Wilhelm Grimm sure knew how to spin a yarn. In 1812, they published the first volume of the first edition of *Kinder- und Hausmärchen*—or, *Children's and Household Tales*. They continued to add, subtract, and edit those tales in subsequent editions throughout the first half of the nineteenth century. Although Disney would have us think otherwise, these stories were far from G-rated. Cannibalism, murder, and scandalous nighttime visits are all to be found in Bantam's *The Complete Fairy Tales of the Brothers Grimm* (2003). Translated and edited by acclaimed folklorist Jack Zipes, this volume includes 250 tales—some of which had never before been translated—making it the most comprehensive there is. It certainly doesn't skimp on the gore. Elizabeth Dalton does somewhat sanitize her 120-story collection, *Grimm's Fairy Tales* (Barnes and Noble Classics, 2003), but with the lower price and more convenient size, it's still a good option. For a truly luxurious (not to mention scholarly) Grimm experience, *The Annotated Brothers Grimm* (W.W. Norton, 2004) is not to be missed. Harvard professor Maria Tatar selects and translates forty stories for the volume, and adds hundreds of fascinating footnotes contextualizing the tales historically, psychologically, and culturally. There's even an introduction by A. S. Byatt and gorgeous color illustrations by legendary painters such as George Cruikshank and Walter Crane. And the whole thing is beautifully clothbound to boot.

THE CONFESSIONS OF NAT TURNER

African-American slave Nat Turner and the heroic slave revolt he led in Southampton, Virginia, in 1831 might have been nearly buried by the sands of time if not for Thomas Ruffin Gray, a lawyer who took it upon himself to write and publish *The Confessions of Nat Turner*, derived from jailhouse conversations with Turner prior to his trial and execution. Docsouth Books (a collaboration between UNC Press and the University of North Carolina at Chapel Hill Library) publishes the unaltered, original text (2011). In *Nat Turner's Slave Rebellion* (Dover Publications, 2006) historian Herbert Aptheker provides his extensive, original research and analysis alongside the text of the confession in an extremely affordable edition. If straight history isn't your thing, you might check out William Styron's controversial Pulitzer Prize–winning *The Confessions of Nat Turner* (Vintage, 1992), a novelization of Turner's life. First published in 1967, Styron's book was strongly criticized by some for its contentious characterization of Turner, but others (including President Bill Clinton!) cite the novel as a powerful exploration of slavery's corruption of morality.

"THE MORTAL IMMORTAL"

Mary Shelley was definitely way into weird science. First, we've got *Frankenstein*, and then we've got "The Mortal Immortal," a short story in which a man drinks a potion granting (or cursing) him with immortality. The story was commissioned for an 1834 issue of the literary magazine *The Keepsake*, and at first it was not well received. The vote's still out with modern critics: some see it as commercial hackwork, while others see it as an expression of Shelley's humorous side. The story is not so easy to find in print today, but the diligent reader can check it out alongside a slew of Shelley's other writing in *The Mary Shelley Reader* (Oxford University Press, 1990) or in the much cheaper and more portable *The Mortal Immortal, and The Evil Eye* (Dodo Press, 2008).

FAIRY TALES BY HANS CHRISTIAN ANDERSEN

Late bloomers are comforted by Hans Christian Andersen's "The Ugly Duckling," the gullible are cautioned by his "The Emperor's New Clothes," and merpeople the ocean over are given hope by "The Little Mermaid." Andersen's fairy tales have inspired films, ballets, theme parks, plays, and countless literary adaptations, but nothing can beat the magic and elegance of the stories themselves, the first volume of which was first published in Denmark in 1835. Anchor's edition, *Hans Christian Andersen: The Complete Fairy Tales and Stories* (1983), translated by Erik Christian Haugaard, is the most thorough and faithful to the stories as Andersen originally

published them. The Oxford World's Classics selection of twenty-eight stories, *Hans Andersen's Fairy Tales: A Selection*, translated by L. W. Kingsland and featuring the original illustrations by Vilhelm Pedersen and Lorenz Frolich, is also excellent. For a super-cheap, super-portable little volume, check out *Andersen's Fairy Tales* (Signet Classics, 2004), translated by Pat Shaw Iversen. In the lavish and erudite *The Annotated Hans Christian Andersen* (W.W. Norton, 2007), acclaimed folklore scholar Maria Tatar pairs a range of Andersen's tales with stunning color images by prominent artists and rich cultural, historical, and social annotations.

"RONDEAU" ("JENNY KISS'D ME")

James Henry Leigh Hunt was a more cheerful, pleasant poet than his brooding English Romantic contemporaries, and for that reason he was, and is, often left out of the canon's party. But his optimistic, charming lyrics like "Rondeau"—better known as "Jenny Kiss'd Me"—are more than worth a gander, as is his remarkably astute literary criticism. *Leigh Hunt: Selected Writings* (Routledge, 2003), edited by David Jesson-Dibley, draws upon a range of Hunt's prose and verse, though it does not include "Jenny Kiss'd Me." Hunt was mentor to many of the giants of English literature—John Keats, Percy Bysshe Shelley, and Alfred Tennyson, among others—so *Leigh Hunt: Life, Poetics, Politics* (Routledge Studies in Romanticism, 2003), which collects essays by leading Romanticists on Hunt's cultural significance, is a fascinating read. The story of Hunt's own life is also worth attention and can be explored in *Fiery Heart: The First Life of Leigh Hunt* by Nicholas Roe (Random House, 2005).

OLIVER TWIST

Oliver Twist might be the most famous orphan in English-language literature (along with Little Orphan Annie), and equally famous is his plaintive, "Please, sir, I want some more." We want more, too! More Dickens, that is. Luckily, we can find *Oliver Twist* (also known as *The Parish Boy's Progress*) in numerous editions. The Penguin Classics edition (2003), which includes the original text as serialized in 1837–1838, is an excellent value. The Norton Critical Edition (1992), edited by distinguished professor and Dickens scholar Fred Kaplan, reproduces the later 1846 edition of the text—the last edition to be substantially revised by Dickens—alongside critical reviews, illustrations, and maps. The 2001 Modern Library edition is a bit easier on the wallet than the Norton edition, but still includes explanatory notes, an appendix, and an introduction from Philip Pullman alongside the 1846 text. If you're not up for Dickens's loquaciousness (he was paid by the word, after all), you'd do well to settle in and watch *Oliver!*, the 1968 Academy Award–winning film adaptation of the novel, itself adapted from the Tony Award–winning Broadway musical of the same name. With jaunty songs like "Food, Glorious Food" and "You've Got to Pick a Pocket or Two," you'll definitely want more.

"THE JUMBLIES"

Anyone who has ever chuckled at a dirty limerick or two can thank nineteenth-century British poet Edward Lear for creating the familiar, jaunty limerick structure. But his "nonsense" verse took other forms, too, as does "The Jumblies," which first appeared in 1870 in *Nonsense Songs*. Like much of his poetry, the absurdity of "The Jumblies" is tinged with a sense of voyage and restlessness. For the voyaging reader with an appreciation for silliness, there is *The Complete Verse and Other Nonsense* (Penguin, 2002), which also includes stories, letters, previously unpublished material, and an introduction by Lear scholar Vivien Noakes. The slightly cheaper and more portable *The Complete Nonsense of Edward Lear* (Faber Children's Classics, 2001), edited by Holbrook Jackson, includes Lear's own original illustrations. For an extra touch of whimsy, go for the stand-alone hardcover *The Jumblies* (Pomegranate, 2010), lavishly and lovingly illustrated by prominent illustrator Edward Gorey. For those who'd like to get to know Lear for the world-traveling artist and outsider that he was, Vivien Noakes has written the biography *Edward Lear: The Life of a Wanderer* (The History Press, 2006).

DER STRUWWELPETER

Thumb-suckers, beware! When Heinrich Hoffman couldn't find a good children's book for his three-year-old son, he went ahead and wrote and illustrated his own, *Der Struwwelpeter,* which translates literally as *Slovenly Peter* and was first published anonymously in Germany in 1845. Even Mark Twain became a fan of the bizarre moral tales and delightfully grotesque illustrations, so he wrote his own English translation in 1891. The collection is available and affordable as *Struwwelpeter in English Translation* (Dover Publications, 1995). For the bilingual reader, the paperback *Der Struwwelpeter auf Englisch* pairs Mark Twain's translations with the original German verse. There's also Iolair Publishing's *Struwwelpeter 2000* (2000), which pairs new English translations by Colin Blyth with the original German. Caution: Blyth also takes the liberty of bringing happy endings to some of the more gruesome tales. The best edition is probably *Struwwelpeter: Fearful Stories and Vile Pictures to Instruct Good Little Folks* (Feral House, 1999), which contains an English translation, horrific new illustrations by Sarita Vendetta, a color reproduction of the original German edition, and an introduction by Jack Zipes, a prominent folklorist specializing in fairy tales and children's literature. Various stories have also been adapted for the stage and screen, and referenced by such diverse public figures as W. H. Auden, Dwight Schrute of The Office, and Pippi Longstocking.

"THE RAVEN" AND OTHER WORKS BY EDGAR ALLAN POE

A midnight visit from a talking bird might sound absurd, but it has become one of the most iconic scenes in American literature. Edgar Allan Poe's "The Raven," first published in 1845, immediately made Poe a household name, and—the true mark of celebrity—began garnering various parodies and pop culture references; it has been adapted for silent films and talkies (in fact, John Cusack stars in a 2012 adaptation), Grateful Dead songs, and comic books, and it has been illustrated by artists as illustrious as Gustave Doré and Édouard Manet. Poe's other gothic tales, such as "The Tell-Tale Heart," "The Pit and the Pendulum," and "The Bells," have garnered nearly as much popular and critical attention over the years. G. R. Thompson's *The Selected Writings of Edgar Allan Poe* (Norton Critical Edition, 2004) is generous and well-curated, with plenty of contextual documents and critical essays illuminating Poe's politics, psychology, and literary styles. It's a hefty volume at a reasonable price. The more conveniently sized *The Portable Edgar Allan Poe* (Penguin Classics, 2006) still covers all the major works, with notes and introduction by J. Gerald

Kennedy. Unsurprisingly, this national treasure has received the full Library of America treatment, so the most ardent of Poe fans can pick up *Edgar Allan Poe: Poetry and Tales* (Library of America, 1984), which contains the complete fiction and poetry as well as extensive notes by editor Patrick F. Quinn. But for those looking for "The Raven" and not much more, *The Raven and Other Favorite Poems* from Dover Publications (1991) is a steal at under three dollars, and still includes a selection of forty-one poems. Luckily for those jonesing for visuals beyond what you'll find earlier in this volume, Poe's work has inspired numerous adaptations. For starters, you'd do well to check out *Maxon's Poe: Seven Stories and Poems by Edgar Allan Poe* by Maxon Crumb in its entirety (Word Play, 1997) and *Edgar Allan Poe's Tales of Mystery and Madness* by Gris Grimly (Atheneum Books for Young Readers, 2004).

JANE EYRE

Bookwormy girls throughout the world rejoice at the triumph of *Jane Eyre*'s plain-Jane bibliophile heroine. Indeed, when English writer Charlotte Brontë first published the novel in 1847 under the pseudonym Currer Bell, she broke a lot of molds with her in-depth exploration of the feelings of a strong, intellectual woman. That exploration has remained compelling over the centuries, inspiring dozens of memorable television, radio, literary, and cinematic adaptations involving such A-list celebrities as Michael Fassbender, Orson Welles, Elizabeth Taylor, and Aldous Huxley. (And yes, some of these spin-offs have included zombies and/or vampires, such as *Jane Slayre* [Gallery, 2010] by Sherri Browning Erwin.) But the gothic novel itself can be enjoyed affordably in Penguin Classics' revised edition (2006), with notes and introduction by Stevie Davies. For a more extensive critical analysis, take a look at the Norton's third critical edition (2000), edited by Richard Dunn to include notes, a selection of Brontë's letters, and essays from such prominent writers and scholars as Adrienne Rich and Sandra M. Gilbert.

WUTHERING HEIGHTS

Charlotte wasn't the only Brontë with a gift for gothic gloom and passion; her sister Emily flaunts her own talents in the novel *Wuthering Heights*, first published in 1847, and, in keeping with familial practice, under the pseudonym Ellis Bell. Charlotte Brontë published a revised edition of the novel after her sister's death. Bedford/St. Martin's second edition (2003), edited by Linda H. Peterson, includes the original 1847 text alongside essays reading the novel from psychoanalytic, Marxist, and feminist perspectives. Oxford World's Classics reproduces the authoritative 1976 Clarendon text, and editor Patsy Stoneman adds additional notes and even includes a selection of Emily Brontë's poems. The Signet Classics edition (2011) is super-affordable and handy, and still includes an introduction and afterword by prominent writers and scholars. Of course, Heathcliff and Cathy's romance is too passionate to stick to the printed page, and has been liberally adapted for the opera, stage, and screen. The 1939 film, staring Laurence Olivier and Merle Oberon, was nominated for the Academy Award for Best Picture, and won the New York Film Critics Circle Award for Best Film.

THE SCARLET LETTER

The Scarlet Letter was an instant bestseller when it was first published in 1850, and over the years has been adapted liberally for film, stage, television, and even opera. Today, it remains widely read in high-school classrooms across the United States. Bedford/ St. Martin's second edition (2005), edited by Ross. C. Murfin, is unbeatable for the psychoanalytic, feminist, and historicist critical essays that are presented alongside the authoritative, 1851 Centenary Edition text. The cheaper and more portable Penguin Classics revised edition (2002), with introduction by Nina Baym, also includes thorough notes on the Centenary text. For the cheapest and barest-bones copies, you could get by with the Bantam Classics and Dover Publications editions, but if you prefer a more sumptuous package, go for the modern, edgy-looking Penguin Classics Deluxe Edition, illustrated by acclaimed fashion artist Ruben Toledo. If your craving for Hawthorne's dark romanticism simply won't be sated by just one novel, pick up the Library of America's *Nathaniel Hawthorne: Collected Novels*, which collects all five. The Bedford/St. Martin's Case Studies in Contemporary Criticism edition (1996) is also a good choice.

MOBY-DICK

A true whale of American literature, Herman Melville's *Moby-Dick; or, The Whale* received mixed reviews when it was first published in 1851. Though none today would challenge this novel's position in the Western canon, it wasn't until World War I and the flourishing of Modernist aesthetics that the book truly seemed relevant to American readers. Today, readers must choose from a plethora of abridged, unabridged, illustrated, and critical editions. Norton's second critical edition, rigorously and elegantly edited by Melville scholars Hershel Parker and Harrison Hayford, includes the MLA-approved Northwestern-Newberry text of the novel, and a slew of glossary terms, historical and contemporary critical essays, and comprehensive footnotes. The Penguin Classics edition, with introduction by Andrew Delbanco and notes by Tom Quirk, is also excellent, and a bit less expensive. Something about the epic struggle central to *Moby-Dick* must cry out for illustration, as the text has been memorably illuminated by cartoonist Tony Millionaire (Penguin Classics Deluxe Edition, 2009, with introduction by Nathaniel Philbrick) and librarian Matt Kish (Tin House Books, 2011), among others. Celebrities ranging from Orson Welles to Laurie Anderson and Gregory Peck to Ethan Hawke have also brought the novel to life on the stage, screen, and radio.

WALDEN

What could be more American than two years of reflection on the self, nature, and society in a secluded cabin in the great American outdoors? Transcendentalist writer Henry David Thoreau's *Walden; or Life in the Woods* is inspired by just such an experience. First published in 1854, Walden has remained an American classic of simplicity and self-reliance. For a cheap edition with just the stand-alone text, take a look at the Dover Publications edition (1995)—at under four dollars, it's a steal. At the other end of the spectrum is the lavish, oversize hardcover *Walden: 150th Anniversary Illustrated Edition of the American Classic* (Houghton Mifflin Harcourt, 2004), containing Scot Miller's spectacular color photographs of Walden Pond and the surrounding area. The Modern Library's *Walden and Other Writings* (2000) gathers all of Thoreau's most significant works into one very reasonably priced volume with an introduction by Ralph Waldo Emerson and commentary from E. B. White and Van Wyck Brooks. If you're looking for an even more comprehensive view of the writer's work, splurge on Yale University Press's clothbound *Walden: A Fully Annotated Edition*, in which Thoreau scholar Jeffrey S. Cramer meticulously corrects the original 1854 text using Thoreau's own notes and glosses the text with references to Thoreau's other works.

LEAVES OF GRASS

Even after publishing the first edition of his poetry collection *Leaves of Grass*, Walt Whitman dedicated his life to revising and expanding the exultant, epic ode to America's virtues and vices. Numerous editions were published during Whitman's own lifetime, resulting in an abundance of editions available today. Penguin Classics' *Leaves of Grass: The First (1855) Edition* reproduces the text as first published alongside an introduction from acclaimed literary scholar Malcolm Cowley (1961). Contrast that with the much-expanded 1892 "deathbed" edition found in Norton's *Leaves of Grass and Other Writings* (2002). The Norton edition definitely packs a wallop of scholarly expertise; edited by Michael Moon of Johns Hopkins University, it prints the 1855 text alongside the 1892 text, as well as a selection from Whitman's notebooks, letters, and newspaper articles, with commentary from illustrious writers like D. H. Lawrence, William Carlos Williams, and Henry James. *Walt Whitman: Poetry and Prose* (Library of America, 1982), edited by Justin Kaplan, also juxtaposes the 1855 and 1892 texts, and includes virtually all of his prose writings. Later generations of American writers—particularly the Beats—embraced the romanticized vagabond lifestyle set forth in *Leaves of Grass*, and thus Whitman lives on in the works of writers like Allen Ginsberg, Jack Kerouac, and Lawrence Ferlinghetti.

THE HASHEESH EATER

It may be difficult to imagine stuffy nineteenth-century men in waistcoats kicking back and getting stoned at their ivory tower institutions, but it seems that's just what American writer Fitz Hugh Ludlow did, perhaps along with his friends Mark Twain and Walt Whitman. His 1857 *The Hasheesh Eater* is a glorious account of his experiences and state of mind under the influence. Naturally, the book's popularity (and controversy) surged after the prohibition of marijuana, and again during the rise of the counterculture in the 1960s and 1970s. Today's cannabis aficionados can explore Ludlow's experiences in *The Hasheesh Eater: Passages from the Life of a Pythagorean* (Theophania Publishing, 2011). For additional commentary, readers should page through *The Annotated Hasheesh Eater* (CreateSpace, 2007) and the biography of the hashish eater himself, *Pioneer of Inner Space: The Life of Fitz Hugh Ludlow, Hasheesh Eater* by Donald P. Dulchinos (Autonomedia, 1998).

ON THE ORIGIN OF SPECIES

Could Charles Darwin have known that his *On the Origin of Species*, first published in England in 1859, would continue to cause controversy well into the twenty-first century? Of course, controversy makes for a compelling read, so those interested in the development of modern science—heck, those interested in the development of humankind!—should definitely check out *On* the Origin of Species: A Facsimile of the First Edition (Harvard University Press, 2001), which exactly reproduces the original 1859 text (many other editions contain the greatly modified and watered-down 1872 edition). Acclaimed Harvard professor Ernst Mayr prefaces the text of this valuable edition. The Penguin Classics 150th anniversary edition also reproduces the 1859 text, with notes and introduction by medical historian William Bynum and a super-snazzy cover design by artist Damien Hirst (2009). Philip Appleman's *Darwin* (Norton Critical Editions, third edition, 2000) is an excellent anthology comprised of generous excerpts of all Darwin's major works and thorough contemporary and historical analytic essays by such scientific geniuses as Steven Pinker, Richard Dawkins, and Stephen Jay Gould. For those interested in Darwin's entire body of thought and work, the website *The Complete Works of Charles Darwin Online* [darwin-online.org.uk] is just that: page images and transcribed text for every last one of Darwin's publications—including all editions of *Origin*—as well as his *Beagle* notebooks, private journal, and unpublished papers and manuscripts. If Darwin's Victorian prose and complex ideas are intimidating, check out the "reader's digest" version, *The "Origin" Then and Now: An Interpretive Guide to the "Origin of Species"* (Princeton University Press, 2011) in which professor David Reznick deconstructs each chapter of the text, adding clear explanation of difficult ideas and citing modern examples.

"THE MESSAGE FROM MOUNT MISERY"

If it were not for brave writers like Frederick Douglass, we would have little inkling of the true horrors of American slavery. His extensive writings and speeches about his experiences as a slave and then a freeman ensure that "our peculiar institution" remains in our memories. For an excellent selection of Douglass's most significant works—including his famous speech, "West India Emancipation"— check out *Frederick Douglass: Selected Speeches and Writings*, edited by the director of the Library of Black America series, Philip S. Foner (Lawrence Hill Books, 1999). Douglass has also been honored with a Library of America volume, edited by none other than Henry Louis Gates, *Frederick Douglass: Autobiographies* (1994), which includes three of his major autobiographical narratives. The Bedford Series in History and Culture edition of the must-read *Narrative of the Life of Frederick Douglass* by Frederick Douglass (Bedford/St. Martin's second edition, 2002) also includes a selection of speeches and letters, and the introduction and notes by David W. Blight put Douglass's writings in literary and historical context. For a less extensive look at Douglass's experiences, pick up *Narrative of the Life of Frederick Douglass* from Dover Publications (1995).

LES MISÉRABLES

To many of us, *Les Misérables* is the long-running, award-winning 1985 musical by Claude-Michel Schönberg. But over a hundred years before Jean Valjean and Cosette hit the stage, they suffered and protested in the pages of Victor Hugo's novel *Les Misérables*, first published to great commercial success in Belgium in 1862. There are three major English translations for *Les Miz* readers to choose from. First is Julie Rose's 2008 English translation for the Modern Library, which features an introduction by Adam Gopnik and is widely considered to be fantastically vibrant and complete.

Second is the Signet Classics edition (1987), translated by Lee Fahnestock and Norman MacAfee; the text is unabridged and based on a translation by Victor Hugo's contemporary, Charles E. Wilbour, but with the language a bit modernized. Lastly, there is Norman Denny's 1976 translation—not technically abridged, but rather heavily edited. It's available, along with Denny's introduction, in the Penguin Classics 1982 edition.

"BECAUSE I COULD NOT STOP FOR DEATH" AND "I TASTE A LIQUOR NEVER BREWED"

American writer Emily Dickinson may be most well known for her hermit-poet lifestyle and dizzying use of the dash. Of course, she's pretty well known for her verse, too—of death, illness, confession, religion, privacy, and gardens—and there are numerous selections, collections, and volumes of criticism to tempt the sensitive reader. Consider Thomas H. Brown's *The Complete Poems of Emily Dickinson* (Little, Brown, and Company, 1960) for a very thorough, accurate text. For the whole shebang bound in cloth and tied with a ribbon, consider splurging on *The Poems of Emily Dickinson: Reading Edition* from Belknap Press of Harvard University Press (1999); the esteemed R. W. Franklin edits the order of the poems into a new, authoritative volume. If you'd rather simply sample the verse without investing too heavily, check out *Selected Poems* (Dover Publications, 1990), which contains 100 poems for under two dollars. And for the scholars among us, there is the wonderful Dickinson companion, *Emily Dickinson: A Collection of Critical Essays* (Prentice Hall, 1990), for which editor Judith Farr brings together a fascinating body of criticism, bibliographies, and chronologies to shed light on the secluded poetess.

LETTER TO GEORGE SAND

As tortured as Madame Bovary may be, her creator was just as long-suffering. Scrupulously devoted to all aspects of style, Gustave Flaubert worked painstakingly to create the perfectly worded sentence. He wrote of his struggles in letters to many of his literary friends, but especially to George Sand. This correspondence between two of the greatest nineteenth-century French writers provides a clear window into history and the minds of two masters of language. Page through the letters in the hardcover *The George Sand-Gustave Flaubert Letters*, translated by A. L. McKenzie (Norilana Books, 2009), with introduction by literary critic Stuart Sherman. Or, check out McKenzie's translation in paperback from Echo Library (2006). For a complete picture of Flaubert's mailed musings, definitely consider a trip to the library for the two-volume *The Letters of Gustave Flaubert*, translated by master translator Francis Steegmuller for Belknap Press of Harvard University Press (1981, 1982). More insight into the Sand-Flaubert relationship, and into Flaubert's life as a whole, can be had in Frederick Brown's critically acclaimed *Flaubert: A Biography* (Little, Brown, and Company, 2006).

ALICE'S ADVENTURES IN WONDERLAND, THROUGH THE LOOKING-GLASS, AND "JABBERWOCKY"

It's hard to imagine a world without Tweedledee and Tweedledum, the Cheshire Cat, and the Mad Hatter. Somehow, the fantastical, nonsense world of Lewis Carroll's *Alice's Adventures in Wonderland* has become as real and necessary as the world we live in. The book received little attention when it was first published in England in 1865. Today, its ubiquity in pop culture—Disney films, a Tim Burton film, stage musicals, ballets, and so on—signals that the book is here to stay. The extremely affordable Bantam Classics *Alice's Adventures in Wonderland & Through the Looking Glass* (2003) also includes the sequel (which itself includes the famous nonsense poem, "Jabberwocky") and an introduction by Morton N. Cohen. For an ultra-cheap edition of *Alice* that still includes all forty-two of Tenniel's illustrations, check out the Dover Thrift Edition (1993). If you're looking for something more substantial, definitely take a peek at the updated *The Annotated Alice*, edited by leading Carroll authority Martin Gardner (W.W. Norton, 1999); the volume includes *Alice*, *Through the Looking-Glass*, explanatory commentary, and all of Tenniel's illustrations.

CRIME AND PUNISHMENT

The intimidating length of *Crime and Punishment* may seem like a punishment in itself, but once entrenched in Raskolnikov's anguish and moral turmoil, readers won't want the book to end. The English-language translation by Richard Pevear and Larissa Volokhonsky is considered one of the best, clearest translations available today; it appears in the Vintage edition of the novel (1993). For a more accessible modern translation, you might want to explore David McDuff's rendering for Penguin Classics (2002). Dover Publications' edition, translated by Constance Garnett, doesn't feature much in the way of introduction or notes, but it sure is cheap and portable for a book of this length. For an edition packing a more scholarly punch, look into Norton's third critical edition, which, featuring Jessie Senior Coulson's translation, illuminates the dense text with essays by a star-studded cast of Dostoevsky admirers and scholars: Czeslaw Milosz, Leo Tolstoy, and Sergei Belov, among others.

VENUS IN FURS

How could a novella titled *Venus in Furs (Ariadne Press, 2003)* not be a totally sexy read? In fact, Leopold von Sacher-Masoch's 1870 Austrian novel is basically an early example of dominatrix erotica. In fact, most editions in print today come from erotica publishers or feature covers you might not feel comfortable displaying on public transportation. Check out the CreateSpace edition, translated by Joachim Neugroschel (2010). For a truly deep exploration of the novel, pay a visit to Gilles Deleuze's rigorous philosophical examination, *Masochism: Coldness and Cruelty & Venus in Furs* (Zone, 1991). Naturally, a book as tantalizing as *Venus in Furs* has seen its fair share of stage and cinematic adaptations. David Ivies adapted the book into a play set in modern times, which can be read (from Northwestern University Press, 2011) or seen on Broadway.

"THE DRUNKEN BOAT"

Most of us cringe at the thought of the poetry we wrote at age sixteen. Not so Rimbaud, who wrote "The Drunken Boat" ("Le Bateau ivre") when he was still a teenager in 1871. In fact, Rimbaud wrote most of his poetry before the age of twenty. Check out Paul Schmidt's *Arthur Rimbaud: Complete Works* (Harper Perennial Modern Classics, 2008), which includes insightful commentary from the editor. Or, take a look at *Rimbaud Complete* from the Modern Library (2003), in which translator and editor Wyatt Mason organizes the poems, drafts, and incomplete pieces chronologically, creating the most complete edition so far collected. For a more curated volume, consider Penguin Classics' *Selected Poems and Letters*, translated by John Sturrock and Jeremy Harding (2005). Rimbaud abandoned his brilliant writings by the time he was twenty-one, embarking on a whole new life as a trader in Africa—why? Learn more about this most enigmatic of writers—inspiration to Allen Ginsberg, Dylan Thomas, Patti Smith, and myriad others—in *Rimbaud: A Biography* by Graham Robb (W.W. Norton, 2001).

MIDDLEMARCH

Often cited as among the best novels in the English language, George Eliot's *Middlemarch* is a classic of realism and narrative irony. Virginia Woolf, Martin Amis, and Emily Dickinson have all praised the 1874 novel, and it remains a staple of the canon today. The revised Penguin Classics edition featuring an introduction by Eliot scholar Rosemary Ashton (2003) is a sure bet, as is the inexpensive Signet Classics edition with introduction by novelist Michael Faber (2002). If you're looking for an edition that sheds a bit more light on what can be a difficult text, try the Oxford World's Classics edition, which features the authoritative 1986 Clarendon edition of the novel as well as an introduction by Felicia Bonaparte, notes, and chronologies. A novel as very English as this has of course received the most appropriate of British treatments—it's been adapted not once, but twice, for BBC productions (in 1968 and 1994).

THE HUNTING OF THE SNARK

Lewis Carroll wore many hats. First of all his, his name was really Charles Lutwidge Dodgson, not Lewis Carroll. What's more, he was a mathematician, Anglican deacon, logistician, photographer, and poet famous for nonsense verses like *The Hunting of the Snark*. Unlike "Jabberwocky," which appears within *Through the Looking-Glass*, "The Hunting of the Snark (An Agony in 8 Fits)" was a stand-alone work first published in 1876, illustrated by Henry Holiday. Join the ramshackle crew on their hunt to "find an inconceivable creature" in *The Annotated Hunting of the Snark*, with extensive notes by Carroll scholar Martin Gardner and Henry Holiday's original illustrations (W.W. Norton, 2002). Or, check out the Melville House graphic edition of the poem, beautifully and surreally illustrated by artist Mahendra Singh (2010).

ANNA KARENINA

When *Anna Karenina* was first published in the 1870s, Russian critics dismissed it as a high society trifle. But some very important people—Dostoevsky, Faulkner, Nabokov, to name a few—knew it was more than aristocratic gossip, and Leo Tolstoy's novel remains a fixture on lit syllabuses today and Anna Karenina a recurring figure in pop culture adaptations. Award-winning husband and wife translating team Richard Pevear and Larissa Volokhonsky did a much-praised translation of the text for Penguin Classics (2003), and Oprah Winfrey selected their edition for her book club in

2004, so you can have extra assurance that it's a good one. The 1918 Maude translation, found in the Norton Critical Edition (1995), contains a selection of Tolstoy's correspondence, diary entries, and other background material. For an affordable, more pocket-sized book, try the Barnes & Noble Classics edition (2003), translated by Constance Gardner and with an introduction by Amy Mandelker. Or, rent one of the many film adaptations of the novel—that is, if you can't catch one of the ballet, opera, or musical performances live.

ADVENTURES OF HUCKLEBERRY FINN

Considering the endless controversy surrounding Mark Twain's *Adventures of Huckleberry Finn*—regarding issues of vulgarity, racism, vernacular language, and so on—it is a testament to the novel's staying power that it has remained a constant favorite and a permanent fixture in the literary canon since its first publication in the United States in 1885. Whether you go for the expurgated versions or not, there are a plethora of editions to choose from. The Penguin Classics edition, edited by Guy Cardwell (2002), is affordable and convenient, and still includes an introduction by Twain scholar John Seelye. The Bedford College Edition (2007) is also quite affordable, and is lightly annotated by Gregg Camfield. If you're looking for a heavier dose of analysis with your text, consider Thomas Cooley's Norton Critical Edition (1998), which reprints the definitive Iowa-California text of the novel for the first time and includes a rich selection of contextual documents. For an edition that eliminates potentially offensive words, check out the NewSouth Edition (2011). This Great American Novel has also gotten the Great American Hollywood treatment several times; coast down the river with the very youthful Mickey Rooney, Drew Barrymore, and Elijah Wood, appearing in 1939, 1985, and 1993 films, respectively.

THUS SPAKE ZARATHUSTRA

Friedrich Nietzsche gets a bad rap as a bit of an egotistical misanthrope. But you might take on an air of superiority, too, if you wrote books as passionate and chock-full of ideas as Nietzsche's *Thus Spake Zarathustra: A Book for Everyone and No One*, first published in Germany in the 1880s. It took a while for the book to catch on in English-language academia, not for lack of available translations. The Penguin Classics edition (1961)—containing a translation by R. J. Hollindale, who has translated several books by Nietzsche (as well as by Goethe, E. T. A. Hoffmann, and other German giants)—is very faithful to the original German. Walter Kaufmann's translation for the 1995 Modern Library edition is also considered very readable and modern and can also be found in *The Portable Nietzsche* (Penguin, 1977)—alongside his translations of three other major Nietzsche works and a selection of letters, notes, and other texts. At under twenty dollars, it's a steal. For a translation that focuses first and foremost on conveying the musicality of Nietzsche's original text, page through Graham Parkes's translation in the Oxford World's Classics edition (2009)—his introduction is particularly illuminating. The Barnes & Noble Classics edition, translated by Clancy Martin, is the cheapest you'll find, and still contains an erudite introduction. If Nietzsche's complex and daring ideas still elude you, you might want to visit the library

to consult the chapter-by-chapter commentary in *Nietzsche's Teaching: An Interpretation of "Thus Spoke Zarathustra"* by Professor Laurence Lampert (Yale University Press, 1989).

STRANGE CASE OF DR. JEKYLL AND MR. HYDE

There's a bit of good and a bit of evil in us all, a bit of civilized man and a bit of animal instinct. Robert Louis Stevenson's *Strange Case of Dr. Jekyll and Mr. Hyde*, first published in England in 1886, explores this divide explicitly and dramatically. The story was an instant hit, and as the dozens of cinematic, radio, and stage adaptations show, the theme of multiple selves within each person strikes a continuous chord in humanity. The novella on its own can be had for near pennies and in perfect pocket-size from Dover Publications (1991). For a bit more context, the Broadview Press second edition edited by Martin A. Danahay (2002) is also a steal, and includes contemporary reviews, historical documents, an updated introduction, and loads more. If Dr. Jekyll and Mr. Hyde aren't enough personality for you, consider the Oxford World's Classics *Strange Case of Dr. Jekyll and Mr. Hyde and Other Tales* (2008), which includes additional stories, essays, and extracts by Stevenson along with valuable notes.

"AN OCCURRENCE AT OWL CREEK BRIDGE"

Nineteenth-century American writer Ambrose Bierce was known for his sardonic wit, dark satire, and a rather modern sense of irony—that is, until he he set off for Mexico to witness the revolution and disappeared without at trace. He left behind a brilliant body of writing, though, including the surprising 1890 story, "An Occurrence at Owl Creek Bridge." For a true survey of his work and critical commentary to accompany it, invest in the Library of America volume *Ambrose Bierce: The Devil's Dictionary, Tales, and Memoirs* (2011) edited by Bierce scholar S. T. Joshi. If you're after an inexpensive and conveniently sized little volume, check out the Dover Publications edition (1994), which includes sixteen stories for only three dollars. Curious about the man who came to be known as "Bitter Bierce" before his ultimate disappearance? The biography *Ambrose Bierce: Alone in Bad Company* by Roy Morris, Jr. (Oxford University Press, 1999) is a good place to start.

THE PICTURE OF DORIAN GRAY

Unlike the eponymous painting, *The Picture of Dorian Gray* has aged well. As befits a book that is largely about vanity, the Penguin Classics for Waterstone's edition (2009) is beautifully designed and clothbound, and contains notes by editor Robert Mighall. For the uncensored version, page through *The Picture of Dorian Gray: An Annotated, Uncensored Edition* from Belknap Press at Harvard University Press (2011), in which editor Nicholas Frankel annotates the original text as it appeared before the most scandalous and homoerotic passages were edited out for Victorian society. Or, you can go the less hedonistic route and read the bare-bones Dover Thrift Edition (1993) for less than four dollars. For a truly stylish ode to the vain self-love that permeates *Dorian Gray*, definitely take a peek at *A Portrait of Dorian Gray* (2008), in which fashion designer and photographer Karl Lagerfeld stages the novel as a luxurious Bohemian world in glamorous film-stills.

CONTRIBUTORS

JASMINE BECKET-GRIFFITH is a world-renowned fantasy artist living in Celebration, Florida. She works exclusively in acrylic paints on wood or canvas. Her trademark wide-eyed girls explore the whimsical, gothic, historical, magical, and the beautiful.

WILLIAM BLAKE (1757–1827) was a poet, illustrator, engraver, printer, and bookmaker of the Romantic era who started to see visions as early as the age of four, poured untold hours of his life into his illuminated poetry printings that were barely recognized during his lifetime, and died in abject poverty without ever knowing how much his work would be revered centuries later. His most enduring works include the poetry collections *Songs of Innocence* (1789) and *Songs of Experience* (1794), for which the text and illustrations were printed from copper plates and each picture was finished by hand in watercolors. A nonconformist, Blake's opposition to the English monarchy—and to the general political, social, and theological tyranny of the time—was palpable in his poetry. His later works, including *Jerusalem* (1804–20), were visionary epics, containing neither traditional plot, characters, rhyme, nor meter, and favoring an exultation of human spirit over reason. In Blake's final years, he was commissioned to create a cycle of illustrations for Dante's *Divine Comedy*, which he worked on till he died.

TERRENCE BOYCE is an Emmy Award–winning multidisciplinary designer and musician residing in Nashville, Tennessee. The nephew of Hawaiian artist James Hoyle, Terrence has since spent nearly twenty years designing for print, web, multimedia, and architectural structures. He is currently working with his wife and frequent collaborator, Huxley King, on a graphic novel, a historical adventure set in 1890s Nashville. You can contact him at his website: wowium.com.

LISA BROWN is a *New York Times*–bestselling illustrator, author, and cartoonist. She lives in San Francisco. You can usually find her at americanchickens.com.

ERAN CANTRELL was fascinated with storytelling from an early age. Her efforts to bring stories to life continue to direct her practice to this day: she is drawn to fields such as book publishing and animation, where narrative is essential. It is her hope that, by creating imagery that is both eye-catching and thought-provoking, she will ultimately contribute to the proliferation of those stories and encourage the same appreciation in others.

BILL CARMAN has worked as a designer, illustrator, and art director at universities, ad agencies, publishers, and large corporations. Holding both bachelor's and master's degrees in fine arts, Bill currently teaches illustration and drawing at Boise State University. He has been included in annuals such

as the *Society of Illustrators*, *Spectrum*, *3x3*, and *American Illustration*, and has even finagled some medals. He was proud to do a children's book with Random House in 2002.

SHAWN CHENG is an artist and cartoonist working in New York City. He creates handmade, limited-edition comic books as a member of the comics and art collective Partyka. His comics have appeared in the *SPX Anthology* and *Best American Comics*; his paintings and prints have been shown at Fredericks & Freiser Gallery in New York and the Giant Robot galleries in Los Angeles and San Francisco. Shawn was born in Taiwan and grew up on Long Island. He studied painting and printmaking at Yale University. Shawn currently lives in Astoria, Queens, with his wife and two daughters.

JASON COBLEY lives with his wife and daughter in Norfolk, in the East of England, where he spends most of his days teaching English to high-school children. He writes about mythical monsters and historical heroes, most notably in his weird Wild West graphic novel *Frontier: Dealing with Demons*, with artist Andrew Wildman (Print Media Productions, 2011) and the children's novel *The Legend of Tom Hickathrift* (Mogzilla, 2012). He has adapted classic texts *Frankenstein*, *Dracula*, *Dulce Et Decorum Est*, and *An Inspector Calls* for Classical Comics; in 2009, *Frankenstein* won an Association of Educational Publishers award. Jason is currently working on an adaptation of Charles Dickens's *The Signal Man* with artist David Hitchcock.

NEIL COHN is best known for his pioneering research in linguistics and cognitive neuroscience on the cognition underlying the comprehension of comics. On this topic, he has spoken internationally, written several articles, and authored the 2003 book *Early Writings on Visual Language*. In addition to the adaptation of "La Belle Dame Sans Merci," which Neil originally drew in college at the age of twenty, his original and adapted graphic poetry is compiled in *Meditations* (2005). Neil is also the illustrator of *We the People: A Call to Take Back America* (2004), with author Thom Hartmann. His work can be found online at emaki.net.

JOHN COULTHART is an illustrator, graphic designer, and comic artist. His book collection of H. P. Lovecraft adaptations, *The Haunter of the Dark and Other Grotesque Visions*, was published worldwide by Creation Oneiros in 2006. He lives and works in Manchester, UK.

MAXON CRUMB was born in Albert Lea, Minnesota, the fourth of Charles and Beatrice Crumb's children, and the younger brother of famed cartoonist Robert Crumb. From the East Coast, he moved permanently to San Francisco in 1973. Maxon is an artist, author, mystic, strict vegetarian, and long-distance road tripper. His meticulous art first gained acclaim with his illustrations for Edgar Allan Poe's stories and poems in *Maxon's*

Poe (Word Play, 1997). Since then, his drawings and paintings have entered collections in Germany, England, France, and throughout the United States. Two of his most notable writings are his extended introduction to *Crumb Family Comics* (Last Gasp, 2000) and *HardCore Mother,* his first work of fiction, about which R. Crumb says: "Beautiful work . . . Maxon in his creative prime." He is represented by Word Play publications (word-play.com). An illustrated biography of Maxon Crumb is in process. (Malcolm Whyte ©Word Play, 2012)

DAME DARCY is known worldwide as an illustrator, writer, animator, fine artist, musician, filmmaker, and doll crafter. She designs, animates, and produces music for and conceptualizes Paper Doll Dreams, an online game based on Meat Cake Comix. She has collaborated with writers ranging from Alan Moore to Tori Amos, and her comic book series, *Meat Cake,* has been published by Fantagraphics Books for twenty years. A new graphic novel, *Hand Book for Hot Witches,* will be released in late 2012 by Henry Holt, and a current graphic novel in the works is the *Black Rainbow Ranch* trilogy, a romantic dark fantasy based on Darcy's life as a teen. A musician with the band Death By Doll, and fashion illustrator for the likes of Anna Sui and others, Darcy is also the founder of the EZ Bake Coven Forum (ezbakecoven.com), a feminist place to connect with other artists and profile your own art, with a gothic Lolita flair. You can find out more at DameDarcy.com, where she can be contacted directly.

An important figure in the 1960s underground comix movement, **KIM DEITCH** was born in Los Angeles during the dwindling days of World War II. After briefly attending art school at Pratt Institute, he began drawing comic strips for *The East Village Other* in 1967. In 1969 he became the editor of *Gothic Blimp Works,* an underground comics tabloid. Since then, his work has appeared in *RAW, Pictopia, Zero Zero, Nickelodeon Magazine, Details,* and *Little Lit.* His 2002 graphic novel, *The Boulevard of Broken Dreams,* was chosen by *Time* in 2005 as one of the 100 best books published since 1923. Deitch lives in New York City.

Using his father Kent Dixon's thoroughly researched rendition of the text, **KEVIN DIXON** has converted the world's oldest epic, *Gilgamesh,* from cuneiform to comix. Kevin is also responsible for the autobiographical series . . . *And Then There Was Rock,* true stories about playing in a crappy loser band. With collaborator Eric Knisley, he produced *Tales of the Sinister Harvey, Mickey Death and the Winds of Impotence,* and the Xeric Award–winning *Flavor Contra Comix and Stories.* His latest non-Gilgamesh project is *Mkele Mbembe,* which has nothing to do with the legendary modern-day dinosaur of Kenya. You can contact him at ultrakevin@hotmail.com.

ALICE DUKE is an illustrator and sequential artist based in the UK. Her comics work has appeared in anthologies by publishers SelfMadeHero (*Lovecraft Anthology Vol. 1* and *Nevermore*) and Blank Slate (*Nelson*). Her illustration work can be found on album covers, in magazines, inside video games, and tattooed on skin. More information is available at alice-duke.com.

HUNT EMERSON has drawn cartoons and comic strips since the early 1970s. He has published around thirty comic books and albums, mainly with Knockabout Comics (London), including *Lady Chatterley's Lover, The Rime of the Ancient Mariner,* and *Casanova's Last Stand.* His characters include Firkin the Cat (a strip of sexual satire that has run in *Fiesta* magazine, UK, since 1981), Calculus Cat (the cat that hates television), PussPuss (yes—another cat!), Max Zillion and Alto Ego (a jazz musician and his saxophone), Alan Rabbit, and many more. His comic strips have been translated into ten languages, he has been awarded several comic strip prizes, and in 2000 he was chosen for inclusion in the exhibition Maîtres de la Bande Dessinée Européenne by the Bibliothèque nationale de France and the CNBDI, Angouleme. You can see and buy his work at largecow.com.

DIANA EVANS is a full-time illustrator and author living in Ontario, Canada. She is self-taught and loves to dabble in all sorts of media. Her work can be found in children's books, magazines, and surface designs. In the future, she hopes to see more of her art on all sorts of surfaces. You can find more of her work on her website, dianaevans.com, and follow daily fun art on her blog dianaevans.blogspot.com.

ANDREA FEMERSTRAND is a conceptual artist and illustrator from Sweden, with a main focus on character and creature designs, storytelling, and storybook illustrations. She's been working on projects for games, movies, children's books, advertisements, and a lot more. Andrea travels a lot by train to get to work, and so most of her paintings have actually been created while sitting on the train, with only a laptop and a wacom tablet at hand. noukah.com

TIM FISH is a Boston-based artist whose comic book stories have been published by Marvel Comics and Oni Press and translated into French, Italian, and Portuguese. Fish is best known for his gay romance series *Cavalcade of Boys,* and its subsequent graphic novels. He has spoken at comic book festivals, community centers, and stores across the US and Europe. You can follow him on Facebook and Twitter via timfishworks.com.

NICOLLE RAGER FULLER is a professional illustrator, with a bachelor of arts in biochemistry from Lewis and Clark College and a graduate certificate in science illustration from the University of California–Santa Cruz. She lives with her husband in Washington, DC.

LAURENCE GANE teaches philosophy at London University and Open University, and is the director of Critical Studies at the Royal College of Art. Gane is also a rock music producer, musician, and filmmaker and video producer.

SANYA GLISIC is an illustrator and printmaker in Chicago, Illinois. She is originally from Bosnia. During her 2010 Artist Residency at Spudnik Press in Chicago, she illustrated, screen-printed, and hand-bound an edition of books based on Heinrich Hoffmann's nineteenth-century *Der Struwwelpeter*. She has contributed to several publications, including *Lumpen Magazine* and *Artifice*, and her work has appeared on the covers of *Newcity Magazine* and *KOSHKA* zine. Her work will appear in the upcoming anthology *BLACK EYE No.2*, published by Rotland Press. Her prints have been included in the Blaque Lyte exhibition at Hyde Park Art Center, as well as other galleries in Chicago. She was awarded the 2011–2012 Artist Residency at the Chicago Printmakers Collaborative. More of her work can be found at sanyaglisic.com.

Originally recognized for his dark yet humorous illustrations for young readers, **GRIS GRIMLY** has transcended beyond the realm of picture books through writing, gallery art, and film. His illustrations can be appreciated in over a dozen best-selling books including *The Dangerous Alphabet* with author Neil Gaiman, his own personally scribed *Little Jordan Ray's Muddy Spud*, the *Wicked Nursery Rhymes* series, and the highly anticipated release of *Frankenstein.* Grimly has also ventured into moving pictures as the director of the demented and humorous independent featurette, *Cannibal Flesh Riot!* He has worked with cult sensation Elvira, directing the opening to her show *Elvira's Movie Macabre* and a music video featuring the Mistress of the Dark. He is currently working on his second featurette, *Wounded Embark of the Lovesick Mind*, and he has signed on to direct the stop-motion feature *Pinocchio*, produced by Guillermo Del Torro.

ALI J's mixed-media artworks are whimsical, dreamy, and invoke the imagination. She creates portraits of characters that are modern, fashionable, and feature red rosy cheeks. Her subjects are everyday people that we can relate to, and she enjoys telling stories through their eyes and facial expressions. Her clients include the *Women's Weekly*, the Australian Copyright Council, Sony/BMG, and Oxford University Press, and her illustrations have appeared on everything from greeting cards to magazines, book, and CDs.

SANDY JIMENEZ is an American comic book artist and film director. Having produced scores of varied and original illustrated stories since graduating from The Cooper Union in 1990, he is best known for creating the independent series "Marley Davidson," and the long-running and critically acclaimed "Shit House Poet" stories for *World War 3 Illustrated*. Recently Mr. Jimenez was designated the Two Boots Pizza in-house artist for 2012, after painting illustrations for the New York City independent restaurant chain's entire 2011 calendar.

A former graphic designer, Brazilian illustrator **KAKO** today works as freelance illustrator for clients from the advertising, publishing, and editorial markets. Recently he was awarded the Gold Lion at Cannes Advertising Festival, the Gold Medal at El Ojo de Iberoamerica Advertising Festival, and Best Illustrator of 2007 at HQMix Awards. His work has been published in several illustration/design books and annuals such as *Communication Arts*, *Society of Illustrators*, the *SPD*, and the *Lurzer's Archive 200 Best Illustrators Worldwide* book. From time to time, he likes to flirt with the comic book world, doing covers for unusual books or telling very short and odd stories.

MICHAEL KELLER, an award-winning journalist and writer, has a bachelor of science in wildlife ecology from the University of Florida and a master's degree from the Columbia University Graduate School of Journalism.

A native of Seattle, Washington, **MEGAN KELSO** first came to comics fans' attention with her Xeric Award–winning minicomic *Girlhero*. Two collections of short stories followed: *Queen of the Black Black* (Highwater, 1998) and *The Squirrel Mother* (Fantagraphics, 2006). In 2007, the *New York Times* asked Megan to create a strip for their Sunday magazine. The resulting story, *Watergate Sue*, ran weekly for six months, in a slot previously occupied by Chris Ware, Seth, and Jaime Hernandez. In 2010, Fantagraphics published Megan's double-Ignatz Award–winning *Artichoke Tales*. Megan is currently at work on a children's book and new collection of short stories. girlhero.com.

MOLLY KIELY is an artist, illustrator, underground cartoonist; Canadian-in-exile in Tucson, Arizona; and stay-at-home mom to a spitfire. She's been drawing erotic comix since 1991, including the *Diary of a Dominatrix* and *Saucy Little Tart* series, and graphic novels *That Kind of Girl* and *Tecopa Jane*. See more at mollykiely.com or mollykiely.tumblr.com.

HUXLEY KING is an editor, writer, and artist living in Nashville, Tennessee. Over the course of her varied career, she has edited everything from Bible commentaries to a tome on Hindu love goddesses; written everything from catalog copy to theater reviews; and illustrated everything from album covers to comic books that deal with the lighter side of substance abuse. Ms. King also dabbles in performance art and can occasionally be found trolling local art galleries in mime makeup or painting murals at Bonnaroo with her art collective, the E Flat Dillingers (eflatdillingers. com). She is currently working with her husband and frequent collaborator, Terrence Boyce, and her partner in creative crime, Maxx Kelly, on a historical adventure set in 1890s Nashville. You can contact her through her website, huxleyking.com.

MATT KISH is a librarian in Ohio. Childhood obsessions with Jack Kirby, Philippe Druillet, and the *Monster Manual* led to this all. He talks to the planets, the results of which can be seen at spudd64.com.

ANDRZEJ KLIMOWSKI has exhibited internationally, with work collected by museums in Europe and the United States. During his acclaimed career, he has designed film and theater posters; directed short, animated films in Warsaw; and designed covers for Penguin, Faber & Faber, Everyman Library, and Oberon Books. His graphic novels include *The Depository*, *The Secret*, and *Horace Dorlan*. Klimowski is a professor of illustration at the Royal College of Art, London. In addition to his adaptation of *Dr. Jekyll and Mr. Hyde* for SelfMadeHero, Klimowski has also adapted *The Master and Margarita*, which his readers will see in Volume 3 of *The Graphic Canon*.

AIDAN KOCH is an illustrator and comics artist working out of Portland, Oregon. Her first graphic novella, *The Whale*, was released in 2010. See more at aidankoch.com.

PETER KUPER is cofounder of the political graphics magazine *World War 3 Illustrated*. Since 1997, he has written and drawn *Spy vs. Spy* for every issue of *MAD*. Kuper has produced over twenty books, including *The System* and an adaptation of Franz Kafka's *The Metamorphosis*. He lived in Oaxaca, Mexico, July 2006–2008, during a major teachers' strike, and his work from that time can be seen in his book *Diario de Oaxaca*. Kuper has been teaching comics courses for twenty-five years in New York and is a visiting professor at Harvard University.

DAVID LASKY has been a published cartoonist since 1989. Among his best-known work is the award-nominated *Urban Hipster*, in collaboration with Greg Stump, and *No Ordinary Flu*, in collaboration with King County Public Health. He is currently working on his first graphic novel, *Carter Family Comics: Don't Forget This Song*, the story the first family of country music, in collaboration with Frank Young.

MAY ANN LICUDINE, a.k.a. Mall, is a painter and freelance illustrator living in La Union, Philippines. With a body of work including music album covers, paintings, and murals, she has won many art awards since her kindergarten graduation, including the Alcala Prize for young illustrators, and prizes from the Cultural Center of the Philippines, the National Library, and the Asia/Pacific Cultural Centre for UNESCO. High-profile commissions have included BBDO Guerrero's "Live Your Dreams" campaign for the Philippine Department of Tourism. Licudine's work has been exhibited around the world.

Born on Long Island, illustrator **ELLEN LINDNER** is the author of *Undertow*, a graphic novel about Coney Island in the early 1960s, and the editor of *The Strumpet*, a transatlantic comics magazine showcasing art by upcoming women cartoonists. See more of Ellen's comics and illustration online at littlewhitebird.com, or take a peek at her sketchbook at ellenlindner.livejournal.com.

In her culturally rich homeland, Ukraine, **OLGA LOPATA** followed a family legacy and pursued her lifelong passion at a prestigious school of the arts in her native city of Kiev. After attaining an advanced degree in fine and commercial art at the Academy of Art in Kiev, where she specialized in book illustration, Olga moved to the US, where she graduated from the Academy of Art in San Francisco. Olga's portfolio—including paintings, illustrations, and sophisticated commercial graphic art—can be viewed at olgalopata.com

DAVE MORICE is a writer, visual artist, performance artist, and educator. He has written and published under the names Dave Morice, Joyce Holland, and Dr. Alphabet. His works include sixty poetry marathons, three anthologies of *Poetry Comics*, the Wooden Nickel Art Project, and other art and writing, including *The Great American Fortune Cookie Novel*, composed entirely of actual fortunes from fortune cookies. He is one of the founders of the Actualist Poetry Movement.

The spiritual lovechild of Jack Kirby and Pablo Picasso, **J. BEN MOSS** is from the artistic no-fly zone called Shreveport, Louisiana. He is the star of many an internet profile "About Me" section, as well as the creator of a bajillion brain-babies that may or may not decide to surface into the full light of day. J. Ben Moss is an actual, real-life literate Southerner who is pursuing his MLA with a concentration in Animation & Visual Effects. He is also father to the two most brilliant and awe-inspiringly beautiful daughters to have ever existed in the entire multiverse. See more of his work at thecreativefinder.com/benmoss or squoog.com.

CORINNE MUCHA is a Chicago-based cartoonist, illustrator, and teaching artist. She is the author of the YA graphic novel *Freshman: 9th Grade Tales of Obsessions, Revelations, and Other Nonsense*, as well as the Xeric Award–winning *My Alaskan Summer*. Her comic strip etiquette column, "Barnyard Etiquette," appears monthly in the *Philadelphia Inquirer*. Find more of her work at maidenhousefly.com.

JORDYN OSTROFF graduated from Brown University, where she studied comparative literature and art history. Originally from Miami, Florida, she now lives in Brooklyn and works variously in art and publishing.

JOHN OTTINGER graduated from the Art Center College of Design as an illustration major who has worked for several years in the toy industry designing toys. He has also illustrated children's books; designed for video games, theme parks, and websites; and has done sculptures for Warner Bros, Dreamworks, Disney Interactive, Universal Studios, Lucasfilm, and Williams Entertainment, among others.

CHRISTOPHER PANZNER is an American fine artist, illustrator, and writer who lives and works in Paris. For many years he worked in the film and television industry, essentially in European animation. Three animated features to which he contributed—the double Oscar-nominated *The Triplets of Belleville*, the Venice Film Festival selection *The Dog, the General and the Pigeons*, and, as associate producer, *Blackmor's Treasure*—were part of an eight-film retrospective in 2006 of contemporary French animation at the Museum of Modern Art called Grand Illusions: The Best of Recent French Animation. He currently illustrates books of contemporary poetry, classics, and is the creator and editor in chief of *LHOOQ magazine*.

JULIAN PETERS is a comic book artist and illustrator living in Montreal. A good portion of his formative comic-book-reading years were spent in Italy, and the masters of the *fumetti* tradition continue to be his greatest sources of artistic inspiration. He has a long-standing passion for history, which he values mainly as a form of escapism; his comics are set in all kinds of different historical eras but never in the present. In the past couple of years, Julian has become particularly interested in exploring the possibilities of combining poetry, the most imagistic of literary forms, with comics, the wordiest of the visual arts, and he has created comic book adaptations of many classic poems from the canons of English, French, and Italian literature.

JOHN PIERARD is an old pro: an Air Force brat until the age of thirteen, he was ejected from that existence and forced to seek work as an illustrator. Some of his main influences have included Rays Bradbury and Harryhausen; Alfred Hitchcock and Stanley Kubrick; Sams Fuller and Peckinpah; Robert Altman; Charles Willeford; and Jim and Hunter S. Thompson—Mort Drucker, Frank Frazetta with a soucon of R. Crumb & Vaughn Bode. John lives in Manhattan with his beautiful wife Wendy and two dogs, and he really likes it a lot.

PIERO is an illustrator, artist, and graphic designer whose work has twice been included in the Royal College of Art in London. He has illustrated many "Introducing" titles.

PMURPHY is an illustrator, designer, animator, and all-around art tinkerer currently living in Portland, Oregon. Moving on from a six-year, full-time designer gig, he moved to the Pacific Northwest from the East Coast to pursue personal and freelance work. He is inspired by his friends, functions of the brain, the occult, and online documentaries. PMurphy is always interested in creative collaborations and can be contacted here: pmurphy.org.

JOHN PORCELLINO was born in Chicago in 1968, and he has been writing, drawing, and publishing minicomics, comics, and graphic novels for over twenty-five years. His celebrated self-published series *King-Cat Comics*, begun in 1989, has inspired a generation of cartoonists. Porcellino currently lives and works in South Beloit, Illinois, the "Sand Capital of the World."

Born in London, **DANUSIA SCHEJBAL** was awarded a British Council Scholarship to study stage design at the Academy of Fine Arts in Warsaw, Poland, and later studied fashion and textiles at Ealing School of Art, London. From 1976 to 1981, she designed sets and costumes for various theaters in Poland. Her career has subsequently seen her as a designer for the Cherub Theatre Company, which received the *Sunday Telegraph* Award for best production at the Edinburgh Fringe Festival for *Macbeth* in 1981. Schejbal has exhibited her critically acclaimed paintings across Europe. Her further collaborations with Andrzej Klimoski on *The Master and Margarita* can be seen in Volume 3 of *The Graphic Canon*.

TARA SEIBEL is an alternative cartoonist, graphic designer, and illustrator from Cleveland, Ohio, who is best known for her collaborations with underground comix book writer Harvey Pekar. Her work has been published in *Chicago Newcity,* the *Austin Chronicle, Cleveland Scene, Juxtapoz Magazine,* the *New York Times,* and the *Los Angeles Times,* among other publications. After receiving a bachelor of fine arts from Edinboro University of Pennsylvania, Seibel illustrated covers for restaurant menus and food packaging, then later worked as a line designer and illustrator for American Greetings before becoming a freelance editorial cartoonist. Seibel has taught illustration courses at Ursuline College in Cleveland. She lives with her husband Aaron, three children, and pets in Pepper Pike, Ohio.

After the success of *Frankenstein*, Irish artist **DECLAN SHALVEY** went on to work on a *Sweeney Todd* adaptation, also for Classical Comics. Credits since include *28 Days Later* for BOOM Studios and *Northlanders* for DC/Vertigo. He is currently illustrating *Thunderbolts* for Marvel Comics.

NATALIE SHAU is illustrator and photographer from Vilnius, Lithuania, working mainly with a mixture of photography, digital painting, and 3D elements. Shau's style is influenced by religious imagery, fairy-tale illustrations, fashion, and fashion photography. In addition to working on her artwork and participating in international solo and group exhibitions, she also creates illustrations for bands, fashion designers, and book publishers, with a client list including Island Def Jam, Actes Sud, and Sony BMG. Her illustrations for the Lydia Courteille jewelry campaign were published in French *Vogue*.

MAHENDRA SINGH is a freelance illustrator in Montreal. He's illustrated a wide range of books and comix, ranging from the verse of D. A. Powell to Martin Olson's *Encyclopaedia of Hell*. He's also the editor of the *Knight Letter*, the journal of the Lewis Carroll Society of North America. Born in Libya to German and Indian parents, married to an Assamese woman and surrounded now by the Quebecois, he regards multiculturalism as an artful dodge and prefers to spend his spare time designing tin-foil turbans for Hindus who no longer wish to hear the voices in other people's heads, taking Buddhist shut-ins to Nirvana concerts, and helping Canadian atheists distribute blank pamphlets on the subway.

In 1980, **SETH TOBOCMAN** was one of the founding editors of the political comic book *World War 3 Illustrated*, a magazine that challenged the politics and morals of the Reagan-Bush era. Tobocman is the author and illustrator of five graphic books—*You Don't Have to Fuck People Over to Survive*, *War in the Neighborhood*, *Portraits of Israelis and Palestinians*, *Disaster and Resistance*, and *Understanding the Crash*—and his illustrations have appeared in the *New York Times* and numerous other publications. He has had a one-man show at ABC No Rio, a two-man show at Exit Art gallery, and group shows at the Museum of Modern Art, the Museum of the City of Ravenna, and the New Museum of Contemporary Art. He currently teaches in the department of cartooning and illustration at the School of Visual Arts. Tobocman's images have been used in posters, pamphlets, murals, graffiti, and tattoos by people's movements around the world, from the African National Congress in South Africa, to squatters on New York's Lower East Side. Most recently he provided placards and banners to Occupy Wall Street.

The coeditor of African-American Classics, **LANCE TOOKS** began his career as a Marvel Comics assistant editor. He has worked as an animator on 100+ television commercials, films, and music videos; self-published the comics *Danger Funnies*, *Divided by Infinity*, and *Muthafucka*; and illustrated *The Black Panthers for Beginners*, written by Herb Boyd. His stories have appeared in Graphic Classics volumes of Edgar Allan Poe, Ambrose Bierce, Mark Twain, and Robert Louis Stevenson, and he collaborated with Harvey Pekar on *The Beats: A Graphic History* and *Studs Terkel's Working*. Tooks's first graphic novel, *Narcissa*, was named one of the year's best books by *Publishers Weekly*, and his four-volume *Lucifer's Garden of Verses* series for NBM Comics Lit has won two Glyph Awards. Lance moved from his native New York to Madrid, Spain, where he's hard at work on a new and very original graphic novel. lancetooksjournal.blogspot.com.

DAVID W. TRIPP lived in Maine for the first half of his life, where he developed his artistic skills in the quiet, rustic environment that only Maine can give. Then in 2001 he moved to Philadelphia and attended the Pennsylvania Academy of the Fine Arts, where he received his undergraduate certificate and MFA. His work can be seen in gallery exhibits and private collections around the world, as well as in numerous publications. You can see more of his art at davidwtripp.com.

EMERSON TUNG grew up watching and falling in love with franchises like *Predator*, *Aliens*, *Star Wars*, and, of course, Saturday morning cartoons. Being exposed to these shows in his younger years might be why stories involving young heroes, monsters, robots, and steampunk airships in fantastical floating islands constantly play in his head today. Tung graduated from the Academy of Art University in 2010 and currently works in a social game company based in the San Francisco

Bay Area. He is also a freelance illustrator and gallery painter, with a client list including Hasbro and Fantasy Flight Games. He was recently featured in the Society of Illustrators Student Show 2010 and *Spectrum 18: The Best in Contemporary Fantastic Art*. emersonart.blogspot.com.

ANTHONY VENTURA has been working as an illustrator since graduating from Sheridan College, though he has been drawing and painting for even longer. He has done work for print, multimedia, advertising, and television, and he currently resides in a hamlet north of Toronto.

RAPHAËLLE VIMONT is part of Supercinq, a graphic design studio located in Paris. The four members of Supercinq graduated from L'École de Communication Visuelle de Paris in 2001. Since then, they have been active in the spheres of music and culture, with which they have strong affinities. Their main fields of investigation are typography and illustration, and their main clients are Printemps department store, VP Records, and Wagram Music.

ELIZABETH WATASIN has worked on thirteen 2D animated feature film favorites. She has written for *Disney Adventures* magazine, and her graphic novel, *Charm School*, was published by SLG Publishing. She's currently working on her storybook, *Fey Dently, Vampyre*; a young adult adventure novel, *Wit's World: Never Was*; and the short story gothic steampunk series, *The Dark Victorian*. She lives with a black cat named Draw in a tree house in Los Angeles.

Originally from Nebraska, **S. CLAY WILSON** relocated to San Francisco in the 1960s where he rose to fame as a founding artist for Zap Comix along with Robert Crumb, Robert Williams, Victor Moscoso, Spain Rodriguez, and Rick Griffin. (Paul Mavrides was later added to this talented roster.) Wilson challenged censorship by depicting wild characters like the infamous Checkered Demon, Captain Pissgums, and Ruby the Dyke (to name a few), making the world a more liberal environment for all artists and cartoonists. In November 2008, he suffered a traumatic brain injury that left him severely impaired. Although he managed to do some drawings after his recovery, his health has declined in the past year, leaving him in need of twenty-four-hour care and unable to draw. A special-needs trust has been created for those who wish to help at sclaywilson.com. Snail mail can reach him at PO Box 14854, San Francisco, CA 94114.

YIEN YIP is currently a freelance illustrator and screen-printing artist who was born and bred in Alberta, Canada. She has been drawing and painting ever since she was a kid; however, like every other member of her family, she decided to be "realistic" and took up accountancy for a bit. After five years in the field and one quarter-life crisis, she packed her bags and got her BAA in illustration at Sheridan College. With a deep love for drawing, screen-printing, some animation, and noodles, she is taking on the illustration world one step at a time.

CREDITS AND PERMISSIONS

Adventures of Huckleberry Finn by Mark Twain was created especially for this volume. Copyright © 2012 by J. Ben Moss. Printed by permission of the artist.

Alice gallery illustration *We're All Mad Here* by Raphaëlle Vimont first appeared in the graphzine *Peau de Lapin* (2008). Copyright © 2008 by Raphaëlle Vimont. Reprinted by permission of the artist.

Alice gallery illustration *Alice and Mad* by Bill Carman first appeared in the exhibition "Curiouser and Curiouser: Inspired by *Alice in Wonderland*" at Nucleus. Copyright © 2010 by Bill Carman. Reprinted by permission of the artist.

Alice gallery illustrations by Kim Deitch are excerpted from *Alice's Adventures under Ground* by Lewis Carroll, illustrated by Kim Deitch (Word Play, 2000). Copyright © 2000 by Kim Deitch. Reprinted by permission of the artist.

Alice gallery illustration *A Mad Tea Party* is an excerpt from the *Psychedelic Wonderland 2009* calendar by John Coulthart. Copyright © 2009 by John Coulthart. Reprinted by permission of the artist.

Alice gallery illustration *The Wasp in a Wig* is an excerpt from the *Through the Psychedelic Looking-Glass 2010 Calendar* by John Coulthart. Copyright © 2009 by John Coulthart. Reprinted by permission of the artist.

Alice gallery illustrations *I see you, Cheshire, Young Queen of Hearts*, and *The Hole in Alice's World* by May Ann Licudine first appeared in the exhibition "Curiouser and Curiouser: Inspired by *Alice in Wonderland*" at Nucleus. Copyright © 2010 by May Ann Licudine. Reprinted by permission of the artist.

Alice gallery illustration *Caterpillar Concept* by Andrea Femerstrand was created for the 2010 Chiustream Sketchaholic contest. Copyright © 2010 by Andrea Femerstrand. Reprinted by permission of the artist.

Alice gallery illustration *Caterpillar* by Olga Lopata was created for Amanda Elo'esh Johnsen's *Go Ask Alice Oracle*, an in-progress Tarot-like deck. Copyright © 2009 by Olga Lopata. Reprinted by permission of the artist.

Alice gallery illustration *Alice and White Rabbit* by Natalie Shau first appeared in the artist's gallery at natalieshau.carbonmade.com. Copyright © 2009 by Natalie Shau. Printed by permission of the artist.

Alice gallery illustration *Mr. White Rabbit* by Emerson Tung first appeared on the artist's blog at emersonart.blogspot.com. Copyright © 2009 by Emerson Tung. Printed by permission of the artist.

Alice gallery illustration of the Queen of Hearts by Peter Kuper was first published in *Alicia en el País de las Maravillas* (Sexto Piso Editoral, 2010). Copyright © 2010 by Peter Kuper. Reprinted by permission of the artist.

Alice gallery illustration of the elephant/bee by Peter Kuper was first published in *A través del espejo y lo que Alicia encontró allí* (Sexto Piso Editoral, 2011). Copyright © 2011 by Peter Kuper. Reprinted by permission of the artist.

Alice gallery illustration *Midnight Tea* by John Ottinger first appeared in the "What's the Use of a Book without Pictures" project organized by Notld Reanimated. Copyright © 2011 by John Ottinger. Reprinted by permission of the artist.

Alice gallery illustrations *Alice Paragraph 162* and *Alice Paragraph 276* by David W. Tripp first appeared in the "What's the Use of a Book without Pictures" project organized by Notld Reanimated. Copyright © 2011 by David W. Tripp. Reprinted by permission of the artist.

Alice gallery illustration *Alice's Adventures in Wonderland* (Paragraph 108) by Christopher Panzner first appeared in the "What's the Use of a Book without Pictures" project organized by Notld Reanimated. Copyright © 2011 by Christopher Panzner. Reprinted by permission of the artist.

Alice gallery illustration *Alice and the Bosch Monsters* by Jasmine Becket-Griffith is part of the artist's series *Alice in Other Lands*. Copyright © 2012 by Jasmine Becket-Griffith. Printed by permission of the artist.

Alice gallery illustration *Alice and Humpty* by Molly Kiely was created especially for this volume. Copyright © 2012 by Molly Kiely. Printed by permission from the artist.

Alice's Adventures in Wonderland and *Through the Looking-Glass* by Lewis Carroll were created especially for this volume. Copyright © 2012 by Dame Darcy. Printed by permission of the artist.

Anna Karenina by Leo Tolstoy was created especially for this volume. Copyright © 2012 by Ellen Lindner. Printed by permission of the artist.

"Auguries of Innocence" by William Blake was created especially for this volume. Copyright © 2012 by Aidan Koch. Printed by permission of the artist.

"Because I Could Not Stop for Death" by Emily Dickinson was created especially for this volume. Copyright © 2012 by Dame Darcy. Printed by permission of the artist.

The Confessions of Nat Turner by Nat Turner and Thomas R. Gray was created especially for this volume. Copyright © 2012 by John Pierard. Printed by permission of the artist.

Crime and Punishment by Fyodor Dostoevsky was created especially for this volume. Copyright © 2012 by Kako. Printed by permission of Levy Creative Management.

Der Struwwelpeter by Heinrich Hoffmann first appeared in a privately published artist book by Sanya Glisic, created at the Artist Residency Program at Spudnik Press Cooperative, Chicago IL, 2010. Copyright © 2010 by Sanya Glisic. Printed by permission of the artist.

"The Drunken Boat" by Arthur Rimbaud was created especially for this volume. Copyright © 2012 by Julian Peters. Printed by permission of the artist.

Fairy tales by Hans Christian Andersen first appeared in *Wilson's Andersen* by S. Clay Wilson (Word Play, 1994). Copyright © 1994 by S. Clay Wilson. Printed by permission of the publisher.

Fairy tales by the Brothers Grimm first appeared in *Wilson's Grimm* by S. Clay Wilson (Word Play, 1999). Copyright © 1999 by S. Clay Wilson. Printed by permission of the publisher.

Frankenstein by Mary Shelley first appeared in *Frankenstein: The Graphic Novel* by Jason Cobley and Declan Shalvey (Classical Comics, 2009). Copyright © 2009 by Jason Cobley and Declan Shalvey. Reprinted by permission of the publisher.

The Hasheesh Eater by Fitz Hugh Ludlow was created especially for this volume. Copyright © 2012 by John Pierard. Printed by permission of the artist.

"How Six Made Good in the World" by the Brothers Grimm was created especially for this volume. Copyright © 2012 by Shawn Cheng. Printed by permission of the artist.

The Hunting of the Snark by Lewis Carroll is an excerpt from *Hunting of the Snark* by Lewis Carroll, illustrated by Mahendra Singh. Copyright © 2010. Reprinted by permission of the publisher, Melville House Publishing, USA.

"I Taste a Liquor Never Brewed" by Emily Dickinson was created especially for this volume. Copyright © 2012 by Diana Evans. Printed by permission of the artist.

"I Wandered Lonely as a Cloud" by William Wordsworth was created especially for this volume. Copyright © 2012 by PMurphy. Printed by permission of the artist.

"Jabberwocky" by Lewis Carroll first appeared in *The Jabberwocky* by Eran Cantrell (self-published via Lulu, 2010). Copyright © 2010 by Eran Cantrell. Printed by permission of the artist.

Jane Eyre by Charlotte Brontë was created especially for this volume. Copyright © 2012 by Elizabeth Watasin. Printed by permission of the artist.

Jerusalem: The Emanation of the Giant Albion [plates 25, 32, 41, 46, 53, 78] by William Blake first appeared in *Jerusalem: The Emanation of the Giant Albion* by William Blake (1804–1820). Reprinted by permission of the Yale Center for British Art, Paul Mellon Collection.

"The Jumblies" by Edward Lear was created by Hunt Emerson as a private commission in 2009. Its appearance here is its first print publication. Copyright © 2009 by Hunt Emerson. Printed by permission of the artist.

"Kubla Khan" by Samuel Taylor Coleridge was created especially for this volume. Copyright © 2012 by Alice Duke. Printed by permission of the artist.

"La Belle Dame Sans Merci" by John Keats first appeared on www.webcomicsnation.com in 1999, and was collected in *Meditations* by Neil Cohn (self-published via BookSurge, 2006). Copyright © 1999 by Neil Cohn. Reprinted by permission of the artist.

Leaves of Grass by Walt Whitman was created especially for this volume. Copyright © 2012 by Tara Seibel. Printed by permission of the artist.

Leaves of Grass by Walt Whitman first appeared in *Poetry Comics: An Animated Anthology* by Dave Morice (Teachers & Writers Collaborative, 2002). Copyright © 2002 by Dave Morice. Printed by permission of the artist.

Middlemarch by George Eliot was created especially for this volume. Copyright © 2012 by Megan Kelso. Printed by permission of the artist.

Les Misérables by Victor Hugo was created especially for this volume. Copyright © 2012 by Tara Seibel. Printed by permission of the artist.

Letter to George Sand by Gustave Flaubert was created especially for this volume. Copyright © 2012 by Corinne Mucha. Printed by permission of the artist.

"The Message from Mount Misery" by Frederick Douglass was created especially for this volume. Copyright © 2012 by Seth Tobocman. Printed by permission of the artist.

Moby-Dick by Herman Melville first appeared in *Moby-Dick in Pictures: One Drawing For Every Page* by Matt Kish (Tin House, 2011). Copyright © 2011 by Matt Kish. Printed by permission of the artist.

"The Mortal Immortal" by Mary Shelley was created especially for this volume. Copyright © 2012 by Lance Tooks. Printed by permission of the artist.

"O Solitude" by John Keats was created especially for this volume. Copyright © 2012 by Hunt Emerson. Printed by permission of the artist.

"An Occurrence at Owl Creek Bridge" by Ambrose Bierce was created especially for this volume. Copyright © 2012 by Sandy Jimenez. Printed by permission of the artist.

Oliver Twist by Charles Dickens was created especially for this volume. Copyright © 2012 by Kevin Dixon. Printed by permission of the artist.

On the Origin of Species by Charles Darwin is reprinted from *Charles Darwin's On the Origin of Species: A Graphic Adaptation* by Michael Keller and Nicolle Rager Fuller. Copyright © 2009 by Michael Keller. Illustrations © by Nicolle Rager Fuller. Permission granted by Rodale, Inc., Emmaus, PA 18098.

"Ozymandias" by Percy Bysshe Shelley was created especially for this volume. Copyright © 2012 by Anthony Ventura. Printed by permission of the artist.

The Picture of Dorian Gray by Oscar Wilde was created especially for this volume. Copyright © 2012 by John Coulthart. Printed by permission of the artist.

Poe montage by Gris Grimly first appeared in *Edgar Allan Poe's Tales of Mystery and Madness* by Gris Grimly (Atheneum Books for Young Readers, 2004). Copyright © 2004 by Gris Grimly. Printed by permission of the artist.

Pride and Prejudice by Jane Austen was created especially for this volume. Copyright © 2012 by Huxley King. Printed by permission of the artist.

"The Raven" by Edgar Allan Poe was created especially for this volume. Copyright © 2012 by Yien Yip. Printed by permission of the artist.

"The Rime of the Ancient Mariner" by Samuel Taylor Coleridge first appeared in *The Rime of the Ancient Mariner* by Hunt Emerson (Knockabout Comics, 2008). Copyright © 2008 by Hunt Emerson. Printed by permission of the artist.

"Rondeau" ("Jenny Kiss'd Me") by Leigh Hunt was created especially for this volume. Copyright © 2012 by Ellen Lindner. Printed by permission of the artist.

The Scarlet Letter by Nathaniel Hawthorne was created especially for this volume. Copyright © 2012 by Ali J. Printed by permission of the artist.

"She Walks in Beauty" by George Gordon, Lord Byron was created especially for this volume. Copyright © 2012 by David Lasky. Printed by permission of the artist.

Strange Case of Dr. Jekyll and Mr. Hyde by Robert Louis Stevenson first appeared in *Dr. Jekyll and Mr. Hyde: A Graphic Novel* by Danusia Schejbal and Andrzej Klimowski (SelfMadeHero, 2009). Copyright © 2009 SelfMadeHero / Danusia Schejbal & Andrzej Klimowski. Reprinted by permission of the publisher.

Thus Spake Zarathustra by Friedrich Nietzsche first appeared in *Introducing Nietzsche* (compact ed.) by Laurence Gane and Piero (Icon Books, 2001). Copyright © 2001 by Laurence Gane and Piero. Reprinted by permission of the publisher.

Venus in Furs by Leopold von Sacher-Masoch was created especially for this volume. Copyright © 2012 by Molly Kiely. Printed by permission of the artist.

Walden by Henry David Thoreau first appeared in *Thoreau at Walden* by John Porcellino (Hyperion, published in association with The Center for Cartoon Studies, 2008). Copyright © 2008 by John Porcellino. Printed by permission of the artist.

Works by Edgar Allan Poe first appeared in *Maxon's Poe: Seven Stories and Poems by Edgar Allan Poe* by Maxon Crumb (Word Play, 1997). Copyright © 1997 by Maxon Crumb. Printed by permission of the publisher.

Wuthering Heights by Emily Brontë was created especially for this volume. Copyright © 2012 by Tim Fish. Printed by permission of the artist.

INDEX TO VOLUME 2

COUNTRY/AREA OF ORIGIN

Photo by Ross Smith

RUSS KICK is the editor of the bestselling anthologies *You Are Being Lied To* and *Everything You Know is Wrong*, which have sold over half a million copies. *The New York Times* has dubbed Kick "an information archaeologist," *Details* magazine described Kick as "a Renaissance man," and *Utne Reader* named him one of its "50 Visionaries Who Are Changing Your World." Russ Kick lives in Nashville, Tennessee, and Tucson, Arizona.

SEVEN STORIES PRESS is an independent book publisher based in New York City. We publish works of the imagination by such writers as Nelson Algren, Russell Banks, Octavia E. Butler, Ani DiFranco, Assia Djebar, Ariel Dorfman, Coco Fusco, Barry Gifford, Hwang Sok-yong, Lee Stringer, and Kurt Vonnegut, to name a few, together with political titles by voices of conscience, including the Boston Women's Health Collective, Noam Chomsky, Angela Y. Davis, Human Rights Watch, Derrick Jensen, Ralph Nader, Loretta Napoleoni, Gary Null, Project Censored, Barbara Seaman, Alice Walker, Gary Webb, and Howard Zinn, among many others. Seven Stories Press believes publishers have a special responsibility to defend free speech and human rights, and to celebrate the gifts of the human imagination, wherever we can. For additional information, visit www.sevenstories.com.